CREATING INTERACTIVE FICTION WITH INFORM 7

Aaron Reed

Course Technology PTR
A part of Cengage Learning

COURSE TECHNOLOGY
CENGAGE Learning™

Australia, Brazil, Japan, Korea, Mexico, Singapore, Spain, United Kingdom, United States

Creating Interactive Fiction with Inform 7
Aaron Reed

Publisher and General Manager, Course Technology PTR:
Stacy L. Hiquet

Associate Director of Marketing:
Sarah Panella

Manager of Editorial Services:
Heather Talbot

Marketing Manager:
Jordan Castellani

Acquisitions Editor:
Heather Hurley

Project Editor:
Jenny Davidson

Technical Reviewer:
Jesse McGrew

Interior Layout Tech:
Bill Hartman

Cover Designer:
Mike Tanamachi

Indexer:
Valerie Haynes Perry

Proofreader:
Kezia Endsley

For product information and technology assistance, contact us at
Cengage Learning Customer & Sales Support, 1-800-354-9706.

For permission to use material from this text or product,
submit all requests online at **cengage.com/permissions**.
Further permissions questions can be e-mailed to
permissionrequest@cengage.com.

Inform was created by Graham Nelson.

All trademarks are the property of their respective owners.

All images © Cengage Learning unless otherwise noted.

Library of Congress Control Number: 2010922092

ISBN-13: 978-1-4354-5506-1

ISBN-10: 1-4354-5506-1

Course Technology, a part of Cengage Learning
20 Channel Center Street
Boston, MA 02210
USA

Cengage Learning is a leading provider of customized learning solutions with office locations around the globe, including Singapore, the United Kingdom, Australia, Mexico, Brazil, and Japan. Locate your local office at: **international.cengage.com/region**.

Cengage Learning products are represented in Canada by Nelson Education, Ltd.

For your lifelong learning solutions, visit **courseptr.com**.

Visit our corporate Web site at **cengage.com**.

Printed in the United States of America
1 2 3 4 5 6 7 12 11 10

To my brother Andrew,
my first and best adventuring companion.

FOREWORD

You are in a maze of twisty little passages, all alike.

It was early 1977 and I was lost, deep in an underground cave system. I'd been exploring it for hours, sometimes walking upright but often crawling through tight passages, marveling at its vast caverns of intricate stone formations, and occasionally even stumbling across ancient bits of treasure: coins, some silver bars, a large and unwieldy nugget of gold. Now I had entered a section of very similar-looking chambers, and was having trouble finding my way back out.

None of this was happening "for real." I was a character in a story, a story I was helping to write. A fellow by the name of Willie Crowther had outlined the story in such a way that readers like myself could guide its course, choosing which directions to explore and how to interact with the creatures and objects I encountered.

The "Choose Your Own Adventure" books by Packard and others had only just started to be published, and fantasy role-playing games (RPGs) such as *Dungeons & Dragons*® were also quite new, and I had not yet heard of either genre. Crowther, who did have some experience with RPGs, had laid out a world much as a "dungeon-master" might, and was guiding me as we together wrote the tale of my adventure. But he had not written it as a "choose your own adventure" book; he had written it as a computer program.

Crowther's program was in many ways very like those books. I would read the description it printed* of my situation in the story, tell it what I chose to do next, and then it would tell me what happened. Unlike the books, though, the program didn't need to give away

---

*This being in the dark ages when most computers didn't have graphical displays or mice, so most programs interacted with people using text.

all my options by making me choose from a list. Instead, I instructed it using short English sentences such as "go west" or "take coins."

Like many who would follow me, I had never before seen a computer program of this sort, and was fascinated by the experience. But the program was incomplete: there were areas that could not be explored, or worse, rooms with no exits. And though there were a few mysteries to be solved (what was scaring that little bird? how can I get that heavy gold nugget out?), the story felt like it needed more motivation than mere exploration. I wanted to add some of my own ideas to the world Crowther had created.

For starters, I felt that there needed to be more reason to explore some of the remote areas of the cave system. Crowther had included a few bits of treasure, and I felt I could use that to give the reader a goal, to find and collect all the treasure. The reader could still explore without regard to the treasure, of course, but ideally the two would coincide: some treasures might be discovered only by thorough exploration, and others might be hard to retrieve, requiring the reader to explore in search of tools or clues. It would be a "puzzle story," one which might stand up to multiple readings.

I wanted Crowther's permission to expand on his work, and also a copy of the "source code" to his program for me to use as a starting point. The program credits where I'd found his name did not list any contact information, but after some effort I located him and he gave me a copy of the program source, asking only that I give him copies of any changes I made. Some of my ideas I discovered were hard to implement, as everything other than description of locations and how to move between them, or picking up generic objects, required special-purpose code in the program. Try to move along a certain passage and special code would check if the snake was blocking the path. Try to climb a steep stair and other code would check if you were carrying the gold nugget, which, a sign had warned, was too heavy to carry up the steps.

I was impressed by how vivid and engaging Crowther's program was given how simple the underlying structures were. That maze of twisty little passages that had trapped me on that earlier visit required nothing more than a set of locations with the same description, connected in ways that were not easily retraced. (That is, leaving one chamber by moving north did not necessarily mean that one entered the next from the south.) But it quickly became clear that I needed to be able to add a wider variety of choices without requiring special code for each.

I stepped back and spent some time thinking about the various special cases in Crowther's program, and about some of the puzzles I wanted to add. Then I rewrote the program, adding new structures that would let me specify many of the previously special cases in a uniform way. Some attempts at movement would simply produce a message describing why the movement was not possible. Some movements would be permitted only if you were (or weren't) carrying certain objects, or if other objects were present, and so forth.

Combining these features, I could specify that a certain attempted movement would, if the snake were present, refuse to move and instead respond, "You can't get by the snake."

With the program thus augmented, I set to work adding treasures, puzzles, more exploration, and even the occasional comedy relief to the story that Crowther had begun. Like him, I titled my version *Adventure* and made it freely available for others to "read." Many did, and they liked it, and word quickly spread. Since they were all sharing the single computer where I'd installed it, it quickly became unable to support the load. Soon I was giving out copies to let people install *Adventure* on other computers.

Some people were so taken by the idea that they decided to write their own story-telling programs, inspired by *Adventure* but not derived from it as my version was from Crowther's. One such group went on to form a company called Infocom, of which more will be said in this book. These early tales continued to be driven mostly by puzzles, perhaps a reflection on the somewhat geeky community doing the writing, and helped drive a perception of such programs as being simply "games," like the graphical story-based games and online fantasy worlds that later evolved from these textual beginnings. But text-based interactive fiction can be just as varied as more traditional books. You'll see some of what I mean in the pages that follow.

In all these works, the biggest obstacle has always been translating the author's vision into a form the reader can experience and interact with. When I rewrote Crowther's program into *Adventure*, the first thing I added was simpler ways to include many elements Crowther created, with the goal of making it easier—or at least possible!—to add some of the more subtle features I wanted. The Infocom people, whose story-based games were far more complex than *Adventure*, designed their own "virtual machine"—a machine simulated by a program—and a special programming language for the task.

The virtual machine outlived its creators, with others developing a new language called Inform in which to create more works for it. That language has evolved over the years, becoming both more versatile and easier to use. Its most recent incarnation, Inform 7, provides the expressive power of its predecessors in a more natural form, to make it accessible to authors who are not necessarily programmers.

I still read interactive fiction, and am often amazed at the depth and quality of literature being produced in the field. In this book, Aaron Reed describes how to write IF using Inform 7, the latest version of the language designed to re-create the experience of the original Infocom games. I hope you enjoy it, and perhaps someday I will find myself exploring *your* world, as we write another story together!

Don Woods
Los Altos, California
June 21, 2010

Acknowledgments

I am indebted to the many people who helped make this volume possible.

Several generous souls read drafts of the manuscript and offered feedback that dramatically improved it, including Kevin Jackson-Meade, Jesse McGrew, and Richard Smyth. Thanks also to my editors Heather Hurley and Jenny Davidson, and their colleagues at Cengage Learning, for their work in bringing this project to life.

The example game, *Sand-dancer*, would not be nearly so magical without the contributions of its co-designer, Alexei Othenin-Girard, or the beta testers who worked to iron out its complications: Duncan Bowsman, Jacqueline A. Lott, Juhana Leoinen, Sharon R., and Stephanie Camus.

The team behind Inform 7 deserves accolades both for creating such an elegant system for writing interactive fiction, and for patiently answering questions and responding to feedback from its many users. A heartfelt thank you to Graham Nelson, Emily Short, and the rest of the Inform team for all they've given us.

Countless kindnesses, favors, ideas, and moments of moral support were given me during the writing. I'd like to thank Richard Bartle, Amber Fitzgerald, Michael Mateas, Peter Mawhorter, Andrew Plotkin, Ben Samuel, Jason Scott, Emily Short, Don Woods, and my friends and family.

I found great inspiration from two graduate courses taken at the University of California Santa Cruz while writing: Noah Wardrip-Fruin's "Playable Fictions" and Warren Sack's

"Software Studies." Both were instrumental in helping shape my thoughts on how to write about code and think about play. Thanks to the faculty and my classmates for the great discussions.

Finally, I want to thank two people who nudged my early life in profound directions: my uncle Bruce, for sharing maps of *Adventure* from his college days and introducing me to stories you could play, and Tim Hartnell, whose book *Creating Adventure Games on Your Computer* first inspired me to try to write my own. It is my fondest hope that this volume helps pass on the sparks of imagination they kindled.

About the Author

Aaron A. Reed has worked as a travel writer, web monkey, offensive T-shirt designer, graphic artist, filmmaker, and murder mystery producer. His fiction has appeared in *Fantasy & Science Fiction* magazine, and his interactive fiction has won acclaim from indie gaming, electronic literature, and new media circles. His 2009 project *Blue Lacuna* has been called "the most ambitious interactive story of the decade" and "as close to interactive literature as I've ever seen," and is the longest work yet produced in the Inform 7 language.

Reed is currently studying at UC Santa Cruz with the Digital Arts and New Media program and the Expressive Intelligence Studio. He hopes to continue developing new forms of participatory storytelling.

TABLE OF CONTENTS

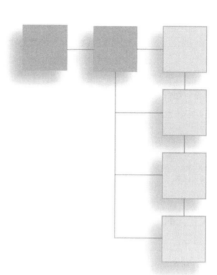

INTRODUCTION: WHY INTERACTIVE FICTION?

The box cover is striking: a whole family, from suit-and-tie father to laughing child clutching a puppy, pulled by the hand through a bright window onto a vivid, fantastical landscape. King Graham, the square-jawed hero of Sierra On-Line's best-selling computer game series, cheerfully leads them into the world of *King's Quest V*, due to be released just in time for the 1990 holiday season with a marketing fanfare unrivaled in the still-emerging game industry.

"Beautiful scenery and amazingly lifelike animation," the box gushes. "Characters that speak to one another using real voices take you into that world for an experience so real… you may forget you're playing a computer game." Not only is the fifth *King's Quest* the first Sierra game to use the new VGA graphics cards (offering a quantum leap from 16 to 256 colors), it's also among the first to come on CD-ROM, heralding a new age of multimedia-enabled games designed to fill those bottomless discs with art and music. (Sierra already helped jump-start the market for add-on sound cards two years previously, luring Hollywood composer William Goldstein to compose the score for *King's Quest IV*, and AdLib or Sound Blaster equipment is rapidly becoming *de rigueur* among serious PC gamers.)

In a segment on the television program *Computer Chronicles,* host Stewart Cheifet introduces Sierra's Stuart Moulder with a smile. "Stuart, we all remember the *old* adventure games, and the painful text entry," he says. Stuart chuckles. "But this is another story, isn't it?"

"It is," Stuart responds as he demonstrates the game. "For one thing, the old text-driven approach is gone now. In this game your character is controlled through a series of icons... everything's done with the mouse, there's no typing at all. …with the CD-ROM's storage capacity, instead of reading text, you can hear the text spoken to you by actors. …no typing in words, no 'I didn't understand what you said.'"

"And obviously great graphics," Cheifet says, bending in to peer at the ten-inch screen. "I mean, look at that, it's like watching a cartoon on TV."

Meanwhile, software outlets quietly dump their last remaining text-only games into the bargain bin to accommodate the VGA and CD-ROM titles that show off newer PCs. The final products from Infocom, once the leading publisher of "text adventures"—or, to use their preferred term, "interactive fiction,"—have nearly vanished from retail shelves. After making a name with the popular *Zork* series in the early '80s, Infocom focused not on chasing emerging technologies for graphics and sound but on improving their stories. Their games became better at understanding their players; their authors began to include prominent novelists like Douglas Adams and James Clavell. Infocom's ad campaigns, dismissive of early multimedia technology, bragged that graphics would never match the power of imagination: one two-page spread in *Analog* featured a human brain pulsing with a golden glow, below the huge banner "We stick our graphics where the sun don't shine."

But declining sales and mismanagement have scattered and shrunk the Infocom team, which closed the doors on its original Cambridge home in 1989. *King's Quest V* will go on to be the top-selling PC game of the year, and plans for *King's Quest VI* include an elaborate computer-animated intro sequence and a fully produced musical number. Sierra will soon begin constructing a multi-million dollar blue-screen studio for incorporating live actors into their games. Meanwhile, Infocom's final title, *Journey: The Quest Begins*, is marked down from $39.95 to $19.95 and then $9.95. Nobody wants it.

Interactive fiction has failed, just another short-lived fad in the early days of home computing, unable to compete with the superior technology superseding it.

Time passes.

Twenty years later, in 2010, a website tracking interactive fiction called the IFDB adds a newly written story to its archive every four days on average. Projects to bring interactive fiction (IF) to cell phones, web browsers, and game consoles proliferate. Thousands of dollars in prizes are awarded annually to winners of online IF competitions, the oldest now in its sixteenth year. A browser-based multiplayer *Zork* spin-off, *Legends of Zork*, continues to expand, and vintage Infocom games routinely sell for hundreds of dollars on eBay. Teachers in elementary and middle schools use IF to teach logic, problem-solving, and game theory, and new media and digital arts courses at universities around the world hold classes that study IF; a scholarly analysis, *Twisty Little Passages*, continues to be highly ranked on Amazon.com seven years after its first publication. *Get Lamp,* a documentary about the medium's history, gets heavily Slashdottted upon release; TextFyre, the first company seriously selling text adventures in two decades, releases the first game in its third series.

Long viewed only through the lens of nostalgia or even pity, IF is increasingly claiming a place alongside hypertext fiction and digital poetry as a serious medium of expression and storytelling, and alongside casual games and downloadable entertainment as a thoughtful, mature alternative to more violent or repetitive fare. While still not commercially successful again, some IF stories are increasingly viewed as artistically so.

The *King's Quest* series made it to a poorly received eighth installment, before fading from the spotlight as the corporate conglomerates that absorbed Sierra divided and then largely ignored its intellectual property. There are no current plans to revive the series.

The comparison is not to say that graphical games have failed (far from it) but to reveal one of interactive fiction's most striking qualities. Divorced from the technological arms race, unconcerned about chasing the latest graphics fad or interaction scheme, IF has had time to develop and mature over the past three decades into a distinct, unique, and vibrant medium. The mainstream game industry wants to create interactive movies, but interactive fiction strives for a goal that's haunted the human subconscious for centuries longer, dreamed or fretted about by Stephenson, Borges, Swift, Voltaire, and countless other thinkers. Interactive fiction is participatory literature. It not only talks back to its reader, but listens, too.

Why write IF now? Why work in a digital medium thirty-five years old, instead of playing on the bleeding edge of technology?

There are as many answers as there are IF authors, but for me, the truth lies in the older, less elegant term Infocom wanted people to forget about: text adventures. Text predates the computer, electricity, and the printing press: it is in many ways the foundation of civilization. Text can outlast the technology used to inscribe, print, or transmit it; the great texts of the past may outlive the printed book itself. And adventure is a driving force of the human condition. The need to discover, to explore, to experience—without necessarily shooting anything along the way—is stronger than ever in an age where every inch of our planet has been mapped, claimed, and conquered. Indeed, such a world needs adventure even more.

Graphics cards come and go, but text endures. And adventure is forever.

The Power of Text

Interactive fiction has often been dismissed as inferior to mainstream games for being "only text." Curiously, though, we don't feel a game like Charades lacks anything for being "only gestures," or that checkers suffers from being "only pieces." Many make the mistake of judging IF as a technological artifact of the time in which it was created, rather than on its own merits or faults as a game-playing system.

The criticism falls even flatter from the perspective of story. Dickens, Lovecraft, and Tolkien all got along just fine with "only text." I'm not sure that, were any of them alive in our century, they would decide vertex shaders, voice acting, and a good physics engine were necessary to tell their stories. One can almost hear them suggesting such things might in fact be distractions.

The first step to understanding interactive fiction is to embrace its text-only nature as a feature, not a bug—an advantage, not a limitation. Let's quickly go over some of the reasons.

Single-Developer Games

Major works of interactive fiction can be created by single authors, a feat nearly impossible in any other mode of digital storytelling. Between 2006 and 2009, I spent my spare time working on *Blue Lacuna*, a full-length IF novel (and perhaps the longest interactive fiction yet written) that provides something like 18 to 25 hours of entertainment. Over roughly the same period of time, it took a team of more than 70 people to create *Batman: Arkham Asylum*, a well-reviewed game but one which could be played through in half the time, even with gameplay often consisting of repetitive combat.

Why this huge disparity? A science fiction entry in the 2009 IF Competition, *The Duel that Spanned the Ages*, featured this sentence in its introduction:

> "All around him, the Machines' fleet and orbital stations are blasting away at his tree ships, burning the mighty trunks like firewood."

Let's think about what it would take to realize this sentence in a mainstream multimedia game. We'd need to hire conceptual artists to design the ships in the fleet of the Machines, their orbital stations, and also the tree ships of the protagonist. Each individual ship design would need several iterations to find a version that pleased the game's director. Once signed off, the sketches would be turned over to a team of modelers, who would create each ship in 3D and texture them. The organic tree ships would probably take a lot of work to get right. At the same time, a team of programmers would be building an engine capable of rendering lots of ships on screen at the same time (or contracting with an animation studio, if budget only allowed the sequence to be realized as a non-interactive cutscene). The engine would need a lighting system that can not only light the ships in a realistic manner (even in the dark void of deep space), but also deal with the "blasts" fired by the enemy ships. (Do they give off light? Do particle effects have to be added to the engine? What is the effect when blasts hit a target?) The fire consuming the tree ships would also be a considerable challenge: creating realistic fire might require significant R&D effort, not only to look visually compelling and realistic but to incorporate dynamic firelight effects into the engine's lighting system. We'd also need to record or license sound effects—for the blasts firing and striking, the tree ships burning, perhaps ambient noise like pilot cockpit chatter—and probably record a symphonic orchestral soundtrack to lend the scene the appropriate gravitas. The composer would need to write the track as well as perform it (or possibly hire guest performers, which may be a budget and scheduling nightmare) and then someone would have to mix the recording into a final form and compress it to fit on the game media. We would probably also need to hire voice actors to narrate the events of the scene. And this is before we find a team of quality assurance testers to find all the things that don't work and need to be fixed.

As IF, all the author had to do was write those twenty-two words.

While there will always be a market for multi-million-dollar entertainment requiring teams of hundreds to produce, our greatest stories often come from the undiluted visions of single artists. IF lets that sacred space exist in the realm of digital, participatory stories.

Prototyping

Perhaps counter-intuitively, IF can be a useful tool for designers of multimedia games as well. The speed with which game mechanics and plot events can be mocked up and iteratively improved makes IF a wonderful medium for prototyping any sort of interactive story.

As illustration, this book's example game, *Sand-dancer*, contains multiple locations, plot-advancing setpieces, over a dozen locations and several puzzles, four characters that can be interacted with, flashbacks, weather and lighting effects, and other elements: yet the process of building a prototype in Inform 7 took only about a day's work. A day after finalizing the design, I had a playable version that, while basic, still gave me a sense of the story's consistency, interest, and playability. It forced me to answer key questions like "What is the nature of the player's role in this story?" and "Is this going to be any fun?" These are the sorts of answers it's good to have before spending countless hours, not to mention any amount of money, on a story-based game.

Demographics

IF's text-based nature also makes it accessible to audiences disenfranchised from other styles of computer game. Blind fans of IF are a large and enthusiastic component of the online community. Gamers with disabilities who are unable to keep up with reflex-based shooters are delighted to immerse themselves in the slower-paced mental challenge of interactive fiction. The more mature and often less violent tone of some IF stories can also appeal to an older audience with the patience and attention span to appreciate them.

Compared to the mainstream game industry, the audience for IF may be small—but it's surprisingly broad.

Literary Quality

The written word can do things even the most expensive multimedia cutscene cannot. Here are some snippets demonstrating the wide range of genres and tones found in modern interactive fictions. Many of these are not the sorts of moments you expect to find in mainstream games:

"She listens intently, expressing no reaction—no judgment, no amusement, no boredom or distraction—and you find yourself straying into more personal territory. Not dark secrets, but incidents that have no bearing on anyone but you. Standing on the porch of a friend's house while the Santa Ana winds stripped branches off the palm trees and made the telephone poles bend and sway, restless with the electricity in the air. The sort of thing that would make little impression now, but which at the time seemed wonderful and strange."—*Galatea*, Emily Short (2000)

"I began to have my doubts about Mr. Booby almost as soon as the balloon had made its ascent from Berkeley Square."—*To Hell in a Hamper*, Jason Guest (2003)

"Calm down. All you have to do is write a thousand words and everything will be fine. And you have all day, except it's already noon."—*Violet*, Jeremy Freese (2008)

"A man could go mad trying to describe the desert to another man—it's easy enough to talk sand, mind you. It's harder to get down to brass tacks with endlessness and loneliness, to talk the truth about anything, really, except the long white curves of the desert. But they're not even curves, really. Maybe closer to waves, maybe closer to doodles drawn by a half-asleep Picasso."—*Blue Chairs*, Chris Klimas (2004)

"In the beginning was the Word, and it was hungry."—*Slouching Towards Bedlam*, Daniel Ravipinto and Star Foster (2003)

"Parts of the city like this one give you a special tingle and suggest that Santa Claus and Jesus will be able to coexist in peace."—*Book and Volume*, Nick Montfort (2005)

"You are standing in a circle of hot, white light in the midst of a great darkness. …In the center is a glittering stainless steel table and, suspended beyond that, the silver throne of the Inquisitor… criticised by many for his leniency, his reliance on mercy, but he still is an imposing figure, floating in mid-air, surrounded by a dozen black video screens and surveillance cameras."—*Kaged*, Ian Finley (2000)

"Rowdy Juanita stands behind the bar, a six shooter in each of her upper set of hands, a third being reloaded by her lower arms."—*Gun Mute*, C.E.J. Pacian (2008)

"Your corpse is now just so much meat scattered across the grass, but enough of your face remains that you can tell that, yes, it's definitely you the dogs are eating."—*Shrapnel*, Adam Cadre (2000)

Good writing can evoke visuals and sounds, but also tastes and smells, textures, emotions; it can reveal the mental state of the viewpoint character or other characters; it can create multiple layers of reality, narration, and truth; it can use metaphor, rhythm, dramatic irony, stream of consciousness, and other techniques refined over centuries of tradition.

For the last twenty years, digital games have been trying their hardest to be like films. Maybe some of them should try being like literature instead.

Why Inform 7?

Inform 7, first publicly released in 2005, is the preeminent design system for IF today. Its lineage can be traced in a fairly straight line all the way back to *Zork*, the first interactive fiction released by Infocom.

By the early 1990s IF had been declared dead on arrival, but a growing online community was celebrating their favorite games and even making some of their own. The hero of *King's Quest* was losing his luster, but a different, less fictional Graham was equally willing to lead people into new realms of storytelling magic. In 1993, Dr. Graham Nelson of Oxford University announced he had created both a new language for creating interactive fiction, and a compiler for this language that produced files readable by the many existing Infocom interpreters. Of his "Infocom-format compiler," called Inform, Nelson modestly wrote "It is not a marvelously well-written program, but it does work, and it is documented."

Twelve years later, after nearly 100,000 newsgroup posts mentioning Inform and something like a thousand stories written with the language, Nelson announced Inform 7, a radically new language entirely. While the old Inform was "a computer programmer's tool which aimed to be welcoming to creative writers," Inform 7 "aspired to be the other way around": a tool for making interactive stories that's been designed first and foremost for writers, not coders.

Why choose a language like Inform 7 over a more traditional general-purpose programming language like C or Python? Why choose it over other IF design systems, such as TADS 3 or even Inform 6? A few of the biggest reasons are outlined below.

Natural Language

Inform 7 uses a natural language (NL) syntax that lets authors use English sentences to create their story worlds, which Graham Nelson calls "a radically humanising interface for the writing of interactive fiction."

Inform 7 is not the first programming language to have an NL structure—the effort dates back at least to 1959 and the creation of COBOL—and experts have accused similar systems for being long-winded and lacking clarity. While traditional programming languages are better at solving traditional programming problems, Graham Nelson asserts (and I agree) that the writing of interactive fiction is *not* one of these problems.

Take, for example, this sentence of real Inform 7 code (adapted from an example in Nelson's 2005 paper "Natural Language, Semantic Analysis, and Interactive Fiction"):

> Every turn when a container (called the sack) held by someone visible (called the unlucky holder) is bursting, say "[The sack] splits and breaks under the weight! [if the player is the unlucky holder]You discard[otherwise][The unlucky holder] discards[end if] its ruined remains, looking miserably down at [the list of things in the sack] on the floor."

Here is the same snippet rewritten in Inform 6, which has a more traditional programming structure:

```
[ Initialise s;
    ! start a daemon for every sack object in game
    objectloop (s ofclass sack) {
        StartDaemon(s);
    }
];
Class sack
    with daemon [ unlucky_holder;
        ! check to see if sack is bursting and its owner is visible
        unlucky_holder = parent(self);
        if ((self.bursting == 1) && TestScope(unlucky_holder, player)) {
            print (The) self, " splits and breaks under the weight! ";
            if (unlucky_holder == player) {
                print "You discard";
            } else {
                print (The) unlucky_holder, " discards";
            }
            print " its ruined remains, looking miserably down at ";
            WriteListFrom(child(self), DEFART_BIT + ENGLISH_BIT);
            print " on the floor.^";
        }
    ],
    has container;
```

Both versions produce identical games, but the first is easier to understand, since it reads like a natural English sentence. We still must learn the kinds of sentences Inform understands, to be sure—but we can guess, and are likely to remember without needing reference material, what "every turn" means much more easily than "StartDaemon(s)". The first version likewise does not need clarifying comments, because the words explain themselves—whereas in the second version, we feel obligated to remind the reader that "TestScope" relates to whether or not something is visible; to translate the code into human-readable text. One of the great innovations of Inform 7 is reducing the need for this extra layer of translation between the writer and the compiler.

Since IF communicates with the player in plain English, and the player communicates back in plain English, it seems only natural that the author should be able to do the same thing. Or, in Nelson's words, "the natural language for writing IF is natural language."

A subtler benefit of natural language is the playful creativity engendered by a fuzzier boundary between coding and writing. Soon after Inform 7's release, people began writing source texts that were not only functional games, but functional poetry. The following limerick, which is also a complete and valid Inform 7 program, plays on the old text adventure clichés of lamps and dark spaces:

> The Hole Below is a dark room.
> The description is "Cavernous gloom."
>   The lamp is in Seoul.
>   Before going in Hole,
> instead say "You will meet a grue soon."

Accessibility

Inform 7 compiles stories into one of two formats, z-code and Glulx, both of which can be played with an appropriate interpreter program on an astonishing variety of devices. IF interpreters have been written for the Mac OS, Windows, Linux, UNIX, Commodore 64, PalmOS, iPhone, Android, JavaScript, Java, Flash, Silverlight, Xbox, Game Boy, a number of long-dead systems and probably systems not yet invented at the time of this writing.

As a result, your stories will be playable on nearly any type of computational system imaginable, with no extra work on your part, and as the fan community continues to write new interpreters at a steady pace, your stories will still be playable and enjoyable ten or twenty years in the future on computer systems we can't even imagine yet.

IF also tends to be much simpler, computationally, than mainstream games, meaning neither you nor your audience needs to have the latest, greatest hardware. IF theoretician Nick Montfort went so far as to release "hardback" editions of his story *Winchester's Nightmare*—installed on cheap, aging laptops.

Community

A supportive and vocal community of Inform authors and players can be found online, offering advice, playtesting, and active discussion on the theory behind interactive narrative. Other online resources include a dedicated wiki, databases of games and reviews, tutorials, screencasts, and more detailed documentation.

URLs to some of the best resources at the time of publication can be found at the end of Chapter 2. Up-to-date links will also be maintained at this book's website for as long as possible.

Your best long-term bet to find the community, of course, is by typing "Inform 7" into your favorite search engine.

Extensions

Inform 7 was designed from the ground up to make it easy to package useful source texts as "extensions," which allow authors to easily add more functionality to their games or customize built-in behavior. The official website hosts hundreds of extensions, all freely available for download and use within your own stories. You can incorporate a tutorial extension, for instance, which will teach your readers how to play an IF story. You can grab another that prints an on-screen map of the territory explored. There are extensions to add specific types of objects to your game world, like horses or ropes, and others to add systems for combat, conversation, or magic. Why recode the wheel?

Navigating This Book

Intentions

I wrote this book to help you learn how to tell an interactive story with Inform, regardless of whether you have any interest in learning how to program.

Chapter by chapter, you'll construct a full example game along with me, gaining the vocabulary, comfort, and familiarity necessary to launch into your own projects once finished. While we won't cover all of Inform's advanced functionality, or every one of its dozens of built-in systems, I'll help you learn where to find the parts you need, and the skills to create similar systems on your own.

Don't expect a history of IF in this book—for that I recommend Nick Montfort's excellent *Twisty Little Passages*. This is also not a replacement for a comprehensive reference manual, which the built-in documentation and a forthcoming book by Graham Nelson will cover, nor is it a book on game design or IF theory, though we'll touch on a little of both as we go along.

Finally, this isn't a book that will teach you how to write programs in any language (for that I recommend *Processing: A Programming Handbook for Visual Designers and Artists*). Our focus will be strictly on using Inform 7 to write interactive fiction, without spending much time on abstractions without practical examples.

Naming Conventions

Consistent language is an important component of any instructional book, so briefly, here's the rationale behind certain nomenclature choices.

Scholars of interactive stories have often struggled with what to call the pieces they talk about. Are they stories, or games? Are the people who interact with them readers, or players? The most useful answer, of course, is that they are both, but then which terms should we use to refer to them? While some have proposed the creation of new words like "story-game" or "reader-actor," I find these constructions too self-conscious, and terms like "inter-actor" too much of a mouthful. Instead, I'll use **game** and **player** in contexts most concerned with interaction, and **story** and **reader** when we're talking about narrative, and trust you to follow me across both terminologies.

And what do we call a single work of IF? The emerging consensus, and the one this book adopts, is to call it **an interactive fiction**, as in "*Photopia* is an interactive fiction about memory and death." This seems less redundant than something like "interactive fiction story," and less awkward than something like "work of IF."

While most programming languages use the term "source code" to describe what the user generates, Inform and this book use the term **source text** to mean the same thing, a nod to the readability of Inform's natural language sentences.

Finally, I'll most often refer to "Inform 7" as simply **Inform**. This is not only easier to type and read, it's also a reminder that this version of Inform is a completely new language. It's not really the seventh version of anything, but a wholly unique paradigm for IF creation.

Info Boxes

As you progress through the book, you'll see several types of boxed text.

CAUTION Cautions note potentially confusing elements or pitfalls to watch out for.

Source text blocks contain sentences of Inform source text. Many of these are meant to be typed in to your local copy of the example game as we build it: those that do will always indicate where in your source text the block should go.

Sometimes you'll see illustrative source text not meant for the game:

> This will still be styled like source text, but will be visually distinctive.

PROGRAMMER'S NOTE

Programmer's Notes contain info of interest to people with prior programming experience. For the most part, this book ignores conventional programming lingo and standards, but experienced coders may want to check out these blocks to better understand how Inform's concepts relate to the larger programming world.

 Tip boxes contain supplementary info and sometimes point to information about more advanced functionality glossed over in the main text.

Many common Inform constructs can be understood by multiple syntaxes. We'll sometimes demonstrate these with a sidebar like the one seen here.

New Concept

First method.

Second method.

Exercise

Finally, the occasional exercise lets you test the concepts you've just learned in a non-guided way. One possible implementation of each exercise can be found at the end of its chapter. Exercises are always optional: you can include the given answer or your own solution in the example game as you build it, or leave them out.

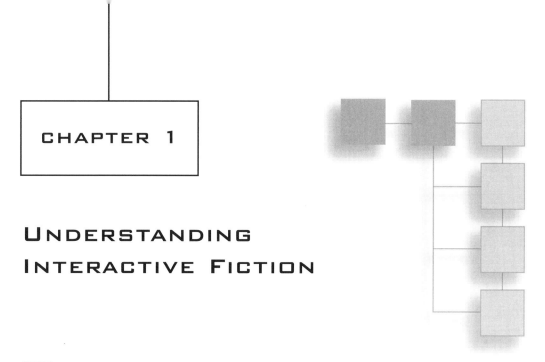

CHAPTER 1

UNDERSTANDING
INTERACTIVE FICTION

Before you start creating your own interactive fiction, it's important to understand the medium: its strengths and weaknesses, its tropes and clichés, its language, pacing, and flow. If your experience with IF is limited to hazy memories, and especially if you've never encountered an interactive fiction before, this chapter provides a useful overview of what IF is like and what it can do.

Blue Lacuna: An IF Excerpt

Let's start by looking at an existing IF story in mid-stride. Below I've adapted a portion of *Blue Lacuna*, an interactive fiction I released in 2009, into a sample transcript. The transcript should offer a brief taste of what playing IF feels like. After the excerpt, I'll break down the details of what's going on.

> Of course, as with anything, learning by doing trumps simply reading about an experience. I highly recommend downloading and exploring *Blue Lacuna* (Figure 1.1) or any of the hundreds of other freely available interactive fictions online for yourself. Tips for finding and playing IF and some recommended stories can be found later in the chapter.

In this excerpt, the player explores a seemingly abandoned tropical island. The capitalized words after each **prompt** (the > character) represent commands typed by the player, and all the other text is a response from the story explaining what happened next.

Figure 1.1
The cover art for *Blue Lacuna* (2009).

>*LOOK*

Beach, Near the Log Cabin
The beach widens here in the middle of its sweeping curve around the lagoon, rising in graceful white dunes to the sudden black slope of the old lava flow. Up against the flow is built a log cabin, looking long-neglected but still intact. Pristine white sand stretches in a great arc around the lagoon.

The beach stretches away back south towards the cluster of boulders or north to the rocky rise, or you could also wade down into the lagoon. The cabin lies up the beach.

A gull walks carefully along the sand, occasionally poking at something with its indigo-tipped beak.

>*EXAMINE GULL*

These seem larger and more streamlined than most you've seen, and their long yellow beaks are tipped with a vivid indigo rather than red. But their cries sound just as you'd expect.

>*PET GULL*

The gull leaps into the air with a raucous call, flapping up in a broad spiral to join its fellows.

>*UNDO*

Beach, Near the Log Cabin
Okay, I've taken back your last move.

>*EXAMINE CABIN*

The small cabin lies well up above the high water mark, but stains and crusted salt near its base indicate spring tides have reached it in the past, and give the small building the feel of a place abandoned. The cabin rests flush against the black lava flow behind it.

>*ENTER CABIN*

You clamber up the slipping sand past seaweed and shells at the high-water mark, then onto sturdier ground, before finally arriving at the building. First peering cautiously through the doorway, you step inside.

Abandoned Cabin
Sand drifts around the open doorway, spilling out in tiny dunes across the wooden floorboards, undisturbed. Bare, water-stained walls frame a small room, empty and abandoned save for a manta ray skeleton hanging from one wall; some frayed ropes tied to one beam are the only other hint of past furnishings.

The room's sole other feature is a wooden box discarded in a corner.

Two smaller interior doorways lead north to a bright porch or east to a darker interior. You can also step back outside.

>*NORTH*

You duck through the small doorway into a windowed porch.

Cabin, The Studio
High, narrow windows admit steep slants of daylight into the studio. The floor is stained with paint and clay, and artisan tools litter the surface of a wall-to-wall workbench, though everything seems to be under a layer of thick dust, as if undisturbed for years.

On the rough plank walls to the east and west, exactly opposite each other, hang two spectacular paintings.

The only exit is back south to the front room of the cabin.

>*EXAMINE PAINTINGS*

Which do you mean, the left painting, or the right painting?

>*LEFT*

You step up and study the incredible artistry.

A gently rolling hilltop of lemon-yellow and milky-white wildflowers, fantastically profuse, explodes from the surface of this painting. A large gathering of smiling people in simple clothes of brown and crimson pick the flowers, laughing and smiling: children, parents, aunts, grandmothers, all so richly detailed that you can almost hear them laughing and calling out to each other. The smell of dusty dry pigment somehow suggests the first day of spring, and fresh mountain breezes in a sea-blue sky. Beyond the hilltop a storybook village basks in late morning haze, thatched roofs and cobbles ringed by balding mountaintops, rounded and emerald green.

Carved into the rough-hewn frame is a word in an unfamiliar language.

>*SOUTH*

You return to the larger front room of the cabin.

Abandoned Cabin

>*LOOK*

Abandoned Cabin
The white glow of the beach through the open door is brilliant; your eyes struggle to adjust to the dim interior of the cabin instead.

The room's sole other feature is a wooden box discarded in a corner.

Two smaller interior doorways lead north to the brightly-lit studio or east to the tiny storage room. You can also step back outside.

>*EXAMINE BOX*

You blow sand and dust off as you kneel to examine it, brushing years of neglect from its detailed surface. The box is a perfect cube, each side about the length of your forearm, carved from inter-locking pieces of wood which fit together seamlessly without nails or mismatched joins. Intricate carvings cover every surface. Salt crusts the lower third, where the wood is swollen and discolored.

>*OPEN IT*

You can't see any signs of hinge or latch.

>*SHAKE IT*

You rock the cube back and forth. It seems lighter than it should be, and you can hear something shifting around inside.

>*X CARVINGS*

The carvings, impossibly tiny, make up one immense, tropical scene. Splashing dolphins segue seamlessly into beaches littered with shells, tall, graceful palm trees, laughing children, and fanciful animals. You could study these carvings for hours without taking in all the detail.

Along the top of the cube, worked into the design, are five oval indentations.

>*TOUCH INDENTATIONS*

You slip your fingers into the indentations along the top and push with your other hand. The top rotates open easily, revealing a delicate sketchbook.

>*READ SKETCHBOOK*

You open the sketchbook and study the first page.

The first drawing shows a stunning portrait study of two girls, maybe ten or eleven. Long black hair frames unsmiling but beautiful faces, trapped between the carefree whimsy of childhood and some premature pain that strips it away. At first you take them for twins, though subtle differences of appearance suggest otherwise, because of their nearly identical expressions. Though they look out at you and not each other, some bond strong even for sisters connects them, forged perhaps in loss and strengthened by necessity of reliance, each upon the other.

It looks like you could see more if you turn the page.

>*SAVE*

Ok.

Hopefully, the transcript has given you a sense of what IF is like. Though this may not be the most exciting or drama-filled moment in the story, it demonstrates the fundamental partnership between author and player that defines IF. In the next section I'll explain what's going on in a little more detail, and tell you how to play IF on your own computer.

How to Play Interactive Fiction

Nearly all IF comes in the form of packaged **story files.** These are platform independent, meaning the same story file runs on many types of computers (just as the same PDF or MP3 works on a Mac, PC, or smartphone). However, you first need a program for your system that understands these files (such as iTunes to open MP3s on a Mac, or Windows Media Player to open them on a PC). This program is called an **interpreter.**

Finding and Installing an IF Interpreter

Story files come in several formats, depending on which language their author used to create them and what technical capabilities the story required. Inform 7 produces story files in one of two formats: **z-code** or **Glulx**.

z-code story files are best for small or medium stories. They do not offer advanced style or multimedia capabilities. Z-code story files typically end with the extensions .z5, .z8, or .zblorb.

Glulx story files are best for long stories or those which need advanced style and multimedia effects. Glulx stories typically end with the file extensions .ulx or .gblorb.

While z-code and Glulx are similar, they have different specifications (think DVD versus Blu-Ray), and therefore you will need a separate interpreter program for each format. Some interpreters conveniently come with built-in support for multiple formats. At publication time, my favorite multi-format interpreter for Windows machines was Gargoyle (http://ccxvii.net/gargoyle/) and for Macs, Zoom (Figure 1.2) (http://www.logicalshift.co.uk/unix/zoom/). However, as interpreters and URLs frequently change, try checking the website for this book or searching online for something like "Windows z-code interpreter" for the most up-to-date results.

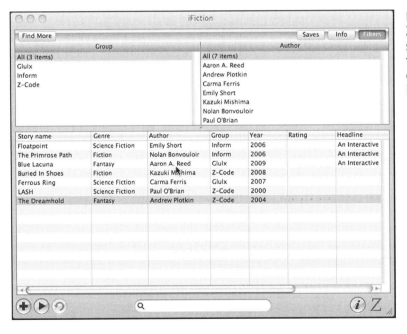

Figure 1.2
Zoom's iTunes-like story browser on the Mac helps you organize your interactive fiction.

You may also see story files written with another IF design system, such as TADS, which generates story files with the .gam extension. These require their own interpreter (or one capable **CAUTION** of running multiple formats).

Once you've located an interpreter, you'll need to download and install it. This should be a quick and simple process: just follow the instructions on the interpreter's website or in a readme file within the download.

The interpreter may automatically associate itself with files ending in the appropriate extensions, which means double-clicking a story file will launch it. If this doesn't work, you can launch the interpreter, select File > Open, and then choose the story file you wish to play.

 Increasingly, interpreters are written for the web on platforms like JavaScript and Flash. In most **TIP** cases, using a web-based interpreter means just clicking a link and selecting the game you wish to play from a list of pre-populated options. However, it still makes sense to have your own local interpreter. You can play any game at all, not just pre-selected ones; you can customize the appearance to something you're comfortable reading; and most crucially, you can test your own stories locally without needing to upload them to the web.

Finding Stories to Play

Once you have an interpreter, where do you find stories to play?

Since the rise of graphics, text-based games have been perceived, rightly or wrongly, to have little commercial value. As a result, nearly all the interactive fiction of the past two decades has been released for free on the web. Small file sizes and widespread availability means it's the work of only a moment to download a story and start playing.

Try browsing the recent winners of an IF competition (like the long-running IF Comp at http://www.ifcomp.org/) to find high-quality stories to play. Another great resource, the IFDB (http://ifdb.tads.org/), hosts themed lists and reviews hundreds of interactive fictions in every genre imaginable.

Here are a few of my personal favorites:

Bronze by Emily Short. A twist on a classic fairy tale, heavy on exploration, and good for beginners.

Slouching Towards Bedlam by Star Foster and Daniel Ravipinto. Enter a steampunk adventure set in a dangerously different London.

Hunter, in Darkness by Andrew Plotkin. Wriggle through wet cave passages and stalk your quarry. Short and gripping.

1893: A World's Fair Mystery (Figure 1.3) by Peter Nepstad. Explore a meticulous recreation of the historic Chicago World's Fair.

Shade by Andrew Plotkin. Magical realism and hidden secrets in the predawn gloom of a modern apartment.

The Gostak by Carl Muckenhoupt. If you don't speak the language, can you still play the game?

Photopia by Adam Cadre. A classic of inevitability and tragedy.

See the section "Resources for Learning More" in Chapter 2 to find other places to look for IF to play.

Figure 1.3
Cover art for *1893: A World's Fair Mystery.*

Playing IF

Okay—you've got an interpreter, and you've opened a story file with it. Now how do you actually play?

It may seem intimidating at first, but it's not difficult to learn to play IF. What follows covers all the basics.

Command Prompt and Syntax

The atomic unit of IF is the **turn**. During each turn, the game prints text describing what your character sees and experiences in the fictional story world, and you respond with an imperative command describing what you want the character to do next. No time passes in the story world until you submit the next command. This call and response forms the basis of all interactive fiction.

Some IF commands are one word, a verb such as LISTEN or LOOK, but most require two: a verb followed by a noun, like OPEN DOOR. The story usually understands pronouns and adjectives, but almost never requires them: an exception is when the extra words resolve ambiguity, such as OPEN GREEN DOOR. Some commands need both a subject and a direct object, as in ASK DOCTOR ABOUT EMILY.

Any valid IF command does one of three things:

1. Observation: Returns information passively about the state of the world.
2. Action: Causes a change in the state of the world.
3. Action Out of World: Performs a "meta-action" on the program running the story world, not the story world itself.

Here are some common examples of each of these three types of action.

Observation	Action	Action Out of World
LOOK	TAKE [something]	SAVE
EXAMINE [something]	OPEN [something]	UNDO
LISTEN	UNLOCK [something]	QUIT
INVENTORY	GO [direction]	RESTART
WAIT	ASK [someone] ABOUT [something]	

IF commands most commonly involve moving through physical spaces, examining your environment to better understand the story world, and manipulating objects to advance the plot.

Room Names

Space in IF is divided into specific areas called **rooms**. When the player moves to a new room, or types LOOK, the story prints the room name in bold, followed by a line break and the room's description.

Descriptive Text

The vast majority of IF is written in the second person, present tense—*you* are the person experiencing the events, and they are happening *now*. In regular fiction this style can be difficult to identify with, but perhaps because of the more immediate nature of IF, second person present tense has become the standard voice for the medium.

Well-written text in IF broadcasts relevant information about the story world. Any objects specifically mentioned imply significance, even if only as conveyers of background and flavor. One of the most common verbs in IF is EXAMINE, which reveals more details about a specific nearby object (if, of course, the author has provided these details).

Manipulating Objects

A computer can much more easily simulate a person's stuff than the person himself, so many interactive fictions rely on details of setting and props to carry the plot. In most stories, you can TAKE and DROP things (and review what you're carrying with INVENTORY). You can also CLOSE and OPEN, LOCK and UNLOCK, or TURN ON and TURN OFF appropriate items. Authors can easily add new commands, so a story with a guitar would very likely respond to the verb PLAY.

Abbreviations and Shortcuts

Many commonly used commands have single letter abbreviations to save typing:

Command	Abbreviation
EXAMINE	X
INVENTORY	I
WAIT	Z
GO NORTH	N (and so on for all compass directions)
UP	U
DOWN	D
OOPS	O (see "Actions Out of World" below)

Another useful shortcut that nearly all IF interpreters support: players can press the up arrow key multiple times at the prompt to cycle through previously entered commands.

Disambiguation

If you type a word that might refer to more than one visible object, the story asks a disambiguation question. EXAMINE TRAIN in a certain story might result in "Which do you mean, the express train or the toy train?" At the next prompt, you can type a single clarifying word (like TOY) or a whole new command to try something different instead.

Actions Out of World

Use SAVE and RESTORE to bookmark your place in a story and return to it later. RESTART lets you begin again from the first turn. Typing UNDO "takes back" the previous command entered; in some interpreters, you can do this multiple times in a row. OOPS corrects a single word in your last command (so after EXAMINE TOY TRAN you could type OOPS TRAIN, or just O TRAIN, and the story would continue as if you'd typed EXAMINE TOY TRAIN the first time).

Misunderstood Commands

When you type something the story doesn't recognize, it tells you it's confused and no time passes in the story world: you can immediately try something else without consequence. While the most commonly misunderstood commands are simple typos and misspellings, the system that deals with your input (called the **parser**) will also be confused by attempts to use verbs or nouns it doesn't understand (such as SNICKERSNACK JABBERWOCK in a story where neither word has been implemented), non-imperative commands (like THIS IS HELLA COOL YO), overly complex commands (like DO PICK UP THE CIGAR, THERE'S A GOOD FELLOW), and, in most games, attempts to converse with the game or game characters in unstructured English sentences (like WHAT DID YOU SAY ABOUT MY MOTHER?).

The IF command prompt promises a certain amount of magic. Unlike nearly any other game interface, it potentially understands a nearly unlimited set of commands—the English language. Many games take advantage of this flexibility to offer magical moments hard to replicate in other media. The sudden realization that your character can perform an action you didn't think he could; the witty wordplay in games like Rob Dubbin and Adam Parish's *Earl Grey*, where you can transform objects by adding or removing single letters from their names; the flash of delight when you realize what topic will force an uncooperative character to talk—all these are moments when IF's text parser really shines.

The flipside to this magic: the parser can't understand everything. Many new players grow jaded or disillusioned by a sequence of misunderstood commands. As an author, make sure your audience knows what sorts of commands are likely to be fruitful: we'll focus on how best to communicate this in the chapters ahead.

The Nature of Interactive Fiction

We've seen how to play interactive fiction, but we still haven't defined what makes it unique as a medium. What is IF at its core?

Story vs. Game

"Games and stories don't mix," said sci-fi author Orson Scott Card in 2007. "In a game, the players have a simple motivation: To win within the rules. In a story, the teller of the tale has the motive of entertaining, and the characters in the tale have their own motives, which are rarely simply 'to win.'" *Doom* creator John Carmack once expressed a similar sentiment even more bluntly: "Story in a game is like story in a porn movie. It's expected to be there, but it's not that important."

The belief that games and stories are fundamentally incompatible is surprisingly common, especially considering some of the highest-rated and best-selling game series of recent years, including the *Elder Scrolls*, *Grand Theft Auto*, *Metal Gear Solid*, *Fallout*, and *Half-Life* franchises, all have strong narrative components. To counteract this misconception, it's worth refreshing our definitions of story and game to make it clear how the two activities both resemble and differ from each other.

Game

A **game** provides a play activity structured by a set of rules that participants agree to abide by while participating. Games present challenges that must be overcome using the rules of the game: the challenge should be difficult but possible to achieve for at least one player. The challenge often represents some real-world difficulty, providing a way for players to rehearse the act of problem solving in a safe and consequence-free environment.

Story

A **story** introduces a protagonist who must fight against an opposed force in order to achieve a desired goal. A storyteller determines the arc of the protagonist's journey, adding details to keep the audience's interest, and ensuring that suspense is maintained until the protagonist is able to achieve victory, despite seemingly insurmountable odds. Stories transmit cultural information and give societies common touchstones and points of reference.

These two definitions certainly vary quite a bit, but I also see many overlapping points between them. Both games and stories create a special "space" used to experience an alternate reality, with all participants agreeing to abide by the rules of that space (the game board/suspension of disbelief). Both involve difficult challenges that can nevertheless be overcome (by the players or protagonist). Both have mechanisms to provide structure (rules/genre conventions), and we are meant to learn lessons in both that can be applied to the real world.

My personal belief, and one I hope readers of this book will share (or at least entertain), is that games and stories can not only mix, but can also harmonize to form novel experiences that neither can engender alone. When story and game fuse into a single experience, that experience becomes a collaboration between two people: the player navigating the game, and the author telling the story. Both parties should have an active role in shaping the experience: the author must give the player opportunities to participate in the story in meaningful ways, and the player must respect the author's story world and have a genuine desire to explore it. When this collaboration works, it can be a truly magical experience.

The game/story debate deserves much more attention than the glib summary provided here. A great and seminal introduction to the topic is Janet Murray's *Hamlet on the Holodeck*. More recently, *Second Person* collects essays from dozens of gamemakers and storytellers grappling with these same questions. I highly recommended both books for anyone interested in telling interactive stories.

Solving Puzzles

Inform's creator Graham Nelson once called interactive fiction "a narrative at war with a crossword," and theorist Nick Montfort places IF within the ancient storytelling tradition of the riddle. Like crosswords and riddles, IF cannot be taken in passively: it demands participation from its audience. While the reader of a novel advances the narrative by turning the page, readers of IF must become players as well. Often this play takes the form of a series of **puzzles** that need solving before the story can continue.

In traditional fiction, the protagonist strives to achieve a goal while the antagonist places a series of obstacles in the way. In an interactive story, it's up to the player, not the protagonist (who mindlessly obeys the player's orders), to overcome these challenges with his or her own skills. In the mainstream video game world, these skills are often reflex and dexterity, since action translates well to both the tactile feedback of buttons and controllers and the visual feedback of the screen. But the written word is more suited to logic and argument. Just as print fiction tends to challenge its protagonists with more social, psychological, or cerebral problems, interactive fiction challenges players not with physical tasks but with mental or observational ones.

Puzzles provide challenge and interest, but also pacing: they slow the player down long enough to understand and synthesize the details of the story world. They also can act as a gateway mechanism, ensuring that the plot does not advance until all necessary story prerequisites have been met.

IF without puzzles is certainly possible, and has grown in popularity as the medium has matured. Puzzles are often poorly matched to a story's narrative, and can undermine its dramatic potential (see "Bad Puzzles" below). Even so, they remain the easiest way to add pacing, gameplay, and challenge to your interactive fictions. Understanding a little about the tradition and tropes of the puzzle will also help you navigate the many existing stories that include them. Below I'll quickly summarize the major types of puzzles common to IF.

Observation

If you watch the 2003 film *The League of Extraordinary Gentlemen*, it makes no difference if you understand the details of the plot or the geography of its alternate 19th century London; the film will continue regardless. But if you play the 2003 IF *Slouching Towards Bedlam*, also set in an alternate 19th century London, to reach and make sense of the end of the story you *must* understand the details of your environment and why the events you experience are happening. IF stories require that you look closer than you would at a film or even a book. For this reason, EXAMINE is probably the most commonly used IF command, and examining details of the environment is the most common first step towards solving a puzzle.

First-person shooters are all about moving through levels as quickly as possible, often offering achievements or high scores for fast times. Conversely, IF rewards smelling the roses (sometimes literally, as in Nolan Bonvouloir's magical time-travel fantasy *The Primrose Path*). It's usually much more like playing detective than playing action hero, more about experiencing the journey than claiming the reward. Puzzles often hinge on an assumption that players will be moving slowly and carefully enough to uncover details necessary to solve them.

Tasks

As in many other types of interactive stories, IF often requires the player to take a certain series of actions before the story can advance: finding a key for a door, convincing another character to help, discovering the function of a device and correctly operating it, and so on. Tasks are much like quests in mythology: they provide obstacles for the protagonist to keep him from achieving his goal too quickly, and a reason for him to move through the story world and let us discover it along with him.

However, for players, tasks can often feel like jumping through hoops. In poorly written games and even in some well-written ones, the justification for a task can feel weak and artificial. Keeping tasks tightly integrated to the ongoing story is crucial.

Lateral Thinking

Well-crafted IF rewards thinking outside the box, something easier to do with a text parser than with a game controller. One famous story drops the player into an unfamiliar character seemingly trapped in a dead-end landscape, and slowly hints and teases until the player realizes his character can FLY to escape. Nick Montfort's *Ad Verbum* features linguistic challenges like a room where the player can only type words beginning with the letter E. *Slouching Towards Bedlam* reveals disturbing truths about the nature of the central character's world that profoundly change the player's understanding of what certain commands can do.

Good Puzzles

A good puzzle provides challenge to a player, but also provides opportunities to meet that challenge. It exists for a reason connected to the story, not just as a speed bump. It reveals something about the story world and the characters within it. It's fun to fail at solving, and fun to solve. A good puzzle makes players think, but rewards them for thinking. A good puzzle should be interesting and fair.

Bad Puzzles

Of course, many games feature puzzles that are neither interesting nor fair. The entire genre of the adventure game became tainted by a reputation for arbitrary puzzles solved by using seemingly unconnected items together. Authors can easily fall into a trap where they feel they must demonstrate their cleverness to players, that players are somehow an enemy they must outwit. Designing good puzzles is hard, but designing hard puzzles is not necessarily good. We'll talk more about puzzle design as the book continues.

What IF Does Well

IF is a unique medium with its own strengths and weaknesses. Let's quickly go over some of the things it does particularly well.

Stories about Props and Settings

Motion pictures are best at telling stories through intriguing visuals. Radio drama excels at stories heavy with dialogue and set in interesting-sounding places. And interactive fiction's strongest storytelling tools are objects and settings.

While the old dramatist's saw that "stories are about people" holds true across media boundaries, it's hard to get people right in an interactive medium. Screenwriters and novelists have the luxury of pre-planning all the scenes in which their characters appear and converse with each other, but in interactive fiction one of the conversants—the player— might say anything at all, making dialogue exponentially more difficult to construct. We'll talk about how to deal with this problem in future chapters, but one of its consequences is that IF stories often focus on a single character (the player character) or on the spaces inhabited by and props important to the other characters.

Emily Short's *Floatpoint* begins with the player character landing on an alien world as a newly appointed ambassador. By first walking from the landing port on the outskirts in to town, then through town to your new office, exploring and settling in, you learn about the story's setting, about the back story that's happened before your arrival, and about your own character as he reacts to the things you see. The details of the environment you choose to interact with provide additional information to fill out the picture. Though there are brief conversations with other characters during this sequence, the bulk of the action and interest comes from the setting and props.

Stories about Investigation and Exploration

In his book *Cybertext: Perspectives on Ergodic Literature,* Espen Aarseth says "A reader, however strongly engaged in the unfolding of a narrative, is powerless. He cannot have the player's pleasure of influence: 'Let's see what happens when I do *this.*'" But, Aarseth continues, in stories that are "ergodic" (requiring effort by the reader to advance) the reader becomes the player, gaining power over the environment and a freedom to participate in it. The simple joy behind this empowerment—discovering what's around the next corner, or behind the next locked door—was at the heart of the earliest interactive fictions, and still continues to be a large part of the charm in modern IF.

Nearly all interactive fiction lets players explore an unfamiliar environment, and it's usually one populated with things to investigate and sometimes puzzles to solve. Some memorable settings from modern IF games include a sinister trailer park in the Mississippi bayou (*Lydia's Heart*), a haunted Arctic research station (*Babel*), Shakespearean London (*The King of Shreds and Patches*), fragmented memories of the Holocaust (*Buried in Shoes*), an elaborately recreated World's Fair in Chicago (*1893: A World's Fair Mystery*), a castle steeped in Japanese mythology (*The Moonlit Tower*), the post-apocalyptic ruins of a Civil War plantation (*LASH*), and an abandoned afterlife (*All Hope Abandon*). In each of these works much of the joy comes from the feeling of immersion in and exploration of these meticulously recreated environments, without the focus on hurry and combat that goes with graphical shooter games.

Stories about Mechanics and Systems

Because IF excels at interactions with objects, as well as playful exploration, it's a medium well suited for presenting complex systems the player must discover, experiment with, and master. Some stories may feature actual machines with puzzles built around activating and operating them; others, such as Adam Cadre's *Varicella,* are based around mastery of complicated social dynamics. Emily Short's *Damnatio Memoriae* requires the mastery of an elaborate magic system tying one object to another, while Dan Shiovitz's *Bad Machine* and Carl Muckenhoupt's *The Gostak* present seemingly incomprehensible surfaces that become more and more clear with investigation.

What's Harder with IF

As with any medium, IF has weaknesses too. Let's go over some of the things that aren't as effective in this medium.

Stories about Action and Reflexes

Interactive fictions, unlike movies or plays, do not unfold in real time, which means they are less suited to stories about lightning-fast reflexes or adrenaline-soaked action. This is not because of the medium's foundation in written language—certainly many adventure novels feature these qualities—but has more to do with its central "call and response" dynamic. Most action games feature simultaneous player input and game output, but IF is turn-based: the action must halt for the player to read the story's text, consider what to do next, and type the chosen command. As with chess, or something like a court room trial, the structure of the experience dictates a more thoughtful, considered approach. This tends to translate into more thoughtful, considered stories.

This is not to say it's impossible to create action IF (see *Gun Mute*), nor is it impossible to create a thoughtful shooter game (see *Deus Ex*). But certainly, both cases are more challenging than playing to the strengths of your chosen format.

Stories about Precise Spatial Relationships

Some types of games—from *SimCity* to *Tetris* to *Starcraft*—rely on the precise positioning of dozens or hundreds of elements, and the player's understanding of the meanings of these positions. IF is a poor choice for this sort of game simply because language is inherently imprecise. We don't say a book is 2.87 meters away; we say it is "nearby," a word which has a much different meaning than if we're talking about a nearby city. We've already seen how this ambiguity is also a strength of IF (writing "blasting away at his tree ships" does not require a multi-million dollar budget), but for describing precise arrangements of elements, it's a weakness, and IF is not the best tool for that sort of gameplay.

Length

How long should an interactive story be? What amount of work is required to make an IF story?

Most IF written in the past 20 years has provided a play experience of one to two hours. This places it in the same range as the literary short story. However, though a quick author could write a short story in a single afternoon, an IF of the same length requires a much greater time commitment.

A good rule of thumb is the Rule of 60. If you want to create an IF story that will take someone one hour to play, you'll probably have to spend at least 60 hours designing, building, and testing it. This means if you can work on it an hour a day, you should expect to spend about two months on the project. Games with more or less complicated puzzles, mechanics, and ideas, of course, will take more or less time to create.

While many authors have created novel-length stories (ahem!), these take exponentially more time: the rule of 60 breaks down as complexity increases. I'd highly recommend that your first few IF projects be short story length or even shorter. It's very easy to start off with an incredibly ambitious first project and get lost in the woods. Come up with an idea and try to decide what the simplest way to tell that story is. You'll get a bigger sense of accomplishment for actually finishing something, more feedback, and can get started on your next, better story right away.

Sand-dancer: **The Example Game**

As you read through this book, we'll construct together an interactive fiction called *Sand-dancer*. As you reach the last chapters, you'll have seen the process of creating and building this small but real story all the way through, from first line to final polish.

So that you have some idea of the overall shape of *Sand-dancer*, I'm including my concept document for the game below. I like to write a document like this once the design is mostly finished but before I begin coding. It lays out all the major challenges of the game—all the systems that need to be designed and all the components of the story and setting. As I'm creating the game, I can refer back to this document to see what still needs to be built, and make sure I'm sticking to my original vision for the story.

PROGRAMMER'S NOTE

If you've programmed before, you may be familiar with the concept of the "design document," which lays out the design and functioning of a program in explicit detail. I've found that interactive fiction projects rarely need such a detailed design write-up. Partly this is because so much of the infrastructure is provided by using a language like Inform 7, but it's also that IF stories are simulations of worlds, so you can often describe all the important behavior using completely non-technical terms.

The Concept Document

The story begins with a crash: waking up behind the wheel of a pickup careening out of control. You've come to a stop having driven off the road into the desert night of the American southwest: lonely and cold. Fuel dribbles from the punctured gas tank, and the tracks behind the truck disappear into pitch blackness. The highway is nowhere in sight. An electrical tower and abandoned utility building are the only signs of civilization within the range of the truck's dying headlights.

You explore the desert around the tower. Distant coyotes howl, hares flee from the fading headlights of the truck, and little dun-colored lizards (sand-dancers, grandmother used to call them) scurry through the sand. Storm clouds cover the moonless sky and the desert is pitch black outside the light. You find a flashlight and poke through the abandoned interior of the tower's utility building. As you explore, things uncovered trigger memories bubbling under the surface, traumatic events which appear in your "emotional baggage."

Through these memories, you learn that your character is Nakaibito Galvano ("Knock"), a high school dropout, working two jobs, with a girlfriend on the reservation 40 miles away. The conflicting mythologies of your white hippie grandmother, Mexican stepfather, and absent Native American dad overlay these memories: stories of three spirit animals

Figure 1.4
The cover art for
Sand-dancer.

watching over you, dreams for the future and the grimness of your present. You were on a midnight drive home from work to see your girlfriend, having made an important decision, when you dozed off and drove off the road. The decision, its nature still unclear to the player, weighs heavy on Knock's mind.

In one room of the utility building is an old shortwave radio. On it you raise a BLM ranger with a strangely familiar voice who gives you two options: try to fix the truck and get back to your girlfriend, or camp out at the station for the night and wait for help to come in the morning. Indeed, around the building are items that could move you towards either goal, but Knock does not have the strength or courage to retrieve them.

But the open desert seems to call, whispers of sand skidding through sage. Once you've spoken with the voice on the radio and lit up the building by activating the emergency lights, you can chase a skittish hare into the desert, until you stumble over a root and fall into a half-hidden burrow. Awakening, you discover you are not alone.

In the burrow is the rabbit, one of Knock's spirit guardians. His huge black eyes glint in the dim light; his lightning-fast heartbeat fills the room. The rabbit is a strange mixture of Native American folklore and 21st century cynicism: some of the aphorisms he spouts are from *Family Guy*. The rabbit offers to trade one of his talents, strength or courage, for one of the troubled memories you've uncovered. After you choose, he vanishes, but not before reminding you there are two other spirit animals watching you. As you regain your senses, stumbling groggily back towards the tower, rain begins to fall.

With the help of your chosen talent, you can advance towards one goal: camping out or fixing the truck. The goals begin to take on a larger importance: trying to get home tonight would reaffirm a commitment to Knock's girlfriend, while staying the night suggests that Knock needs to make time for himself, instead.

But the building seems different now, subtly changed. The voice on the radio seems to know more than it should, the crackling static like the hissing of sand. The voice asks if you know who you really are, taunts you, threatens you. Knock finally realizes why it sounds so familiar: it is his own voice.

If Knock is ever unsure what to do, the player can try smoking a cigarette to think the problem out. This quickly becomes a slippery slope, though: the more the player smokes, the more likely Knock is to smoke by himself without the player requesting it, weakening his resolve to quit.

Shortly after acquiring a goal item, the storm clears up, and the desert calls you once again. Deep in the sand you meet the next spirit animal: the Coyote, sneakier and less comforting than the rabbit. He preaches freedom, and looking out for yourself before anyone else, and also forces Knock to confront the hard truth he's been trying to keep from thinking about all night: his girlfriend is pregnant. Though there's no money to start a family, she wants to keep the baby.

The Coyote offers another choice of talents, this time costing two memories: either luck or scent. He too vanishes, but not before warning that the last spirit animal is the most dangerous of all.

Using the Coyote's power brings you even closer to your chosen goal. But as you do so, the ground begins to shake. Sand pours in through the window of the building and you must flee to the roof, where the final spirit animal is waiting: an enormous lizard, Sand-dancer himself. As he speaks, dangerous and sinister, millions of tiny lizards scurry through the desert around the tower, leaving intricately elaborate patterns in the sand.

Sand-dancer lays out the truth behind your choice. For three memories, he offers you one of two talents: honor, with which you can fix your truck and return home to your girlfriend, committing to a life together; or spirit, choosing the freedom of the open road, abandoning her and your roots for a life on your own.

But Sand-dancer smiles. There is another choice, he tells you. If you give up all your memories to him, you can buy freedom, the most powerful gift of all. With it you can remake the world so that the baby was never conceived, erase it from the past, the present, and the future. There will be no problem to solve, no hardship to suffer. His raspy tongue snakes out and the lizards below writhe, waiting for your decision.

Each choice provides its own conclusion to Knock's story. It's up to the player to decide which one is right.

What It Will Teach Us

Sand-dancer is strongly plotted, without many forking branches: it is certainly much closer to story than game. But it still touches on several strengths of IF: exploration, a mature story world, and meaningful choice. Few mainstream video games feature Native American mythology or teen pregnancy as thematic elements, which lets us explore ground that hasn't been mined to death already by other interactive stories. Throughout the game the player makes choices (which memories to retrieve, which goal to work for, what attitude to take with the spirit animals) that mirror the game's ultimate resolution, and the player defines how those choices are meaningful.

To build *Sand-dancer*, we'll need to learn how to describe this story world to Inform and let our players experience it. In the next chapter, we'll learn how to download and install Inform, and in Chapter 3, we'll begin creating *Sand-dancer*.

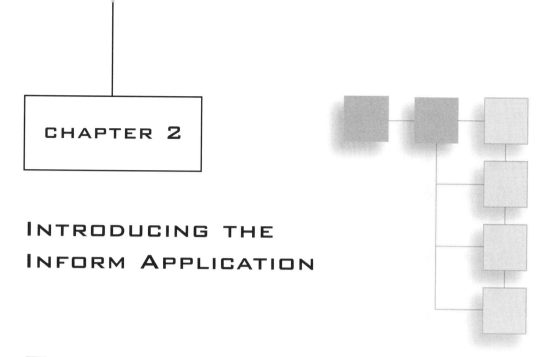

CHAPTER 2

INTRODUCING THE
INFORM APPLICATION

Inform 7 is not just a programming language, but a free application that helps you organize, write, and release your interactive fiction projects. This means that a single download is all you need to get started making your own IF.

After you've installed Inform, we'll get familiar with how it's laid out and how its design helps authors of interactive stories do their work. By the end of this chapter, we should have the tools we need to start writing *Sand-dancer*.

Installing Inform

You can download Inform 7 from http://inform7.com. Click the Download link and then look for the latest release that matches your computer type—Mac, Windows, or Linux.

Installing for Windows

On a Windows machine, double-click the .exe you just downloaded to launch Inform's install wizard. Click Next and choose a folder where you'd like to install the application—the default setting is probably fine. Click Next again and choose the Start menu folder where you'd like Inform to live—again, use the default if you don't have a preference. Finally, click Install and the wizard will do its magic.

When you see a message that installation is complete, click the Finish button. Inform can be launched by navigating through the Start menu to the relevant folder—Inform, unless you changed it—and selecting Inform.

Installing for Mac

On an Apple Mac system, double-click the .dmg file you downloaded to open the Inform disk image. After a moment a window with the large title "Inform" should appear. You want to drag the Inform icon inside to your Applications folder. You may need to open a second Finder window (by pressing Command + N) to do this.

Once the file has been copied, you can eject the disk image—under the Devices header in the Finder, click the eject icon next to Inform7—and you can now start Inform by clicking its icon in the Applications folder. As with any Mac application, you can keep Inform's application in the dock even when it's not running: hold Control, click the dock icon, and select Options > Keep In Dock.

Installing for Linux

Inform for Linux is available both as a command-line compiler or a Gnome-based GUI application, with packages for a number of different distributions. I'll assume if you're running Linux you already know what you're doing and don't need detailed installation instructions.

Getting Started

When you first open Inform, you'll see a window (Figure 2.1) that asks whether you'd like to start a new project, reopen the last project you worked on, or open an existing project. An Inform **project** consists of all the source text that defines a single interactive fiction, along with related material for testing and releasing.

Click Start a new project. On a Mac, you'll be asked what type of project you want to create. In nearly all cases, you can just select New Project under Inform 7—the other options are for more advanced scenarios.

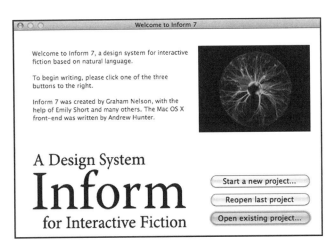

Figure 2.1
The first thing you see when you open the Inform application.

Next, Inform wants to know where the project should be stored, and what it should be called. The application creates a folder with the name you give it at your desired location, which will hold your project and Inform's internal work files. You can also store additional materials related to your game, such as cover art, in certain folders within the project directory—we'll talk more about this towards the end of the book.

 On a Windows machine, you can make the project name different from the filename, and must enter the author's name by hand. Mac projects inherit an author name from the user logged in to the system.

Once you finish this step, you'll arrive at Inform's refreshingly simple main interface (Figure 2.2).

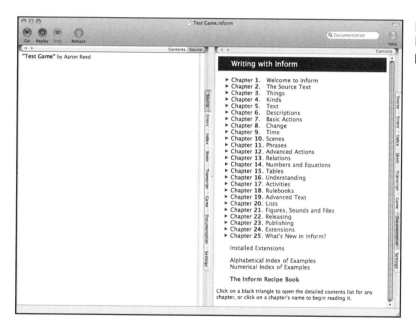

Figure 2.2
Inform's "facing pages" interface.

The Facing Pages

Whenever you're working with Inform, you always see two tall pages, like the facing pages of a book that provide windows into different aspects of your project. The tabs along the side (Mac) or top (Windows) allow you to decide what each page displays. Learning to navigate between these different views, called **panels**, is vital to getting anything done in Inform, so let's talk first about what each panel is for.

CAUTION The Mac, Windows, and Linux Inform applications are all a little different from each other and work in slightly different ways, because each one is actually a separate project by a different designer. I'll try to point out major differences in interface or functionality as we go along.

The Source Panel

In a new project, the Source panel (by default shown on the left page) seems as blank as a fresh sheet of paper at first glance. Look towards the top, though, and you'll see something like:

"Test Game" by Aaron Reed

This is actually the first line of **source text** for your project, defining its title and author, and all the rest of the words that make up your IF masterpiece will be written below it.

Syntax Highlighting

Depending on your settings, the story title may appear in bold, unlike the rest of the line. The Source panel can use syntax highlighting to automatically style different parts of your source text—prose, logic, section headers, comments—in visually distinctive ways (see Figure 2.3). This lets you see at once if, say, something has gone wrong with a quotation mark, and eases navigation through longer passages of code.

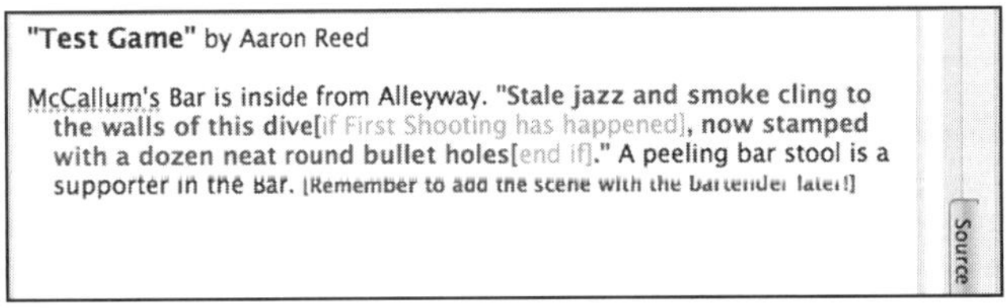

"**Test Game**" by Aaron Reed

McCallum's Bar is inside from Alleyway. "Stale jazz and smoke cling to the walls of this dive[if First Shooting has happened], now stamped with a dozen neat round bullet holes[end if]." A peeling bar stool is a supporter in the Bar. [Remember to add the scene with the bartender later!]

Source

Figure 2.3
A close-up of the Source panel, showing a paragraph of Inform 7 code using syntax highlighting.

If you're on a Mac and don't like the way the syntax highlighting looks, you can tweak the style (and other details about how your source text appears) by selecting Preferences from the Inform menu and perusing the Styles and Intelligence tabs.

The Contents Tab

The Source panel can also show only the part of your source text you're currently working on. Inform lets you insert divisions to add hierarchical organization, just like a book (just like this book, for that matter). In an IF adaptation of *The Wonderful Wizard of Oz*, for instance, you might begin with a heading like:

Chapter 1 -- The Kansas Prairie

Headings must be their own paragraphs (with blank lines before and after) and begin with a heading word (in ranked order, they are Volume, Book, Part, Chapter, and Section). Your chapter on Kansas might be contained within a larger, earlier heading:

> Part I: Locations

…and it might contain smaller headings within it:

> Section - Gathering Storm Clouds

You'll notice that after you've typed the heading word and a space, you can have anything you want that helps you categorize your project: letters, most symbols, words, descriptive subtitles, or nothing at all.

It's not necessary to use every level of heading, and subheadings are not required to be at the next level down. It's perfectly acceptable to have a Section immediately inside a Volume.

If dividing your work with headings strikes you as a waste of time, then listen up: by organizing your source text this way, Inform understands your project well enough to offer you all kinds of helpful tools and shortcuts. One of these can be seen by clicking the Contents button above the Source panel in a project with headings. This shows you a clickable table of contents for your project (see Figure 2.4).

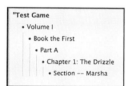

Figure 2.4
The Contents tab (in the Source panel), summarizing a source text that uses all five levels of heading.

Clicking any heading will open all the source text underneath it in the Source panel, and show arrows at the top and bottom of the page to let you "turn" to the headings before or after. This serves much the same purpose as white space dividing chapters in a printed book: it lets you focus only on the content at hand, without distraction from the beginning or ending of other material.

To return to the original view showing your entire source text, click Contents again and select your game's title at the very top of the list.

Organizing your project with headings has all kinds of other benefits, so it's good to get in the habit of doing so from the beginning. If nothing else, it's vital for keeping track of where you are in larger projects (see Figure 2.5). Imagine trying to read this book if all the chapter, section, and subsection divisions were removed.

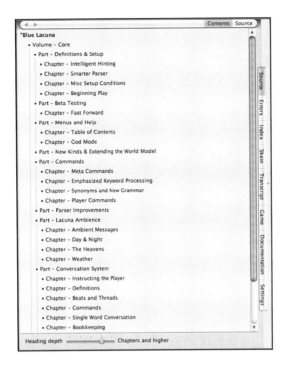

Figure 2.5
An example of the
Contents tab for a
large Inform project.

The Game Panel

If you're following along with Inform, try adding a few blank lines under your title in the
Source panel and typing the following:

    Section - Kitchen

    Kitchen is a room.

Press the green Go! button in the upper left of the application, and after a few moments,
your application should look like Figure 2.6. You can also press F5 (Windows) or Command
+ R (Mac).

Notice that Inform has switched the right page to the Game panel. This is where you'll test
your stories as you develop them, playing through them the same way your readers will
once your project is complete.

You should now be able to type commands at the **prompt** (the > symbol) in the Game
panel—try WAIT, GO EAST, and JUMP. Nothing too exciting is happening yet, but you
can see that you are indeed interacting with a story world already.

If you make any changes to your source text, you'll need to click Go! again—this is called
compiling your project—to place a fresh, updated copy in the Game panel. This pattern
of playing, adjusting your source text, and recompiling is the core of developing projects
with Inform.

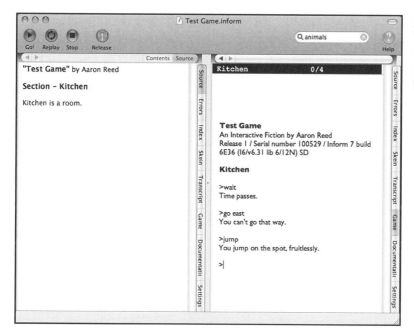

Figure 2.6
Figure 2.6
The Game panel showing the simplest possible example game.

PROGRAMMER'S NOTE

Clicking the Go! button compiles your project to a temporary z-code or Glulx file, with a lot of debugging routines added in. The Game panel then loads this temp file with an appropriate interpreter application. The Release button compiles a clean copy without debugging verbs, and lets you save it wherever you like.

The Errors Panel

If something in your source text is unclear to Inform when you recompile by clicking Go!, the right page will switch to the Errors panel rather than the Game panel. Here, you'll find a **problem** message, a friendly attempt to diagnose what's wrong with your source text and advice on how best to fix it.

Try mangling our single line of code:

    Kitchen iss a room.

Now recompile and watch what happens (it should look like Figure 2.7).

Inform tells us it no longer recognizes "iss" as something it knows about, so it can't make sense of the sentence, and, as a result, can't generate a story for us to play. Click the orange arrow icon in the problem message to jump to and highlight the source of the confusion.

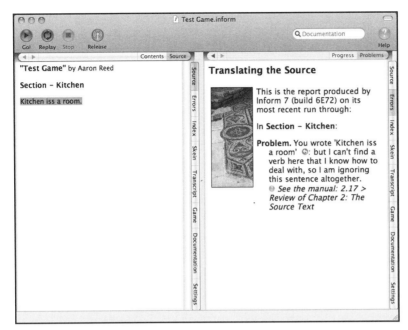

Figure 2.7
The Errors panel, reporting a problem message. I clicked the orange arrow link in the problem message, so the culprit paragraph is highlighted in the Source panel.

(This is somewhat unnecessary here, but becomes increasingly useful the longer your project becomes.)

Some problem messages, including this one, also include a second section in italics that directs you to the part of the documentation Inform guesses is most relevant. Click the blue question icon in these segments to jump to the appropriate page in the docs.

> Remember how I told you there were multiple benefits to organizing your code with headings? Here's another one: Inform also told us the error was found within Section – The Kitchen. The larger your project becomes, the more useful this signposting is to narrow down the bit of your source text that's confused Inform.

If you see the Errors panel instead of the Game panel when you compile, fix each error Inform finds one by one until your game successfully compiles and runs again.

The Documentation Panel

Inform comes with built-in documentation that explains in detail every feature of the language and application environment. You can browse this resource with the Documentation panel. The amount of information here can be daunting when you're first getting started, but the writing style is friendly, and hundreds of short examples provide helpful illustrations.

We'll talk more about the built-in docs in a minute, but note that the documentation is searchable. Click on the search bar with the magnifying glass in the upper right of the Inform application, type a search term, and press Enter (see Figure 2.8).

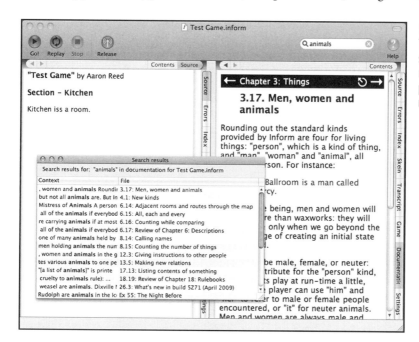

Figure 2.8
The documentation search window and a relevant page displayed in the Documentation panel.

If you'd like to search within the body of the documentation page you're currently viewing, press Ctrl + F (Windows) or Command + F (Macs). In fact, you can do this to search within almost any Inform panel.

The Other Panels

More advanced tools for testing, debugging, and releasing your game reside in the other panels. We'll introduce these as they become useful to us. The first few chapters of the built-in documentation describe these panels in detail, so feel free to read up on them if you're curious now.

Notice that both the left and right page have "back" and "forward" buttons at their top-left corners. These will step you forward and back through the material that page has recently displayed—even across panels. So if you clicked through three pages in the Documentation panel, then clicked Errors, and then Source, the page's back button would take you through each of those five locations in reverse order, switching between panels as necessary.

Using the Built-In Documentation

As you work through this book and become a more and more advanced Inform author, you'll find yourself referring with increasing frequency to the Documentation panel. Whereas this book is designed as a tutorial to ease you into making IF projects, the official documentation is the comprehensive source for the finer points of how Inform works, and is the key to unlocking the full potential of the very powerful and sophisticated Inform 7 language. It's worth taking a moment to understand how to navigate the documentation and use it most effectively.

The Documentation panel actually contains two manuals, each serving a different purpose (see Figure 2.9). You can switch between the two manuals with links at the bottom of each one's table of contents.

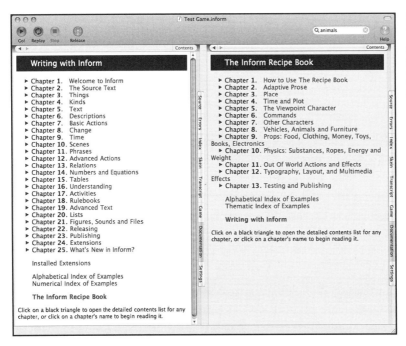

Figure 2.9
Inform's two built-in manuals: "Writing with Inform" in a Documentation panel on the left page, and "The Inform Recipe Book" on the right.

Writing with Inform

When you first open the Documentation panel, you see "Writing with Inform," which has a white background. If you'd like to learn more about a certain aspect of Inform's functionality—concepts like Text, Actions, Phrases, or Relations—this is the place. Click any chapter name to see the sections within it, and click a section to bring it up on the page.

While browsing the documentation, you can use the large forward and backward arrows in the black header bar to move from section to section, and the circle and arrow icon to go back to the table of contents. This functionality is also available at the bottom of each page.

Most sections of the documentation end with one or more examples. Click the name of an example to see its code and an explanation of how it works. The examples are excellent and are a great way to see easy or even complicated concepts in action (see Figure 2.10).

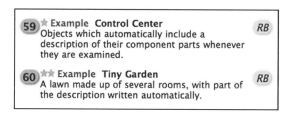

Figure 2.10
Over four hundred examples like this one can be found through the Documentation panel.

Each example is actually a complete source text that will compile and run on its own. Click the square icon next to the first line of an example's source text to paste it into the Source panel—you'll want to make sure this panel is empty first. You can then compile and run the example game, and even try changing it in the Source panel and recompiling to see what happens.

The Inform Recipe Book

The second part of the built-in documentation, recognizable by its tinted background, is "The Inform Recipe Book," which reinvents the hundreds of examples in "Writing with Inform" into an à la carte menu of common IF problems and solutions. This manual is great if you have something specific to do and want to know how to do it. If your story involves windows, weather, magic words, bicycles, ropes, or math (to name a few out of hundreds of examples), the Recipe Book will give you practical examples of one (or often, several) way to create them.

Note that the examples in both manuals have star ratings from one to three, which indicate whether they are of simple, intermediate, or advanced complexity. Some of the three-star material is beyond the scope of this book.

Extensions

An **extension** to Inform is like one of the documentation's examples wrapped up in a box you can easily use in your own project. There are extensions to implement certain types of vehicles, containers, or weapons; some that add elaborate conversation systems or simulate physics; others that add new commands for players to use or change the way output is reported; even some that change fundamental aspects of the IF experience in new and interesting ways. Figure 2.11 shows some examples.

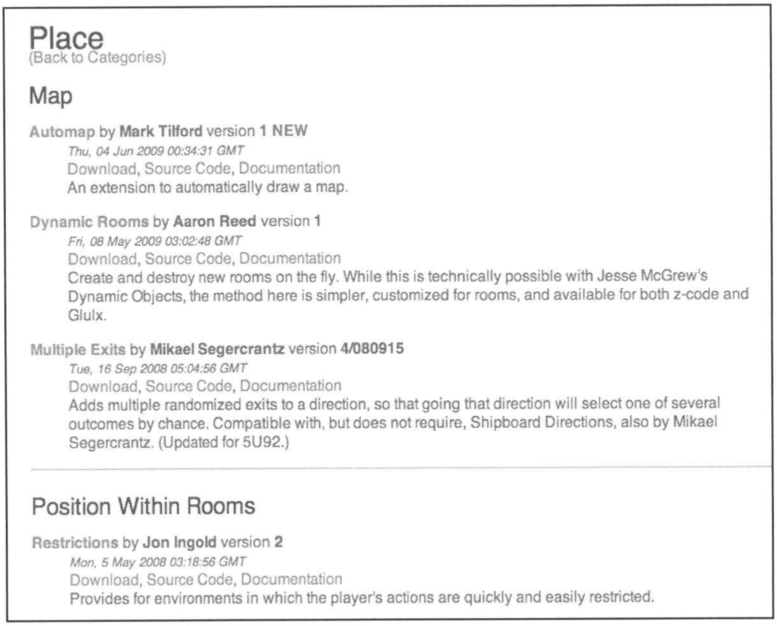

Place
(Back to Categories)

Map

Automap by **Mark Tilford** version **1 NEW**
   Thu, 04 Jun 2009 00:34:31 GMT
   Download, Source Code, Documentation
   An extension to automatically draw a map.

Dynamic Rooms by **Aaron Reed** version **1**
   Fri, 08 May 2009 03:02:48 GMT
   Download, Source Code, Documentation
   Create and destroy new rooms on the fly. While this is technically possible with Jesse McGrew's
   Dynamic Objects, the method here is simpler, customized for rooms, and available for both z-code and
   Glulx.

Multiple Exits by **Mikael Segercrantz** version **4/080915**
   Tue, 16 Sep 2008 05:04:56 GMT
   Download, Source Code, Documentation
   Adds multiple randomized exits to a direction, so that going that direction will select one of several
   outcomes by chance. Compatible with, but does not require, Shipboard Directions, also by Mikael
   Segercrantz. (Updated for 5U92.)

Position Within Rooms

Restrictions by **Jon Ingold** version **2**
   Mon, 5 May 2008 03:18:56 GMT
   Download, Source Code, Documentation
   Provides for environments in which the player's actions are quickly and easily restricted.

Figure 2.11
A few of the hundreds of extensions available on the Inform 7 Extensions page.

Inform was designed to make it easy for authors to include extensions in their projects, and I very much encourage you to do so. Extensions are the shoulders of giants to stand on until you grow into one yourself. If you just want to include an extension and use its functionality without worrying about how it works, that's great; if you want to open it up and find out how it ticks, that's even better. Either way you've saved time and moved your project forward.

You can find the library of Inform extensions at inform7.com (look under "Write" and then "Extensions"). Extensions are categorized in a similar way to the Recipe Book. As you browse through the possibilities, you can view their instructions or source code online. Click the name of the extension to download it to your computer.

 All the extensions on the Inform 7 website are freely available for any sort of use in any sort of project. You don't need to worry about getting permission from anyone to use them.

To install a downloaded extension, open Inform and select File > Install Extension. Find the file you just downloaded and click Open. The extension is now ready to be used (see Figure 2.12). You can include it in your story by typing a line like the following in your source text, specifying both the extension's title and author:

    Include Rideable Vehicles by Graham Nelson.

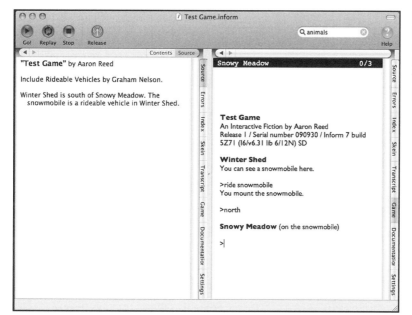

Figure 2.12
Once installed, it's easy to use an extension to add cool new functionality to your project.

Extensions come with their own documentation to let you know how each one is meant to be used. To access this, open the Documentation panel, make sure you're at the white "Writing with Inform" table of contents, and click Installed Extensions at the end of the chapter list. Click on the extension in question to see its documentation page, often complete with examples.

You already got some useful extensions when you installed Inform: go ahead, take a look. "Menus by Emily Short," for instance, lets you easily add a menu of options to your game.

If you want to look at the source text for any extension, just select File > Open Extension and choose the extension in question. Extensions are usually written in regular Inform with only some minor structural differences.

On the Windows application, the extensions that come bundled with Inform, including the useful Standard Rules, are not stored in the same place as any extensions you download yourself. If you'd like to view their contents, the built-in extensions can be found in Program Files\Inform 7\Inform7\Extensions.

CAUTION Be careful about modifying extensions you plan to reuse in the future. If you want to play around, it's best to make a copy of the extension and import it under a different name, so the original, functional version remains intact.

Resources for Learning More

A thriving interactive fiction community lives online, along with a huge range of free IF to play, reviews, tips, discussions, and tools. Here's a quick guide to some of the best places to look for more information.

The Inform Website

I've mentioned the official Inform website (http://inform7.com, Figure 2.13) several times already, because it really is one of the best resources for Inform authors. In addition to the extensions page, you can also find additional tutorials and reference docs, news, materials for teachers using Inform in classrooms, example games with source code, and lots more great stuff.

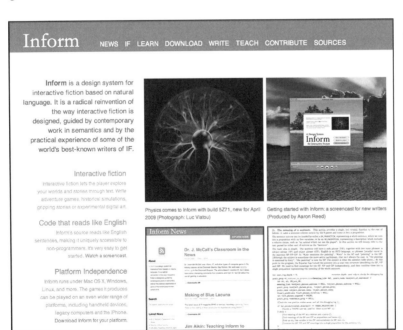

Figure 2.13
The home page of the official Inform website.

PROGRAMMER'S NOTE

Inform is a private project, but the author releases the source for all of its components as they grow stable and less likely to change radically. Some of the compilers and application code, as well as related tools, had been released by press time with extensive comments and documentation, with the release of the remaining code planned for the future. Visit the official site to find out what code is currently available.

The Interactive Fiction Community Forum

While there are a number of places online where IF authors and players gather, one of my favorites at press time was the Interactive Fiction Community Forum (http://www.intfiction.org/forum). This is a great place to ask technical questions or engage in discussions on the craft and theory of IF.

The traditional home of the IF community has been in the two Usenet newsgroups rec.arts.int-fiction and rec.games.int-fiction (Figure 2.14). While the unmoderated wildlands of Usenet are becoming increasingly unfashionable in the modern world, you can still find advice and the occasional on-topic discussion there.

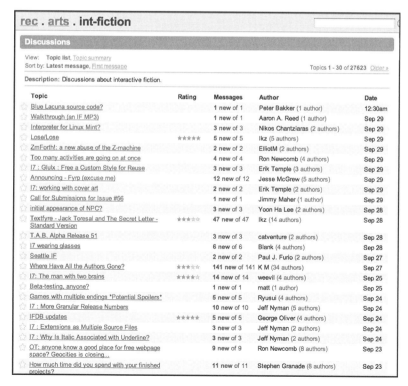

Figure 2.14
Some recent discussions in rec.arts.int-fiction. All the threads beginning with "I7" (and many of the ones that don't) are about Inform 7.

IFDB

The IFDB (http://ifdb.tads.org) is the best source for information on the IF stories authors have already told. You can find the fictions themselves, instructions on how to download and play them, reviews, user-created lists (see Figure 2.15) and polls, and other community-building resources. The vast majority of the IF indexed on the site is available for free download with a single click.

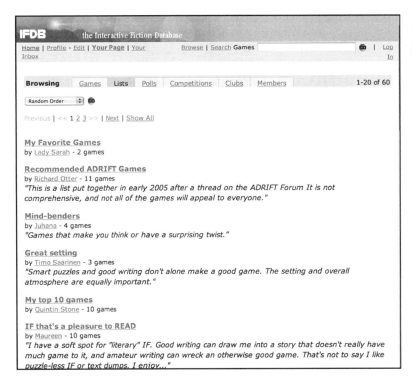

Figure 2.15
Some of IFDB's user-created lists of notable IF.

Planet IF

Planet IF (http://planet-if.com) is a news aggregator that pulls from dozens of blogs about interactive fiction and experimental digital games in general. Not all of the stories here are strictly IF-related, but they are all of interest to authors of playable narratives, and Planet IF is rapidly becoming the best source for in-depth commentary and critique of the medium.

IFWiki

Yes, everything has a wiki, and we have a pretty good one (http://ifwiki.org). The home page of IFWiki typically displays an overview of upcoming competitions and recent award winners in the IF world. Digging deeper, you can search for information about specific games, authors, programs, or even IF tropes and conventions. And, as you'd expect from a wiki, everything is editable and constantly being improved and updated by visitors.

CAUTION   It is, of course, quite likely that some or all of these resources may no longer be available by the time you read this. Since "IF" is a difficult thing to effectively index, a quick search for "interactive fiction" should pull up contemporary equivalents in whatever dystopian future you find yourself in.

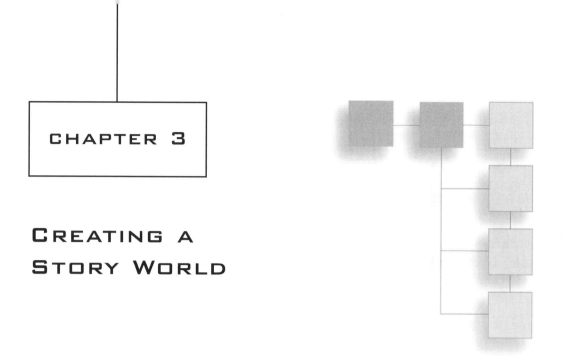

CHAPTER 3

CREATING A
STORY WORLD

Good storytellers hold universes in their heads. From erudite novelists to grizzled old men around campfires, every person who tells a story creates a mental image of characters, props for them to use, places for them to inhabit, and events for them to experience. Human storytellers carefully select the words that best reveal to their audience the state of the world in their imaginations.

To teach a computer with no imagination how to tell a story, we must first explain to it our **story world**—the places, things, people, and plans that make up a narrative. Only then can the computer select appropriate words to explain that story to an audience sitting at a keyboard, and only then can it understand what the audience types back.

Inform lets us use declarative sentences in natural-sounding English to define a story world. These sentences can be as simple as "Tom is a person," or as complicated as "Instead of attacking Tom when something lethal is held, now every nearby watchdog owned by Tom hates the player."

Over the next few chapters, we'll learn how to construct these sentences so Inform understands our meaning. In the process, we'll build, one sentence at a time, a complete interactive fiction called *Sand-dancer*. Breaking from the "text adventure" clichés of dungeons and trolls, *Sand-dancer* tells a contemporary story of a young man alone in the Arizona desert on an involuntary journey of dark mythology and irrevocable choices. (More details about *Sand-dancer* can be found in Chapter 1.)

You can follow along with the construction in your local copy of Inform by adding each sentence as it appears. Each snippet of source text contains a label indicating which heading and subheading it should be placed under, sometimes indicating that one or both headings need to be added. After adding each line, you can recompile the story by clicking the Go! or Replay buttons to begin interacting with the updated version within seconds.

Some source text only serves to illustrate a point, and should not be added to *Sand-dancer*. These cases will be printed with a gray background.

Sometimes, you'll be given a challenge to add your own twist to *Sand-dancer* in the form of an exercise to create something. One way to complete each exercise can be found at the end of the chapter, but you're encouraged to try to solve these problems yourself, to make sure you fully understand the concepts involved.

The official website for this book contains full source texts for the evolving *Sand-dancer* as it appears at the end of each book chapter. You can also play the full version of the game and view its complete source text online.

Building the Foundations: Rooms and Directions

Go ahead and create a new Inform project called "Sand-dancer." Review Chapter 2 if you need help installing Inform or creating a new project.

The Room

Space in most interactive fictions is divided into discrete chunks called **rooms**. Props and characters (including the player) can be in only one room at a time, and this simplifies concerns about distance and visibility: the player can see and touch just the things in the same room (see Figure 3.1).

Defining a room simply says that a space exists where characters and props can be. Inform makes no assumptions about the size of the room or its makeup—it can be an outdoor location, despite the name, or a space without clear conceptual boundaries at all.

Let's add the first sentence to *Sand-dancer*. We'll want to create two headings also, to keep our text organized: one called Part - Setting that will contain all the locations for our story, and a subheading underneath called Chapter - Around the Tower. Our first sentence will be within this chapter subheading. Make sure the title, headings, and first sentence each get their own paragraph (separated by blank lines).

    Middle of Nowhere is a room.

When you're done, your source text should look like Figure 3.2, and you should be able to successfully compile it by clicking the Go! button without receiving any problem messages.

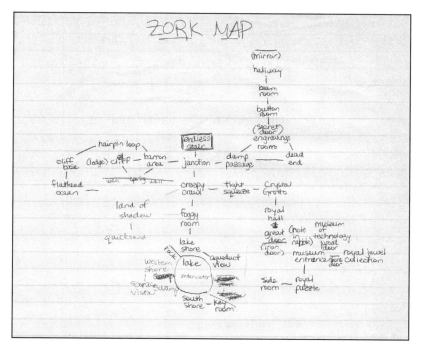

Figure 3.1
Early IF often required drawing elaborate maps of the story world, like this map of part of *Zork* by Mellicious; modern stories tend to be easier to navigate.

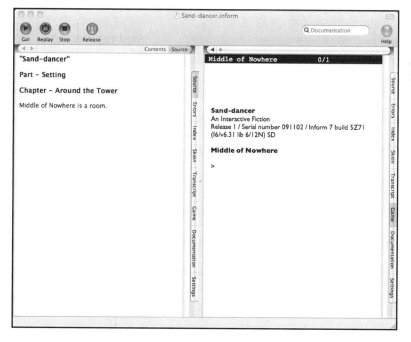

Figure 3.2
If you've been following along, your Inform application should look like this.

Something that's not in any room can't directly take part in the ongoing story: it's like a prop in a play that lingers backstage. This is why defining a room is the sole action Inform requires of you: without it, the player character would not exist within the story world, and no story could be told. Inform assumes unless told otherwise that the player begins the story in whichever room you define first.

But how does the sentence we wrote create a room? Inform understands certain declarative sentences containing the word "is"—present tense of the verb "to be"—as commands to create things in the initially empty story world. These sentences are called **assertions**. By declaring a thing to be, we make it so. Middle of Nowhere is now a specific place in our story world.

But hang on. Can we just write anything we want? What if we replace this line with:

> There is a room called Middle of Nowhere.

If we click the Go! button to compile our story, we see that this seems to do the same thing. What about:

> You can get to a place known as Middle of Nowhere.

This time, rather than a playable game, Inform has given us a problem message. "I can't find a verb here that I know how to deal with," it says. Herein lies the first and perhaps most important point to remember about writing stories in Inform: *though your story text looks like natural language, Inform does not understand all natural language.* It understands a specific set of phrases constructed in a specific way, and only those constructions will result in playable stories.

So how do you know what Inform understands and what it doesn't? Each time this book introduces a new construction, you'll see a sidebar like the one on this page, which shows all the valid ways to write the sentence in question. Anything other than these will confuse or be misunderstood by Inform. If you recompile and get a problem message, make sure you're using a valid format in the contested sentence.

Make sure you change your first sentence back to the original "Middle of Nowhere is a room." before continuing.

Defining a Room

- Middle of Nowhere is a room.
- There is a room called Middle of Nowhere.

Rooms can also be declared in relation to other rooms—for more on this syntax, see the next section.

Linking Rooms Together

People have written interactive fictions that take place in a single room. (Jeremy Freese's *Violet* is a recent example.) But a typical IF has multiple locations, which means we need a way to connect them together so the player can move between them. While the relationships between locations in a play or a film tend to be ambiguous, IF (and games in general) tends to involve discrete spaces and the movement between them as part of the experience of play.

CAUTION

Well, but why? Why is the movement between places a common trope in games, and often skipped entirely in novels and movies?

One theory goes that when someone participates in a shared story space—the implied story of conquest in chess or football, the elaborate epic tales of a tabletop role-playing game, a well-crafted interactive fiction—he must feel he has control over his alter-ego in that space. His actions may be restricted by game rules, but even if he has no agency at all—as in a game governed by the random roll of a die—he still expects, sometimes even insists, on moving his "piece" himself. In a similar vein, allowing your player to control his alter ego in your story world, to move at will from one location to another, helps make the story participatory and encourages him to engage with your world, rather than passively observe it.

Traditionally, the IF player moves between rooms with compass directions, typing commands like GO NORTH, NORTH, or just N (all equivalent). The use of compass directions can be traced back at least to 1975 and the original interactive fiction, *Adventure*, originally created by a caver involved in survey and mapping projects in the Mammoth cave system in Kentucky.

TIP

For an excellent history of this genre- and industry-defining game, I highly recommend *Somewhere Nearby is Colossal Cave: Examining Will Crowther's Original 'Adventure' in Code and in Kentucky*, by Dennis G. Jerz, freely available online. Check this book's website for a link to play the original *Adventure* in your browser.

Many IF authors have experimented over the years since with alternate systems of navigation, but compass directions have the virtue of being commonly known, easily visualized, precise, and easy to abbreviate ("N," "NE," etc.). The use of compass directions (even in story contexts without a compass) has become a genre convention, in the same way moviegoers understand that the characters onscreen can't hear the musical soundtrack.

Inform defines the eight cardinal and intermediate directions (north, northeast, east, southeast, south, southwest, west, and northwest), as well as up and down, and in and out. Rooms can be connected to each other along any of these directions.

We can create rooms in isolation, or we can define them in relation to already existing rooms. Let's add another sentence to our source text, in Part - Setting, Chapter - Around the Tower:

> Crumbling Concrete is north of Middle of Nowhere.

If you compile and run this game, you'll see that we can now type NORTH or N to move to our second room, called Crumbling Concrete, and south again to return to Middle of Nowhere. If we were to draw a simple map, it would look like Figure 3.3.

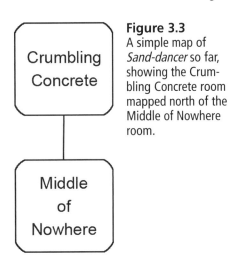

Figure 3.3
A simple map of *Sand-dancer* so far, showing the Crumbling Concrete room mapped north of the Middle of Nowhere room.

Defining a Room in Relation to Other Rooms

- [A room called] Crumbling Concrete is north of Middle of Nowhere.
- North of Middle of Nowhere is [a room called] Crumbling Concrete.
- Middle of Nowhere is a room. North is Crumbling Concrete.
- Crumbling Concrete is north of Middle of Nowhere and south of Base of the Tower.
- Crumbling Concrete is north of Middle of Nowhere, south of Base of the Tower, and outside from Staging Area.

"A room called" is stronger and should be used in room names containing special words like "and" or direction names. For more natural-seeming vertical connections, "up of" can be replaced with "above," and "down of" with "below," as in "Attic is above Kitchen." You can also replace "of" with "from" at your discretion.

The sidebar demonstrates several sentence formats we can use to make this read more easily. Let's quickly sketch out the rest of the map for the first portion of *Sand-dancer*. Add the next paragraph to Part - Setting, Chapter - Around the Tower:

> Base of the Tower is north of Crumbling Concrete. A room called Weed-strewn Rust is east of Crumbling Concrete and southeast of Base of the Tower. Backtracking is south of Middle of Nowhere.

Notice that you can more or less name rooms whatever you want. The name of a room becomes the way Inform understands it internally, the way you'll refer to it in later source text, and the way it's described to the player. Names can have multiple words (though beyond six or so gets confusing), but aren't allowed to contain certain punctuation marks, which Inform reserves for its own use (including . , ; : ( ) [ ]). If you capitalize letters in your name, your usage will be preserved when the game displays that name, although you can refer to the object later in your source text with whatever casing you like.

PROGRAMMER'S NOTE

In programming terms, Inform is case-insensitive, except that the casing of an object's printed name (and in some situations, its article) is preserved.

Regions

Quite often, a group of adjacent rooms in your story world will have something in common, in a way that ties in to your plot or game mechanics. Inform calls such a grouping a **region**. We can create and populate regions quite easily. Add the next paragraph at the top of Part - Setting, Chapter - Around the Tower:

> Around the Tower is a region. Middle of Nowhere, Backtracking, Crumbling Concrete, Base of the Tower, and Weed-strewn Rust are in Around the Tower.

CAUTION Regions must be defined before they're mentioned elsewhere in source text, to help ensure your meaning is comprehended by Inform.

If you add the above code and recompile, you shouldn't notice any difference in the generated story, since putting a room in a region doesn't produce any effect visible to the player. But as we learn more advanced techniques to make things happen in our story world, having similar rooms organized into regions will give us added flexibility in creating global game effects.

Regions cannot overlap each other. You can, however, declare that one region is entirely enclosed by another, with a line like:

```
The small region is in the large region.
```

My IF *Blue Lacuna* broke its tropical island setting into about a dozen small regions. All but a few of these were declared to be in another region called Outdoors. This let me easily write global rules to, for example, decide whether the player should be able to see the sky from a certain room, while also giving me the power to write rules based on the smaller subregions like Volcano Caldera.

Sand-dancer has three regions, in total: Around the Tower and Office Interior divide the main parts of the map into two useful chunks. The final region, Tower Vicinity, encompasses both, useful for checking whether the player is in the "normal" part of the world or other, special areas.

Let's go ahead and create these regions and their rooms. Make a new heading called Chapter - Office Interior (which should be the second heading underneath Part - Setting):

```
Staging Area is inside from Crumbling Concrete. Foreman's Office is north of
    Staging Area. Break Room is east of Staging Area and south of Storage Room.
    Roof is above Storage Room.

Office Interior is a region. Staging Area, Foreman's Office, Break Room, and
    Storage Room are in Office Interior.
```

Now, after all other room and region definitions in Part – Setting, add the line:

```
Tower Vicinity is a region. Around the Tower and Office Interior are in Tower
    Vicinity.
```

Structuring Your Source Text

We've only taken some baby steps into the water, but before we go any further let's put on our wetsuit. There are a few things you ought to know about authoring source text that will come up again and again as we go on.

Spacing and Ordering

Extra spaces and single line breaks within your source text are for the most part purely aesthetic. A double line break will be treated the same as a sentence-ending period, but otherwise has no effect on the way Inform understands your game.

Heading divisions are the only significant structural dividers Inform pays attention to. Each heading line, as well as the game's title, should be in its own paragraph.

We'll come to more complex statements later on that require specific line breaks and indentation, but for now, feel free to structure your source text however seems logical. I like my source text to read like a book, so I tend to put several related sentences together in a single paragraph, and separate each paragraph with a blank line.

The order of sentences in your source text mostly doesn't matter to Inform, but in certain cases referring to something like a region or a relation before you've formally defined it can result in problem messages. You can generally fix these by moving the definition before the line that's causing a problem.

Headings

I gave you a lecture about the importance of headings in Chapter 2, but it's worth reiterating here: headings save time. Dividing your source text using any or all of sections, chapters, parts, books, and volumes will make a world of difference in the ease with which you can alter, improve, and fix your story.

Remember that you can use the Contents tab of the Source panel to view only a particular heading and everything underneath it. Try clicking the Contents button in the upper right of the Source panel, then selecting Chapter - Office Interior to see this in action. You can click the up arrow in the top center of the window to jump to the previous heading (Chapter - Around the Tower), or click Contents again and then select the project title (*Sand-dancer*) to return to your original view of the entire source text.

Using "It"

As a handy shortcut, you can say "it" in your source text instead of the most recent thing you created. So instead of:

> Middle of Nowhere is a room. Middle of Nowhere is south of Crumbling Concrete.

…you could say:

> Middle of Nowhere is a room. It is south of Crumbling Concrete.

Take care with this construction, however. If you reorder your code, "it" might start referring to something completely different. It's also easy to write a sentence where it's unclear which of several things "it" might be referring to, which can lead Inform to assume the wrong one and your story to behave unexpectedly. Unless there's exactly one noun in the previous sentence, it's best to spell out your intentions more clearly.

CAUTION   "It" is an example of a word that has special meaning to Inform and which it's probably best to keep out of the names of your own things. Other words in this category include *have, has, wear(s), contain(s), support(s), relates, and, are, am,* and *with*.

If you do want one of these words in a thing's name, you can preface the assertion creating it with *a thing called* or use the printed name property (described in Chapter 6) to override its display name.

Comments

Sometimes you may want writing in your source text that isn't meant for Inform—notes to yourself, experiments, alternate versions of particular sentences, or explanations of complicated concepts. Fortunately, there's a simple way to tell Inform to ignore something: wrap it in square brackets.

> Middle of Nowhere is a room. [Not too exciting yet, but soon!]

Inform understands that the second half of that line—the **comment**—is for your benefit, not its own.

Experienced programmers will tell you that comments are your friends. While less crucial in Inform than in other languages, you can still use them to explain your thought processes as you're writing, and you'll find they increase your own understanding of what you're doing, assist other collaborators or friendly authors helping fix your bugs, and serve as a sanity check that what you're doing makes sense. There's nothing like explaining something to somebody else (even if it's only yourself) to get a firmer grasp on a concept.

Making Things

Rooms and the connections between them chart the geography of your story world. Next, we'll talk about what exists within this geography: the props and backdrops that fill out your fictional universe. We'll start with Inform's atomic unit of worldbuilding: the thing.

What Are Things?

Inform's basic object type is called the **thing**, and it makes up nearly all the "stuff" of your story. Let's add our first two things to *Sand-dancer*, in Part - Setting, Chapter - Around the Tower:

> A tumbleweed and a rusty tin can are in Base of the Tower.

The above assertion creates two things, called *tumbleweed* and *rusty tin can*. Not only will these names be shown to your players when they encounter these items, but all the words you use in the name can also be typed by players to refer to them. The sentence also places these two things in the room Base of the Tower. They may not stay there for the whole game, but that's where they'll begin it. We can see how these objects behave and respond to interaction by recompiling (see Figure 3.4).

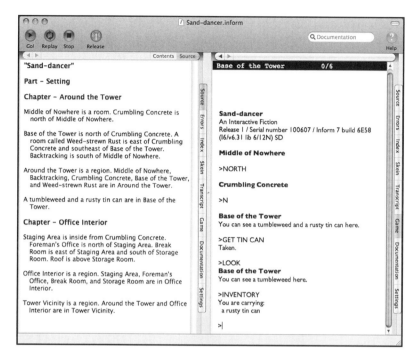

Figure 3.4
A short transcript of proto-*Sand-dancer* showing interaction with our first two things.

Defining a Thing

- A tumbleweed is a thing.
- There is a thing called a tumbleweed.
- A tumbleweed is in Base of the Tower.
- A tumbleweed and a rusty tin can are in Base of the Tower.

If you use one of the first two lines to define a thing without a location, it won't be encountered by your players, since it cannot be found somewhere the player can navigate to. The utility of this will become more obvious once we learn how to change the location of things in later chapters.

Articles

When you create a thing, you use an article like "a" or "the". Inform makes assumptions about how to describe your thing based on your choice of article.

- Creating "a bat" or "the bat" will result in your thing being described as "a bat" in lists and "the bat" individually. (Note that Inform doesn't care about "a" versus "an" when creating objects; it automatically uses the grammatically correct form when describing your thing.)

- To force the definite article "the," use the stronger declarative form "a thing called the bat" in your assertion sentence. This will result in descriptions like "You can see the bat here."

- If you use "some," as in "some scattered papers," Inform understands the new thing to be plural, and will refer to it as such, perhaps using *are* instead of *is* when mentioning them.

- If you use no article at all, as in "ENIAC is a thing," then Inform assumes the new thing is a proper noun, and refers to it as such, as in "You can't do that to ENIAC."

After your initial assertion creating a thing, you can use *a*, *the*, or no article at all whenever you refer to it: Inform will not read any meaning into your choice of article.

 We can override Inform's assumptions about plurality and articles by explicitly setting the indefinite article property of a thing: see the section on "Plural Things" in Chapter 10 for more about this in the built-in documentation.

Properties

Sometimes, we'd like to provide more details to Inform about the nature of a thing when we create it. To do so, we can use a word called a **property**. You can think of a property much like an adjective, except that properties always have opposites, and one of the two states is the default for any newly created thing.

Let's look at a few examples of properties common to all things.

Portable/Fixed in Place

As you noticed if you played around after creating the tumbleweed, most things can be picked up and carried around. This is because they have the **portable** property defined by default.

This is often not what we want, so we can use the opposite property **fixed in place** for things either too big, too inaccessible, or too ethereal for the player to take. Let's create an example in *Sand-dancer*, in Part - Setting, Chapter - Around the Tower:

    A tall Saguaro is in Middle of Nowhere. It is fixed in place.

You can also use a property much like an adjective when first defining the thing. The following line would be equivalent to what we wrote above:

    A tall Saguaro is a fixed in place thing in Middle of Nowhere.

CAUTION One of the easiest and most common bugs to be found in IF story worlds is the unexpectedly portable thing. My own work has seen testers happily walking around carrying pneumatic tube systems, bonfires, or in one case, an entire beach.

Described/Undescribed

By default, most things are **described**, meaning Inform will mention them when listing the contents of the player's location. If a thing is **undescribed** instead, Inform will omit it from this listing.

This doesn't seem very useful at the moment, but sometimes we've already mentioned an object in a piece of prose, or have an object players might try to interact with that's not particularly important to the story. Since we mention the weeds in our room name for Weed-strewn Rust, we ought to create them, but since they're just scenery and not important to the plot, we can give them this property (in Part - Setting, Chapter - Around the Tower):

> Some yellowing weeds are fixed in place and undescribed in Weed-strewn Rust.

Another thing we could create as undescribed is electrical tower in our Base of the Tower room:

> A huge electrical tower is in Base of the Tower. It is undescribed and fixed in place.

Lit/Unlit

Inform has a conceptually simple mechanism for modeling light and dark: if anything visible to the player has the property **lit**, including the room itself, the player can see everything in that room; otherwise, darkness reigns. Rooms are lit by default, but the existence of this property hints at the early days of IF, when players spent much time searching for sources of light to explore caves and dungeons.

Exercise 3.1

Try creating things called "some scattered newspapers" and "a withered cactus" in whatever locations you feel are appropriate, making sure the story uses the correct articles. Use appropriate properties so that, for instance, the player can't take items when it would be inappropriate. Feel free to add a few objects of your own devising.

Positioning

We've seen how things can be "in" a room. On an abstract level, we can say that the room **encloses** its contents. Some things can enclose other things, like the player: if we type TAKE TIN CAN from the appropriate location, the can is now enclosed by the player (who is in turn enclosed by the room called Base of the Tower). We can verify this by typing INVENTORY (or just I).

We can think of the objects in our story world existing in a diagram like a tree, as shown in Figure 3.5.

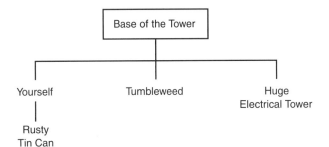

Figure 3.5
A diagram showing the tree structure for the Base of the Tower room.

Positioning things on the object tree in proper ways maintains the illusion of a coherent story world, in the same way theatres employ people to track where each prop and costume needs to be for every scene of a play.

A node on the tree encloses everything that falls beneath it, no matter how many levels down. So the room encloses the player, and it also encloses anything enclosed by the player.

PROGRAMMER'S NOTE

The parent of any item in Inform's object tree is called the **holder**; likewise, the first item enclosed by something is the **first thing held by** it.

We use "in" to say what room something is enclosed by. In the next few sections we'll talk about some of the other major forms of enclosure.

Holding and Wearing

As we've seen, the player (and, indeed, all characters in your story world) can enclose things, but we don't say something is "in" a person—instead, we say that a thing is either **carried** or **worn** by that person. Add this to *Sand-dancer*, under a new heading called Part – Mechanics (placed before Part - Setting) and a new subheading inside that called Chapter - Beginning the Story:

> The player carries a pack of cigarettes and a lighter. The player wears a denim
>   jacket.

Unless we tell Inform otherwise (such as via the "fixed in place" property) all things we create can be carried, but only certain ones can be worn. (Anything worn at the start of play, obviously.) For things that don't begin as worn by someone, but should correctly respond to commands like WEAR and TAKE OFF if found, we give the **wearable** property. We could have said this instead of the second sentence above:

> The denim jacket is a wearable thing. It is in Middle of Nowhere.

Or:

> The denim jacket is in Middle of Nowhere. The denim jacket is wearable.

Supporters

For a thing itself to contain other things, we need to make it a specific **kind** of thing. A kind in Inform is a subcategory with certain rules and behaviors already attached.

PROGRAMMER'S NOTE

Inform's kinds work much like classes in traditional programming languages. Kinds can be inherited from parent kinds. Multiple inheritance is not allowed.

One of Inform's two built-in kinds that deal with things enclosing other things is the **supporter**. A supporter is a kind of thing that other things can be on top of. A dinner plate, a table, and a treadmill are all examples of supporters. Add this to *Sand-dancer* in Part - Setting, Chapter - Office Interior:

> A half-collapsed desk is a supporter in Foreman's Office. On the desk is a rusted
>   key.

Almost any time you mention a single item in your source text, you can also mention multiple items at once. We could replace the second sentence above with "On the desk are a rusted key, a coffee cup, some stale french fries, and a crumbled wrapper." Inform would create all four objects on top of the desk. Likewise, the player could collect a group of objects from disparate places, and the game would allow us to put them all on the desk (by typing, in fact, PUT ALL ON DESK).

The above construction also illustrates another time-saving assumption of Inform: if you don't specify the full name of an object, Inform assumes you mean the first thing under the current heading with a name containing one of the words you used. So in the second sentence, "the desk" is understood to mean the same thing created in the previous sentence ("A half-collapsed desk is…").

As a result, you can create a "wire mesh cage" in one chapter and a "lion cage" in another, and say "the cage" within each chapter without the wrong one being understood.

When in doubt, you can always use the full name of the thing in question.

A supporter does not hide or prevent access to the items it supports, so you should be able to recompile, travel to the Foreman's Office room, and type TAKE KEY. We could formally describe this series of events by saying that the desk **supported** the key, but now the player **carries** it. The thing that **enclosed** the key changed from the desk to the player.

Creating Supporters

- There is a supporter called a half-collapsed desk.
- A half-collapsed desk is a supporter.
- A half-collapsed desk is in Foreman's Office. On the desk is a rusty key.
- A half-collapsed desk is in Foreman's Office. The desk supports a rusty key.
- A half-collapsed desk is in Foreman's Office, supporting a rusty key.

Enterable/Not Enterable

Supporters can be defined with a property called **enterable**, which means they can enclose the player (or any other character). If we created a supporter called the bumper car, the player could type ENTER CAR to climb aboard, and EXIT to disembark.

Since the damaged desk probably couldn't support the player's weight without collapsing, we accept its default property of **not enterable**, and don't need to change any of our source text.

Containers

The second way a thing can enclose another thing is if it is a **container**. Containers represent things that other things can be physically inside. Add the next line to *Sand-dancer*, in Part - Setting, Chapter - Office Interior:

> A wire mesh cage is in Break Room. In it is an emergency blanket.

Wait a minute—where's the word "container?" Again, we're relying on Inform's ability to make assumptions. Containers are the only kind of thing that can have something "in" them. (Remember, rooms are different than things.) Since we situate the emergency blanket in the cage, Inform infers that the cage must be a container.

We can still use the more explicit form for clarity, or if we don't have anything to put in our container just yet:

> A wire mesh cage is a container in Break Room.

Figure 3.6 shows a brief transcript of interaction with both our container and our supporter. Notice how Inform describes each enclosing item, explicitly telling players its status.

Creating Containers

- A cage is a container.
- There is a container called a cage.
- In/Inside the cage is a blanket.
- A blanket is in/inside the cage.
- The cage contains a blanket.

Note that "in" and "inside" can be used interchangeably in this context.

CAUTION It's important to remember that Inform does not come with built-in encyclopedic knowledge of nouns. It understands certain abstract concepts that define a supporter or container—such as the fact that you can't put a container inside—but it does not understand the meaning behind the words you use to name your things. If you create a container called a matchbox, and a thing called a yacht, your game will happily allow you to put the yacht inside the matchbox, even though that probably wasn't what you intended. We could also pile up an entire city's worth of things onto a supporter called "the delicate china saucer." Teaching Inform concepts like size or fragility must be done using relations and rules, which we'll explore in detail as we move forward.

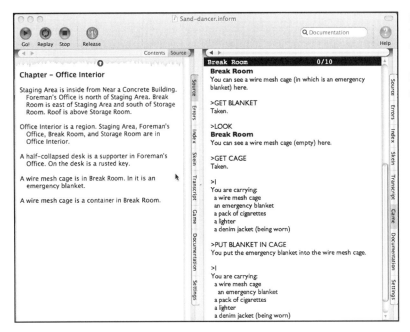

Figure 3.6
Two brief interactions with our proto-*Sand-dancer*, demonstrating a container and a supporter.

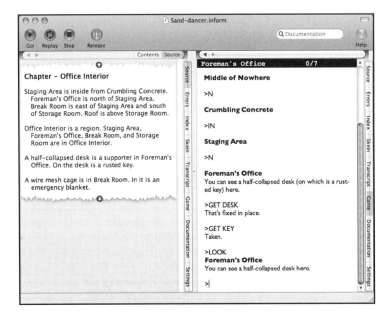

Inform's containers are more complex than its supporters. They can be enterable or not enterable, as with supporters, but they have several unique properties as well.

Open/Closed

Containers, unlike supporters, can be either **open** or **closed**. If we add the next line to *Sand-dancer* in Part - Setting, Chapter - Office Interior:

> The cage is closed.

…and go back to the Break Room location, the game no longer tells us the contents of the cage. Containers are open by default (meaning their contents are both visible and touchable), but we've overridden this assumption with a more specific declaration.

Remember, we can declare properties more succinctly by using them much like adjectives in our initial declaration of things. We could have said simply this earlier on:

> A wire mesh cage is a closed container.

Openable/Unopenable

Containers also have a more subtle property defined by default: they are **unopenable** (as opposed to **openable**). If you try the command OPEN CAGE in the game, you'll see indeed that it doesn't work. We can override this easily enough: add the next line to *Sand-dancer* in Part - Setting, Chapter - Office Interior:

> The cage is openable.

We could have done this instead, all as one line:

> A wire mesh cage is a closed openable container.

Why would you want something closed and unopenable? A glass display case with no way for the player to get inside might be one example. A container that's open but unopenable, on the other hand, might be something like a cup: it can contain something like water or a toothbrush, but you can't open or close it.

Containers can also be **locked** or **unlocked**, and you can create things that function as keys. *Sand-dancer* never uses this functionality, and modern IF audiences rarely find stories about locating missing keys to be interesting, but look up "Locks and keys" in the built-in documentation for further information.

Transparent/Opaque

Containers can also have the property **transparent** to indicate that their contents can be seen even when closed—they are by default **opaque**, the opposite. The contents of a closed transparent container are still untouchable, meaning players can see but not take the things inside a closed glass box, or, in *Sand-dancer*, our wire mesh cage. We'll also add one other property to our cage, since it's bolted to the wall. Add the next line to *Sand-dancer* in Part - Setting, Chapter - Office Interior:

> The cage is transparent and fixed in place.

Exercise 3.2

Add a few containers or supporters as background scenery in the building. Some examples might be a wastepaper basket, a rusted filing cabinet, and an overturned bookcase. Use appropriate properties to make these objects behave as the player would expect.

Custom Kinds and Properties

We've seen how to create things of an existing kind like a supporter, and we've seen how to give our things properties related to their kind (like a container's ability to be transparent or opaque). But real power lies in creating our own kinds and properties.

Creating New Kinds

Creating a custom kind is quite easy. Add this in Part - Setting, Chapter - Office Interior:

> A window is a kind of thing.

When creating a new kind, make sure you assert its existence before you create any objects of that kind. Otherwise, Inform might get confused.

We can now create "windows" just as we could create containers and supporters. Add this next bit to the same place:

> A pane of cracked glass is a window in Staging Area. A dust-covered window is a window in Foreman's Office. A tiny frosted window is a window in Break Room.

Why do we say "window" twice when creating the second and third things? It's because the first time, "window" is part of the name of the object—"the dust-covered window"—and the second time, we're stating the kind of the object—a window. It sounds redundant, but it's the same as writing an English sentence like "'The Kentucky Fried Movie' is a great movie!"

Default Properties for New Kinds

If we recompile, however, we can see that our windows do not seem different from any other thing in our game. This is precisely right: until we define how they differ from the norm, newly created kinds have no distinguishing features.

One way we can differentiate a kind is by defining which properties it has, and what their initial values are. Add this to *Sand-dancer* in Part - Setting, Chapter - Office Interior:

> A window can be open. A window is usually closed.

In the first sentence, we state that the new window kind has the built-in property open/closed, meaning every window we create will be in one of these two states. Supporters, for example, don't have a line like this, meaning it doesn't make sense to try to OPEN or CLOSE them when playing (if you try to do this, you'll see a message like "That's not something you can open."). To affect this, we use the **can be** construction followed by an existing property (in either of its two states).

Once we've established that a kind can be open or closed, we should also say the default state a new thing of that kind should be in. **Usually** in the second sentence makes this happen, establishing that newly created windows should by default be closed. We can, of course, explicitly create an "open" window. Add this in Part - Setting, Chapter - Office Interior:

> The tiny frosted window is open.

CAUTION It should be noted that letting windows be open or closed does not imply anything else about how they work. In particular, they haven't gained the ability of containers or supporters to enclose things. We'll have to write our own rules for how an open window differs from a closed window, which we'll do in a later chapter.

Sometimes, however, a property is such an inherent part of a kind that we should not allow its default to be changed. It should pretty much never be allowed for the player to pick up a window and carry it around, for instance. We use the word **always** instead of usually to make this true. Let's add to *Sand-dancer* in Part - Setting, Chapter - Office Interior:

> A window is always fixed in place.

TIP Each of these words has opposites: instead of "always fixed in place," an equivalent phrase would be to declare something "**never** portable." Less common is **seldom**: "seldom open" is equivalent to "usually closed."

One last thing for our window kind: remember the distinction between open and openable. We've said that windows can be open, and that they are usually closed, but we also have to say that they are able to be opened and closed by game characters, and whether they actually are by default. Add this in Part - Setting, Chapter - Office Interior:

> A window can be openable. A window is usually openable.

As it happens, we want to override this for one of our windows. Add this in Part - Setting, Chapter - Office Interior:

> The tiny frosted window is unopenable.

Every Inform project silently includes an extension called "The Standard Rules," which defines all of the standard actions, kinds, and rules that form the baseline of a consistent story world. The Standard Rules defines containers, for instance, including lines like "A container can be open. A container is usually open and unopenable."

Knowing this, it's good to add that you can also use the words learned above to override the Standard Rules. If you're creating a story with very accessible containers, for example, you could add the line "A container is usually openable." to your story text. If we had a story where nothing could be picked up and carried around, we could even make a more sweeping statement like "A thing is always fixed in place."

Contradictory Inform assertions tend to be resolved by treating the last assertion in the source text as true. The Standard Rules are included at the very beginning of a project, so any assertions in your source text will override them. When including other extensions, you can choose where in your source to place them, which in some cases can affect whether their assumptions or your own take precedence.

Making Your Own Properties

We've seen how to make a new kind and use existing properties with it, but we can also make our own properties, and attach them to any kind (even predefined ones like "container"). To do this, we use a construction like the following:

> A window can be large or small.

We can even create properties with more than two states:

> A container can be small, medium, large, or extra large.

…and in either form, we can apply our other rules as usual:

> A window is usually small. A container is usually medium.

But predefined properties like open and closed have observable effects in the story world. How does Inform treat a medium container differently than an extra-large one? It does-n't, at least not until we write rules and actions that only work on objects with our new properties. For now, we'll just set up some basic properties we'll need later on in *Sand-dancer*, and come back to fill out the details later. Add this in Part - Mechanics, under a new subheading called Chapter - Memories:

> A memory is a kind of thing. A memory can be retrieved or buried. A memory is usually buried.

Memories instantiate the back story in *Sand-dancer*. Certain objects in the story world are linked to memories; as the player finds the objects, the memory's *buried* property flips to *retrieved*.

Exercise 3.3

Create a new kind for plants, and add a few desert-appropriate examples to some exterior rooms. The player shouldn't be able to take plants, and they should have a new property that describes whether they are dead or alive. Retrofit any appropriate existing objects (like the tumbleweed) to fall into this class.

Relating Things to Each Other

We've made some connections between parts of our story world already: we know that Crumbling Concrete is north of Middle of Nowhere, and that the wire mesh cage contains the blanket. But these are only spatial relationships. Real stories have much more compli-cated connections between their elements: plans and the steps needed to complete them; hierarchies of material value or aesthetic judgment; complex relationships between mem-bers of a family or friendship group. To model these more abstract but richly detailed con-nections, Inform gives us an extremely powerful tool called relations.

Defining Relations

A **relation** defines one way in which the rooms, things, or properties in your story world connect to each other. You've already encountered at least one example of a relation: con-tainment, which creates the concept of one or more things being inside another thing, and support, for things resting on top of something else. Inform's Standard Rules include both of these because it's hard to tell stories involving physical objects without these basic con-cepts. Part of the key to unlocking the power of Inform is to identify what sort of connec-tions are equally basic concepts in the story you are trying to tell, and creating relations that accurately instantiate these connections.

In the last section, we created a kind of thing called a memory, and explained that memories were connected to certain objects in our game world. Here's how we introduce this concept to Inform. Add the next line to *Sand-dancer* in Part - Mechanics, Chapter - Memories:

> Suggestion relates various things to one memory.

Let's unpack the meaning of this sentence. "Suggestion" defines the name of our new relation, and could be any word—I chose it over something like "implication" or "connection" because it's fairly specific, and says exactly what the relation is. Next, the verb "relates" lets Inform know we're creating a relation.

Finally, we have "various things to one memory," which defines the specific type of relation we're creating. In this case, we're saying that any number of things, of any kind (containers, windows, or just plain things) can each suggest exactly one thing, which must be of the kind memory. We had to define our initial concept a little more precisely in order to create this line: if we wanted things to be able to suggest more than one memory each, we might have said "various things to various memories," and we've also implied that it's okay for multiple things to suggest the same memory (otherwise, we'd have said "one thing to one memory"). Also implicit in the "various to one" relation is that the connection only works in one direction: we cannot say that a memory suggests a thing, because that's not the way we've decided it should work.

These two aspects, number and reciprocity, react in various ways to form the major types of relations you can create in Inform.

Relation Type	Number	Reciprocal	Rxample Relation
various Xs to one Y	many/one	no	fealty
various Xs to various Ys	many/many	no	admiration
one X to various Ys	one/many	no	fatherhood
one X to one Y	one/one	no	apprenticeship
one X to another	one/one	yes	marriage
Xs to each other	various/various	yes	meeting

The distinctions between some of these may seem subtle at first glance, but they are all unique cases. You could correctly say the knight has apprenticed his squire, but not that the squire has apprenticed the knight, which makes "one X to one Y" a non-reciprocal relation. On the other hand, you can correctly say both that "Tom is married to Katie" and "Katie is married to Tom," demonstrating the difference with the reciprocal relation "one X to another." And note that a knight can only apprentice one squire at a time (one/one), while Tom has no restrictions on the number of children he can father, at least theoretically (one/many).

Inform also supports relating people in groups, such as by nationality, and conditional relations that only hold true in certain circumstances. For details on these more advanced features, see the "Relations" chapter in the Inform documentation.

Relation Verbs

We've defined the nature of our "suggestion" relation, but we don't have a way yet to connect objects with it. In the same way we use built-in verbs like "is," "holds," "contains," and even "relates," we need to teach Inform a verb that will let us assert that things are related by suggestion. Here's how we do it: add this to *Sand-dancer* in Part - Mechanics, Chapter - Memories:

> The verb to suggest (he suggests, they suggest, he suggested, it is suggested, he is suggesting) implies the suggestion relation.

What's with the flashback to high school Spanish all of a sudden? Due to the vagaries of natural language (and English in particular), Inform doesn't try to guess the different forms of speech any newly defined verb might take. It doesn't look so difficult in this case, but imagine even a fairly innocuous verb like "to become": Inform would be hard-pressed to know that "became" or even "becoming" (with the dropped "e") were different conjugations of the same word.

As a result, whenever we declare a new relation verb (which fortunately doesn't happen that often) we need to spell out the conjugation in each of the five forms likely to be used by you or Inform when discussing that relation. We'll flash you back to fifth period even harder with this handy little table:

Tense	Conjugation
Infinitive	to suggest
Present singular	he suggests
Present plural	they suggest
Past	he suggested
Past participle	it is suggested
Present participle	he is suggesting

Once we go through this drudgery for a relation, though, Inform can understand our use of it no matter what context we're talking in. Add this to *Sand-dancer* in Part - Mechanics, Chapter - Memories:

> The last day of high school is a memory. It is suggested by the tumbleweed.

Which is exactly equivalent to:

> The tumbleweed suggests a memory called the last day of high school.

As mentioned earlier, a lot of the "built-in" concepts we've already learned are simply parts of the Standard Rules included in every Inform game, made using the same techniques we've been learning here. For example, here's a portion of the Standard Rules' definition of the support relation:

> The verb to support (he supports, they support, he supported, it is supported, he is supporting) implies the support relation.

It's important to note that relations are purely abstract. The above sentence alone does not imply anything about how objects should behave when placed on supporters, and our new "suggesting" relation doesn't do anything exciting yet—that will come later. Relations simply define how the important things in your story world are conceptually connected.

Let's create another of the important relations in *Sand-dancer*. An important theme of the story is that the player must make choices that limit his options—that "you can't have it all." The player must commit to one of two possible plans for escaping his predicament. At several moments of the game, it will be useful for Inform to understand which plan the player is pursuing. To implement this, we'll create a new kind of thing called a plan, and a relation that connects relevant objects to plans. Add this in Part - Mechanics, under a new subheading called Chapter - Plans:

> A plan is a kind of thing.
>
> Requirement relates one plan to various things. The verb to require (he requires, they require, he required, it is required, he is requiring) implies the requirement relation.
>
> Staying the night is a plan. Staying the night requires the emergency blanket and the canned oranges.
>
> The roll of duct tape and the gas can are required by a plan called Fixing the truck.

Note that there's nothing functionally different about the way we defined the two plans—the difference just serves to illustrate again the benefits of declaring all the conjugations in the verb definition.

Tools

Inform comes with a number of tools, both in the application's panels and through special testing verbs you can use when playing your game, that help ensure it correctly understands the intentions behind your source text. If something fails, generating a confusing problem message, these tools can help you find what's being misunderstood.

The Index Panel: World

I haven't yet asked you to open the Index panel within Inform, mostly because it contains a lot of information that can be overwhelming when you're just getting started. You've learned enough now, however, to start making sense of it.

If you open the Index panel in a project you've successfully compiled, you'll see a number of tabs along the top that offer different perspectives on how Inform has understood your source text. Click the World tab and you should see something like Figure 3.7.

The tab shows a map of the rooms we've created, color-coded by region and showing the directional connections between them. Names are abbreviated using the initial first letters of the room name—so Crumbling Concrete has the label "CC."

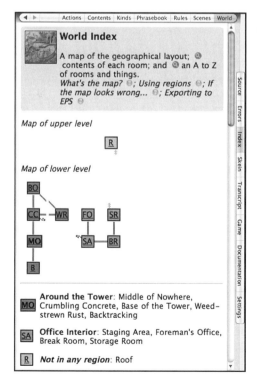

Figure 3.7
The World tab of the Index panel for *Sanddancer*, showing the map we've created.

CAUTION Something that's not necessarily obvious but worth pointing out: Inform's model of rooms and directions has no concept of distance. One room may be "east" of another, but how far east? A mile, or twenty feet? Is the next room to the east the same distance away, or not? Where are rooms "inside" from other rooms spatially situated? Nothing in the model requires your rooms to fall into a grid, or have connections that even make sense in two-dimensional space. As a result, Inform may not always be able to successfully draw a sensible map in the World tab. However, this does not mean its internal understanding of that space is necessarily flawed, which the rest of the tab's contents should reveal.

Directly underneath the map is a breakdown of your story's regions, and which rooms are assigned to each one. Scrolling through *Sand-dancer*'s info, we can see that Roof is currently not in any region. You can get to this room from within the building, so it makes sense that we forgot to assign it to the Around the Tower region, which represents all our outdoor spaces.

This oversight wasn't at all apparent from viewing our source text or playing the game, and demonstrates how the World tab's alternate perspectives on your story can be useful. Let's fix this in *Sand-dancer* before moving on. Add the following in Part - Setting, Chapter - Around the Tower:

> Roof is regionally in Around the Tower.

Recompile, go back to the World tab's map, and click the abbreviated name of one of the rooms. You'll jump down the page to a more detailed description, naming the room in full and listing its exits, as well as showing all the things within it at the start of play. The small orange arrows will jump to the paragraph in your source text where you created the room or thing in question.

Finally, at the bottom of the page, you'll find another version of the same information, this time presented as an alphabetical index of all rooms, things, and even directions in your story—again, with orange arrows that take you straight to the assertion sentence in your source text.

If you scroll back to the top, you'll see that the first few lines in the gray title box act as a table of contents: click the gray magnifying glass icon to jump to each section of the World tab. The remaining text in italics cross-reference useful sections in the "Writing with Inform" documentation, like the one on creating regions. Click the blue question mark icon to open these pages in the Documentation panel.

The World tab helps you see what's going on in your story world, and should be one of the first places you look when problems arise, if the problem message and source text aren't enough for diagnosis.

The TREE Testing Command

Switch back to the Game panel of *Sand-dancer*, and type TREE at any prompt. You should get a list of output like that seen in Figure 3.8. (You may have to press Enter a few times to show the whole list—the scrollbar on the right-hand side will let you go back and see the earlier text.) What is all this information?

```
(property_numberspace_forcer)
fixing the truck (47)
spending the night (48)
roll of duct tape (49)
gas can (50)
canned oranges (51)
Middle of Nowhere (52)
  yourself
    a pack of cigarettes
    a lighter
    a denim jacket (being worn)
Crumbling Concrete (53)
Base of the Tower (54)
  a tumbleweed
  a rusty tin can
  a huge electrical tower
Weed-strewn Rust (58)
Backtracking (59)
Staging Area (60)    --
  a pane of cracked glass
Foreman's Office (62)
  a half-collapsed desk
    a rusted key
  a dust-covered window
Break Room (66)
  a wire mesh cage
    an emergency blanket
  a tiny frosted window
Storage Room (70)
Roof (71)
Tower Vicinity (72)
```

Figure 3.8
Part of the results of the TREE testing command for our proto-*Sand-dancer*.

The TREE testing command shows all rooms and things in your story world and where they're currently positioned on the object tree. For enclosing objects like rooms or containers, contents are indented and listed underneath the parent.

You might notice a few things you didn't expect to see—a list of every direction inside something called the compass, for instance—as well as mysterious objects with names wrapped in parentheses, like (Inform Parser). Certain names are also followed by numbers representing Inform's internal code for that item. Most of this info is irrelevant, but it's an interesting peek behind the scenes.

If you want to pare down the amount of information, follow TREE with the name of a specific room or thing. Try TREE BREAK ROOM to see this in action. As another example, the output from TREE YOURSELF should look very similar to the output for INVENTORY.

The TREE command always shows you the current, live state of the story world: TAKE something and type TREE again, and you'll see the item move from being under its starting room to being under "yourself"—the name of the thing that represents the player. Also, like all testing commands, TREE only works within the Inform application, not in a final released game.

TREE is another way of verifying that Inform's idea of your story world's contents corresponds with your own. If TREE reveals that something isn't where you think it should be, that's a sign that you may have a miscommunication in your source text.

The SHOWME Testing Command

Another useful testing command is SHOWME. Typing SHOWME by itself provides similar information to using TREE with a location name, but more commonly we add the name of something in the story world. Type SHOWME TUMBLEWEED for some useful information about this thing, what kind it belongs to, and its properties.

 CAUTION If you do this, you'll see a few properties listed that we haven't covered yet. The **edible** property, for instance, lets you EAT a thing to make it disappear from the story world; see "Food" in the Inform documentation for details.

SHOWME lets you ensure that you and Inform are on the same page about what the properties of a thing should be at a given time. If you can't seem to TAKE something that you thought should be portable, and SHOWME reveals it's currently fixed in place instead, you've learned something very useful about solving the problem.

The RELATIONS Testing Command

One last testing command for now: type RELATIONS at any prompt to show the different relations you've defined, and the objects currently making use of them. In *Sand-dancer*, the output should look like Figure 3.9.

```
>RELATIONS
Suggestion relates various things to one memory:
  The tumbleweed >==> the last day of high school
Requirement relates one plan to various things:
  Staying the night >==> the canned oranges
  Staying the night >==> the emergency blanket
  Fixing the truck >==> the roll of duct tape
  Fixing the truck >==> the gas can
```

Figure 3.9
The output of the RELATIONS command in *Sand-dancer*.

Once again, this opens a window into Inform's understanding of the story's relations, letting us see if it matches our own. It's clear at a glance that each of our plans connects to exactly two items via the requirement relation, which we expected from our source text. Surprises here would indicate that we're not setting up our relations in a correct and unambiguous way.

We'll go over more testing commands and tabs in the Index panel as we go on, but these three tools are foundational. Knowing everything you know now, we're ready to turn to a more artistic side of world-building: crafting the words and descriptions used to make our story come to life.

Exercise Answers

Exercise 3.1

Create some objects, making proper use of articles and basic properties. This could go in Part - Setting, Chapter - Around the Tower:

> Some scattered newspapers are in Weed-strewn Rust. A withered cactus is fixed in place in Backtracking.

Exercise 3.2

Add a few containers or supporters as background scenery in the building. The best place for this is Part - Setting, Chapter - Office Interior:

> A wastepaper basket is an open unopenable fixed in place container in Foreman's Office. A rusted filing cabinet is a closed openable fixed in place container in Storage Room. An overturned bookcase is a fixed in place enterable supporter in Staging Area.

Exercise 3.3

Add a new kind for plants. Put this in Part - Setting, Chapter - Around the Tower:

> A plant is a kind of thing. A plant is always fixed in place. A plant can be living or dead. A plant is usually living. Some yellowing weeds are an undescribed plant in Weed-strewn Rust.

At least one thing we've already created could fall into this category: the tumbleweed. You could add this sentence to retrofit it into our new class:

> The tumbleweed is a dead plant.

We'll also need to move our block of code defining the plant class to the top of the Around the Tower chapter, because otherwise when we start calling things "plants" Inform won't yet know what we mean.

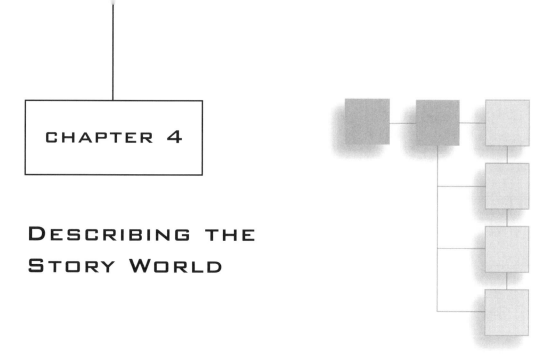

CHAPTER 4

DESCRIBING THE STORY WORLD

An Inform story knows how to list the items in your story and report on basic actions like picking them up and putting them down. But Inform is not a writer. To create a unique story world with character and flavor, you need to teach Inform how to describe it.

To do this, you'll use two tools: static, pre-authored **text**, and dynamic, flexible **text substitutions**. Working in tandem, both kinds of description help bring your story world to life, while keeping it flexible enough for players to clearly see the impact of their actions.

The Description Property

The most basic way of describing the world is with the **description** property, which both rooms and things can use. A room's description displays when the players first visit, and whenever they type LOOK thereafter, while an object's description shows up when the players try to EXAMINE it. The description property holds a **string** (a piece of quoted text) which contains words meant not for Inform to process, but for the players to read. Together, room and object descriptions provide the basic details that create your story world in readers' minds.

Descriptions for Rooms

As players move around, they keep tabs on their location through the bolded room name printed after each movement turn. But since exploration is a key component of the joy of IF, we want to reward it with something much more exciting and rich: interesting, world-building, descriptive prose that sets the tone of your story and fills in its details (Figure 4.1).

Figure 4.1
As you're writing descriptions, a helpful way to get a feel for a place is to search online for images. Here's one of thousands of photos tagged "new mexico desert" on Flickr (photo by Flickr user folkrockgirl).

Room descriptions serve two purposes. First, they fulfill many *story* functions. They:

> Tell the reader what kind of story this is: its genre, its tone, and its focus.

> Establish the details of setting that lets the reader imagine himself in the story world.

> Explain details of geography and environment that will become relevant to the story.

But room descriptions have many *game*-related functions as well. They must also:

> Clearly define how the room connects to its neighboring rooms, and in what compass directions.

> Draw attention to parts of the environment that are worthy of further exploration, while leaving out unimportant details.

> Describe any spatial relations that are important to navigating or understanding the story world.

Writing room descriptions, then, requires careful consideration of both dimensions: game and story. Your descriptions must be interesting from a storytelling perspective, but also provide the information needed to navigate your world's game-like challenges.

Let's add our first room description to *Sand-dancer*. Remember, everything within quotation marks is meant for the player, not Inform. (The application displays quoted text in a visually distinct style, to help remind you of this.) Add the following to Part - Setting, Chapter - Around the Tower:

> The description of Base of the Tower is "Behind the building a steel girder rises from the sand, one of three legs of the huge electrical tower looming like some gargantuan spider into blackness above you. A tumbleweed drifts lazily against the rusted metal among scrawny weeds and bits of trash. The desert stretches in all directions except back south towards the building."

Let's look at this description and see how it functions both as narration and information.

> "Behind the building" and "looming... into the blackness above you" establish the spatial geography of this area.

> We mention the girder and tower, the tumbleweed, the weeds and the trash, enough nouns to paint a picture of the area without overwhelming the player (or the author, who will have to create each of these things to maintain a consistent story world).

> The final sentence explains the single connection from this room, while the word "back" emphasizes the temporal logic of how the player got here.

> The words "sand" and "desert" remind us of the larger setting these rooms are part of, the New Mexico desert, while the metaphor of the spider suggests the theme of watchful animals and imparts a suggestion of danger.

Note, too, what we don't mention. Realistically, there might be all kinds of things we'd expect to find in such a setting: small rocks, scorpions, a warning sign or fence, animal bones, a dirt road. But unlike in static fiction, every object we mention here requires effort to integrate into Inform's vision of our story world. By keeping things simple, we create a more tightly focused and internally consistent reality to simulate.

Room descriptions can also suggest further courses of action. The room description for one room in Eric Eve's *Snowquest* ends with this sentence: "So far as you can see nothing grows here; the ground is quite bare apart from an abundance of snow lying deep and crisp and uneven." Can you think of something you'd like to do in this location? After a moment's thought, you might try to DIG, which would reveal something hidden under the snow. The description of the snow is carefully crafted: *deep* suggests something major could be hidden underneath, while *uneven* implies something is. The word *crisp* suggests an unbroken expanse waiting to be disturbed.

Setting the Description Property

- Base of the Tower is a room. The description of Base of the Tower is "Behind the building... ".
- Base of the Tower is a room. The description is "Behind the building... ".
- Base of the Tower is a room with description "Behind the building... ".
- Base of the Tower is a room. "Behind the building... ".

Note that except for the final shortcut form, each of the other three forms can be used to set other properties you might define or learn about later.

If we recompile with our new description and visit Base of the Tower, though, we see an annoying problem (Figure 4.2). By default, any things in a room are listed together in a separate paragraph after the room description. But what if we've already mentioned them in our room description—as we do above with the tumbleweed?

To fix this, we can usually give the duplicated items the **scenery** property. Scenery is fixed in place and usually behaves like something undescribed (two properties we learned about in Chapter 3). Recall that something *fixed in place* cannot be picked up and moved around by the player, and something *undescribed* will not be mentioned by Inform. In this case,

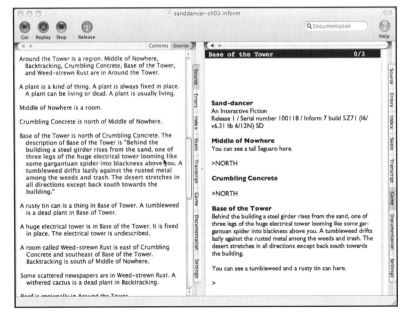

Figure 4.2
The default method of description causes some objects to be listed twice.

this is just what we want: since we've mentioned the tumbleweed within our room description, Inform shouldn't describe it again later; and it's not something we want the player to be carrying about. Let's find the definition for our tumbleweed within the same section and add immediately after:

The tumbleweed is scenery.

Recompile, and voilà: problem solved.

CAUTION Room descriptions probably shouldn't include portable things. If the player picks something up and moves it elsewhere, and you've enshrined its presence into a room description, your story world now has a gaping inconsistency. Maintaining a coherent story world is one of many small things that earns the respect of your players and encourages them to keep playing, rather than give up in frustration.

Text Substitutions and Getting BENT

As mentioned earlier, descriptions—and most groups of words wrapped in quotation marks—are ignored by Inform and only shown to the player. But there's a hidden danger here: nothing stops us from describing things to the player differently than we describe them to Inform. It's all too easy to create a story world that seems inconsistent to the player by mentioning things in our room description we have not created in our story world.

In fact, we've already done it. Type EXAMINE GIRDER into your copy of *Sand-dancer* while in the Base of the Tower room, and see what you get back: "You can't see any such thing." But weren't we just told we could see a steel girder rising from the sand?

We told the player, who has added the girder to her mental picture of the environment, but we never told Inform. It doesn't exist in the computer's model of the story world. Therefore, attempts to interact with it produce only errors: Inform has no idea such an object exists. Another way of saying this is that we haven't **implemented** the girder. Implementation problems are a huge source of player frustration with IF, and arguably one of the leading causes for its reputation for being obtuse and obsolete.

Most modern authors try to solve this problem by hoping they can remember to implement all the objects they mention in their room descriptions. But this approach is fraught, much like trying to keep two address books always up-to-date with the latest information. You're very likely to update one and forget about the other.

I'd like to introduce you to a method I've found useful for addressing the implementation problem: BENT, or Bracket Every Notable Thing. In your *Sand-dancer* code, revise the description for Base of the Tower to add square brackets around the important objects, so it looks like this:

> The description of Base of the Tower is "Behind the building [a steel girder] rises from the sand, one of three legs of [the huge electrical tower] looming like some gargantuan spider into blackness above you. [A tumbleweed] drifts lazily against the rusted metal among [scrawny weeds] and [bits of trash]. The desert stretches in all directions except back south towards the building."

What do these brackets mean? We've encountered our first example of a text substitution.

Text substitutions are phrases within strings that are meaningful to Inform, activated by wrapping them in square brackets. Instead of printing a text substitution verbatim, Inform replaces it on the fly with whatever that text currently signifies. In this case, Inform understands a bracketed thing as a request to show the name of that thing.

Why would this be useful—isn't the result here exactly the same as if we'd omitted the brackets? If you recompile after making the above change, you'll see one reason the BENT method is useful (Figure 4.3).

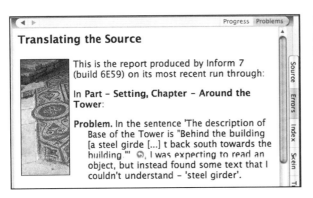

Figure 4.3
A problem message resulting from the BENT method.

Recall our missing girder. Previously, Inform skipped right over the phrase "a steel girder" in our room description. But by wrapping this phrase in brackets, we've told Inform we expect it to know what these words mean. It doesn't, so it gives us a problem message: "I was expecting to read an object, but instead found some text that I couldn't understand – 'steel girder.'" Inform knows it's expected to recognize this object, but it doesn't—because you haven't created it yet.

So, for our story to compile, we must create the steel girder object, thus bringing Inform's model of the story world up to date with the one promised by our description. BENT keeps us from writing descriptions our parser can't cash.

But why is it important that things like the steel girder exist in our story world in the first place, if they're not important to the plot? Two reasons: these bits of unimportant scenery add to your story's *consistency* and its *character*. If all the objects you mention are recognized by Inform, your players will receive far fewer contradictory messages and will find it easier to stay immersed in your world. And these scenery objects can add to the flavor of your environment and introduce unique opportunities for bits of description and exposition.

How do we know which things are notable and which aren't? The astute may have noticed we left several nouns unbracketed earlier: building, sand, legs, blackness, metal, and spider, for instance. Why?

The blackness, as an omnipresent aspect of the environment and something the player is unlikely to try interacting with directly, isn't worth implementing. Legs and metal are synonyms for the girder: in a later chapter, we'll teach Inform to recognize these extra words, but for now we can ignore them. The reference to "gargantuan spider" was only metaphorical, and thus if the player tries something like EXAMINE SPIDER it makes sense for the story to respond with "You can't see any such thing." Finally, we're actually going to go back and bracket building and sand in a moment after we introduce the concept of backdrops, which appear in more than one location.

Getting BENT has a few other benefits, too. If we change the name of a thing in one place, we'll get a problem message reminding us to change its name everywhere else. More importantly, BENT thinking forces more careful consideration about which things you really need to tell your story and paint your scene, and which ones are irrelevant and merely adding unnecessary headaches or clutter. Each additional thing in your story world increases its complexity and the odds that somewhere down the line that thing will cause problems or need fixing. Think BENT from your very first description and you'll save yourself trouble later on.

When getting BENT, it's important to note that the object's full name, just as it appeared when you created it, will always be displayed, even if you shorten the name within the text substitution. We'll see in Chapter 6 how to customize the way a thing is described.

Let's get back to *Sand-dancer*. To correct the problem messages produced by our unimplemented objects, let's quickly create them in a new paragraph following our room description:

A steel girder, some scrawny weeds, and some bits of trash are scenery in Base of the Tower.

We create all of these things as scenery, so Inform won't mention them on its own and the player can't move them around. Note also that we use the indefinite article "some" to let Inform know which things represent plural objects.

When using text substitutions to say names, the choice of article tells Inform how to describe each thing. Saying [the thing] will use the definite article (usually "the") while [a thing] will use the indefinite article (usually "a" or "some"). You can also just say [thing] to print the name without any article, or [A thing] and [The thing] to begin the article with a capital letter. In the description for Base of the Tower, we used several of these forms, depending on what seemed most natural in each context.

Exercise 4.1

Try creating a new room north of Base of the Tower called Against the Fence. Give it a description and populate it with a few items. Keep in mind the room description's dual purpose: to tell the story, and to assist with the game. Decide whether you want to mention any fixed in place items in the room within your room description, and adjust their properties accordingly so the player will not see them described twice. Remember BENT (Bracket Every Notable Thing) and add any newly created things to the story world.

Descriptions for Things

Things can have a description property too, which holds the text printed if the player EXAMINEs that thing. Let's add our first thing description to *Sand-dancer*, in the same section as our work on the Base of the Tower room:

> The description of bits of trash is "Worthless and forgotten, drifting against snags like non-biodegradable snow."

As with rooms, descriptions of things serve several purposes. They flesh out the environment, provide bits of color, and sometimes reveal a lot about the player character by the way he or she chooses to describe something. But additionally, descriptions also indicate to the player whether this thing is important to your story.

This is worth repeating: *a thing's description should make clear whether or not that thing is important to the story.*

The easiest way to indicate a thing's unimportance is to not give it a description at all. Inform's default message, "You see nothing special about {the thing}," serves this game purpose just fine. However, it drops the ball on the story side, neither keeping the player immersed in the story world nor adding flavor or character. Our description above for the trash adds a bit of color without misleading the player as to its importance. Notice the careful construction: the descriptive sentence includes no nouns except the metaphorical "snow" and the vague "snags." There is nothing further for the player to examine and nothing that suggests taking further action. Imagine, instead, that the description read like this:

> The description of trash is "Aluminum pop cans, newspaper pages, plastic bags, and other junk rest in precarious piles underneath the steel girder."

Applying BENT to this description reveals how many things we've suddenly implicitly created: cans, pages, bags, junk, and piles. Adding each of these to our story world would just clutter it with red herrings and introduce more possibilities for bugs. In addition, the "precarious piles" implies actions like PUSH or SEARCH, and the irrelevant spatial word "underneath" suggests LOOK UNDER GIRDER: players trying these actions will be frustrated to find they produce no results. We've introduced extraneous information and misled the player.

On the other hand, what if we *did* want the player to search the trash? How could we convey this? Perhaps with a description more like:

> The description of trash is "Mostly inconsequential, and stacked high enough you can't even begin to take stock of what might be here with just a cursory glance."

We haven't introduced any extra things to implement, but we've implied there might be more here than is immediately obvious. The original description suggests no further course of action, but this version does: the phrase "what might be here" implies something hidden, and the verb "take stock" implies action—we could be even more clear and work the word SEARCH into the sentence, if we liked.

But in *Sand-dancer*, the trash is unimportant, and our description suggests no further avenues of discovery. The player reads it, enjoys the response and bit of detail, finds nothing further to pursue, and moves on to try something else.

 A subtle point worth drawing attention to: Inform understands the English convention of putting a closing period inside a quotation mark. Each of the lines above does not need another period after the final quotation mark because the one inside does double duty. This also works with question and exclamation marks.

Exercise 4.2

Try writing descriptions for some of the scenery items you created in the last chapter's exercises. Keep in mind that your description should not introduce extraneous nouns, and should clearly indicate to the player whether or not this item merits further investigation. (It's okay if you want to make something seem important, though you don't have the tools to make it so yet!) Remember too that object descriptions are a great way to set tone and reveal small pieces of story.

Backdrops

Let's add a few more room descriptions to *Sand-dancer*, still in Part - Setting, Chapter - Around the Tower:

> The description of Middle of Nowhere is "The [tire tracks] from the south stop abruptly here, but where the hell are you? The [desert sand] and clumps of pale [sagebrush] are all your dimming [headlights] pick out before barely reaching a [concrete building] to the north."

> The description of Backtracking is "It's quieter and darker over here, the black desert night bleeding in. Your [tire tracks] are hardly visible in the [desert sand], and you can barely make out the way north back to your truck."

You'll notice we've used a few things (the tire tracks and the desert sand) in both rooms. But can't things only be in one room at a time? A special kind of thing called the **backdrop** breaks this rule. Backdrops can be in more than one room at a time, but otherwise are just like scenery: they are fixed in place, so they can't be taken, and they're not described (because you've presumably mentioned them already in description text). Let's create the new backdrops, at the top of Chapter - Around the Tower (but after our region definition):

> Some tire tracks are a backdrop. They are in Middle of Nowhere and Backtracking. The desert sand, some sagebrush, and the concrete building are backdrops. The desert sand is in Around the Tower. The sagebrush is in Around the Tower. The concrete building is in Around the Tower.

We can assign backdrops to either a group of rooms, or an entire region (such as Around the Tower, which encompasses all our external rooms). Even though we might not refer to the desert sand in every exterior room, the player will rightfully assume that it's there and may try to interact with it, so the broad placement makes sense.

(If you like, go back and bracket [the sand] and [the concrete building] within the existing room descriptions. You might also change the definition for the huge electrical tower created in the previous chapter to make it a backdrop in the Around the Tower region.)

If we recompile, Inform reminds us we still need to create the headlights. We'll do so momentarily.

More Descriptive Tools

The description property is the basic unit of textual exposition, but Inform provides us other tools as well to help describe the player's surroundings.

Initial Appearance

We mention the tire tracks, but why haven't we mentioned the player's pickup truck, which should also be present in the Middle of Nowhere room where the story begins?

By convention, important objects in IF receive their own paragraph of text after the room description, and the truck falls into this category. Let's make a pass at creating it and see what happens. Add the next line in Part - Setting, Chapter - Around the Tower, underneath the Middle of Nowhere description.

> The pickup truck is an enterable openable transparent closed fixed in place
>   container in Middle of Nowhere.

This seems like a complex definition, but let's break it down: we've seen all these properties before. The pickup is an *enterable container* because we can get inside it; it's *openable* because it has doors, and *closed* because when the story begins, those doors are closed. It's *transparent* because we should be able to see and refer to things inside of it even when the doors are closed (through the windows, of course, though we won't implement those as separate objects). Finally, it's *fixed in place*, perhaps surprisingly, because over the course of *Sand-dancer* the truck will never move from this location. In one of the possible endings we'll fix it, but only in the story's conclusion, after the player's last chance to enter a command. The truck, then, never needs to move during the course of our story: as far as Inform is concerned, it's as immobile as the Statue of Liberty.

> This illustrates a subtle point about the potentially misleading nature of natural language source text. Remember that the sentences you write have a very precise meaning to Inform. If you noticed the Rideable Vehicles extension in the list of built-in extensions by Graham Nelson, you might have been tempted to include it and write "Your pickup truck is a vehicle," but this would be a mistake: the pickup, *as an object in the Sand-dancer story world*, never needs to move, and thus should not be a vehicle, even though we might use that word in real life.

You can set the player's starting location by simply asserting it. Try adding:

> The player is in Base of the Tower.

Unless we include an assertion like this, the player will begin in the first room defined in the source text. In our case, that's Middle of Nowhere, which is what we want, so remove the assertion above to restore the correct behavior.

Now that we've created the pickup, we can add the headlights, and introduce another useful tool.

> Some headlights are part of the pickup truck.

This does just what it sounds like: lets Inform know that the headlights are connected to the pickup truck and don't need their own description, and also that the player can't pick them up and carry them off. In the Standard Rules, this behavior is created as a relation called "incorporation," using sentences like:

> The verb to be part of implies the reversed incorporation relation.

("Reversed" simply meaning that "the headlights are part of the pickup truck" is equivalent to "the pickup truck incorporates the headlights.")

What does the room description for Middle of Nowhere look like now when we recompile? As seen in Figure 4.4, the description of the truck is technically accurate, but doesn't capture much flavor. It's certainly more generic than the way a real storyteller would set the scene.

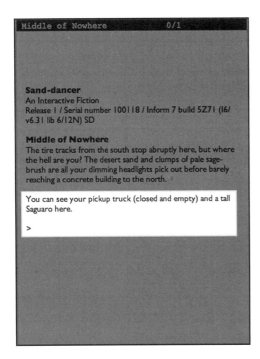

Figure 4.4
The default description is often not the most exciting.

For objects that require more character, Inform provides another string property called **initial appearance**, which holds text describing an item's appearance in a room. Let's add an initial appearance property to the truck.

> The initial appearance of the truck is "Your poor old [pickup truck] ticks and
>   groans, smashed gracelessly against [a tall Saguaro]; [whiffs of evaporating
>   gasoline] linger in the chill air." Some whiffs of evaporating gasoline are
>   scenery in Middle of Nowhere.

Now our room description reads much more naturally. But note that we've overridden Inform's ability to automatically describe the status and contents of the truck as a container. We'll learn how to add this ability back in later in this chapter.

Setting the Initial Appearance Property

- Your pickup truck is a thing. The initial appearance of pickup truck is "Your...".
- Your pickup truck is a thing. The initial appearance is "Your... ".
- Your pickup truck is a thing with initial appearance "Your... ".
- Your pickup truck is a thing. "Your... ".

 Just as we can set the default values for either/or properties like "open," we can also set default values for properties containing strings. Recall the "window" kind we made in Chapter 3. We could add the following line to its definition in Sand-dancer:

The description of a window is usually "Dusty glass panes."

Now every window will have this description. As usual, we can override it for a more specific window:

The description of the tiny frosted window is "Can't imagine this ever provided much light."

We can do the same thing with initial appearance, and any other property.

Exercise 4.3

Try adding an initial appearance to a portable object somewhere in the story world. Recompile and see how the object is described when you first encounter it, after picking it up and dropping it, and after leaving and returning to its location. You should be able to learn something useful about the behavior of initial appearance.

More Text Substitutions

We can do more with text substitutions than just print the names of things. Much more, in fact. But for now, let's introduce three useful phrases that start allowing your text substitutions to provide more functionality: numbers, lists, and randomness.

Number

We can use text substitutions to display how many things in the story world match a given description. We'll use this later in *Sand-dancer* to, among other things, determine how close the player is to achieving one of the two story goals they can strive for. Though it's not very realistic, as an example for now add the following line, still in Part - Setting, Chapter - Around the Tower:

> The description of Crumbling Concrete is "The building is nondescript, with [the number of windows] windows."

If we start a text substitution with **number of** (or *the number of*) followed by a description of a group of things, Inform will display the appropriate figure at the time that text is printed. In this case, we'd see a message like "The building is nondescript, with 3 windows."

If we want the number to be printed "three" instead of "3," we can add "in words" to the end of the text substitution, like [the number of windows in words].

When describing things to count (or for any other purpose), you can use adjectives to narrow your search. It's good to know some useful adjectives built in to Inform. A **visible** thing is one that the player currently sees, usually meaning that it's in the same room and not inside a closed opaque container. An almost equivalent adjective is **touchable**: something could be visible but not touchable if it was inside a closed transparent container, like a glass box. Rooms are **visited** if the player has occupied them for at least one turn since the story began, and **adjacent** if they are exactly one map connection away from the player. We can refer to the room the player occupies with **location of player** or just **location**.

If we had other buildings in our game, we could ask for [the number of windows regionally in Office Interior] to get just the ones placed in rooms inside this building. We could also ask for [the number of open windows] or perhaps [the number of visible closed windows]. Once we learn more about actions, we could write a diagnostic action that displays [the number of things] or [the number of rooms in Office Interior] or [the number of unvisited rooms].

Lists

Using *number of* counts the things matching a description, but the **list of** keyword actually specifies those things. Replace our earlier description for Crumbling Concrete with:

> The description of Crumbling Concrete is "The building is nondescript. The windows include [the list of windows in Office Interior]."

If we recompile, we can see the description this produces (Figure 4.5). Inform automatically constructs the list as a valid English phrase. If nothing matches the given condition, the word "nothing" is printed.

As might be expected, starting your list with "the" uses the definite article for each list item; with "a," the indefinite article; and with nothing, no article is used.

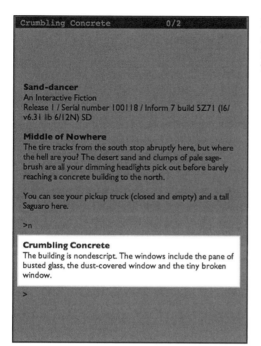

Figure 4.5
A room description showing a list of things.

Frequently when using lists, you'll need some text just before or after the list to vary based on how many items were in the list, such as saying *is* versus *are*. The extension Plurality by Emily Short, which comes with Inform, contains a number of text substitutions to deal with situations like this, such as [is-are]. Go ahead and include it at the top of your source text now.

Exercise 4.4

Can you use lists and Plurality to modify the initial appearance of the pickup truck to list its contents in a natural-sounding way?

Random

Finally, the keyword **random** will show just one of the possible matches. Change our earlier description again to read:

> The description of Crumbling Concrete is "Your headlights glint off [a random window in Office Interior] in the building."

Now, instead of a list of all windows, we see only one: we might get a sentence like "Your headlights glint off a pane of busted glass in the building."

Exercise 4.5

Give one window an initial appearance that describes a reflection of a random appropriate thing in the room. Recompile, and try moving different things into this room to see how the description changes.

Random Choices of Text

A more complicated text substitution using randomness lets Inform make a random selection from several strings of text. Replace our description one more time with the following:

> The description of Crumbling Concrete is "Mostly nondescript, but your eyes
>   linger for a moment on [one of]the peeling paint[or]a half-collapsed
>   wall[or]the dusty windows[at random]."

The [one of] text substitution tells Inform that we're going to give it a list of alternatives, separated by [or], and concluding with [at random], and that it should select a single one to print. The above might generate the sentence "Mostly nondescript, but your eyes linger for a moment on a half-collapsed wall." The sentence might be different the next time the room is visited.

 Inform lets you get much more picky with your randomness by replacing "at random" with other options, such as "sticky random" which will choose once and then keep that choice for the rest of the game, or "in random order" which will not display any text a second time until all options have been printed once. We'll talk about this in more detail in Chapter 7.

Conditional Descriptions

Descriptions can also vary based on more complex criteria. In this section we'll talk about how to use conditions, definitions, and custom adjectives to create more flexible descriptions.

Conditions

So far, all the instructions we've given Inform have been static: declarations of the way things are when the story begins. But in the last section, we introduced adjectives (like "visible"), which change from turn to turn based on outside conditions like whether or not the player holds a light source. On any given turn, a phrase declaring the state of one of these adjectives—such as "the truck is visible"—is either **true** or **false**.

We call such a phrase a **condition**. Other true conditions we could think of for our story world include:

> the dusty window is closed
>
> the dusty window is a window
>
> the tumbleweed is fixed in place
>
> Middle of Nowhere is north of Backtracking
>
> Base of the Tower is not visited

Some false conditions might be:

> the tire tracks are portable
>
> the tumbleweed is not a thing
>
> Backtracking is down from Base of the Tower

Conditions can even involve categories of nouns:

> every window is closed
>
> any window is visible
>
> any thing is fixed in place

All conditions have three parts in an exact order: first the noun or descriptive clause, an assertion verb (usually "is"), and lastly an adjective. Many conditions remain either true or false throughout an entire story. Some might change only once (such as rooms changing from not visited to visited). Some could potentially change every turn (such as the open/closed status of a window). But each will always be either true or false at any given moment.

Conditions can be more complicated than this, checking for specific numbers or ranges of numbers: "at least three windows are open" is a valid condition. We'll talk more about this in Chapter 7, or see the sections "All, each and every" and "Counting while comparing" in the Descriptions chapter of the built-in docs.

The built-in adjectives are useful, but what if we want to create our own? Fortunately, we can, by making a definition.

Defining New Adjectives

A **definition** creates a new adjective that will be either true or false on any given turn according to the exact parameters we specify. We teach Inform a new definition using the following syntax:

```
Definition: a thing is important if it is not a backdrop.
```

Let's look at this sentence piece by piece. The word "definition" and a colon mark the beginning of a definition sentence. We start with the kind of thing we're creating a definition for: in this case simply "thing," the most generic category, but we can also make definitions that apply to specific kinds, like "window" or "person." Next, the verb "is," followed by our adjective: in this case we've chosen the word "important." (This could be any word that doesn't already have a special meaning to Inform.) Finally, we say "if," and end with a condition. We use "it" within the condition to mean the thing we're testing this definition on. We can even use "its" to reference a property of the thing in question, like *its description.*

At first glance, this may seem like merely a convoluted way for making synonyms for other adjectives. Definitions become more powerful when we realize that our conditions may be more complicated, linked by the words "and" and "or."

> Definition: a thing is important if it is not a backdrop and it is not scenery and it is visible.

The linking word "and" means that for a given thing, each condition must be true for the "thing is important" condition to also be true. If we had used "or" instead, any one of the subordinate conditions could have been true to make the whole definition true.

Creating a Definition

- Definition: a thing is important if it is not a backdrop.
- Definition: a thing is important: if it is not a backdrop, [decide] yes.
- Definition: a thing is important: if it is not a backdrop, [decide] yes; otherwise, [decide] no.
- Definition: a thing is important: if it is not a backdrop, yes; if it is held by the player, yes; otherwise, no.

The use of "decide" is optional in this context. Useful synonyms include "something" (in place of "a thing"), "someone" (in place of "a person"), and "somewhere" (in place of "a room"). You can also use "he" or "she" in place of it, which makes definitions involving people sound more natural.

Now we have the power to make much more complicated and useful conditions. In a moment, we'll demonstrate adding a few to *Sand-dancer.*

Whenever we create a definition for a new adjective, Inform also defines an opposite adjective by adding "not" before your chosen name. The above example would also create the definition "not important," and we could write conditions testing whether "the tin can is not important." If we want to use our own word for the opposite definition (say, "irrelevant") we can add "rather than irrelevant" after our adjective in the definition: so the example above would begin "Definition: a thing is important rather than irrelevant if...".

Using Definitions

Let's add a few real definitions to *Sand-dancer*. Since light is important to our story, we'll create definitions that will let us determine the dominant light source in a room at any given moment.

First, we'll create the things that represent light sources in our story world. To do this, we need a new kind, the **device**. Devices have the property **switched on** or **switched off**; the player can use the SWITCH ON and SWITCH OFF (or TURN ON/TURN OFF) verbs to change this state. Add the following to *Sand-dancer* under the appropriate room definitions in Part - Setting, Chapter - Office Interior:

> The flashlight is a portable device in Foreman's Office.
>
> The emergency lights are a fixed in place device in Storage Room.

We've already created the headlights, but we need to let Inform know that they're a device, too: back in Part - Setting, Chapter - Around the Tower, add this after your headlight definition:

> The headlights are a device. They are switched on.

We'll come back and define these things in more detail later, including making them actually work to produce light: for now, we just need to tell Inform they exist.

Next, let's make a definition that knows which rooms are within reach of the pickup truck's headlights. (This is a purely arbitrary choice based on aesthetics, so it's something Inform can't figure out for itself.) Under Part - Mechanics, create a new heading called Chapter - Lights and add the following beneath it:

> Definition: a room is within range of headlights if it is Middle of Nowhere or it is Backtracking or it is Crumbling Concrete or it is Base of the Tower.

Now, we'll create three more definitions for each of the three light conditions. Add these in the same section:

> Definition: a room is lit brightly if it is regionally in Tower Vicinity and emergency lights are switched on.
>
> Definition: a room is lit by headlights if it is not lit brightly and it is within range of headlights and headlights are switched on.
>
> Definition: a room is lit by flashlight if it is not lit brightly and it is not lit by headlights and flashlight is enclosed by it and flashlight is switched on.

A bit more complicated, but let's unravel the logic behind these. We're creating adjectives made up of multiple words (such as *lit by headlights*), which is no problem as long as these phrases don't have a preexisting meaning for Inform. The other potential point of confusion is that our lights are hierarchical: we want the illumination from the emergency lights to trump the headlights, and the headlights to trump the flashlight. If any two of these sources compete within the same room, the more dominant source should win. This is why the *lit by headlights* definition invokes the *lit brightly* definition, to ensure that only one of these will be true for a given room at any one time.

Exercise 4.6

Create two new adjectives, "recognized" and "unfamiliar," which identify rooms that are nearby and either seen or not seen by the player. You might find the use of the existing adjectives *adjacent* and *visited* to be useful.

Using Conditions

By themselves, these definitions don't do anything. How do we actually use conditions and definitions within our source text?

One way is to put them inside text substitutions. If we'd made the "important" definition, we could have a description indicate [the number of important things], or maybe [the list of important unheld things]. But definitions become much more useful once we introduce conditional tests.

When we include an assertion such as:

    The blanket is in the wire mesh cage.

...we're declaring the way we want the story world to be at the start of play. However, we can also test whether that condition holds true at any given moment. We do this by simply adding the special word "if" to the beginning of the phrase:

    if the blanket is in the wire mesh cage

We've now created a **conditional test**, and while these can't stand alone like declarative sentences, one useful place they can be used is within a text substitution. A conditional test lets us show one of two pieces of text: the first if the condition is true, and the second if it is false.

Add the following description to *Sand-dancer*, after the flashlight's definition in Part - Setting, Chapter - Office Interior:

    The description of flashlight is "[if flashlight is switched on]Emitting a good,
        strong beam: thank god it works.[otherwise]Cold blue metal, and hefty."

The syntax here is a fairly straightforward five parts: 1) the conditional test, 2) the text to be printed if the test is true, 3) [otherwise], 4) the text to be printed if the test is false, and 5) optionally, [end if] if you want more text following that shows regardless. The Inform application's syntax highlighting helps you see if you've missed a bracket or otherwise gotten the structure wrong.

PROGRAMMER'S NOTE

Programmers may be more used to saying "else" than "otherwise"; in Inform, the two words are interchangeable.

If we leave out parts 3 and 4 of this syntax (the "otherwise" and its associated text), then nothing will be printed if the conditional test is false. In addition, we can add additional tests in the form of [otherwise if flashlight is held]; we can have any reasonable number of these we like, before concluding with an optional final [otherwise] if none of the earlier tests were true.

One shortcut: if your conditional test is checking just a property or adjective of something, and it's within the description or initial appearance of that thing, you can omit the thing's name from the test. In the example above, you could replace [if flashlight is switched on] with [if switched on] to produce an identical effect.

Conditional Text Substitutions

- The description of flashlight is "Sturdy and heavy[if flashlight is switched on], currently turned on[end if]."
- The description of flashlight is "Sturdy and heavy[if switched on], currently turned on[end if]."
- The description of flashlight is "Sturdy and heavy[if flashlight is switched on], currently turned on[otherwise/else]currently turned off[end if]."
- The description of flashlight is "Sturdy and heavy[if flashlight is switched on], currently turned on[otherwise/else if flashlight is not held], too far away for you to see any details[otherwise/else]currently turned off[end if]."
- The description of flashlight is "[if switched on]Bright and useful.[otherwise/else]Sturdy and heavy."

Exercise 4.7

Using the definitions created in the previous exercise, create a description for the player character's lighter that discourages him from smoking if there are currently any unfamiliar rooms.

Describing *Sand-dancer*

Now that we've learned the tools we need, let's start doing some real description writing for our example game.

Filling in Detail

Let's add a few more room descriptions to *Sand-dancer*, making use of our light level definitions and newfound skills to vary the descriptions based on whether the dominant light source is the truck headlights, the flashlight, or the emergency lights. Replace our temporary room description for Crumbling Concrete room (in Part - Setting, Chapter - Around the Tower) with the following:

> The description of Crumbling Concrete is "This [building] must've been some sort of utility structure for [the huge electrical tower] to the north, now abandoned[if lit by headlights]: [fragments of glass] sparkle faintly in the beam of your headlights[otherwise if lit by flashlight]: it seems dead and alone in the dusty beam of your flashlight[end if]. Tendrils of [sand] spill through the empty doorframe leading in to a [if lit brightly]brightly lit[otherwise]dark[end if] interior; you could also walk around to the east or head south back to your truck." Some fragments of glass are scenery in Crumbling Concrete.

Note the care taken in spacing and punctuation around the conditions and text substitutions. At the end of the description's first sentence, but before our closing period, we check to see if either of two light conditions are true: if they are, we add a descriptive clause to the sentence, before printing the final period in all three cases (after the [end if]).

Let's modify some of our existing descriptions to reflect the light level. Adjust these two room descriptions within the same section:

> The description of Middle of Nowhere is "The [tire tracks] from the south stop abruptly here, but where the hell are you? The [desert sand] and clumps of pale [sagebrush] are all [if lit by headlights]your dimming [headlights] pick out before barely reaching[otherwise if lit by flashlight]your flashlight picks out, other than[otherwise]you can see in the glow of[end if] [the concrete building] to the north."

> The description of Base of the Tower is "Behind [the concrete building] [a steel girder] rises from [the sand][if lit by flashlight]; you shine your flashlight up towards the tower looming above you[otherwise if lit by headlights], one of three legs of [the huge electrical tower] looming like some gargantuan spider into blackness above you[otherwise]; far above you [a red warning light] blinks on and off[end if]. [A tumbleweed] drifts lazily against the rusted metal among [scrawny weeds] and [trash]. The desert stretches in all directions except back south towards the [if lit brightly]glow of the [end if]building." A red warning light is scenery in Base of the Tower.

If you recompile, you can test these descriptions by finding and using the TURN ON/TURN OFF verbs on the three light source objects: the headlights, the flashlight, and the emergency lights. If you don't remember where they are, the SHOWME or TREE debugging verbs might come in handy (see Chapter 3). Note that, for now, descriptions will not be accurate if all three light sources are switched off: in a future chapter, we'll make it so the player can't see anything at all in this situation.

In the same section, let's add a description after our declaration of Weed-strewn Rust:

> The description of Weed-strewn Rust is "Behind the rather small [building] is nothing but a scraggly patch of [yellowing weeds] and dirt near [a leaking pipe], littered by [a collection of rusted barrels] and some [scattered newspapers]. Desert stretches in all directions; back west is the front of the building."

> The scattered newspapers are scenery in Weed-strewn Rust. [You might have already created these in Exercise 3.1.] A collection of rusted barrels and a leaking pipe are scenery in Weed-strewn Rust.

Let's go ahead and add descriptions for a few objects, too, to start building in some character and flavor and making *Sand-dancer* feel more exciting. This is the kind of thing that doesn't strictly need to be done until later in the process, but filling in the details of your story world right away helps make it feel real, and makes it easier to visualize yourself in that environment and imagine what might happen there.

Immediately below our scenery items for Weed-strewn Rust, add the following:

> An overturned barrel is a fixed in place supporter in Weed-strewn Rust. A weather-worn guidebook is on barrel. The initial appearance of barrel is "[if the number of things on barrel is at least 1]Atop one [overturned barrel] [is-are a list of things on barrel].[otherwise]The top of the [overturned barrel] is stained with rust.[end if]".

> The description of guidebook is "Most of the pages are faded or worn away, but flipping through, it looks like a guide to local animal life. You could try looking up various animals in it."

Here we do a couple of new things. In the room description, we count the number of items to generate one of two variations on the barrel's description, and also use a list text substitution to say what's on top of the barrel, since we're replacing Inform's normal description. (You might wonder why this is necessary, but remember since the barrel is a supporter, the player might place other objects on top of it.) Prefacing a request for a list with "is-are" will use the appropriate article: "is" for a single item and "are" for multiple items.

In our description of the guidebook, we imply that the command LOOK UP will do something useful, which indeed it will eventually—just not yet.

Keeping Things Organized

Feel free to create more descriptions for rooms and things in *Sand-dancer*. We may offi-cially define them later, but you can feel free to keep your own version or the new descrip-tion as you like. The environment is still mostly static, but in the next chapter we'll start learning how to let players use active verbs to cause real change in the story world.

But first, let's take a moment to keep our source text organized. You may have already found it difficult to find the right section to add something or make changes. You can always use Ctrl + F (Command + F on Macs) to search for text within the Source panel; but this isn't always the best solution. It's worth taking a moment now to go through your source text and organize it: make sure room descriptions are next to room declarations, and all the sentences setting the properties of a thing are adjacent to each other.

Try creating a new subheader for each room: the first might be called Section - Crumbling Concrete. Within each section header, lay out your declarative sentences in a sensible order. Move any objects within a room into the appropriate section, and give each significant object its own paragraph, to make it easy to find. Take a moment to do this now. When you're finished, you should have something that looks a lot like Figure 4.6.

Now, from the Contents tab of the Source panel, you can easily click on a specific part of your story world and see all relevant descriptions and things at a glance. The convenience gained is well worth the time spent in clean-up.

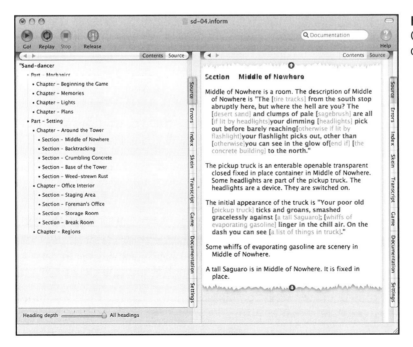

Figure 4.6
Cleaned-up source code for *Sand-dancer*.

Extensions for Controlling Description

A number of Inform extensions exist to help customize the way descriptions of the environment appear, which you can use to add functionality and ease of use to your game.

 A reminder: to install an Inform 7 extension, visit the Inform home page and find the list of user-submitted extensions. Locate the extension you want, click the Download link, and save it to your computer. Then, from within the Inform application, click File > Install Extension and select the file you downloaded. You can now view the extension's documentation in the Documentation panel under Installed Extensions, and incorporate an extension into your story by typing a sentence like "Include Exit Descriptions by Matthew Fletcher" in your source text.

Extensions for Describing Rooms

<u>Exit Descriptions by Matthew Fletcher</u> will add a line after the player moves or looks that lists all of the exits from the current location. If an adjacent room has been visited before, the extension prints the name of the room as well as the direction it's in. This makes it easier for players to see at a glance what directions they can move in, rather than having to search through each room description for that information.

Try downloading and installing this extension, then add the following near the top of your local copy of *Sand-dancer*:

    Include Exit Descriptions by Matthew Fletcher.

If you've correctly added the extension, you should see something like the left side of Figure 4.7.

 If you decide to use this extension with *Sand-dancer*, you might want to rewrite the room descriptions to not mention the exits, since this information is now presented in a more straightforward format below. On the other hand, the mechanical listing lacks flavor and might keep your players from immersing themselves in the story world by the constant game-like distraction. Most extensions come with trade-offs, and it's up to you to decide whether the advantages outweigh the side effects for your particular project.

<u>Exit Lister by Eric Eve</u> also helps the player navigate, but this time the information about available exits is placed in the **status line** at the top of the screen. Traditionally, this black bar is used to show the name of the current location, the number of moves the player has made since the story began, and the current score. The <u>Exit Lister</u> extension adds a second line with navigation information. Rooms that are unvisited are printed in red, providing a visual cue as to which rooms still need to be explored.

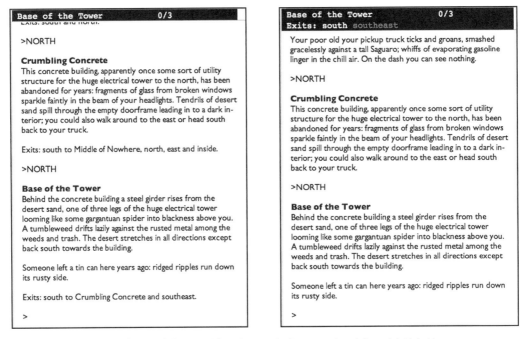

Figure 4.7 On the left, *Sand-dancer* with <u>Exit Descriptions</u>; on the right, with <u>Exit Lister</u>.

An even more elaborate status bar replacer is <u>Automap by Mark Tilford</u>. This extension attempts to draw a simple map of the current location and surrounding rooms by using text characters in a much larger status bar.

If you like, try downloading and installing all three extensions (although try them one at a time, since each one provides roughly the same functionality). How does each change the experience of play? Do some go too far or not far enough? These are all ultimately personal questions, and may change from one project to the next. Familiarizing yourself with the contents of Inform's extensions page is time well spent: it's always a relief to realize someone else has already solved tough problems for you.

Extensions for Describing Things

<u>Room Description Control by Emily Short</u> is part of a comprehensive library of extensions designed to let authors affect how Inform describes the miscellaneous objects at the end of a room description. For instance, when used with <u>Tailored Room Descriptions by Emily Short</u> it will eschew the "(which is open)" style of parenthetical property descriptions, and instead describe these in standard prose. A full description of this suite of extensions goes well beyond the concepts we've covered so far, but the curious should feel free to download and consult the extension's documentation.

Keyword Interface by Aaron Reed draws more attention to objects in room descriptions by highlighting them in blue (see Figure 4.8). It also changes the standard interface so that typing an object without any verb is the same as using the verb EXAMINE. Keyword Interface easily integrates with games designed using the BENT system.

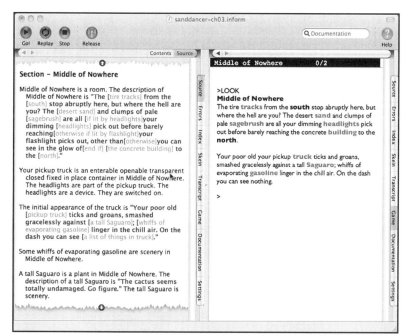

Figure 4.8
Sand-dancer with Keyword Interface by Aaron Reed.

(By default, scenery things are not highlighted by Keyword Interface; add the sentence "When play begins: now every thing is keyworded." to your source text to override this. You can also try bracketing direction words such as [south] to see the direction highlighting as well.)

This approach, which I used in my story *Blue Lacuna*, makes it easy to see at a glance the important items and directions. Some people like this, while others think the colored words detract from the experience of reading the prose. In the end, again, it's up to the aesthetics of the author.

You should now have a fundamental grasp of how to set the stage for your interactive fiction. In the next chapter we'll learn how to make more interesting things happen on that stage.

Exercise Answers

Exercise 4.1

Create a new room called Against the Fence. You can make whatever you want of this room, but a few tips. If your room descriptions lead to problem messages, make sure your bracketed things do not have extra words that are not in the name of your item. Something else to watch out for are things with similar names: Inform may become confused about the difference between a "log" and a "withered log," for instance. You could correct this by giving the first thing a longer name (like "smaller log").

Exercise 4.2

Add descriptions for some scenery items. Here are a few examples:

> The description of scattered newspapers is "Garbage, even if they weren't smeared and streaked illegible." The description of rusted filing cabinet is "Almost looks like an antique. How long has this place been deserted, anyway?"

Exercise 4.3

Add an initial appearance to a portable object.

> The initial appearance of rusty tin can is "Someone left a tin can here years ago: ridged ripples run down its rusty side."

With some experimentation, you should see that the initial appearance of something is only printed before that thing has been moved. This lets your initial appearance include descriptive details that might only be true before the player has interfered: "The purple flower glistens with dew, waiting to be picked."

Exercise 4.4

Modify the pickup truck's initial appearance to list its contents.

> The initial appearance of the truck is "Your poor old [pickup truck] ticks and groans, smashed gracelessly against [a tall Saguaro]; [whiffs of evaporating gasoline] linger in the chill air. On the dash you can see [a list of things in truck]."

Exercise 4.5

Give a window an initial appearance that reflects a random portable object.

> The initial appearance of pane of cracked glass is "In a pane of cracked glass you catch a momentary reflection of [the random portable thing in location]."

Using "portable" means we won't accidentally pick something unusual like the window itself, and a happy side effect is that there will always be at least one object to reflect: the player character (who is portable rather than fixed in place).

Exercise 4.6

Create two adjectives, "recognized" and "unfamiliar," to help determine which connected rooms the player has been to. These could be put under Part - Mechanics in a new heading called Chapter - Recognized and Unfamiliar.

> Definition: a room is recognized if it is adjacent to location and it is visited.
> Definition: a room is unfamiliar if it is adjacent to location and it is not visited.

Why couldn't we create both definitions in a single sentence, using the "recognized rather than unfamiliar" construction? It's because the two are not exact opposites of each other: both require a room to be adjacent to be considered a match.

Exercise 4.7

Create a description for the lighter that encourages exploration before smoking. This requires and should go in the section from the previous exercise, Part - Mechanics, Chapter - Recognized and Unfamiliar.

> The description of lighter is "[if the number of unfamiliar rooms is at least 1] You'll want a smoke before long, but for now you're itching to see what else is around.[otherwise]Now that you've got your bearings a little, a smoke does sound nice.[end if]".

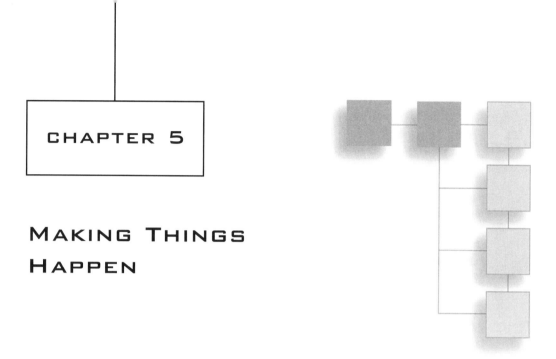

CHAPTER 5

MAKING THINGS HAPPEN

In the last chapter, we introduced the concept of the condition: a phrase, like *the blanket is in the wire mesh cage*, that's either true or false at any given moment. So far, I've shown you two ways to use conditions. Used as assertions, they set the initial state of a story when play begins:

    The blanket is in the wire mesh cage.

When prefaced by "if" in conditional text substitutions, they do one thing if the condition is true and another if it is false:

    if the blanket is in the wire mesh cage

But if we want to change the story world, we need a way to cause something to be. The special word **now**, when placed at the start of a condition, makes it so:

    now the blanket is in the wire mesh cage

As with "if," though, "now" can't start a sentence in Inform; the line above won't stand on its own. We can put if statements within conditional text substitutions, but what about now statements? Where do they go? To answer, we need **rules,** things that happen as a result of player actions or author instructions. Rules, and collections of them called **rulebooks,** lay the foundation for dynamic and interesting story worlds.

To use rules effectively, we also must understand the difference between the verbs a player uses to control the story and the **actions** these become. Understanding actions and how to write rules for them will expand your world-building toolset enormously.

CAUTION
Keep in mind that "now" can't make impossible or vague things true. Not every condition can have a "now" placed in front of it. Inform would allow none of the following:

now the player is a window

now the description of Middle of Nowhere is a rusty tin can

now the emergency lights are open

You can't change the kind of any thing, including the player, in the middle of play. The description of a room must be some text, not an object. And the emergency lights don't have the property openable, so we can't set them to open (although we may grant new properties during play, so if we first said *now the emergency lights are openable* this would be okay).

Rules and Actions

Rules and actions often go hand in hand, but we'll start by looking at them separately. We'll begin with rules.

The Basis of Rules

Description conveys story, as we explored in the previous chapter, but game requires action. If we broke down all the ways we've told Inform about the world of *Sand-dancer*, we might get a list like this:

- a map of the physical spaces where the story takes place (the setting)
- the items, costumes, and backdrops to be found there (the props)
- the details of what the setting and props look and feel like
- (and later) the characters who inhabit that setting and use those props

If we were creating a non-interactive entertainment, such as a short film, you might see only one major thing lacking from this list: the story. But since we're creating an interactive experience, we also need the interactivity: the player's ability to influence events in the story world in a significant way. Both elements require the ability for authors to dictate changes in the story world in responses to certain situations.

Every Inform game contains the Standard Rules, which teach the story world basic concepts: there are things called containers that other things can be inside of; you need light to see things; you can't put a container inside itself; and so on. But a specific story world like *Sand-dancer* has its own basic concepts: that some things trigger memories; that the desert can't be visited until enough light has been found; that certain steps can't be taken until a spirit animal has granted Knock a talent. A significant part of authoring an interactive story is teaching it all the special cases and exceptions that make it unique from all other stories, one by one.

These changes and the conditions that trigger them are called **rules** in Inform, and they look like this:

> Carry out switching on the flashlight: now the flashlight is lit.

This is an action rule, the first and most common type of rule you'll deal with. Action rules change the way Inform responds to player commands. We'll come back to rules soon, but first, let's stop and define actions more clearly.

Actions

Every time the player types a command, the parser tries to match it to one of the actions your story knows about. We always refer to Inform's actions in the gerund form (ending in "ing"): so the player command EXAMINE THE FLASHLIGHT becomes the Inform action "examining the flashlight."

PROGRAMMER'S NOTE

Programmers may be flustered by the cavalier way we've thrown around the articles "a" and "the" in our Inform code. For the most part, these two words act like white space: including or omitting them doesn't change the meaning of a sentence, in either player input or author code. Exceptions include assertion sentences (where the article makes implications about a thing's plurality) and within text substitutions (where the article indicates which article to use when describing the object).

Actions can stand alone (like waiting), have one noun (like examining the flashlight), or two nouns (like putting the key on the desk).

By default, Inform recognizes 80 actions. Some of these come with built-in synonyms, so a total of 143 verb words may be used by players out of the box. Later in the chapter, I'll show you how to see a full and interactive list of all of these, but the following table summarizes some common verbs and the action they translate to.

When dealing with actions, the special word **noun** means the direct object of the player's most recent command. If the player had typed WEAR JACKET, resulting in the "wearing the jacket" action, noun would be set to the jacket. You can also ask for the **second noun** in commands with an indirect object.

Most actions happen in the story world, but some (such as SAVE) happen outside of it. These are called **out of world actions**, and we'll see later on that they work slightly differently than other actions.

In Chapter 6, I'll show you how to add new verb synonyms and create your own actions, but the stock set gives us a good starting vocabulary.

Common Command Verbs and Resulting Actions

Player Command	Inform Action
ATTACK [something]	attacking something
CLIMB [something]	climbing something
CLOSE [something]	closing something
DRINK [something]	drinking something
DROP [things preferably held]	dropping something
EAT [something preferably held]	eating something
ENTER [something]	entering something
EXAMINE/X [something]	examining something
EXIT	exiting
GET IN/INTO/ON/ONTO [something]	entering something
GET OFF [something]	getting off something
GET OUT/OFF/UP	exiting
GET [things]	taking something
GO INTO/IN/INSIDE/THROUGH [something]	entering something
GO [direction]	going something
GO [something]	entering something
INVENTORY/I	taking inventory
JUMP	jumping
LISTEN TO [something]	listening to something
LOOK AT [something]	examining something
LOOK INSIDE/IN/INTO/THROUGH [something]	searching something
LOOK UNDER [something]	looking under something
LOOK/L	looking
OPEN [something]	opening something
PICK UP [things]	taking something
PULL [something]	pulling something
PUSH [something]	pushing something
PUT ON [something preferably held]	wearing something
PUT [things preferably held] DOWN	dropping something
QUIT/Q	quitting the game
REMOVE [something preferably held]	taking off something
RESTART	restarting the game
RESTORE	restoring the game
SAVE	saving the game
SEARCH [something]	searching something
SIT ON/IN/INSIDE [something]	entering something
STAND ON [something]	entering something

Player Command	Inform Action
STAND UP	exiting
SWITCH OFF [something]	switching off something
SWITCH ON [something]	switching on something
TAKE OFF [something]	taking off something
TAKE [things]	taking something
TASTE [something]	tasting something
TOUCH [something]	touching something
TURN OFF [something]	switching off something
TURN ON [something]	switching on something
WAIT	waiting
WEAR [something preferably held]	wearing something

Action Rulebooks

Each of Inform's actions comes with a set of six rulebooks that govern their behavior. These fall naturally into two groups. The three **action default rulebooks** control the standard behavior of an action. These come pre-populated with rules for all built-in actions that enforce the basic underlying reality and consistency of any story world. The three **action exception rulebooks**, on the other hand, start out empty, letting you override the standard behavior for particular actions in particular situations. By learning about both sets, you can make actions produce any result you like.

Action Default Rulebooks

These three rulebooks exist for every action in your story world. Together, they define how the action behaves and what it does. They enforce consistency and logic: for example, declaring that only portable things can be taken, or visible things seen.

The three action default rulebooks are check, carry out, and report:

- An action's **check** rulebook decides whether that action is possible in the present circumstances.
- If the action is possible, its **carry out** rulebook enacts the changes in the story world that result from it.
- Then, the action's **report** rulebook tells the player the results of the successful action.

Each action has all three rulebooks, and together they make the action work.

Check

As an example, let's consider the wearing action. Recall that things defined with the wearable property behave like clothing: the player can WEAR and TAKE OFF these things. Let's look at simplified forms of all of the wearing action's action default rules to better understand the logic governing wearing.

Here's the first rule:

```
Check wearing something not wearable: say "That's not something you can
    wear." instead.
```

Action rules usually begin with the name of the rulebook (in this case, it's "Check wearing.") An action rule defined in this fashion will be consulted any time that action runs. Usually, however, you want to make a rule only apply in a particular situation. You can add a description after the rulebook name to limit the rule to running only when the noun matches the description (in this case, when the noun is "something not wearable"). Finally, a colon indicates that the next sentence will explain what happens if this rule applies.

Creating an Action Rule

- Check wearing: ...
- Check wearing when {a condition}: ...
- Check wearing {a thing}: ...
- Check wearing something {a property or adjective}: ...
- Check wearing {a description}: ...
- A check wearing rule: ...
- A check wearing rule when {a condition}: ...
- A check wearing rule (this is the can't wear what's not clothing rule): ...

Our check wearing rule uses a new command, this one triggered by the word **say**. This simply shows some text to the player. As with any quoted text, these messages can contain text substitutions to say more complicated things.

The rule's say statement ends with the word **instead**, which immediately stops processing the action. No further rules or rulebooks will be consulted. The action has failed, and control returns to the player to try another command. If you like, you can move this word to the beginning of the phrase in question, which sometimes makes a rule a bit more readable: the line below is exactly equivalent.

```
Check wearing something not wearable: instead say "That's not something
    you can wear."
```

So what does this rule do? Pretty straightforward: only things with the wearable property can be worn. If the player typed WEAR CACTUS, this check rule would see that the cactus is not wearable, and tell the player why the command is unsuccessful through the "say" phrase. Without this rule, the player would be allowed to wear anything, which would not necessarily produce a very believable story world.

The wearing action has two other rules in its check rulebook. Let's take a look:

> Check wearing something not held: instead say "You can't wear something
>   you're not holding."

> Check wearing something worn: instead say "You're already wearing that."

Each rule in a check rulebook is consulted, one at a time, until either they've all been consulted or one of them stops the sequence with a phrase beginning or ending with "instead." Assuming the noun is in fact wearable, the next rule requires that that the player be holding it. Finally, the third rule makes sure the player is not already wearing the object in question. Together, these three ensure that, within constraints of the system we've created, the wearing action on a particular thing makes sense at a particular time.

Carry Out

If no check rules stop the action with "instead," Inform proceeds to the carry out rules to find out what the action actually does. Most actions, including wearing, have only a single carry out rule:

> Carry out wearing: now player wears the noun.

Simple and straightforward. We make the item worn, and that's all that needs to be done.

Report

The action has been performed, but the player doesn't know its results. The report rulebook conveys this information, and again, most actions have just a single report rule:

> Report wearing: say "You put on [the noun]."

Remember from the previous chapter how descriptions have to serve both story and gameplay purposes at once? In a similar way, action default rules must notify two separate entities about a successful action: the story world (via a carry out rule) and the player (via a report rule). But this doesn't mean both rules convey identical information: we may change the story world in ways we don't want the player to know about, while at the same time describing minor or aesthetic details of the action that don't concern the code running the story world.

The wearing action's report rule, however, simply tells the player that the thing has been worn, using the text substitution [the noun] to say the item along with its definite article.

Like check rules, carry out and report rules can be limited to more specific circumstances by following the rulebook name with a description. You can also specify that a rule applies only when a certain condition holds true by adding the keyword **when** followed by the condition. We could make an additional report rule applying only when the player is in the right region as follows:

> Report wearing when location is in Around the Tower: say "[The noun] provides some protection from the cold."

 The ordering of rules within a particular rulebook can be complex, but at a basic level, rules of equal complexity are consulted in the same order they appear in your source text. We'll talk more about rule ordering later in this chapter and in Chapter 10, and you can also look up "Sorting and indexing of rules" and "The Laws for Sorting Rulebooks" in the Rulebooks chapter of the built-in documentation.

PROGRAMMER'S NOTE

Programmers and other morbidly curious folk can view the Standard Rules directly within Inform. From the File menu, select the Open Extension option and look under author Graham Nelson to find them. Among other treasures, you'll find the action default rulebooks for every built-in action. The Standard Rules crawl with advanced syntax and confusing concepts, but browse through them to explore the detailed infrastructure Inform creates for even a brand new, empty story world.

In some ways, it might seem that everything in the wearing action's action default rulebooks is common sense: of course you can only wear wearable things! But nobody's figured out yet how to give common sense to computers, except in the relentlessly literal way seen here. Inform does not share our cultural database of associations and definitions, and *wearable* is just a sequence of characters to it, signifying nothing. The job of the action default rulebooks is to provide that definition, to the level of detail simulated by the story world.

Exercise 5.1

Of course, Inform only knows as much common sense as we program into it. The built-in rulebooks have no way to indicate that, for example, a man with large feet cannot wear a small woman's shoe, or that one cannot take off socks if shoes are being worn. If any of these concepts were somehow important to our story, we would first instruct Inform about the relevant concepts (men's shoes versus women's shoes; sizes for footwear and feet). How would you do this? Once the concepts were in place, check rules would be needed to enforce them: how might these begin?

Action Exception Rulebooks

The action default rulebooks (check, carry out, and report) describe the default behavior for actions in your story world. Since these rulebooks are pre-populated with sensible rules for common actions, you'll rarely have to make your own. Frequently, though, you'll want exceptions for particular cases that don't match the workings of Inform's default model. In these situations, use one of the three **action exception rulebooks** to intervene.

- A rule in the **before** rulebook makes an adjustment to the story world before an action is attempted.

- A rule in the **instead** rulebook overrides the normal behavior of an action and does something different.

- A rule in the **after** rulebook changes how the result of a specific successful action is described to the player.

You'll probably use the intensely useful action exception rulebooks more than any other rulebooks. Let's go over each of them in detail, in order of most commonly useful.

Instead

The most commonly used action rulebook is *instead*. An instead rule tells Inform to do something other than the normal behavior in a particular circumstance.

 Instead rules are always for specific situations. If you want the default behavior of an action to change, override its check or carry out rules. We'll see how to modify existing actions like this in Chapter 6.

Often, instead rules exist to better explain why something can't happen. For example, if you try the command TAKE TUMBLEWEED in our current version of *Sand-dancer*, you'll get the same message that's seen for every static object: "That's fixed in place." This is produced by a rule like the following in the Standard Rules:

Check taking something fixed in place: instead say "That's fixed in place."

We gave the tumbleweed this property because we don't want the player carrying it around. But in this case, the translation between Inform's properties and our real-world definitions isn't entirely accurate: the tumbleweed isn't fixed in place in a literal sense, so this response seems incongruous to the player, and reveals the irrelevant infrastructure of our story world.

Let's improve this situation with our first instead rule. Add it in Part - Setting, Chapter - Around the Tower, Section - Base of the Tower:

Instead of taking the tumbleweed: say "Let it blow on. Wherever it's going is bound to be better than here."

Now, instead of a window into the mechanical details of your story world, you've provided a window into the environment and the attitude of the main character: a big improvement. You've also provided a more plausible reason why the player can't take the tumbleweed: the main character can't be bothered to.

Note that we don't need an "instead" with our "say" phrase here because it's implicit in the name and behavior of this rulebook. Triggered instead rules stop the action after running. Also note that we can say either "instead" or "instead of" when naming this rulebook.

We can also make rules that apply more broadly than to individual objects. Add the next line in Part - Setting, Chapter - Office Interior:

> Instead of opening a window: say "It looks like these windows have been rusted
>   shut for years."

In the light of instead rules, what's the value of check rules? After all, couldn't we achieve the same effect as above with a rule like this?

> Check opening a window: instead say "It looks like these windows have
>   been rusted shut for years."

Technically, either rule produces the same effect. But it's easy to forget the extra word "instead" in a check rule that causes it to fail an action, which can lead to annoying bugs in your story. More importantly, check rules are conceptually designed to control default behavior, whereas instead rules for are particular circumstances that override that default behavior.

Exercise 5.2

Try writing a few instead rules yourself for actions that will fail, like taking something fixed in place, eating something inedible, or performing a command that normally produces no result, like jumping or singing.

After

While a "report" rule displays the result of a successful action to the player (such as "You open the box."), you often want more specific responses in more specific situations. An "after" rule overrides the default "report" rule for a certain case.

The pickup truck in *Sand-dancer*, for instance, is openable, but the default text describing a successful opening action sounds awkward when used in this context. Add the next line, in Chapter - Around the Tower, Section - Middle of Nowhere:

> After opening the pickup truck: say "The door creaks open with difficulty, rusted
>   joints straining."

An after rule also stops the action by default, so the standard report rule text won't show up. Let's add another rule for parity:

> After closing the truck: say "You slam the door shut."

Just as instead rules can provide better descriptions for particular failed actions than the default check rules, after rules provide better descriptions for particular successful actions than the default report rules. And again, we could have written the above as a "Report opening the pickup truck" rule: but we'd have to remember to add "instead" to our say phrase to stop the default message, and conceptually, this rule, as an exception, is a better fit for the "after" rulebook that's designed to deal with exceptional cases.

Before

Sometimes before dealing with a player action, we want to tweak the story world (perhaps to make the action more likely to succeed) or describe some small preliminary action to the player. In modern IF it's considered pedantic to make players open unlocked doors by hand before going through them. We can add this convenience to the pickup truck with a before rule like the following, added to Section - Middle of Nowhere below your definition of the truck:

> Before entering truck when truck is closed: try opening the truck.

Something new here: saying **try** and an action causes Inform to immediately attempt to perform that action, as if the player had tried it. The new action's six rulebooks are consulted, and only when the new action has succeeded or failed does the original action continue from where it left off. Here, if the opening action succeeds, the state of the truck changes from open to closed, our "After opening the pickup truck" rule runs to display a custom message, and then control returns to the "entering" action, which describes the results in its default report rule.

Again, let's add a second rule for parity:

> Before exiting when player is in truck and truck is closed: try opening the truck.

 Notice that the "exiting" action in the Standard Rules has no direct object—Inform knows "exiting" but not "exiting the truck." Later in the chapter, we'll talk about the ACTIONS and RULES testing commands that help divine the sometimes mysterious behaviors behind the built-in actions.

Try recompiling and running the game now and getting in and out of the truck, and closing and opening the door, to observe the behavior. The responses and behavior are much improved from the built-in defaults.

When writing rules, always make sure the player's mental map of the world corresponds with Inform's. What would be the problem with a rule like this?

Instead of exiting when player is in truck: now player is in Middle of Nowhere.

While this rule solves the immediate problem of worrying whether the truck is open or closed, it violates the player's mental model of the world. Unless told otherwise, the player will assume a closed door remains closed; trying to get back in to the truck now would produce a refusal with the justification that the truck is closed, but if the player's just left with no problems, this will seem incongruous.

Using Rulebooks

An Inform story consults the exception rulebooks and default rulebooks in a specific order seen below. Together, the six rulebooks offer fine-grained control over when and how to interfere with the normal behavior of an action. Deciding which rulebook to use takes practice, but learning the order they're consulted in makes for a good first step:

Rulebook	Type	Description	Then...
Before	Exception	"Wait... in this case *before* you do that, do this!"	...go on
Instead	Exception	"Don't do that in this case... *instead* do this."	...stop
Check	Default	"Let's *check* to make sure that's okay."	...go on unless the phrase contains "instead"
Carry out	Default	"OK, let's *carry out* the results."	...go on
After	Exception	"In this case, this is what happened *after*."	...stop
Report	Default	"Otherwise, *report on* what normally happens."	...go on

This may seem a little overwhelming, but we'll spend the rest of this chapter working through the implications of these six rulebooks, and teaching you the differences and how to know when to use each one.

CAUTION   Out-of-world actions (such as saving the game or quitting the game) do not have exception rulebooks: it is illegal to make a rule such as "Instead of quitting the game," for instance. If you have reason to modify the behavior of these actions (and such should only be done for good reason!), use the default rulebooks check, carry out, and report.

Use Instead to Redirect Actions

One nice trick: combine *instead* and *try* to redirect actions. Frequently you'll find that you really want several actions to produce the exact same result. Rather than duplicating rules and responses for each instance, you can simply redirect the secondary actions. Let's add this bit of color to *Sand-dancer*, in Chapter - Around the Tower, Section - Middle of Nowhere:

> Instead of touching the Saguaro: say "Yeah, you did that once as a kid, on accident. Not happening again." Instead of taking the Saguaro: try touching the Saguaro.

Now the commands TOUCH SAGUARO and TAKE SAGUARO produce the same effect.

Making Action Rules More General

Sometimes you want rules that are still exceptions to the normal behavior, but apply in broader situations than a particular action on a particular object. Let's add some general rules to *Sand-dancer* to see this in action.

We've already seen that rules can apply to kinds, not just things. Recall the rule we made in Chapter - Office Interior applying to the window kind:

> Instead of opening a window: say "It looks like these windows have been rusted shut for years."

Rules can be made more specific simply by adding adjectives. Change the above to:

> Instead of opening a closed window: say "It looks like these windows have been rusted shut for years."

Similarly, we can create exception rules that apply to ranges of actions. Change the above again to:

> Instead of opening or closing a closed window: say "It looks like these windows have been rusted shut for years."

For longer runs of actions, we can simply list them all: "taking, touching, rubbing, or smelling" for instance.

When creating rules applying to multiple actions, all the actions you list must have the same number of ancillary nouns: zero, one, or two. You couldn't add "looking" to the list above, since the looking action has no noun and the others all take one.

Action default rules (check, carry out, report) must apply to single actions only: "Check opening," never "Check opening or closing."

Even more broadly, we can say **doing anything** to mean any action at all. Back in Chapter
- Around the Tower, Section - Middle of Nowhere, add the following:

> Instead of doing anything to whiffs of evaporating gasoline: say "Fading away in
>   the chill night air, but enough to tell you something on your truck's busted
>   bad."

Now any action, from examining the whiffs to smelling the whiffs, will produce the above
message. For exceptions, add **other than** to the end:

> Instead of doing anything other than smelling to whiffs of evaporating
>   gasoline: ...

...and now you could create a second "Instead of smelling the gasoline" rule to define the
more specific behavior. You can include multiple actions in an "other than" list, too.

So far all the rules we've seen produce only a single effect. It's also possible to have one rule
do multiple things by using a semicolon instead of a period at the end of each sentence
until the last one. Imagine that we also wanted to keep track of whether Knock's pickup
truck was locked or unlocked—we don't, but if we did, we might have a rule like this:

> Before exiting when player is in truck and truck is closed and truck is locked:
>   now truck is unlocked; now truck is open; say "(first unlocking and opening
>   the door)".

You can string together any number of phrases this way, and they'll run in order of appearance when the rule is triggered.

 As noted in the final column of the table in "Using Rulebooks" above, each action rulebook
specifies whether its rules stop the action immediately or continue onwards. You can override
this behavior with the phrases **continue the action** (to continue executing rules even in a
rulebook that would normally stop) or **stop the action** (to stop executing rules immediately
even in a rulebook that would normally continue). For example, normally only the most specific "after" rule will run for any given action, but if you wanted to let all matching "after"
rules run, potentially printing several different messages, you could add a semicolon and *continue the action* to the end of each rule.

Action Rules in *Sand-dancer*

Now that we know how to use rules, we can start adding puzzles to *Sand-dancer*—obstacles for the player to overcome. In the process, we'll get practice recognizing which action
rulebook to use in a given situation.

Let's start by adding some room descriptions for the inside of the building, to set the stage. Put these in the appropriate sections within Part -Setting, Chapter - Office Interior:

> The description of Staging Area is "[if location is not lit by flashlight and location is not lit brightly]Faint [shafts of light] from your dimming headlights seep through a boarded-up [pane of cracked glass], but you can barely make out anything of the interior[otherwise]It's obvious this place has been abandoned for years. Cold night air breathes through [holes in the roof] and everything is strewn with [sand] and [patches of mold]. Other rooms lie north and east[end if]."

> The description of Foreman's Office is "[if location is lit by flashlight]You sweep the beam of your flashlight around[otherwise]The stark emergency lights illume[end if] this tiny office, probably once where the boss sat under [a dust-covered window]. The only exit is to the south."

> The description of Break Room is "Shadows and grime linger in dark corners of this dismal room with just one [tiny frosted window]. Some [rotting picnic tables] strewn with [layers of sand] and [crumbling trash] are pushed against one wall, and open doorways lead west and north."

> The description of Storage Room is "The walls are lined with [bare metal shelves], [if location is lit by flashlight]casting strange patterns of shadow as you sweep your flashlight beam around[otherwise]rusting away[end if]. The break room lies back to the south and a [utility ladder] climbs through [a broken skylight] to the roof."

Most of these windows were created when we set up the window kind previously; you might want to move their declarations to the appropriate room sections, to help you remember their locations. While we're poking around, since we plan to always mention windows within room descriptions, let's modify the kind to make windows undescribed by default. Up near the window definitions in Chapter - Office Interior, add:

> A window is usually undescribed.

We'll quickly create the other bracketed scenery objects (remember to get BENT!) in the appropriate sections for each room. Since we mention the sand in multiple places, we'll create a backdrop object for it and place it in the Office Interior region. Put each sentence below in the appropriate Section for the room in which each object appears.

> Some shafts of light, some holes in the roof, and some patches of mold are scenery in Staging Area. Some rotting picnic tables and some crumbling trash are scenery in Break Room. Some bare metal shelves, a utility ladder and a broken skylight are scenery in Storage Room. Some layers of sand are a backdrop. They are in Office Interior.

We've actually already created a sand backdrop, the "desert sand." We've decided to create a second one here because the two represent distinct elements: the desert sand is used to refer more to the endless desert outdoors, and the layers of sand to much smaller scattered drifts in our abandoned building. We might want to describe the two differently, make different rules about them, and so on.

It's important to note that we couldn't call one of these just "sand," however, because otherwise there's no way for Inform to be certain which one we're referring to. Watch out when creating similar objects and make sure their names are distinguishable from one another.

Sometimes when getting BENT you might want to start a sentence with a bracketed thing that omits the article, perhaps for a sentence like "Piles of trash litter the corners." Unfortunately, while Inform recognizes the difference between [A something] and [a something], and will capitalize the article appropriately, it won't do the same for the actual name of a thing: so [Piles of trash] and [piles of trash] both result in the entirely lowercase "piles of trash". The quickest way around this is to simply remove the brackets from the item in question, although you'll lose the advantages of BENT for this object. Another solution is to check out the <u>Mentioned in Room Description by Ron Newcomb</u> extension, which, among other useful functions for BENT authors, gives more control over capitalization.

Note that not all of our rules about light will work correctly yet, since we haven't fully instructed Inform how our flashlight, headlights, and emergency lights affect the model world—we'll do that later in the chapter.

Before we continue, let's tell Inform something minor but significant about our story. Add the following assertion near the top of the story, under the title but before the first heading:

> Use no scoring.

This is an example of a **use option**, which sets up certain baseline assumptions about how your story should operate. Since *Sand-dancer* (and many modern games) don't include the idea of a score, this omits references to "points" in the status line or ending text, and axes related verbs like SCORE, uncluttering our story world just a little.

Now that we've laid the framework for this area of the game, let's add *Sand-dancer*'s first puzzles.

The Duct Tape

Our story outline requires Knock to collect a series of items leading towards one of two goals: fixing his truck and getting home, or surviving the night in the desert. To make progress towards either goal, he first needs a talent from the first spirit animal, the rabbit. So that the choice of talents has meaning, we want the player to clearly understand how a certain talent will help advance a certain goal.

Let's start with the "fixing the truck" goal. For a busted fuel line, a roll of duct tape might be a good quick fix. Since one talent the player can choose from the rabbit is courage, let's put the duct tape in a hole infested with spiders and prevent Knock from taking the tape without courage.

First, though, we need a way of tracking which talents the player has. We'll do this simply by instantiating them as things that the player can either be holding (after a spirit animal gifts them) or not. The talents will appear in inventory listings: slightly surreal, but then again our story as a whole is slightly surreal. It works. In Part - Mechanics, add a new heading called Chapter - Talents, and put this within it:

> A talent is a kind of thing. strength, courage, luck, scent, honor, spirit, and freedom are talents. [Note the uncapitalized "strength": we don't want the talents to have articles, but we also don't want them to be capitalized like proper nouns.]

Remember comments? The above bracketed text is purely for our own benefit as we read the source text; Inform will ignore it.

We'll come back and add more rules to define talents later, but for now this is all the scaffolding we need.

First things first: let's make the hole. Find Part - Setting, Chapter - Office Interior, Section - Staging Area in your source text, and add the following below your room declarations:

> A hole in the floor is a fixed in place open unopenable container in Staging Area. "The floor has half-collapsed near one corner, revealing a hole criss-crossed with [cobwebs]."
>
> Some cobwebs are in the hole. A roll of duct tape is in the hole.

That's it for our description. Everything else is rules.

First, let's prevent the player from taking the duct tape without courage:

> Instead of taking something enclosed by the hole when player does not hold courage: say "[one of]You reach your hand towards the hole, then pull back with a start as you brush cobwebs. Nightmare visions of fat black spiders shudder through your brain. No way are you reaching in there.[or]Yeah, sorry, but you're not putting your hand in there.[stopping]".

The [one of][or][stopping] text substitution here is another variation on the [at random] text substitution we introduced in the last chapter. Here, each phrase will be shown once per occasion until the final phrase is reached, and on subsequent occasions the final phrase will be repeated. The result in this case is that the first message will only be displayed once, and then the shorter message each time thereafter.

We can recompile and see this rule in action, but how do we test whether the player can in fact take the duct tape if they've got courage? We haven't yet created any way for Knock to obtain it. One quick solution is to add a temporary line like "The courage is in Staging Area." to our source text. Now we can just pick it up ourselves and see if our "instead" rule is working (see Figure 5.1). Try this out for yourself.

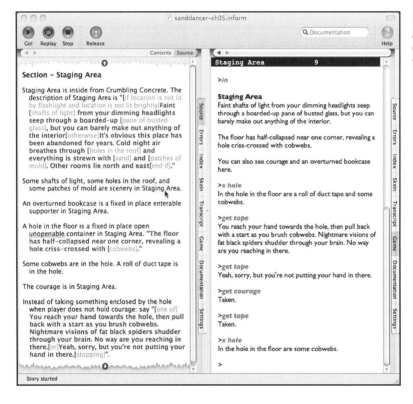

Figure 5.1
A demonstration of our first instead rule for a puzzle in action.

The message "Taken." isn't a terribly exciting reward for this important story moment, so let's write an after rule to make this occasion more memorable. We want an after rule rather than a report rule because this is a specific case, not a default behavior for taking:

> After taking the duct tape: say "[one of]You reach down into the hole, brushing
>   the cobwebs away impatiently, and pull out the duct
>   tape.[or]Taken.[stopping]"; now cobwebs are off-stage.

Note our use again of the [one of][or][stopping] construction, to show one message the first time, and a second on all subsequent occasions. In this case, we only want our special message once, and if the player later drops and picks up the tape again, the normal text should be restored.

The cobwebs create a physical object to represent the player's fear, but after retrieving the tape, they're no longer important to the story. The *now something is off-stage* phrase takes a thing out of the story world entirely. If you need it again later, you can bring it back on-stage with a phrase like *now cobwebs are in hole in the floor*. You can also test whether something has been taken out of play by checking whether it is **on-stage** or **off-stage**.

Writing this rule revealed another possibility: what if the player tries to take the cobwebs first, after they have courage but before taking the duct tape? We don't want the player carrying them around, so let's deal with that possibility too:

> Instead of taking cobwebs when player holds courage: say "You impatiently
>   brush the cobwebs away."; now cobwebs are off-stage.

…and our after rule should be subtly altered, too:

> After taking the duct tape: say "[one of]You reach down into the hole[if
>   cobwebs are on-stage], brushing the cobwebs away impatiently,[end if] and
>   pull out the duct tape.[or]Taken.[stopping]"; now cobwebs are off-stage.

It's useful to think through all the possible states your story world can get into. Another player action that might not have occurred to us: putting things in the hole, since it's a container. This could be a problem, especially since at first the player can't get things back out of the hole, but also because not all the portable items in our story can sensibly fit inside. Since there's no good reason to put anything in the hole, let's write a rule that prevents doing so:

> Instead of inserting anything into the hole: say "Sounds like a good way to lose
>   something forever."

CAUTION   Whenever you restrict player actions to make life easier for yourself, take care that your restriction has an adequate story justification. If it doesn't, players may feel resentful and lose their respect or suspension of disbelief. The adventure game cliché of a knee-high wall impassable to the mighty dragon-slaying hero is an example of a gameplay restriction with poor story justification.

One last point: once the cobwebs are gone, we no longer want to describe them in the initial appearance for the hole in the floor. In fact, the hole itself doesn't have much importance after the tape has been taken, so let's change its initial appearance to the following text:

    "The floor has half-collapsed near one corner[if duct tape is in the hole],
        revealing a hole criss-crossed with [cobwebs][end if]."

Note that we've put the conditional text substitution immediately after the word "corner," without a space, so that if the condition is not true the next character shown will be the concluding period.

That's it for the duct tape puzzle. Recompile and test, and see if you find any situations we overlooked. Once you're satisfied, make sure to remove the test line making the courage easily accessible.

The Emergency Blanket

The player's other alternative is trying to stay the night in the desert and wait for help in the morning. Let's make finding a blanket the first item necessary for this path.

We've already created a wire mesh cage in Chapter 3 as a fixed in place transparent closed container, and placed an emergency blanket inside it. Let's complicate matters by making the cage locked, and unable to be opened without the talent of strength to break through the rusting mesh. In Part - Setting, Chapter - Office Interior, Section - Break Room, add this:

    The cage is locked.

An immediate problem with locked things is that players might assume the correct solution is to find the right key. Locks and keys were a staple of early text adventures, but these hunt-and-fetch puzzles are much less interesting to modern audiences. We created a rusted key as set dressing earlier: let's go ahead and create a clear response for an attempt to use this on the cage, indicating that unlocking it is not the answer.

> Instead of unlocking cage with rusted key: say "You sling the key into the lock, but as you turn it, the rusted metal snaps off inside. The crumbling fragments fall to the ground as you slam your fist against the wire mesh in frustration. This is not your day."; now rusted key is off-stage.

Now, to get inside:

> Instead of attacking closed cage when player holds strength: say "You grip the mesh in one hand and pull, and realize it's so rusted you can easily peel it back. The door rips free and you drop it to the floor."; now cage is open; now cage is unopenable; now cage is not lockable.

By making this rule apply only to the "closed" cage, we ensure that this rule will only apply once: running it causes the cage to become open and no longer openable or lockable, since the door has been destroyed.

Thinking through possible states, we can see a few other options: the player might try to attack the cage before gaining strength, or after already opening it. Let's create rules for these two situations:

> Instead of attacking closed cage: say "You try to get a grip on the mesh to rip it open, but you're just not strong enough."
>
> Instead of attacking cage: say "You've already ripped it open. No point in going mental."

This serves to illustrate an important point about rules: they apply in order of specificity. We've created three rules that apply to attacking the cage, but each for a successively less specific situation. The rule with the "when" clause is most specific, and thus, in the situation it describes, will match before the less specific rule with an adjective (closed) or the even less specific rule that applies whenever the player attacks the cage. And since these are "instead" rules, which stop the flow of the action immediately after running, the later rules are never reached in the more specific situations; were these before rules, however, all matching rules would get a chance to run. Again, refer to "The Laws for Sorting Rulebooks" in the built-in docs for gory details on rule ordering.

So now we've created *Sand-dancer*'s first two puzzles, and the beginning of the player's choice of which path to take. Hopefully you're starting to get a good sense of how to consider and construct sequences that bring action, not just description, into your story.

Exercise 5.3

Try creating a long-expired first aid kit discovered underneath the blanket. Give this all likely properties and create some rules to control plausible attempts to use it.

Debugging Actions and Rules

When working with actions and rules, it's sometimes difficult to know exactly what action results from a particular command, or which rule is interfering with a particular move. Inform provides several diagnostic tools to better understand what's going on inside your story.

The Index Panel: "Actions" Tab

If you switch one of the Inform application's two pages to the Index panel, you'll see a row of tabs along the top. The left-most tab, "Actions," presents a wealth of useful information on actions and action rules: not only the ones you create, but all those built in to the Standard Rules as well.

This Actions Index (Figure 5.2) contains a lot of information, but it's divided into easily navigable categories. Let's get familiar with them.

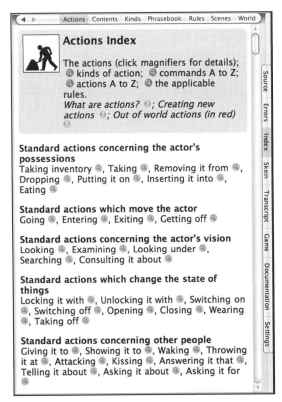

Figure 5.2
The Actions Index for a newly created Inform story.

List of Actions

The first section lists all actions possible in your story, organized into broad categories like "Standard actions concerning the actor's possessions." (The actor in question is usually the player, but in Chapter 9 we'll talk about how other characters in your story can also perform actions.) Custom actions, when you start to make them, will show up in their own category, "New actions defined in the source." Any actions created because of an extension you've included will be listed in their own category as well.

Next to each action is a magnifying glass icon. Click this to show a subpage of the Actions Index on that action, including useful information like the number of nouns it takes, whether it requires light to perform, a detailed prose description of its function, all the commands the player can use that result in this action, and a list of all the rules that concern it, including again both the built-in Standard Rules and any you've defined yourself. Clicking the orange arrow next to a custom rule jumps to and highlights that rule in your source text.

PROGRAMMER'S NOTE

Though it's best not to meddle without fully understanding them, you can easily remove (or **unlist**) any of the Standard Rules from a particular story. Position the cursor at a blank spot in your source text, then from the Actions Index click the purple box before "unlist" in the block for a built-in rule. A sentence will be inserted into your source text that removes that rule from your story. Deleting the inserted sentence will restore the default behavior.

 The Standard Rules all have names that describe their function: under the taking action, for instance, we see a very sensible check rule called "the can't take yourself rule." You can give your own rules custom names by adding a parenthetical clause before the colon in a rule declaration, beginning with "this is the" and ending with "rule":

> Instead of dropping a talent (this is the talents are forever rule): ...

This makes it easier to remember which rules do what when perusing your story's index. Naming your rules becomes vital when you start writing extensions, because of another advantage: named rules can be manipulated, reordered, or removed during play.

You can return to the main Actions Index page by clicking the large "Back to full view" link at the very top of the panel.

Kinds of Action

We won't talk in detail about kinds of action until Chapter 10, but they're another way of creating general rules that apply to wide varieties of situations. If you're curious now, look up "Kinds of action" in the built-in documentation for more details. If you've created any kinds of action in your source text, each will be listed here, along with the specific actions that comprise them.

Commands A to Z

Next comes a full list of all verbs and command forms your story recognizes. Again, this includes not only built-in verbs, but also any synonyms that you or an included extension have added, helpfully alphabetized. Clicking the magnifying glass here will jump you to the detailed information page for the corresponding action.

Below this is a list of all your story's actions (rather than verbs), again in alphabetical order.

Rules A to Z

Finally, all of your custom rules are listed, sorted into the appropriate rulebook: before, instead, or after. If you've created any custom default rules (check, carry out, or report) they'll be listed on the individual pages for the action they apply to, rather than here. Click the blue question mark icon next to a rulebook's name to jump to the documentation page for that rulebook.

All told, the Actions Index contains a huge amount of information on the details of interacting with your story world. It's worth exploring to learn how the actions in the Standard Rules function. Don't forget about this great resource as you continue working on your project.

Next, let's talk about some testing commands that are also helpful when dealing with actions.

ACTIONS

The ACTIONS testing command, when used in an unreleased story, turns on a mode that shows every action attempted, regardless of whether it was generated by the player or by a "try" phrase. It also shows whether the action succeeds or fails. Type ACTIONS OFF to disable this mode.

For example, let's look at the result of the command GET IN TRUCK when standing outside our pickup truck (Figure 5.3). You can see how the before rule we created earlier causes the "opening the truck" action to run, before the original entering action resumes.

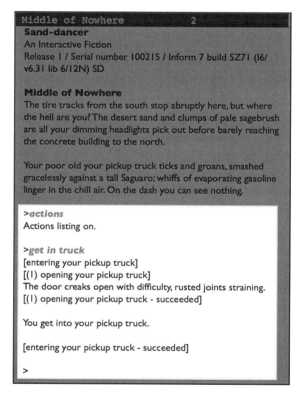

Figure 5.3
The results of an entering command with actions debugging turned on.

```
Middle of Nowhere              2
Sand-dancer
An Interactive Fiction
Release 1 / Serial number 100215 / Inform 7 build 5Z71 (I6/
v6.31 lib 6/12N) SD

Middle of Nowhere
The tire tracks from the south stop abruptly here, but where
the hell are you? The desert sand and clumps of pale sagebrush
are all your dimming headlights pick out before barely reaching
the concrete building to the north.

Your poor old your pickup truck ticks and groans, smashed
gracelessly against a tall Saguaro; whiffs of evaporating gasoline
linger in the chill air. On the dash you can see nothing.
```

```
>actions
Actions listing on.

>get in truck
[entering your pickup truck]
[(1) opening your pickup truck]
The door creaks open with difficulty, rusted joints straining.
[(1) opening your pickup truck - succeeded]

You get into your pickup truck.

[entering your pickup truck - succeeded]

>
```

ACTIONS can also be useful to find out what action results from a particular command. This is helpful if the verb you're thinking of isn't the same word used in the name of the action (for instance, GET translates to the action "taking"). Of course, you can also use the Actions Index in the Index panel to find this same information, but sometimes it's quicker to try the command in your story and see what ACTIONS reports.

Exercise 5.4

Using either of the methods you've learned, identify the actions resulting from each of these commands: "PUT DOWN CIGARETTES." "GO TO TRUCK." "GET OUT." "I."

RULES

Similar to ACTIONS, RULES activates a mode that shows the relevant rules consulted as a result of a player command, as well as any other rules triggered by the story's operation. Type RULES OFF to disable this mode. See Figure 5.4 for an example of this with the same command.

Figure 5.4
The results of the same command with rules debugging turned on.

Here's another place where the naming of rules via parenthetical clauses becomes useful: when debugging your game with the RULES verb, you can more easily see at a glance which rule is having what effect.

Note that just because a rule "applies" does not mean that it matched; only that it was consulted in the current situation. If you type RULES ALL; however, you'll get a much longer list of rules which include all the ones that could potentially apply in this situation, even if it turns out they do not. Be warned, this list can be very long, but can sometimes be useful in getting a detailed overview of all the things your story does on any given turn. (In a large game like *Blue Lacuna*, RULES ALL lists several thousand rules for any given turn!)

Making More Things Happen

Let's close out the chapter by fleshing out *Sand-dancer*'s world with some more scenarios, using rules to construct the cause-and-effect logic behind them and to describe them more dramatically. You'll have the opportunity to help design these, to solidify your growing knowledge of action rules.

Light and Dark

Let's finish the model of light and dark we started to build in the last chapter. Inform already has a pre-built model of light and darkness, but in a story with a setting so powerfully defined by light or its absence, it's too simple for our needs.

Inform's model sets every room as either lighted or dark, and every item as either lit or unlit. If either the room or a visible object provides illumination, the player can see; otherwise, he can't see anything (even the room name) or interact with any unheld objects. For *Sand-dancer*, we want to modify by this by introducing the notion of variable levels of light. We already began to implement this in the previous chapter by creating definitions for each of our three light levels: lit brightly, lit by headlights, and lit by flashlight. But we still need to leverage these definitions into actual changes to the model world, by making appropriate rooms lighted or dark when our various light sources are turned on and off.

First of all, let's reverse Inform's assumption that rooms are usually light, except for the rooms initially lit by the player's headlights when the story begins. Add this to Part - Mechanics, Chapter - Lights:

> A room is usually dark. Middle of Nowhere, Backtracking, Crumbling Concrete, Staging Area, and Base of the Tower are lighted.

Next, let's begin with a rule for our brightest light source, the emergency lights. In Part - Setting, Chapter - Office Interior, Section - Storage Room, add this:

> The initial appearance of the emergency lights is "Mounted to the wall is a control panel for the building's emergency lights. They are switched [if emergency lights are switched on]on[otherwise]off[end if]."
>
> After switching on the emergency lights: now every room regionally in Tower Vicinity is lighted; say "With a sharp buzz, a whiff of static and an electrical groan, bare light bulbs flicker on throughout the building."

We use "after" because we want the action to happen and produce its normal state change in the game world (setting the emergency lights device to on)—which rules out "instead", which would have overridden this default behavior. If we didn't want any custom text, we could have used a "carry out" rule to make the rooms lighted, and let the built-in "report switching on" rule display a stock message ("You switch the emergency lights on.")

Of course, we also need a companion rule for switching off. But this one needs to be considered with more care.

> After switching off the emergency lights: now every room regionally in Tower Vicinity is dark; if headlights are switched on, now every within range of headlights room is lighted; say "The lights flicker and die out."

When we were making rooms lighted, we did not need to care if some of them were already illuminated by another light source, since the emergency lights overpower all other light sources. But when turning them off, we need to consider that other light sources might be present and switched on. The easiest way to do this is to make all rooms dark, then relight those that match the "within range of headlights" definition we created in the previous chapter. If the headlights are not on, it's safe to just turn all the lights off and leave it at that.

 Inform's natural language syntax sometimes produces sentences that sound odd as English. If you're having trouble parsing the second now phrase above, remember that we defined within range of headlights as an adjective. Despite the fact that it contains multiple words, we can use it just like any other adjective:

> now every room is lighted;
>
> now every *visited* room is lighted;
>
> now every *within range of headlights* room is lighted;

It sounds strange since in English we'd normally put an adjectival phrase like this after the noun, but Inform normally expects adjectives only before the noun.

> If you want to include an adjective after the noun, you can preface it with the phrase **which is** to make your meaning clear to Inform. Another way we could have written this phrase is:
>
>   now every room which is within range of headlights is lighted;
>
> In fact, using this format we can create our own adjectival phrases: we could write a phrase like *now every thing which is worn by the player is lit*, or even *now every thing which is worn by someone who is not the player is lit*.

Getting back to our after rule above, note also that this is our first use of an "if" outside of a conditional text substitution. By following the condition with a comma, you indicate that the next phrase will happen only if the condition holds true. We'll talk more about how to use "if" like this in Chapter 7.

Let's go ahead and create two similar rules for the headlights, again making use of the definitions created earlier. Put these in Part - Setting, Chapter - Around the Tower, Section - Middle of Nowhere:

    After switching on the headlights: now every within range of headlights room is
        lighted; say "The desert springs into existence around you."

    After switching off the headlights: if emergency lights are switched off, now
        every within range of headlights room is dark; say "You click the headlights
        off[if emergency lights are switched off and flashlight is switched off]and
        blackness swallows you up[otherwise if emergency lights are switched off
        and flashlight is switched on and flashlight is visible], leaving only the ghostly
        beam of your flashlight[end if]."

Again, we must check to ensure that it makes sense to change the illumination level: in this case, only if the emergency lights are switched off.

Finally, our third light source: the flashlight. Since this is a portable light source, we don't have to adjust the lighted/dark properties of rooms, and since we're happy with the default message for this simple object, we'll use a carry out rule instead of an after rule. Put this in Part - Mechanics, Chapter - Lights:

    Carry out switching on flashlight: now flashlight is lit. Carry out switching off
        flashlight: now flashlight is unlit.

> Remember, the lighted and dark properties are for rooms, and the lit and unlit properties are for things.

We've now enhanced Inform's built-in light/dark model to more effectively tell our story. Discovering how to light up the building gives the player a motivation when the game first begins, and in the process of doing so he'll discover memories and set the stage for the story to come.

Let's complicate this process a little (thus giving the player some more interesting actions to take) by creating a sequence where the player has to find the flashlight in the dim Staging Area room before exploring the rest of the building.

First off, the Staging Area should be too dim at first to see anything in much detail, so let's give everything in the room the undescribed property. Remember, scenery is undescribed by default, and objects contained by something undescribed are effectively undescribed since the player won't know they exist, so all you have to worry about is the hole in the floor (plus any other objects you've added yourself to this location). Add this to Part - Setting, Chapter - Office Interior, Section - Staging Area:

> The hole in the floor is undescribed.

Let's make a desk with a flashlight in its drawer that the player can discover by touch.

> A metal desk is a fixed in place undescribed supporter in Staging Area. A drawer
>   is an openable closed container. It is part of metal desk. The flashlight is in
>   drawer.

If you recompile now, you'll see a good example of problem messages that occur when you contradict yourself in source text. Elsewhere we said that the flashlight was on the desk in the Foreman's Office: since it can't be in two places at once, Inform lets us know this is unacceptable. You can click the orange arrow next to the old definition to jump to and highlight it in the source panel, then delete it, turning the flashlight definition into just:

> The flashlight is a portable device.

We should probably move this definition into Part - Mechanics, Chapter - Lights, too.

Let's say the player discovers the desk by bumping into it while trying to move in the nearly-black room. First, we need to set up a property that distinguishes the dim room from the lit-enough-to-see room. Back in Chapter - Office Interior, Section - Staging Area:

> Staging Area is either dim or bright. Staging Area is dim.

Now we're ready to write some rules. Let's set up the discovery of the desk:

> Instead of going to a room regionally in Office Interior from dim Staging Area:
>   say "You take a step and crack your shin against what feels like a metal desk.
>   Ouch." Instead of going nowhere from dim Staging Area: try going north.

"Going nowhere" is a special variation on the going action which matches if the player tries to move in a direction where there is no valid room connection. Here, we use the instead/try trick to redirect this to show the same message as going a valid direction.

The player shouldn't be able to examine anything in the dimness, so let's add a rule to account for that:

> Instead of examining anything in dim Staging Area: say "You can hardly see anything in here; touch is about the only way you could navigate."

We hint that touch is the way to proceed. Let's make the command TOUCH DESK fruitful:

> After touching desk in dim Staging Area: say "You feel around the edge of the desk, and find that it has a drawer."

Of course, the next step is to try to open the drawer:

> After opening drawer in dim Staging Area: say "You slide the drawer open by feel in the darkness. Something large and lumpy rolls around inside-- a flashlight?"

We'll add another instead/try rule to redirect an action players might attempt:

> Instead of opening desk: try opening drawer.

Then:

> After taking flashlight in dim Staging Area: say "Yeah, it's a flashlight all right. You grip it in sudden relief, turning it in your hands till your finger finds the switch."

Note that the above and below rules both check to make sure the player is still in the right location, since these otherwise could occur elsewhere. Finally:

> Before switching on flashlight in dim Staging Area: now metal desk is described; now hole in the floor is described; now Staging Area is bright.

> After switching on flashlight: say "Your surroundings spring into brightness around you."; try looking.

Try recompiling and testing this sequence, then wandering around and observing the effects when you turn on and off the various light sources in various combinations. Our conditional text substitutions go a long way towards painting an atmospheric environment that feels responsive to the actions of the player.

One last thing: you might discover that if you turn off the last remaining light source, and it's not portable (the headlights or the emergency lights) you can't turn it back on again. This is because Inform's default world model assumes that in darkness, anything not held is inaccessible. This is a little too restrictive for most games. One easy work-around is to download and include the extension <u>Small Kindnesses by Aaron Reed</u>, which adjusts this and many other minor implementation details to be more friendly.

Navigation Restrictions

The player shouldn't be able to visit the deep desert until later in the game, and earlier their access to various areas is restricted. Let's implement this. First, add the desert as a room under a new heading in Part - Setting called Chapter - The Open Desert.

> The Open Desert is a room. The Open Desert is west of Base of the Tower, north of Base of the Tower, east of Base of the Tower, west of Crumbling Concrete, west of Middle of Nowhere, east of Middle of Nowhere, west of Backtracking, south of Backtracking, east of Backtracking, north of Weed-strewn Rust, east of Weed-strewn Rust, and south of Weed-strewn Rust.

We'll define how movement within the desert works in the next chapter, but for now, this connects it on all sides to the rooms in the Tower Vicinity region.

When the game first begins, the area is lit only by the dying headlights of Knock's truck. Our descriptive text implies that the headlights are wavering and the truck's battery is at risk. Though we won't actually simulate this in our story world, it gives the player an early motivation to explore and find another light source, and also an excuse for why the player can't explore the desert until later.

> Instead of going to Open Desert when location is lit by headlights and flashlight is not held and flashlight is not switched on: say "Outside the wavering glow of your headlights, it's black. Pitch. Storm must have rolled in; there's no stars above, no anything but blackness around. Only the smell of the desert tells you it's still out there."

Finding the flashlight isn't enough: we also want the player to have switched on the emergency lights, to find the way back:

> Instead of going to Open Desert when flashlight is held and flashlight is switched on and emergency lights are switched off: say "You heft your flashlight nervously, licking your lips, but decide not to head out into the desert just yet. [if headlights are switched on]Your truck lights are already starting to dim, and with[otherwise]With[end if] how dark it is, you're not sure you could find your way back."

Once the player has activated the emergency lights, the desert is open—however, for realism's sake (and because our descriptions will mention it) we want to ensure the flashlight is held first.

> Instead of going to Open Desert when flashlight is not held or flashlight is not switched on: say "Without a light, on a night this freakishly dark, that's insane."

While we're at it, let's add one more rule, this one to explain why the player can't try to follow the truck's path back to the road. In Chapter - Around the Tower, Section - Backtracking, add:

> Before going south in Backtracking: say "[first time]You stare back down the
>   pickup's path uneasily. The tracks are swallowed by blackness, quickly
>   melding, blending, and vanishing into a maze of ATV tracks, coyote trails,
>   rocky outcrops, and shadows. You squint at the horizon. There's no distant
>   sweep of headlights, no sound of trucks shifting through lonely gears.
>   Nothing. Nothing at all. [only]You're way off the road, and there's no chance
>   at all of finding it again in this demon dark." instead.

The [first time][only] substitutions can surround text that should only appear the first time this say phrase is encountered. Here, we use them to generate a long introduction only seen once: subsequent attempts produce just the last sentence, "You're way off the road..."

The Roof

Let's add a puzzle that prevents access to the uppermost part of the building until one of the two talents has been acquired. This will make the player feel talents are useful in more than one situation.

Let's start by adding a description for the Roof, which we previously defined as above the Storage Room. In Chapter - Office Interior, create a new header called Section - Roof, and add:

> The description of Roof is "From the roof of the building, you can see [the huge
>   electrical tower] rising up in front of you. At your feet is the way back down."
>
> Some metal rungs are a fixed in place thing in Roof. "Some [metal rungs] once
>   led to a control room higher up the tower, but the lowest ones are well above
>   your head. You'd have to jump out into space to grab the bottom rung. You
>   could also go back down."

The rungs are a good way to restrict access to the upper levels, but how can Knock overcome this obstacle? Let's say that with courage, he can make the leap to grab the bottom rung and haul himself up; or, with strength, he can push a huge metal barrel underneath to gain access.

Our description hints the word "jump," to tie in with the built-in jumping action, but to simplify things we'll reroute jumping to going up. We also add a custom "going nowhere" message to prevent the normal outside message about wandering off into the desert from displaying:

> Instead of jumping when location is Roof: try going up. Instead of climbing or
>   entering metal rungs: try going up.
>
> Instead of going nowhere when location is Roof: say "It's a drop off on all sides."

Let's also make the room above, so we have somewhere to go up to, and the barrel.

> The Control Center is up from Roof. Control Center is regionally in Office
> Interior. A huge metal barrel is a fixed in place supporter in Roof.

Now, the rule:

> Instead of going up in Roof when player does not hold courage and huge metal
> barrel is not placed correctly: say "The metal rungs have rusted away and
> crumbled; the lowest are well above your head. You don't have the courage to
> make the jump."

Once courage is found, we don't want to interfere with the ability to go up: but we do want to display a unique message describing the extraordinary way this movement occurs.

> Report going up from Roof when player holds courage: say "[first time]You
> gather your courage and leap off the edge of the roof. Your hands grasp the
> metal of the bottommost rung, scraping and sliding, but holding. [only]You
> pull yourself up the rungs into the control center. Hey, it wasn't that hard
> after all."

(Easy to say once you've acquired some supernatural courage.) We don't use an "after" rule here because that would stop the action; instead, after showing our unique message we'd like to continue on to what normally happens next: displaying the name and description of the newly arrived-in room.

The barrel can be in one of two places: under the rungs or not close enough. This seems like a good candidate for an adjective.

> The huge metal barrel can be placed correctly. It is not placed correctly.

Note that because we have other barrels in our game, we'd better use the full name of the item to ensure Inform understands which one we mean. For similar reasons, we've made the path up a set of rungs to avoid using the word "ladder" again.

Now we can describe the barrel, indicating its position in the process:

> The description of the huge metal barrel is "[A huge metal barrel] stands upright
> and intact nearby, [if placed correctly]directly underneath the bottom rungs
> [otherwise]large enough you could climb up on top of it[end if]."

We don't want to actually let the player climb on the barrel, to simplify:

> Instead of entering or climbing the placed correctly huge metal barrel: try going
> up. Instead of entering or climbing the huge metal barrel: say "Yeah, you
> could get on top of it, but while it's over here you couldn't reach a whole lot."

Normally, Knock can't move it:

> Instead of pushing the not placed correctly huge metal barrel when player does not hold strength: say "You push against the side, but you're not strong enough to move the barrel."

...but if he's gained the talent of strength, he can:

> Instead of pushing the not placed correctly huge metal barrel when player holds strength: now huge metal barrel is placed correctly; say "Heaving, you push against the barrel, and with a horrible grating noise, it slides across the roof till it rests underneath the metal rungs."

And now we can report on successful movement:

> Report going up from Roof when huge metal barrel is placed correctly: say "You climb up on the barrel, reach, grab the bottom rungs, and pull yourself up."

One other fiddly bit: we don't want the player to be able to push the barrel a second time.

> Instead of pushing the placed correctly huge metal barrel: say "Push it any more and it'll fall off the roof. Keep it here and you can get to the rungs."

We're already starting to build up a story world with goals, complicated states, and customized behavior. In the next chapter, we'll talk about better understanding the intentions of the player, and creating your own actions and verbs.

Exercise Answers

Exercise 5.1

Enhance Inform's knowledge about wearing. An easy way to simulate this is to just make both shoes and people have large and small sizes. You could create the appropriate kinds, then define new properties:

```
A shoe is a kind of thing. A sock is a kind of thing. Shoes and socks are
    always wearable. A shoe is either men's or women's. A shoe is either
    large or small.
A person is either large-footed or small-footed.
```

Once these are created, we can make check rules that take these new properties into account:

```
Check wearing a small shoe when player is large-footed: ...

Check wearing a women's shoe when player is male: ...

Check taking off a sock when a shoe is worn: ...
```

Exercise 5.2

Create a few more instead rules. These can be whatever you want, but here are a few examples:

```
Instead of attacking a window: say "Looks like a lot of other people beat you
    to it."

Instead of entering half-collapsed desk: say "It's already on its last legs."

Instead of singing: say "You try to sing some classic rock, but it just makes
    the silence around you even creepier."
```

Exercise 5.3

Create an expired first aid kit. The easiest way to simulate something not visible until a prerequisite action occurs (in this case, taking the blanket) is just to move it on stage at the time that action takes place.

> A first aid kit is an openable closed portable container. Some moth-eaten bandages are in first aid kit.
>
> After taking emergency blanket when first aid kit is off-stage: now first aid kit is in cage; say "As you pick up the blanket, you find an old first aid kit underneath it."
>
> Instead of inserting anything into first aid kit: say "It's really not the best place to store stuff."
>
> Instead of wearing bandages: say "You don't need them."

Exercise 5.4

Identify actions resulting from player commands.

The ACTIONS verb shows us that:

> PUT DOWN CIGARETTES becomes "dropping the pack of cigarettes"
>
> GO TO TRUCK is not an understood action
>
> GET OUT becomes "exiting"
>
> I becomes "taking inventory"

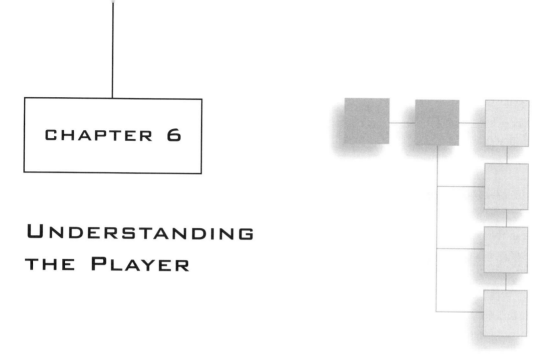

CHAPTER 6

UNDERSTANDING THE PLAYER

An IF story can't just speak clearly; it should listen clearly, too. We've focused till now on the structure of a story world and the way it's described to the reader, but we'll now turn to the words the story gets back—the commands typed by the player. Though the parser and the Standard Rules do the heavy lifting to turn a player's words into actions our story can understand, we can help by making our own language more precise, by teaching a story more ways of referring to its actions and objects, and by helping players whose words are unclear or ambiguous to be better understood.

Players may also want to perform actions that aren't normally recognized by the story world, and authors may wish the built-in actions behaved differently. We'll talk about how to modify actions as well as create new ones from scratch.

 As *Sand-dancer* continues to grow, you may eventually get a message that Inform "ran out of space" when you try to compile. This is because your version of Inform is defaulting to the very small z-code format for story files. To fix this, go to the Settings panel, and select either "Z-Code version 8" or the much roomier "Glulx," then recompile.

Understanding Synonyms

For our first trick, we'll teach Inform to recognize a wider range of words than it knows by default.

Synonyms for Nouns

When we create a new thing, Inform automatically understands all the words in its name as referents. Consider our definition for *Sand-dancer*'s rusty tin can, for instance:

> A rusty tin can is in Base of the Tower.

The player can use the words *rusty*, *tin*, or *can* to refer to this thing and be clearly understood.

Less obviously, the player can place these words in any order or combination. You've probably noticed that *can* is an acceptable abbreviation, but *rusty* alone is equally valid, along with *rusty can, can rusty*, or even *can tin rusty rusty can tin* for those feeling particularly Dada. The parser could care less: it knows which object you mean.

But often you'd like additional words not in a thing's name to be understood, too. Extra adjectives in a room or object description that refer to a certain thing ought to be fair game for the player to type. Take *Sand-dancer*'s flashlight: though it's just defined as "a flashlight," in relevant descriptions the words *beam, cold, blue, metal, hefty, large, lumpy, something,* and *switch* are all used. While the simplest way of ensuring these all get understood is to lengthen the item's actual name, in this case that would be fairly ridiculous:

> The cold blue hefty large lumpy metal flashlight is a portable device.

Not particularly elegant, and since the full name is used every time the item is mentioned, not particularly concise, either. It's also an incomplete solution. What about words like *beam* or *switch,* which couldn't be shoehorned into the item's name, or alternate nouns such as *light* or *something*?

To tell Inform about a thing's synonyms, we use *understand rules*. These include single words or multiple words separated by slashes to add to the parser's vocabulary. Let's add our first understand rule just after the flashlight's definition in Part - Setting, Chapter - Office Interior, Section - Staging Area:

> Understand "beam/cold/blue/metal/hefty/large/lumpy/something/switch" as the
>   flashlight.

We can even understand whole phrases of multiple words, although each run of these should appear as its own quoted text:

> Understand "flash light" or "light" as the flashlight.

Now the player can say *light* or *flash light* to refer to the flashlight, but not *flash* by itself. This is sometimes what you want, and sometimes not; generally speaking, the more inclusive single words with slashes approach is the better way to go. You can have as many understand rules as you like for a given item, and their effects are cumulative. As seen above, the word "or" (or "and") combines multiple understand rules into a single sentence.

Exercise 6.1

Look through your *Sand-dancer* code for places where synonyms are needed. Go ahead and create understand rules to implement them.

Printed Name

Sometimes instead of changing the words understood, you'd like to change the words displayed, without modifying the name of a thing in your source text. This can be useful for things with very long names, very short names, or names containing words likely to confuse Inform (like *and*, *is*, *with*, or *the*). We can modify a thing's display name by giving it a **printed name** text property.

Let's say we wanted to create something with the word *and* in its title, like the book *The Old Man and the Sea*. Normally, Inform would assume you were creating two objects, so:

    The Old Man and the Sea is in Study.

...would actually create two things, one called *the old man* and one called *the sea*. One way to get around this involves the optional *called* syntax for defining objects:

    In the Study is a thing called The Old Man and the Sea.

...but this might create problems elsewhere in your source text, especially if your story contained any seas or old men. Another solution: give the book a simpler name and modify its printed name.

    The Hemingway book is a proper-named thing in Study with printed name
        "The Old Man and the Sea".

(Two quick points: the **proper-named** property simply omits using an article in descriptions, and note that we keep the period outside the quoted text in this case because we don't want it displayed as part of the object's name.)

Now the player will be understood if they say *book* or *Hemingway*. But, important: note that the parser won't recognize *the old man and the sea*, since printed name affects only a thing's appearance, not its vocabulary. You'll most often want to combine its use with an understand rule:

    Understand "old/man/sea" or "old man and the sea" as the Hemingway book.

Another example comes from Infocom's best-selling game without Zork in the title, Douglas Adams's adaptation of his novel *The Hitchhiker's Guide to the Galaxy*. The player character owns an object with a curious (and later on, immensely useful) ability to keep turning up no matter how many times you try to throw it away. Were *Guide* written in Inform 7, this item's declaration might look like this:

> The aunt thing is in bathrobe. The printed name is "thing your aunt gave you which you don't know what it is". Understand "thing your aunt gave you" or "thing my aunt gave me" as the aunt thing.

The large number of vague words in the printed name might conflict with other items, so we leave all that within the quoted text unprocessed by Inform. The understand rules allow for the most likely identifiers the player might type, taking into account the possible reversal of pronouns.

Synonyms for Verbs

You can also create new synonyms for existing verbs with a similar kind of understand rule, adding **the command** to make the distinction:

> Understand the command "snatch" as "get".

This simply means that the first quoted verb will be understood in player commands to mean precisely the same thing as the second. Verb synonyms always apply to a particular verb, rather than a more abstract action (like the taking action).

Verb synonyms are most useful when the phrasing or context of some descriptive text suggests a nontraditional verb. If your character was broke and desperate and something in your prose mentioned "a very snatchable purse," the player may well expect SNATCH PURSE to be understood. Thanks to the understand rule above, it would.

Understanding Less

Rarely, your problem is that you want your story to understand not more words, but fewer.

Understand as Something New

Sometimes there's a verb you want to get rid of. Maybe you have other plans for it, maybe it's not at all relevant to your story world, or you may just have taken a disliking to it. For instance, the verb "shut," as defined by the Standard Rules, refers to the closing action. If the player types SHUT UP, the story will assume he wants to try the action "closing (the direction) up," which produces the eyebrow-raising response "You must name something more substantial." If confrontational conversations were part of your story, a first step to correcting this would be disassociating the verb "shut" from the closing action. To do so, you'd write a normal understand the command rule, but instead of a second verb word, use the phrase **something new**:

> Understand the command "shut" as something new.

Despite the implication, you don't actually need to create anything new: your story simply stops understanding "shut" as a verb, and the response to SHUT UP is now "That's not a verb I recognise," which is at least more accurate if not (yet) more useful. Momentarily we'll see how to make new actions (shushing, perhaps) and tie commands (like SHUT UP) to them.

If you want to get rid of an action entirely, look it up in the Actions tab of the Index panel to find all its associated verbs, then understand each one as something new. This ensures the player can never request that action, effectively eliminating it from your story.

Inform, the brainchild of an Englishman, defaults to British spellings for words like "recognise" where they appear in built-in messages. There's a use option that will change these to American spellings, for those on (or writing stories set on) the other side of the pond. Sand-dancer is set in New Mexico, so let's add this line near the top of our source text:

> Use American dialect.

Keep in mind that this only affects built-in messages: any text you write yourself within quoted strings will stay as you wrote it, so feel free to use any flavour of English you like. (And see Chapter 10 for some tips on using Inform to write games in languages other than English.)

One rarely used action in the Standard Rules is rubbing, which does nothing by default except show the message "You achieve nothing by this." Since we aren't planning on adding any responses to rubbing things in *Sand-dancer*, we can get rid of this action entirely by overriding all the verbs that refer to it. Checking the Actions tab of the Index panel, we see that "rub" is the only affiliated verb, so the following line should do the trick (in Part - Mechanics, under a new header called Chapter - Customizations):

> Understand the command "rub" as something new.

Privately-Named

On rare occasions, you'll create a thing with a name you don't want the player to be able to use. You can give something the **privately-named** property to keep the parser from recognizing any of the words in its name. Later in the chapter, we'll create a puzzle involving some cans of food and a can opener. Let's make the opener now. Go ahead and create a new heading Section - Control Center in Chapter - Office Interior, and add:

> A can opener is in Control Center.

If the player types a command like EXAMINE CAN near both the food and the opener, however, he'll get an annoying disambiguation message ("Which do you mean, the cans of food or the can opener?"). If we think about it, we don't ever want the word CAN by itself to refer to the can opener... but by default Inform understands every word in a thing's name as referring to it. How do we get around this?

The solution is to make the can opener privately-named and define more explicitly how the player can refer to it. Add this:

> The can opener is privately-named. Understand "opener" or "can opener" as the can opener.

This effect could be undone by later changing the thing to **publically-named**.

CAUTION The privately-named property is only useful in specific and unusual circumstances. Deploy it only when absolutely necessary, since it can easily frustrate or confuse your players.

To better understand what's going on with all the new material we've introduced in this section, it's helpful to explicitly describe what happens when you create a thing. The words in the thing's name serve three purposes, as seen in Figure 6.1: how it's referred to in your source text, how it's described, and what words the player can use to refer to it. The privately-named property, understand rules, and printed name text property all let you change Inform's default assumption that all three are the same.

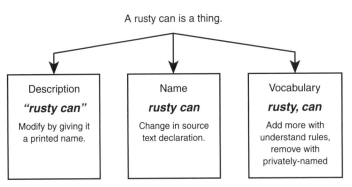

Figure 6.1
The three results of creating a thing.

Creating New Actions

The Standard Rules define 80 actions traditionally useful for interactive fiction, a set which has evolved over the past few decades into a fairly robust and standardized group. 143 verbs are understood as referring to these actions. But the Oxford English Dictionary contains some 25,000 verbs. While you may never need to create an Inform action for the verb *to quinkle* (to go out, like a light), a story of medium to high complexity often finds a need for at least one or two actions not encompassed by the basic set.

Creating an action requires both telling Inform the number and sorts of nouns it can be used with, and what command forms the player can use to invoke it. Once the action has been created, you'll define its behavior using the action default rulebooks we learned about in the last chapter (check, carry out, and report).

Creation

We've given our main character in *Sand-dancer* a pack of cigarettes and a lighter, so it makes sense that smoking should be an action. In our concept document, we wrote that smoking would produce hints on what to do next, but at increasing risk to Knock's resolve to quit.

> You may not feel that encouraging teen smoking is an appropriate thematic element for *Sand-dancer*, even if there are consequences. As with every aspect of *Sand-dancer*'s design, feel free to omit this mechanic, or come up with your own alternative. Maybe in your story world Knock clears his head by pacing, knuckle-biting, or singing. Maybe hints and brooding could be merged. It's up to you.

The first step is to create the new action: smoking. Add our action declaration under a new header called Chapter - Smoking, in Part - Mechanics:

    Smoking is an action applying to one thing.

Defining New Actions

Smoking is an action {out of world} applying to one {visible} {carried} thing {and one direction} {and requiring light}.

The bracketed phrases are optional.

out of world declares that this action affects the game, not the story itself: save, quit, restart, and so on are all defined as out of world actions.

visible in this context is a subtle distinction meaning an object only needs to be seen for this action to be performed on it, not **touchable** too (which is the default). **carried** means the player must be holding the item.

The {and one direction} demonstrates how you would create an action applying to two different kinds of things; in this case, perhaps to define a new command like HURL GRENADE TO THE NORTH.

and requiring light means the action can't be performed in the dark, which would be appropriate were we to create a quinkling action after all.

We declare the action in gerund form, add "is an action applying to," and then set the number of nouns the action takes: either "nothing," "one thing," or "two things." Some optional more advanced forms can be seen in the definition sidebar.

The smoking action now exists, and if we recompile, it appears in appropriate places on the Actions tab of the Index panel. However, we also need to create one or more commands to allow the player to trigger this action. Add this next:

```
Understand "smoke [something]" as smoking.
```

The number of bracketed clauses within the quoted text describing the action's grammar must match the number of associated nouns we declared in the action's definition.

The bracketed clauses can also refer to kinds of values, such as [text] or [direction], or more complex but rarely needed qualifiers (see the "Advanced Actions" chapter of the built-in documentation for details). In simple cases like our smoking action, [something] assumes a currently visible thing. You can instead say [any thing] to mean an object anywhere in the story world, regardless of whether it's currently visible to or anywhere near the player.

We can define as many understand rules as we like for an action to create different verbs or different syntaxes for invoking them, as long as they contain the correct number and kinds of bracketed clauses. We might create a second rule like the following:

```
Understand "light up [something]" as smoking.
```

Definition

Recompile *Sand-dancer* and try to smoke various things (see Figure 6.2). The parser will correct you if you try to use the wrong number of nouns, or a command structure unlike any of our understand rules for this action. But if the command is syntactically valid, all that happens is that a new prompt is immediately printed. What's going on?

Since we haven't defined any rules for when smoking is allowed to happen or what takes place when it does, the story takes our definition quite literally: we are always allowed to smoke something, and nothing at all happens when we do. To make our new action useful, we must create action default rules to tell Inform how it works.

Let's start with the check rules. First of all, the player should really only be able to smoke cigarettes:

```
Check smoking when noun is not pack of cigarettes: instead say "Sounds like
    something your high school buddies would try."
```

Also, the player can't smoke without a lighter:

```
Check smoking when lighter is not held: instead say "You pat your pockets, but
    can't seem to find your lighter."
```

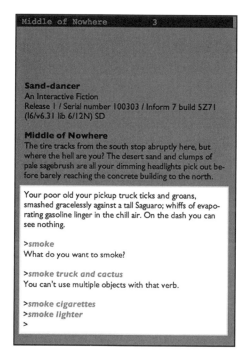

Figure 6.2
An example of a newly created but unimplemented action.

The player ought to be holding both of these props, but we can use a before rule to assist him in this:

> Before smoking when lighter is not held and lighter is visible: say "(first taking the lighter)"; try silently taking lighter. Before smoking when pack of cigarettes is not held and pack of cigarettes is visible: say "(first taking the cigarettes)"; try silently taking pack of cigarettes.

The word **silently** added to a try phrase means the report rules for that action will be skipped, which is useful for actions which probably seem automatic and not noteworthy to the player character.

What happens when we smoke? For the moment, nothing: we'll later keep track of how many cigarettes have been smoked, but for the moment, nothing changes in the story world as a result of smoking, so we don't need a carry out rule.

We want to report to the player some information about the current state of the story, though. To use this, we'll create a series of report rules, and make sure each one runs only in the appropriate circumstances, building a custom paragraph.

Let's add the first rule to begin this process. We saw in the last chapter that rules are ordered the same way they appear in the source text, except that more specific rules trump more general ones. We can also set a rule to be **first** or **last** in its category by adding one of these words to the start of its definition:

> First report smoking: say "You pull out a cigarette and flick it into life. Thoughts tumble through your head."

We can now create a series of "report smoking" rules that will run after this "first report smoking" rule in the order we define them. Since we don't want to affect the ordering by making some seem more specific than others, we'll use "if" within the rule to only print text if the appropriate condition is met.

> Report smoking: say "Well, you're still stuck here. [run paragraph on]".

The text substitution in this line requires some explanation. Though Inform normally handles line breaks automatically for us, on occasion it needs a little hand-holding. Two text substitutions are available to add new line breaks, **line break** and **paragraph break**, and another can suppress automatically generated breaks, **run paragraph on**.

Normally, Inform places a line break after strings ending with terminal punctuation (periods, but also question and exclamation marks), and before running a new action rule. That's not quite what we want here: we'd like to have multiple report rules generate a single paragraph. So we say "run paragraph on" at the end of each one to indicate this. The extra space before the text substitution is simply to make sure each sentence has a space before the next one.

Let's create our last rule, to round out the framework.

> Last report smoking: say "[paragraph break]And you still haven't quit smoking. You crush the butt under your heel and wonder what to do next."

That [paragraph break] is needed to cancel out the [run paragraph on] at the end of the report rule that most recently ran; in other words, to restore the normal formatting.

Now, we can add any number of report smoking rules we like to make a dynamic response to smoking that will appear in a single paragraph. Remember, by default these will appear in the order specified in your source text. Let's add a rule to report on the status of the lights.

> Report smoking: say "[if location is lit brightly]You've finally lit the place up a little[otherwise if location is lit by headlights]It's dark outside the beam of your headlights[otherwise if location is lit by flashlight]It's pitch black outside the beam of your flashlight[otherwise]It's darker than you can remember it ever being[end if]. [run paragraph on]".

Next, we'd like to talk about the player's progress towards meeting a goal. To do that, let's start by reminding the players of the talents they have:

> Report smoking: if the player holds a talent, say "Some weird shit went down in the desert, but you do feel like you have more [list of talents held by player]. [run paragraph on]".

To talk about the plans more specifically, we need a few more definitions. One useful built-in adjective is **handled**, which indicates that an object has been held by the player at some point in the story, even if they aren't holding it any longer. Knowing this, we can write a definition to tell us whether the player has made progress toward one of our two plans. Skip back up to Chapter - Plans, and add this under the paragraph about the requirement relation:

> Definition: a plan is in progress if a handled thing is required by it. Definition: a plan is complete if two handled things are required by it.

Now, if the player has ever held one of the objects that a plan requires, that plan will be considered in progress.

While you're still in Chapter - Plans, let's add some printed names for the plans so they'll display more appropriately for the player:

> The printed name of fixing the truck is "fixing your truck and getting out of here". The printed name of staying the night is "spending the night here".

Now we can create some more report rules. Back down in Chapter - Smoking:

> Report smoking: if there is an in progress plan, say "You've found [the list of handled things which are required by a plan], but you still need something else if you're going to finish [a random in progress plan]. [run paragraph on]".

If the player has only made progress towards one goal, the above message is most appropriate. If, however, they've been inconsistent in their choice of talents so far, this might prejudice the player towards whichever of the two plans is selected at random. Let's modify the above rule to account for this possibility:

> Report smoking: if there is an in progress plan, say "You've found [the list of handled things which are required by a plan], but [if the number of in progress plans is 2]you can't see how they're going to be helpful together[otherwise]you still need something else if you plan on [a random in progress plan][end if]. [run paragraph on]".

In the next chapter, we'll learn some techniques that will let us add context-specific hints to smoking. All we'll need to do is write more report smoking rules.

CAUTION Inform's internal mechanism for generating appropriate line breaks and spacing is more complex than it might appear. It's often difficult to adjust its behavior without understanding why things are going wrong to begin with. Use the related text substitutions sparingly and only when necessary, rather than throwing them about willy-nilly to micromanage lines and paragraphs.

Remember, too, that IF stories can be played on a wide variety of devices with drastically varying font sizes and screen widths (or even devices lacking these attributes entirely, such as the BrailleNote e-reader for the blind that came preinstalled with my game *Gourmet*). Using line breaks to align text or create other visual effects may work on your monitor, but may just make things worse for someone else.

Creating actions is easy, but as the remake of *The Day the Earth Stood Still* demonstrated, just because you can doesn't mean you should. Every action you create is currency your players will try to spend on any and every object in your story. Thinking through and implementing all the ways a new action might be used requires significant effort, but your alternative is either to write a series of instead rules explaining why the action doesn't work in seemingly sensible contexts, or explaining away all other attempts to use it with a glib refusal (like we do when trying to smoke anything other than the cigarettes; this may not always be as appropriate a technique). In a few pages we'll see how to understand verbs that don't result in actions, which can often be a good intermediary step.

Really think through whether an action is necessary before creating it, and you'll save yourself headaches down the line.

Modifying Existing Actions

We've seen how to create our own actions, and how to add new synonyms for existing actions, but what if you want to go further and actually change how a built-in action works? To do so, you'll need some more tools.

Adding New Action Default Rules

While you can always add your own action exception rules, it's also equally valid to add new action default rules for existing actions, if something about your story world fundamentally changes the workings of an existing action.

Let's say we had a story involving lots of objects that could be hot or cold. We could do something like this:

```
A thing can be hot or cold. Report taking a hot thing: say "Ouch! [The noun]
burns your fingers."
```

As we saw with smoking, report rules are cumulative rather than mutually exclusive, so this will also show the default message "Taken." We could add "instead" if we did want it to stop the action and not proceed to the next rule.

 The Standard Rules are included after your source text, so any new action default rules you write will be ordered before them.

New carry out rules let actions make additional changes to the model world. Our thermally minded story might also have:

> A person can be either comfortable or burned. Carry out taking a hot thing: now the player is burned.

New check rules can be used to create additional requirements for performing a default action. We might prefer to disallow taking hot things entirely:

> Check taking a hot thing: instead say "It's way too hot to pick up."

Replacing and Removing Rules

On occasion, your story world changes enough that one of the built-in action default rules needs to be modified.

Sand-dancer, despite its fantastical details, takes place more or less in a world whose rules act as expected, so we rarely need to meddle with the default actions. But imagine a story where odor was important, perhaps one where the player character was (or became!) an animal. Ordinarily, the built-in smelling action doesn't do anything: it merely responds with the message "You smell nothing unexpected." If we consult this action in the Actions tab of the Index panel, we see this message comes from the action's sole rule, the "block smelling rule."

Recall that rules can optionally be given a name. The block smelling rule might look something like this:

> Check smelling (this is the block smelling rule): instead say "You smell nothing unexpected."

Every action default rule in the Standard Rules has a name. An advantage of named rules is that you can replace them with different rules in your source text:

> A thing can be smelly or odorless. Check smelling something odorless (this is the sophisticated block smelling rule): instead say "You smell nothing unexpected."

> The sophisticated block smelling rule is listed instead of the block smelling rule in the check smelling rules.

Now, attempts to smell something that has odor will survive to reach any other check, carry out, or report rules you cared to write to enhance the smelling action.

You can also remove a rule entirely:

> The block smelling rule is not listed in the check smelling rules.

Now any attempt to smell would survive to be carried out and reported.

Remember, you can use the Actions tab of the Index panel to review all of the built-in action default rulebooks for Inform's standard actions.

 Messing with the built-in action default rules can produce unexpected side effects and should only be done with care, and after examining the action's implementation in-depth. More infor-
CAUTION mation can be found in the built-in documentation, under the "Listing rules explicitly" section.

Other Ways of Understanding

Briefly, here are a couple of other tricks to help Inform understand a wider range of player commands.

Understand as a Mistake

Occasionally you want your story to respond to something unusual the player typed, without the work involved in creating a whole action for it. One way of doing this is called **understanding as a mistake**.

Since our story starts with a pickup truck, a reasonable player command is DRIVE. Since this impulse will never succeed within the context of *Sand-dancer*, there's not much point in making an action for it. Instead, let's catch all attempts to input a driving-related command and respond appropriately. Add this in Part - Setting, Chapter - Around the Tower, Section - Middle of Nowhere:

> Understand "drive" or "drive [pickup]" or "start [pickup]" or "turn on [pickup]" or "turn key" or "shift" or "steer" or "brake" as a mistake ("Your truck's not going anywhere in this condition.").

The player sees the quoted string within the final parentheses after typing a command matching the syntax given earlier. This is great shorthand to broaden your story's vocabulary for actions that don't produce any effects. You can even add "when" clauses by putting them after the parenthetical, so for instance we might want to add *when pickup is visible* after the closing parenthesis above.

Anything that requires more complexity should probably be created as a real action.

Understanding Things by Their Properties

With a little help, Inform can understand an adjective or property of a thing as another word the player might use to refer to it. Add the following to *Sand-dancer* (in Part - Mechanics, Chapter - Memories):

> Understand "memory/memories" as a memory.

If the player typed BROOD ABOUT MEMORY, and there was only one memory available, the command would be understood the same as something like BROOD ABOUT LAST DAY OF HIGH SCHOOL. In *Sand-dancer*, this is often useful since we might use the word "memory" without any specific thing having that word in its vocabulary.

We can also understand something by a property. Add the following in Part - Setting, Chapter - Office Interior:

> Understand the open property as describing a window.

Now the player can type EXAMINE OPEN WINDOW, and the game will understand that to mean any thing in the window kind that has the property open, without you needing to put any of these words (or the property's opposite, closed) into understand rules for these items.

Exercise 6.2

How could you help Inform understand a command like TOUCH DEAD PLANT when standing by something matching this description?

Disambiguation

What happens if more than one object is available that might match a typed command? If, say, the player types EXAMINE MEMORY when three memories have been discovered? The result would be a question like "Which do you mean, grandma's stories, meeting Ocean, or the last day of high school?"

This is a **disambiguation question**. These appear in response to commands that might be interpreted as more than one action: say, EXAMINE GREEN in a room containing both a green card and Professor Green. In response, the player can type an additional clarifying word, like CARD, or a new command entirely.

Dangers of Disambiguation

What happens if there isn't a way for the player to give the parser the information it needs? Imagine the player typed EAT ORANGE in a room with both an orange and an orange popsicle. The parser would ask the disambiguation question "Which do you mean, the orange or the orange popsicle?" But, somewhat counter-intuitively, there's nothing the player can type that will clarify: the parser knows the player has already used "orange" to refer to the mystery object, so saying ORANGE again doesn't help. The player can type POPSICLE to refer to the other object, but they'll never be able to answer the disambiguation question in a way that selects the orange.

There are at least two ways around this dreaded disambiguation loop. You can take great care to never give one thing a name that's entirely a subset of another. If you've created a "wooden chair" in one part of your game, don't create a simple "chair" elsewhere, unless you're sure the two objects will never occupy the same space (and there's no special command that might put them both into the same disambiguation question).

If remembering all this seems too stressful, another option is to use my extension Numbered Disambiguation Choices by Aaron Reed. This numbers each option in a disambiguation question and lets the player answer by typing a number, so the above would be replaced with: "Which do you mean, the 1) orange or the 2) orange popsicle?" (The numbers also make disambiguation questions quicker to answer, and more intuitive for players unfamiliar with IF conventions who sometimes think they need to retype the whole command.)

PROGRAMMER'S NOTE

Disambiguation for the player often becomes necessary because of ambiguity on the part of the author. In programming terms, Inform 7 has almost no concept of namespaces: every thing can be referenced and modified from any part of the code, including across extensions. This has been known to cause hair to rise on the back of some programmers' necks, but in practice it rarely causes problems unless your story becomes very large or very full of similarly named objects.

Does the Player Mean

As we've seen, Inform's model of how words map to things is very simple: any combination of the words in a thing's name can be used to refer to it. The parser does not weigh nouns and adjectives differently, and in fact cannot distinguish between them. This simplifies creating objects, but can cause the parser to seem less intelligent when one word much more obviously refers to something than another.

>EXAMINE NOTE

Which do you mean, the suspicious note or the dessert wine with a note of almond?

Even more obvious is when human authors and players know something about the relationship between actions and objects that Inform does not understand:

>EAT ORANGE

Which do you mean, the delicious orange or the orange wallpaper?

In cases like these, it can be helpful to teach the parser that one action is more likely than another. We do this by writing a **does the player mean** rule. To fix the second problem above, we could say:

Does the player mean eating the delicious orange: it is likely.

Or, more generally:

Does the player mean eating something edible: it is likely.

As in other situations where actions are mentioned, we can use lists or qualifiers, too:

Does the player mean doing something with the scrap of orange note paper:
    it is unlikely.

By default, every valid action is rated "it is possible." There are five potential options:

> it is very likely
>
> it is likely
>
> it is possible
>
> it is unlikely
>
> it is very unlikely

If any action in the list of those being considered places higher on this list than the others, that action is assumed to be the one the player meant. The parser notes its clarification before continuing:

>EAT ORANGE

(the delicious orange)

Juicy and delicious.

Avoiding Ambiguity

Avoid disambiguation questions whenever possible. They break the sense of immersion in a story, and usually make it seem less intelligent, since the player always believes his command's intention is obvious. They can break your game entirely if you accidentally create a thing without enough adjectives to distinguish it from another thing. They can sometimes reveal hidden objects that you didn't want the player to know about yet, or objects whose names look inappropriate in the form of a list.

Though the parser's built-in disambiguation system normally does an admirable job at resolving unclear commands, and "does the player mean" rules can clarify obvious cases, a better solution is to construct your story so as to minimize ambiguity in the first place. Try distinguishing items from each other via different nouns, not just different adjectives: instead of a *blue book* and a *green book*, try a *used paperback* and a *bestselling novel*. Compound words are also helpful: a *chess piece* and a *chessboard* don't require disambiguation if you remember to always describe them consistently. For portable objects, think about whether they really need to be portable or can do their job in a particular room or region, thus reducing possible name conflicts with objects elsewhere in your game. If so, write rules to keep them in their designated areas.

Helping the Player Participate

Though the rules and properties we've learned in this chapter help your story better understand its players, your words do even more to help them. Careful use of language tells players how to proceed, and remaining conscious of the cues your prose suggests can immensely improve the quality of the dialogue between your story and its audience.

Using Words Deliberately

Remember getting BENT? Bracketing every notable thing enforces parity between the words your players read and the ones your story understands, and keeps the contract implied by that blinking command prompt. The promise of interactive fiction is communication in the same language between player and story, and that promise is broken if the story uses a word but claims not to understand when the player tries to use it back. Keeping the promise is what's really behind the best descriptive writing in IF.

Besides remembering to get BENT, here are some other tips to help keep the promise.

Describe Things Consistently

If you create a *chessboard* and then call it a *chess board* in its description, a *chess set* in the room description and a *game of chess* in an instead rule, you're being sloppy. And if you're already being sloppy, you're likely to forget to add an understand rule to cover all these variations. Players won't be sure which term to use, disambiguation questions are more likely, and internal name overlaps in your source text become a risk.

Don't do this. Instead, pick a single term and use it consistently everywhere you refer to that object. Stick with *chessboard* everywhere, and the consistency and repetition encourages the players to also use that word, making less frustration and less effort on both sides.

Clearly Advertise New or Unusual Verbs

Creating a new verb also creates a problem: how will the players know what it is and how to use it? Sometimes, such as for the smoking action we made earlier, the verb is implied by a prop or situation. You can and should use the verb word in your descriptive text mentioning the item, and especially in action rules related to incorrect usage or interaction. If the verb is particularly unusual, you can capitalize it in descriptive text: this is an IF convention which means "look, a new verb!" to experienced players and is clear enough that even most IF newbies get the hint.

For instance, say we had a game that involved cooking, and we created a new action, stirring, to go with it. The description for the first dish encountered ought to be something like "Smells delicious, but you should stir it first." For even more emphasis, this could be "Smells delicious, but you should STIR it first." Note how we carefully point the players in the right direction, like positioning someone wearing a blindfold: the mention of the new verb is phrased as a suggestion of action, and we use the verb in the same form the players will use it (not conjugated like *stirring* or *stirred*).

Contrariwise, avoid the unnecessary use of verbs the player can't use. A piece of text like "The water looks so refreshing you could dive right in" suggests a verb like DIVE, and players will be nonplussed if they try this and aren't understood. A less misleading alternative might be "The water seems cool and refreshing." Alternatively, you could understand DIVE as a mistake and nudge the players towards a more appropriate command.

Be generous with syntaxes for new verbs. The Standard Rules often understand a variety of not just verb synonyms but also alternate grammars, such as PICK [noun] UP as well as PICK UP [noun]. Especially for unfamiliar commands, it's a good idea to add understand rules for all likely ways players might try to produce the action.

Use Standard Actions Whenever Possible

New IF authors should familiarize themselves with the built-in actions. Experienced players are used to thinking of ways to solve problems using them. To IF veterans, a stuck rock suggests PULL ROCK before something like UNEARTH ROCK or DIG ROCK, since pulling is a familiar, standard action. Creating lots of new actions often only muddies comprehension, so this should be done thoughtfully and not on a whim.

Remember, too, to use the standard actions consistently. Examining is the most common way to get more detail about something, but other standard actions include looking under and searching. Different authors have different ideas about how to make use of these verbs: some hide lots of details in responses to search commands while never using look under, while others might use neither and include all available information in the response to examine. The only poor choice is inconsistency. If examining things is sufficient to turn up required information early in your game, and then you hide something behind a looking under rule later on, you've just created the hardest puzzle in your game, and not a very fun one.

Create Synonyms Deliberately

While you don't need to bust out a thesaurus and make an understand rule for every object in your game, adding synonyms deliberately can greatly enhance the experience of play. Certainly add any adjectives or alternative nouns used to describe the thing in any story text. For compound or hyphenated words like *baseball*, it's nice to add the component words *base* and *ball*. Hyphenated words like *Sand-dancer* deserve both the individual words and an unhyphenated variant: *sand*, *dancer*, and *sanddancer*. Words like *television* should have their common nicknames understood: *TV, set*. If a word is commonly misspelled (such as *cemetery*) adding in a few variations will ease player frustrations (*cementary, cemetary*). Another useful addition is class-based synonyms for common nouns (for *pickup*, perhaps *car* and *truck*).

It might seem like the more synonyms the better. Why not import a thesaurus and understand thousands of words? This sounds appealing, but remember that more synonyms means more disambiguation questions and more opportunities for confusion. Having a command misinterpreted frustrates players more than having a command rejected. If the player tried to SNEAK A COOKIE and got the response "That's not something you can enter," they are much more likely to be annoyed by than sympathetic to the explanation that "sneak" had been defined as a synonym for GO rather than TAKE.

In addition, a huge vocabulary might lead players to think the story can understand anything at all, and then you're left trying to write rules to deal with HOW FAST CAN I GO NORTH WITHOUT BREAKING A SWEAT? or WINK AT THE BARTENDER BUT WAIT UNTIL JESSICA'S NOT LOOKING. Those who have attempted this sort of natural language processing tend to come out of the process several years older and significantly more depressed.

For now, Inform has merely a parser, not a linguist. Rather than trying to hide this, spend your efforts on nudging players towards the vocabulary and syntax your story does understand.

Introduce New Nouns Sparingly

Remember that every noun in your descriptive text is a promise. BENT helps with this, but creating a huge number of useless scenery objects can frustrate both authors (who have to make them) and players (who can't find the useful things hiding in the mountains of set decoration).

Bracket every notable thing, but also make sure it's clear what's notable and what isn't. Structure your prose so objects are mentioned deliberately, not by chance. Streamline descriptions to remove superfluous nouns, and pare down your words until they convey your scene as effectively as possible. "In anything at all," aviator and beloved author Antoine de St. Exupery once wrote, "perfection is finally achieved not when there is nothing more to add, but when nothing more can be taken away."

Details Are Adrenaline, Generalities Are Novocain

I stole this one from theater professor Greg Fritsch, but it works equally well for any form of storytelling, especially interactive ones. Your job is to make your story world so alive the players can picture being there, and believe the story will react when they type a command. Think of specific objects that provide color and texture to a scene, and the particular qualities that make them unique. Use senses other than vision to paint a multisensory scene: what does this place sound like? Feel like? Smell like? Avoid chiché by finding unique ways to describe the scene in your mind's eye, delving deeper than the surface: if it's a dark and stormy night, how dark and what kind of stormy? What does the storm do to the grass, and how does the dark taste?

If this advice seems to contradict the deliberate sparseness recommended in the previous section, it's no accident. Though opposed, both techniques are useful. To describe your story without unnecessary complexity but with enough descriptive detail to paint a vivid scene is a challenge, but a rewarding one.

Extensions to Assist the Player

A wealth of extensions to better understand players can be found on the Inform 7 extensions page. A useful selection is featured below. (Helping new players learn to play interactive fiction is a personal specialty of mine, so you'll notice that several of these are by yours truly.)

> <u>Tutorial Mode by Emily Short</u> overlays a short tutorial onto the beginning of your story that makes use of your own things and locations to teach basic skills to those new to IF.

> <u>Small Kindnesses by Aaron Reed</u> adds a number of commonly-tried commands (such as GO BACK) and alternative syntaxes to a story.

Poor Man's Mistype by Aaron Reed tries to correct misspelled words in player commands.

Limited Implicit Actions by Eric Eve automatically takes preliminary actions such as unlocking locked doors before going through them. The full version (without the Limited) allows authors to define their own rules for new implicit actions.

Smarter Parser by Aaron Reed understands a wide range of command forms often tried by new IFers (like WHAT DO I DO?) and teaches them more appropriate alternatives.

Disambiguation Control by Jon Ingold gives authors fine-grained control over which items appear in disambiguation lists and how they are listed.

Many other extensions are concerned with improving player experience. Informally, I've observed that including several of these extensions more than doubles the rate of successfully understood commands. That's a *huge* improvement for almost no work on the author's part, making players much more likely to stick around long enough to become enchanted by your story. It's really a no-brainer to throw some of these extensions into your project and let your players reap the benefits.

Exercise 6.3

Pick a few of the extensions above and add them to *Sand-dancer*. Recompile and experiment with how they change the experience of play. You can read the documentation for an installed extension in the Documentation panel to find out more specifically what it does and whether *Sand-dancer* might benefit from it.

Back to *Sand-dancer*

In a moment, we'll take our new knowledge and keep extending the world of *Sand-dancer*. But first, let's learn another useful testing command that will be increasingly useful as we go forward.

The ABSTRACT Testing Command

Frequently when working on an unfinished story, you'll find that you'd like to arrange objects in a story world differently: to test some command, you need to be holding something, or be in a certain room, or want something inside something else. In unreleased games, you can use the ABSTRACT test command to make any thing be enclosed by any other thing. (MOVE might perhaps be a better name for this command, except for the higher possibility of it conflicting with an action the author might want to create.)

So, to teleport yourself somewhere in the story world, you could type a command like ABSTRACT ME TO CONTROL CENTER. To instantly acquire an item, try ABSTRACT FLASHLIGHT TO ME. To put something inside a closed container, try ABSTRACT TUMBLEWEED TO WIRE MESH CAGE. Try this and try not to cackle too maniacally with your newfound ultimate power.

CAUTION   As its name suggests, the ABSTRACT command can easily create untenable situations, such as ABSTRACT ME TO FLASHLIGHT, which pretty much brings the session to a halt; similarly, take care when abstracting your way around puzzles to test something that you don't put the story in a situation it would never get into without this testing command. For instance, using ABSTRACT to steal the flashlight creates problems with our code for the Staging Area semi-darkness puzzle, which expects that things will be dark the first time the player enters.

It might be useful to jump ahead to the section "Creating Test Scripts" in Chapter 11 to learn how to quickly input a series of commands that will jump forward to test a particular part of a story.

The Memories

In an earlier chapter, we created the suggesting relation to tie certain things in the story world to objects of a new kind called memory. Memories will be the primary way we reveal the story of Knock's past, but they'll also serve a critical role in interactions with the spirit animals as the player barters with them for talents, especially in the pivotal final scene with Sand-dancer.

A memory is an abstract concept, but in order for players to perform actions with one, they normally need to be able to see it. While we could use advanced trickery to make the relevant memories accessible at the appropriate time (using Inform's concept of "scope"), a more direct approach is for Knock to simply carry any memories he's uncovered in his inventory. Let's create a whimsical container for these called emotional baggage. In Part - Mechanics, Chapter - Memories, add the following:

> The player carries an open transparent unopenable container called emotional baggage. The description of emotional baggage is "Your guidance counselor used to say you're always carrying it with you. You imagine it's kind of ugly, lumpy, and green, and definitely has a stuck zipper."

Of course, normal actions like taking and dropping shouldn't work on this:

> Instead of doing anything other than examining when noun is emotional baggage or second noun is emotional baggage: say "It's not real, bro."

Now, whenever the player encounters an item that triggers a memory, we'll move that memory into the emotional baggage. Since Knock is always carrying it and it's always open, the memory will then be available to relevant commands at any point afterwards in the story. To prevent memories from popping up in disambiguation questions, let's add the following too:

> Does the player mean doing something to a memory: it is unlikely.

The actual implementation of the detection and movement of memories will come in a later chapter. For now, we can use the ABSTRACT test verb to move the memories we create in and out of emotional baggage to see if everything functions correctly.

Once a memory has been uncovered by finding a thing that suggests it, how does the player retrieve the memory? There's nothing wrong with a simple solution here, either: we can just put the memory's description into its description property.

But EXAMINE seems like an odd command to type to relive memories. Let's give them a custom verb. We'll create this and all its rules in one big go: try to follow along. Put this in a new section in Chapter - Memories called Section - Brooding:

> Brooding is an action applying to one thing. Understand "brood about/on/over [something]" or "brood [something]" or "think about [something]" as brooding.
>
> Check brooding when noun is not a memory: instead say "Eh. You couldn't really get into a good brood about that when it's this damn cold."
>
> Carry out brooding: say "[description of noun][line break]"; now the noun is retrieved. [We defined earlier that memories can be either buried (not yet brooded about) or retrieved.]
>
> Instead of doing anything other than brooding to a memory, say "As if. All you can really do is BROOD ABOUT it."
>
> Instead of thinking: say "Most of the thinking you do nowadays comes from either smoking or brooding." [Thinking is a standard action which we'll use to hint the player towards better options.]

Why do we use "say [description of noun]" instead of "try examining noun?" Even if your source text generates an action rather than the player, it still runs all the action's rules; so our check brooding rule would still stop the examining action and we'd never see the description.

Now that we've got our infrastructure in place, let's create some memories. While most players will probably brood about a good chunk of these, we have no way of guaranteeing that a given player will see any given memory, so none of them should contain any vital piece of information necessary for advancing the plot: instead, each memory should add to the picture of Knock's character, like pieces of a puzzle.

Let's create a new heading under Chapter - Memories called Section - Memory Collection. Move and modify the memory we created in Chapter 3 to be underneath it and read as follows:

> The last day of high school is a memory. It is suggested by the tumbleweed. The description is "You didn't expect it was going to be your last day. But that morning you got called in to the principal's office and fat bald Mr. Cox and pissy old Mrs. Burke were there, and they looked kind of like strong animals stalking weak animals, and you knew something bad was up.
>
> Cox said I have here, Mr. Morales (a bad start since you hate that name) a test you took last week in Mrs. Burke's sophomore English class. Questions have been raised (he looked up at Mrs. Burke like he was trying to pass the buck) questions have been raised about the quality of your essay, and whether a student with your academic and behavioral record (he scratched his bloated nose meaningfully) could have plausibly produced such an essay, and you get the idea. They thought you cheated.
>
> No. They knew you cheated, deep in their smug empty hearts. They wanted you to admit it, say you were a cheater and a liar. But you weren't. You wrote that essay, every god damn word, because you really really liked the book for once and wanted to show Mrs. Burke that maybe if they gave people better books to read kids would actually learn something. But they wanted a confession. They wanted a thieving example they could parade in front of the school. Someone of your academic and behavioral and economic and racial background and yeah, screw this shit. So you got up and left and never came back. Drop out, hell. You walked out and you'd do it again."

Note that simply including a real paragraph break within a quoted string is an aesthetically pleasing alternative to the text substitution [paragraph break].

 The source text for *Sand-dancer* as it appears at the end of each chapter is available on the book's website. For longer passages such as the memories, it's probably easier to cut and paste from there into your local version of the story. Or feel free to invent your own memories.

Here are three more memories for Knock. Feel free to modify these to fit your own vision of *Sand-dancer* or Knock's character.

> The player carries a wallet. The wallet is closed and openable. In the wallet is a driver's license and a receipt from Big Jimmy's. The receipt suggests your shit job.

> Your shit job is a memory with description "Juza straddles the 371 like a drunk at last call, smelly and without a plan for the future. Shiny cars whiz by at ninety once in a while, only stopping for gas or directions (hint: not this way). No one ever stops for the stalls selling food and jewelry and blankets and cheap t-shirts that cluster around the dirt turn-off onto the rez. At least, no one buying anything.

> Big Jimmy shook his head when he heard you lived in Oro Oeste. Hell of a drive, kid, he said, popping up his Lumberjacks cap to scratch the straw pate underneath. You should get a place in Hoo-zuh. Little Jimmy'll set you up in that trailer cross the road for almost nothin['].

> Almost nothing. Yeah, exactly what you'd turn into on the cold day in hell you move to Juza. But on the other hand, that was before you met Ocean. Now the road back to Oro Oeste seems longer and longer every night."

> A piece of jade is in pickup truck. A memory called grandma's stories is suggested by the piece of jade.

> The description of grandma's stories is "There are dark spirits who roam the earth, little Knock. Grandma used to say that, holding you tight and stroking your hair. There are dark spirits who roam the earth, but you're not alone. Oh, no. I'm here. (She'd kiss your head and you'd squeeze her back.) But others are watching out for you too. You have three animal guardians, hmm? Spirits who are always watching over you. Oh, you can't always trust them to know what's best. Remember that, Knock. But when you need help, they'll come, and protect you from the worser things in the world.

> Mom would yell at Grandma a lot for filling your head with that new-age bullshit. Grandma grew up white and midwestern and Baptist, but had started wearing things with feathers and playing the pan flute by the time you were born. She seemed to really like having a son-in-law who was Native American or American Indian or Indigenous Peoples or whatever she'd decided the term was that week, and she was pretty pissed when mom left him. Anyway. Her stories were mostly BS, you guess, but some of them stuck with you. When it's dark you still wonder if your spirit animals are out there somewhere, and what the hell is taking them so long to find you."

> The rusted key suggests a memory called meeting Ocean. The description of meeting Ocean is "She was buying a Fresca at Big Jimmy's when you got off your shift, shoving work keys in your pocket, and you stood behind her waiting to get some cigs, almost too tired to notice how cute she was but still noticing, yeah, still noticing.

She turned around and caught you noticing and you were pretty embarrassed and covered in sweat and grease from the garage, so you stepped up and bought some Camels and were pretty surprised she was still there when you turned around.

She told you her name was Ocean Running Deer and she lived on the rez and you told her your name was Nakaibito Morales and you lived in Oro Oeste. She said isn't Nakaibito the name of a town way off west and you told her your mom had picked it off a map because it sounded like a good Indian name. You never tell anyone that story but for some reason you told her. She laughed, sweetly though, and said maybe the two of you should go there sometime and see what it was like. Somehow two weeks later you were dating although you never ended up going to Nakaibito.

And now... no, you can't think about that yet."

Finding Food

After acquiring the first puzzle item (the duct tape or the emergency blanket; we created this puzzle in Chapter 5), the player can return to the desert to meet a second spirit animal and gain a second talent, this time from the Coyote, who offers either luck or scent. After returning, the new talent enables acquiring a second item, advancing the player closer towards one of the two goals (fixing the car or staying the night).

Let's say that with luck, Knock can find some edible canned food among a mostly ruined cache of emergency supplies. Go to Part - Setting, Chapter - Office Interior, Section - Storage Room and add the following lines:

> Some rows of crumbling shelving are a fixed in place supporter in Storage Room. "Rows of crumbling shelving support hundreds of [cans of food], the labels long since aged away."
>
> Some cans of food are on the shelving. The cans of food are fixed in place. Understand "can/hundreds" as cans of food.

Collections of objects can be tricky from a design perspective. If they break down into portable pieces, can the player take one? More than one? How many? Should the description of the collective change after a certain number have been removed? How is one piece described if placed in a different room? Two pieces? More?

You can teach Inform to simulate all this ambiguity, but in most cases, this level of detail is simply irrelevant to a story. Letting players move around individual cans of food would add neither story nor gameplay value to *Sand-dancer*. So instead, we make a single collective object, "cans of food," and then understand the singular word *can* as referring to it.

We should disallow taking this object, since TAKE CAN is a reasonable command:

> Instead of taking cans of food: say "You grab one and turn it over and over in your hand, but water has soaked and crumbled away the label, and you don't have any way to get it open. Your stomach growls a little as you put it back on the shelf." Instead of opening or eating cans of food: try taking cans of food.

We'd like to keep this puzzle off the player's radar until after they've passed their first milestone, so we'll keep the player from finding a can opener until they get to the Control Center via their first talent. We previously put a can opener in the Control Center, but let's give it an initial appearance:

> The initial appearance of can opener is "But hey, on one pile here's a perfectly good can opener."

Once the player has the opener, we can set up our puzzle. Back in Section - Storage Room:

> Instead of taking cans of food when player holds can opener: say "You pull down a can from the shelf, grip it with the rusty can opener, and peel open the lid. Yuck: [one of]moldy peas[or]rotten condensed milk[or]black and mold-covered mushrooms[or]something nasty-smelling and green[as decreasingly likely outcomes]. [one of]Just your luck.[or]Not your lucky day.[or]Some of these should still be good, right?[as decreasingly likely outcomes]".

Here, we use the [as decreasingly likely outcomes] random text variation to add some variety to this message, since it's one the player is likely to see several times. Note the repetition of the word *luck*, which hopefully plants a seed in the mind of the player that sprouts later on, when luck is one of the talents the Coyote offers.

If the player accepts and acquires luck, the action should succeed. So far, we have kept track of success purely by the player acquiring items: with a little imagination, we can do the same thing here, too:

> The canned oranges are a thing. Instead of taking cans of food when player holds can opener and player holds luck and canned oranges are not handled: say "You run your fingers along the cans, waiting until one feels right. There's nothing, nothing, but then... yeah. That's the one. You snag it down, twist it open, and boom: mandarin oranges, unspoiled and delicious. You scarf them down, picking them out segment by segment with your chilly fingers. By the time you've polished them off you're a lot less hungry. You grab the next can down for later."; move canned oranges to player.

Finally, we should respond differently to taking the cans after the player has satiated Knock's hunger:

> Instead of taking cans of food when canned oranges are handled: say "You won't be hungry again till morning."

To try out this sequence, use the ABSTRACT command to acquire talents and move yourself to the Storage Room, then turn on the emergency lights.

> ## Exercise 6.4
>
> Add a memory associated with the lingering scent of mandarin oranges, only triggered after this event happens. Since it can only be achieved by players on the "stay the night" path, connect it to the side of Knock that's thinking about leaving his girl.

Sniffing Out Some Fuel

If the player is on the other path (fixing the truck), a logical complement to the duct tape might be a can of gas, to replace what was lost from the pickup's busted fuel line.

Let's say that the control center above the roof is filled with trash, and though the player character can smell gas coming from somewhere, he can't find it without the Coyote's power of scent. First of all, we need a room description, so let's add it, in Part - Setting, Chapter - Office Interior, Section - Control Center:

> The description of Control Center is "Some kind of electrical control stuff must have happened here once, but it's totally trashed now. Like, [piles of trash], broken equipment, and junk are everywhere. Back down is the only place to go."
>
> Some piles of trash are scenery in Control Center. Understand "broken/equipment/junk" as piles of trash.

Here, again, we've made a collective object rather than a group of individual things. Rather than getting BENT and bracketing each item, we understand all the unimportant nouns in the list as part of the collective. In this case, the individual items aren't really notable enough to merit becoming their own objects: we simply encompass them all within the larger concept of the piles of trash.

We also want to hint that something else is here.

> The smell of gasoline is fixed in place in Control Center. "[if player holds scent]You can clearly smell gasoline coming from under that [sheet of corrugated metal][otherwise]You catch a faint whiff of gasoline coming from somewhere[end if]." Understand "faint/whiff" as smell of gasoline. Understand "gas" as smell of gasoline when gas can is not visible.
>
> Instead of doing anything to smell of gasoline, say "[if player holds scent]It's coming from beneath that [sheet of corrugated metal][else]You can't tell where the smell is coming from[end if]."
>
> Instead of smelling Control Center, try smelling smell of gasoline.

This last rule requires a bit of explanation. Smelling is one of the few standard actions that can have either no nouns or one: SMELL and SMELL GAS are both valid commands. When the parser converts these to actions, however, a missing noun is filled in with the current location, so in this case SMELL would become the action "smelling Control Center." (The listening action works the same way.) So we add an instead rule to redirect SMELL with no noun to a more useful command.

We referenced a sheet of corrugated metal above concealing the gas can. Let's create it but not describe it, so the player will only know it's there after acquiring scent and being told about it:

> A sheet of corrugated metal is an undescribed fixed in place thing in Control Center.

> Instead of searching or taking piles of trash: try looking under piles of trash. Instead of searching or taking or looking under sheet of corrugated metal: try looking under piles of trash. Instead of looking under piles of trash: say "You root around in the trash hopelessly, but there's a lot of it. You don't turn up anything useful."

And now, a more specific rule for players with scent:

> Instead of looking under piles of trash when player holds scent: say "Your sense of smell leads you straight to a [sheet of corrugated metal]. You lift it [if player holds strength]effortlessly [end if]and throw it aside, revealing a gas can."; move gas can to location; now smell of gasoline is off-stage.

And, of course, the gas can itself:

> A gas can is a closed openable container. The description is "It's full of gas." Instead of opening gas can: say "You don't want to spill it."

Note that we intentionally make *gas can* not share any words with *smell of gasoline*, to prevent unnecessary disambiguation questions.

 Why do we bother to describe the gas can as openable, when our instead rule prevents it from ever being opened? The distinction is subtle, but the response to a command like CLOSE GAS CAN reveals the reason. Since no instead rule blocks this, if we'd made the can unopenable the response would be "That's not something you can close," which seems odd. Making it openable changes this text to "It's already closed," which makes more sense.

To test this sequence, use ABSTRACT to get the emergency lights switched on, then acquire the talents you need to get to the Control Center and sniff out the gas.

We've taken *Sand-dancer* from a single line of source text creating its first room to a substantial game, with an explorable map, puzzles to solve, a player character with a strong voice, and plenty of custom rules and actions. In the second half of the book, we'll take this strong foundation and continue to build, learning about how to write more powerful rules, add scenes and pacing, and, perhaps most importantly, create the other characters that Knock must interact with.

In the last few chapters of the book, we'll talk about how to dig deeper into the operation of the parser and the Standard Rules to change basic assumptions about how your story world should operate. We'll spend some time on how to add finishing touches to a game, including testing and debugging, and conclude with a whirlwind tour of advanced Inform 7 and other topics we won't have time to talk about in detail.

If you've taken a look at the source code for any other Inform 7 source games, you might have noticed there are still a lot of things that look unfamiliar. That's in part because I've so far focused much more on story and description than basic programming technique. In the next chapter, I'll fill in some of these gaps and introduce you to some nuts and bolts concepts, including variables, conditional blocks, standalone phrases, and lists.

Exercise Answers

Exercise 6.1

Add synonyms to *Sand-dancer*.

Here's a decent first pass. Each understand rule should be placed next to the relevant object declaration.

```
Understand "car/door/poor/old/dash" as pickup truck.
Understand "head lights" or "head light" or "high beams" or
    "headlight/lights/light/beams" as the headlights.
Understand "cigarette/cig/cigs/smokes" as pack of cigarettes.
Understand "book/pages/page/guide" as guidebook.
Understand "spiderweb/spiderwebs/cobweb/spider/spiders/web/webs" as
    cobwebs.
Understand "ladder/rung" as metal rungs.
Understand "cactus" as Saguaro.
Understand "rusted/metal" as electrical tower.
Understand "weed" as yellowing weeds.
Understand "bare/bulbs/control/panel" or "light bulb" or "light bulbs" as the
    emergency lights.
```

Exercise 6.2

Understand the kind "plant" and the property "dead." If you didn't create the plant kind, flip back to Exercise 3.3 and add it or something similar. We could put this in Part - Setting, Chapter - Around the Tower:

> Understand "plant" as a plant. Understand the dead property as describing a plant.

Exercise 6.3

This is up to your personal preference, but I added these to the master copy of *Sanddancer* at the top:

> Include Small Kindnesses by Aaron Reed. [You may have already added this in a previous chapter.]
>
> Include Poor Man's Mistype by Aaron Reed.
>
> Include Numbered Disambiguation Choices by Aaron Reed.

Exercise 6.4

Write a memory about the mandarin oranges. This or whatever you come up with can go with the other memories in Part - Mechanics, Chapter - Memories, Section - Memory Collection:

> A lingering smell of orange is an undescribed thing. It suggests Ocean's perfume. Before taking cans of food when player holds can opener and player holds luck: move lingering smell of orange to location.
>
> Ocean's perfume is a memory with description "You used to like it. The perfume. But you like how Ocean smells without it better, but she doesn't believe you. She says girls are supposed to smell sweet, like oranges and rose petals. But you've always liked bitter fruits. Tamarind and lemon.
>
> And sometimes, maybe after a fight or something, you'll drive off and that's all you can smell is her orange perfume. And even after smoking three cigarettes with the windows of your pickup rolled down you can still smell it, and it's still too sweet, and you wonder if this is working out. Because it's such a little pointless thing but it drives you crazy. And if a little thing like perfume is driving you this crazy maybe the whole thing is doomed. Maybe Ocean would be better off with some guy who likes orange perfume.
>
> You don't know what's going to happen now."

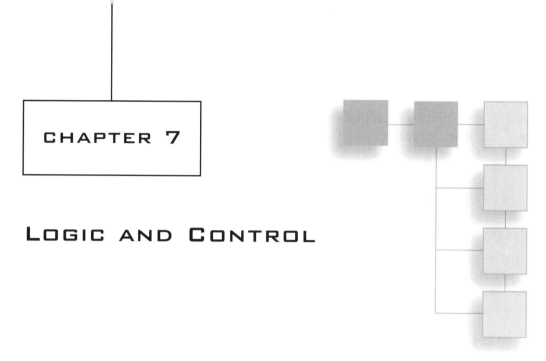

CHAPTER 7

LOGIC AND CONTROL

Many programming books begin with fundamentals like variables, loops, and math, but we've managed to make it through nearly half this book without them. Inform, designed for the highly specific purpose of creating interactive fictions, instead gives us high-level tools like actions, rulebooks, and text substitutions. Behind these tools hides a lot of low-level work. Putting something like [the list of closed windows] in a string of text causes variables to be mustered, lists to be created, loops to run, and grammatically correct output to be generated.

Usually, we needn't be bothered with these details. But as your story grows in complexity, you'll want more direct control over its internals. In this chapter, we'll explore Inform's low-level side, learning how to build more advanced components involving logic, numbers, lists, and randomness.

Logic

Let's start getting our hands dirty by defining conditions more closely, as well as introducing a more precise way to trigger different phrases in response to different conditions.

Conditions

We've already met conditional tests: those phrases beginning with *if* that can be either true or false depending on current conditions in a story.

```
if flashlight is switched on
if location is Staging Area
if the noun is a window
```

We've most commonly encountered conditional tests as text substitutions to display one piece of text if the condition is true and another if it's false, although they've also shown up within rules to make something happen conditionally. In your *Sand-dancer* source, turn to Part - Setting, Chapter - Office Interior, Section - Storage Room and find this rule:

> After switching off the emergency lights: now every room regionally in Tower Vicinity is dark; if headlights are switched on, now every within range of headlights room is lighted; say "The lights flicker and die out."

This after rule declares that three things should happen when the emergency lights are switched off; but the middle phrase only creates a change in the story if the condition *headlights are switched on* is true. This works fine for simple examples, but what if we want more than one thing to happen as a result of a conditional test? Or more than one alternative to be available?

To make more complicated tests, we need a new style of formatting that makes it clear which instructions to run in what circumstances. We use **block indentation** to convey this information to Inform. Go ahead and adjust the rule above in your source text until it looks like the following, using the Tab key to indent lines and noticing the punctuation change from a comma to a colon at the end of the condition:

> After switching off the emergency lights:
>> now every room regionally in Tower Vicinity is dark;
>> if headlights are switched on:
>>> now every within range of headlights room is lighted;
>> say "The lights flicker and die out."

Block indentation is different from the inline style we're used to in three ways:

- Each phrase in the rule is on its own line, with no blank lines in between
- Each phrase after the rule definition is indented by exactly one tab stop
- Each condition ends with a colon, and the phrases that should execute if that condition is true are indented by exactly one additional tab stop

Until now we've been fairly lax about our formatting, but block indentation requires precision. You must stick to one phrase per line, you can't uses spaces instead of tabs to indent lines, and you can't have extra tabs in incorrect places. What you gain with this style of formatting, however, is a clearer at-a-glance picture of the structure and logic of a series of instructions, and the ability to include more than one instruction as part of a test.

Let's expand our rule a bit to make this clearer:

> After switching off the emergency lights:
>> now every room regionally in Tower Vicinity is dark;
>> if headlights are switched on:

```
    now every within range of headlights room is lighted;
    say "The lights die out, except for a ghostly glow from outside that must
        be your headlights.";
  otherwise:
    say "The lights flicker and die out.";
  say "[line break]The generator whines as it powers off, slowly falling silent."
```

When the expanded rule fires, if the headlights happen to be switched on then the two statements following that condition will both run; if not, the one statement following the "otherwise" runs. The final "say" phrase will run regardless of the state of the headlights, because it's indented at the same level as the other main phrases: exactly one tab stop more than the rule's declaration.

We can make conditions more complicated by giving them more than two alternatives. Make the following revision:

```
After switching off the emergency lights:
  now every room regionally in Tower Vicinity is dark;
  if headlights are switched on:
    now every within range of headlights room is lighted;
    say "The lights die out, except for a ghostly glow from outside that must
        be your headlights.";
  otherwise if flashlight is switched on and flashlight is visible:
    say "The lights die out, leaving only the beam of your flashlight.";
  otherwise:
    say "The lights flicker and die out.";
  say "[line break]The generator whines as it powers off, slowly falling silent."
```

Now there are three possible things that can happen in the middle of this rule. The first condition that matches is the only one that runs; so if the headlights are on, the state of the flashlight will never be checked.

Block indentation becomes even more necessary when we nest conditions inside other conditions. Make the changes to the bolded lines, and see if you can work out what this will do:

```
After switching off the emergency lights:
  now every room regionally in Tower Vicinity is dark;
  if headlights are switched on:
    now every within range of headlights room is lighted;
    say "The lights die out, except for a ghostly glow from outside that must
        be your headlights.";
```

otherwise if flashlight is switched on and flashlight is visible:

    say "The lights die out, leaving only the beam of your flashlight.";

otherwise:

    say "The lights flicker and die out";

    if player holds courage:

        say ", but you are not afraid";

    say ".";

say "[line break]The generator whines as it powers off, slowly falling silent."

The comma and following clause appear only if the player has the talent of courage; regardless, the period at the end of the sentence in this "otherwise" clause will be printed.

Nearly anything that can be done with a complex single rule can also be done with multiple rules. The above could be rewritten as follows:

Carry out switching off emergency lights: now every room regionally in Tower Vicinity is dark.

After switching off emergency lights when headlights are switched on: now every within range of headlights room is lighted; say "The lights die out, except for a ghostly glow from outside that must be your headlights."; continue the action.

After switching off emergency lights when headlights are switched off and flashlight is switched on: say "The lights die out, leaving only the beam of your flashlight."; continue the action.

After switching off emergency lights when headlights are switched off and

flashlight is switched off: say "The lights flicker and die[if player holds courage], but you are not afraid[end if]."; continue the action.

After switching off emergency lights: say "The generator whines as it powers off, slowly falling silent."

While both styles are valid, here I prefer block indentation. It makes clear at a glance what happens in what order and under what circumstances. Use whichever style seems most sensible to you in any given circumstance.

PROGRAMMER'S NOTE

Inform's use of block indentation was controversial when introduced, but meaningful white space seems a natural fit for Inform's streamlined NL syntax. If you don't like it, a more traditional alternative using explicit begin and end statements is also available: see "Begin and end" in the built-in documentation's chapter on Phrases for the details. You can mix and match between these two styles at will, as long as each full phrase uses just one of the two internally.

CAUTION   Even though block formatting helps you see the architecture of your logic, problems with complicated rules are frequent. Make sure you fully understand what your rule is trying to do before writing it out, and double-check the indentation with your mental map, walking through it one line at a time. If you're having problems, think of each condition as "owning" the lines indented beneath it, and make sure everything matches up the way it should.

Variables

Another feature of conventional programming we haven't formally introduced is the **variable**. Much like the ones you remember from algebra class, variables are named containers holding values whose contents might vary at different times. Unlike algebraic variables, Inform variables are encouraged to have descriptive names like *the elapsed time* or *Susan's favorite sweater*.

We've already made discreet use of variables. You might remember *location*, which keeps track of the room the player currently occupies. Actually, *player* itself is also a variable that tracks which character the user currently controls—yes, this can change! Other variables we've seen include *noun* and *second noun*, holding the items referred to in the most recent command. *Turn count* is another useful variable, holding the number of turns taken so far. All these variables are created and set to appropriate values by our friend the Standard Rules, which is why we haven't needed to do anything other than use them until now, but learning to create and manage your own variables is a critical skill.

Variable Basics

Variables are useful when we need to remember something for a little while and then retrieve it again. A variable must be created before it can be used. The method for creating a variable differs based on how long we need it to stick around: we'll talk about each of the three possibilities in order of frequency.

Temporary Variables

Very often you'll want a variable that holds something just for a moment, relevant only until the end of the current rule or phrase. The keyword **let** creates such a short-lived variable. So:

```
let chosen item be the rusty tin can;
let selection be a random visible thing;
```

...creates two variables, *chosen item* and *selection*, and places something in each of them. We could then make use of these variables in subsequent parts of the phrase or rule.

To illustrate, let's add a cute little response to *Sand-dancer*. Put this in Part - Mechanics, Chapter - Memories:

> Instead of waiting: let selection be a random thing in emotional baggage; say "Nah, man, better keep busy or else it's back to brooding about [the selection]."

Though the variable name is just *selection*, since it's referring to a thing we can say *a selection* or *the selection* to select an indefinite or definite article.

Changing the contents of a variable is done simply with our old friend "now." We might optionally insert the line below into our instead rule between the two phrases, just in case the player tries this command before uncovering any memories:

> if nothing is in emotional baggage, now selection is a random memory;

You can change the value stored in a variable as often as you like, but you can never change the kind of value that variable can store. For instance, if you tried writing in a rule:

> let selection be a random memory;
>
> now selection is 17;

...you'd get a problem message like that seen in Figure 7.1. Inform says your instructions would be "comparing two kinds of value which cannot mix - an object and a number."

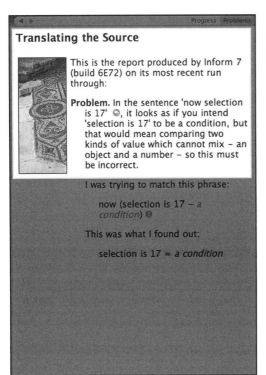

Figure 7.1
A problem message for trying to put the wrong kind of value into a variable.

Pay attention to that last bit: it reveals what kind of values the compiler thinks belong to both your variable and the attempted insertee. Often this message is a sign that you and Inform are in disagreement about what one of these kinds of value should be. In this case, since the first thing we put in the *selection* variable was an object, we can only ever use it to store other objects; 17 is a number, so it's not welcome here.

So what are the different kinds of value? The ones you're most likely to run into are object, number, time, direction, region, truth state, text, and list. (We've also seen thing, direction, and region, which are all specific kinds of object.) Some we've seen before, and the rest you'll learn about as we progress through the book. Note that it's fine to put members of different sub-kinds within the same variable: an object variable can store windows, memories, or devices interchangeably.

If it helps you to remember what kind of value a variable holds, you can create it with an explicit definition instead of an initial value:

```
let selection be an object;
now selection is a random memory;
```

I mentioned **truth state** a moment ago, a kind of value known in other languages as a Boolean. It can hold one of two values: true or false. Conditions evaluate to truth states, and in fact we can store their results in a truth state variable. We use the words **whether or not** to assign such a variable:

```
Check looting:
    let surveilled be a truth state;
    now surveilled is whether or not a policeman is visible;
    if surveilled is true, instead say "Better cool it till the fuzz takes off."
```

In most cases, we could just simplify this to:

```
Check looting when a policeman is visible: instead say "Better cool it..."
```

But in more complicated situations, truth state variables can be a useful bookkeeping tool.

Variables for Things

Another common use for variables is to store information about some item in your story world. An object variable (or **property**) keeps its contents throughout the duration of a story, and can be referenced or updated at any time. To create one, use the keyword **has** in an assertion sentence.

```
The flashlight has a number called battery life.
Every room has a direction called the escape route.
```

To refer to a thing's variable, use **of**, as in *battery life of the flashlight*. The second example creates a series of variables for each room in the map: *the escape route of Staging Area, the* *escape route of Middle of Nowhere*, and so on. As with any variable, the kind of value the variable holds cannot change: the *escape route* of a room could never be a thing or a number.

PROGRAMMER'S NOTE

Inform variables are all public, except for those created by "let" within rules or phrases. IF story worlds tend to be interconnected in extremely complicated ways, with all kinds of systems tightly coupled to each other; enforcing private variables, while good practice in other languages would be more trouble than it's worth here. This does mean that namespace clashes become an increasingly likely possibility in large projects, so best practices include taking care to give variables unique names.

Global Variables

If a variable needs to stick around for the long haul but isn't associated with a particular object, you might want to make it a **global variable**. (Inform calls these "values that vary," but the traditional term seems more descriptive.) Examples include the aforementioned *location* and *player*.

We create a global variable with an assertion sentence specifying its kind of value:

    The favorite item is an object variable.

    The treasure count is a number variable.

Instead of "variable," you can also say "that varies":

    The treasure count is a number that varies.

After creation, you can (and should) declare the variable's initial value with a second assertion:

    The favorite item is the rusty tin can.

    The treasure count is 7.

Changing the value of a global variable works the same as with any other kind of variable:

    now the favorite item is the piece of jade;

CAUTION

Global variables have a bad reputation in other programming languages because they can lead to confusing code. If you define one near the top of your source text and then change its value near the bottom, figuring out later where the variable came from or what it's for can be a challenge. You also risk confusing it with another global variable with a similar name, which again might be buried in some long-forgotten part of your source. While there are legitimate uses for global variables in Inform 7, consider before creating one whether it would make more sense as an object variable or even a temporary variable.

Example: Breaking and Entering

Let's use our knowledge of block indentation and variables to add a bit of a challenge early in the story. Instead of just going straight in to the building, let's say the door is boarded up, so the player needs to break a window to get inside. We'll keep track of whether a window is broken by simply making it open, since an earlier rule prevents the player from using the opening or closing actions on a window.

Let's start with the rule that creates the central action of the puzzle. In Chapter - Office Interior, make a new heading called Section - Windows. Move the existing lines of window code inside, and then add this at the bottom:

> Instead of throwing something at a window:
>
> > let missile be the noun;
> >
> > let broken window be the second noun;
> >
> > move missile to location;
> >
> > now broken window is open;
> >
> > say "[The missile] smashes against [the broken window], shattering it."

Here, we create temporary variables called *missile* and *broken window* and put the direct and indirect object of the player's command into them. We make use of these variables within the rule, but after it's finished, so are they: we can't refer to *the broken window* elsewhere in our source text. We're free to use this name for some other variable elsewhere, since it only exists for this one brief moment.

Since nouns and second nouns are often referred to within action rules and phrases, you can use the special word **called** within the rule definition to quickly create local variables to hold these values. This is exactly equivalent to the rule above:

> Instead of throwing something (called the missile) at a window (called the broken window):
>
> > move missile to location;
> >
> > now broken window is open;
> >
> > say "[The missile] smashes against [the broken window], shattering it."

Once a window is broken, the player should be able to climb through to get inside the building. But how do we know where a window leads? The simplest solution is to revise our definition of windows to make them a kind of **door**, a built-in concept from the Standard Rules. A door sits between two rooms and can allow passage (by being open) or disallow it (by being closed).

We need to tweak our existing window definitions a little to fit this new conception of their purpose. Let's change the declaration paragraph for windows to read:

> A window is a kind of door. A window is usually closed, unopenable and undescribed. Understand "window" as a window. The description of a window is usually "[if noun is open]Just an empty frame.[otherwise]Dusty glass panes."

The understand assertion will let the player type WINDOW to refer to any window, regardless of whether the word "window" appears in its name. Let's also modify our instead rule for opening or closing windows to respond differently when broken:

> Instead of opening or closing a window: say "[if noun is open]It's already busted open.[otherwise]It looks like these windows have been rusted shut for years."

Our source text currently defines some windows, but we need to update them to place them between rooms and be intact. Replace the window definitions in your source with the following paragraph:

> A pane of cracked glass is a window. It is outside of Staging Area and inside from Crumbling Concrete. A dust-covered window is a window. It is outside of Foreman's Office and inside from Base of the Tower. A tiny frosted window is a window. It is outside of Break Room and inside from Weed-strewn Rust.

Inside and outside are two of the standard directions, and they seem natural in this context. A player typing IN from Base of the Tower will try to go through the tiny broken window. ENTER WINDOW also has the same effect.

One slight snag: Inform will complain that we already defined the "in" exit for Crumbling Concrete as leading to Staging Area, not the pane of cracked glass. Let's change the existing exit to use a cardinal direction, and interpose it with a boarded-up door. In Chapter - Office Interior, remove the sentence "Staging Area is inside from Crumbling Concrete" and replace it with:

> A boarded-up door is a closed unopenable undescribed door. It is northeast of Crumbling Concrete and southwest of Staging Area.

Exercise 7.1

The descriptions of the relevant exterior and interior rooms should be modified to mention the new exit through the door, as well as the newly positioned windows. Implement this.

Now that we've set up our windows, we can revise our core rule. Things thrown at a window should probably go through it, not land on the ground. You can ask for **the other side of** a door and get the room it connects to, with respect to the player's current location. Back in Section - Windows, modify our instead rule:

> Instead of throwing something (called the missile) at a window (called the broken window):
>
> now missile is in the other side of the broken window;
>
> now broken window is open;
>
> say "[The missile] smashes through [the broken window], shattering it."

This is better, but it's not taking into account that the player might already have broken a particular window. Let's split our rule into two, to handle both open/broken windows and closed/unbroken ones:

> Instead of throwing something (called the missile) at a closed window (called the targeted window):
>
> now missile is in the other side of the targeted window;
>
> now the targeted window is open;
>
> say "[The missile] smashes through [the targeted window], shattering it."
>
>
> Instead of throwing something at an open window (called the broken window):
>
> say "[The broken window] is already broken."

Let's add some more rules to clean this up. We should explain why the player can't use the boarded-up door (in Section - Crumbling Concrete), and hint at an alternative.

> Instead of opening, entering, or attacking boarded-up door: say "The door won't budge. You slam your hands against the boards in frustration[if pane of cracked glass is closed], causing a nearby window to quiver in the reflected light[end if]." Understand "board/boards/boarded" as boarded-up door. Understand "quiver" as pane of cracked glass.

We also want to take away the easiest solution to getting inside. Back in Section - Windows, add:

> Instead of attacking a window: say "Nice thought, but the last thing you need is a sliced open hand. Maybe if you could get a little distance."

Of course, the above message doesn't make sense after a window's been broken, so:

> Instead of attacking an open window: say "You've already busted it open."

We can add some additional syntax that players might try:

> Understand "climb in/into/through [a door]" as entering. Understand "look through/in/inside/into [a closed window]" as a mistake ("The glass is too filthy for you to see anything on the other side.").

Let's try recompiling and seeing what happens. Figure 7.2 shows a sample transcript. Everything seems okay, except—what's going on right at the end? "You can't go that way?" Didn't we define this connection as being valid?

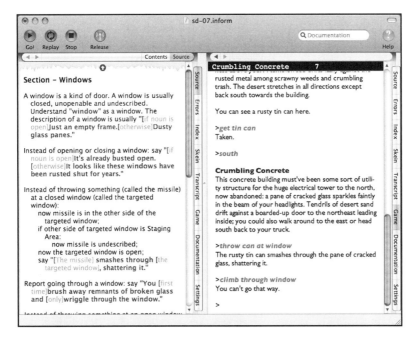

Figure 7.2
Transcript showing our (still buggy) window puzzle in action.

To find out what's gone wrong, let's first verify that the connection between rooms exists. Type the debug command SHOWME WINDOW within the game to examine the window's properties. Down at the bottom, we see "other side: Crumbling Concrete," indicating that yes, the window leads to the correct place. The line above reveals that the window is open, which is also correct.

Another way of verifying this is the World tab of the Index panel. See the squiggly lines leading away from some of your rooms? Those are representing in/out connections, which Inform's poor mapmaker doesn't know where to position; regardless, if you hover your mouse cursor over any connection, you'll see some text after a moment describing it. CC (Crumbling Concrete) shows the text "inside through pane of busted glass to Staging Area," so everything seems to be in order here as well.

Since the world model isn't broken, the next place to check is the logic on top of it. In the game, type the testing commands RULES and ACTIONS to activate diagnostic information. Now try going through the window again and take a look at the output (Figure 7.3).

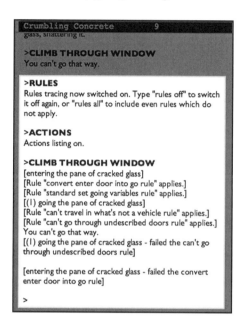

Figure 7.3
Clues to the mystery
of the buggy window
puzzle.

Aha! It appears as if the "can't go through undescribed doors rule" is preventing our movement. We can find out more about this rule from the Index panel's Actions tab. Click on the going action and find this rule. (Remember, Control + F or Command + F search within a page.)

It seems this rule is part of the standard check rulebook for going. The rationale here is probably that undescribed doors might be intentionally hidden until the player discovers them, but that's not how we're using undescribed here. Since we don't plan to use doors anywhere else in our story, there shouldn't be any problem getting rid of this rule. Make sure your cursor in the source panel is positioned on a new line, then back in the Index panel, click the "unlist" box for our mistaken check rule. Alternatively, you can type in the following assertion:

> The can't go through undescribed doors rule is not listed in the check going
>   rulebook.

Hit "Replay," and now you should successfully be able to gain access to the inside of the building.

Let's clean up a few last things before signing off on this puzzle. Sneaking in through a busted window is kind of exciting, and deserves a special response. Normally, the going action provides no report rule: the response is just the description of the new room. Let's add one for this case, printing an extra bit of descriptive detail the first time through:

> Report going through a window: say "You [first time]brush away remnants of broken glass and [only]wriggle through the window."

 Action rules involving the going action can be restricted in many different ways. **going to** matches a destination. **going from** matches an origin. **going through** matches a door (or kind of door). **going with** matches if an object is being pushed from one place to another (rare). **going by** matches movement in a vehicle. **going nowhere** matches for a direction that doesn't lead to another room. There's also **exiting from** an enterable container or supporter.

In Chapter 5, we made the contents of Staging Area undescribed to simulate the nearly-dark state the player first finds it in. However, the thing the player threw inside shows up plain as day. Let's fix this by modifying our "instead of throwing something at a closed window" rule to add the bolded text below:

> Instead of throwing something (called the missile) at a closed window (called the targeted window):
>
> now missile is in the other side of the targeted window;
>
> **if other side of targeted window is Staging Area:**
>
> **now missile is undescribed;**
>
> now the targeted window is open;
>
> say "[The missile] smashes through [the targeted window], shattering it."

Once the player lights the room up, we need to make the thrown item described again, so add the following within the "Before switching on flashlight when location is Staging Area" rule in Section - Staging Area:

> now every handled visible thing is described;

The thrown item will be handled because the player had to have held it at some point to throw it; however, this neatly keeps any fixed in place scenery items in the room from becoming described.

Finally, even though our infrastructure allows the player to break in through any window, our flashlight puzzle really requires that Staging Area be the first room visited. So let's disallow entering through either of the other windows:

> Instead of going through tiny frosted window: say "It's too small for you to wriggle through." Instead of going through dust-covered window: say "It's too high up for you to pull yourself through."

Recompile and test this in action. This is a good addition: it's separated the earliest moments of the story into two sections (exploring outside and exploring inside) and justified the various objects we left littered around such as the rusty tin can, which can now be hurled through windows with aplomb.

Custom Kinds of Variables

Traditionally, programming languages used numbers to represent almost anything. If our story involved a container holding a certain amount of liquid, a classic approach to storing this information would be to create a number variable:

> The jug of milk is a thing. The jug has a number called the liquid level.

But this approach has disadvantages. For one, it's not clear what the number in the *liquid level* variable means. Does a high number correspond to a lot of milk left, or a little? What number represents a full jug? What happens if a number outside the expected range gets accidentally stored in the variable, like minus 137?

Kinds of Value

Inform, and most modern programming languages, encourage us to think in words, not numbers. A better solution is to create what other languages call an enumerated type, and Inform calls a custom **kind of value**. This will be a new kind (like object, number, or text) except that we'll specify exactly what values it's allowed to have.

> A liquid level is a kind of value. The liquid levels are completely full, mostly full, half full, mostly empty, and completely empty.

Now, we can create a *liquid level* variable, and store any of the five values we've created within it. With this approach, we'd simulate our jug of milk like this:

> The jug of milk has a liquid level. The jug of milk is completely full.

This is a big improvement. We don't have to remember which numbers correspond to which liquid levels; it's clear how many allowable states there are, and it's impossible for a *liquid level* variable to get into a disallowed state. Even better, because our states are described with natural language, we can use them directly when describing things to the player:

> The description of jug of milk is "Peering inside, you see that it's [liquid level of jug of milk]."

Once a kind of value is created, we can use it anywhere:

> A gas tank is part of the abandoned car. The gas tank has a liquid level. The gas tank is mostly empty.

CAUTION The options you provide for kinds of value must not conflict with existing keywords defined by Inform. This is why we chose "completely empty" instead of the more succinct "empty"; the latter is already being used as an adjective for lists. If you're trying to create a new kind of value and getting a problem message, look for a phrase like "that seems to involve applying the adjective 'empty' to an object - and I have no definition of it which would apply in that situation." Inform is telling us that it already understands "empty" to have a meaning, so we can't give it another one.

You can see a full list of all of the words Inform and your story have defined in the Phrasebook tab of the Index panel, which we'll talk about in more detail later in the chapter.

The Values Before and After

Usefully, Inform remembers the order of values in your definition, and you can move a variable back and forth through this list by using **the value before** and **the value after**. This is useful for a situation like this where the values are representing a series of steps from one state to another.

```
Carry out drinking jug of milk:
    let amount be the liquid level of jug of milk;
    now amount is the liquid level after amount;
    say "After you finish chugging, you see that the container is now [amount].";
    now the liquid level of jug of milk is amount.
```

If the jug started out with a liquid level of *mostly full*, this code would change it to *half full*. The list wraps around, so the value after the last value is the first value: since in this case that wouldn't make sense, a better implementation of our drinking action might be:

```
Carry out drinking jug of milk:
    let amount be the liquid level of jug of milk;
    if amount is completely empty:
        say "You're out of milk.";
    otherwise:
        now amount is the liquid level after amount;
        say "After you finish chugging, you see that the container is now [amount].";
        now the liquid level of jug of milk is amount.
```

Kinds of value are a great way to leverage natural language to make your source text clearer and more concise. They're a great addition to your toolkit.

Phrases

So far all the programming we've done has been within rules triggered in response to player commands. Each rule contains one or more **phrases** separated by semicolons and describing a sequence of commands to be run when the rule runs.

Named Phrases

We can also create our own sets of commands using a **named phrase**. These are collections of phrases prefaced with **To** and a descriptive name. Named phrases are never automatically called by the system; rather, they can be manually invoked in your source text whenever you want the commands they enclose to execute.

Named phrases are useful when you have a series of instructions that might be run at different times or for different reasons, and you don't want to have to duplicate them in multiple places. Let's imagine our story involves a dramatic tennis match (as does, for example, David Foster Wallace's monumental novel *Infinite Jest*). The start of the match might be triggered by any number of events: a certain elapsed time, a particular action by the player, or a behavior rule of another character. Regardless, we'd want the same sequence of events to happen when it did:

```
To begin the match:
    now player is in Court 9;
    now player holds tennis racquet;
    now opponent is in Court 9;
    now the audience is in Court 9;
    say "The match begins."
```

Now, anywhere in our source text where we wanted to trigger this, we just say:

```
begin the match;
```

...and the sequence we defined will be followed. Afterwards, control will return to the rule or phrase that invoked our named phrase (the **calling phrase**) and continue with the next line there.

PROGRAMMER'S NOTE

What we label as named phrases are called functions, procedures, or subroutines in other languages. The example here shows a function that neither takes nor returns any values, but we'll see in the next few sections how to do these things as well.

Phrases to Decide

Our "begin the match" phrase does some work, but the calling phrase has no way of knowing what it did. Often, you'd like a named phrase to reach some sort of result and report back to the calling phrase. **To decide** phrases have already been introduced (back in Chapter 4) but let's take a closer look at them.

Phrases That Decide

- To decide {what/which} number is the best number: decide {on} 7.
- To decide {if/whether or not} x is the best number: {decide {on}} yes.

In phrases deciding on a truth state, "decide on yes," "decide yes," and "yes" are all equivalent.

The goal of a phrase that decides something is to determine a value for a specified type of variable. Let's say our story required detailed information about the game of tennis. We might need a decision phrase like the following:

```
Tournament play is a truth state variable.


To decide what number is sets needed to win:
    if tournament play is true:
        decide on 5;
    otherwise:
        decide on 3.
```

Decision phrases also begin with "To," and also have a name (in this case, *sets needed to win*) but in between we need some extra info. We start with **decide which** or **decide what** (both equivalent), specify a kind of value, and add the word **is**. We might "decide which liquid level is not enough milk," for instance, or "decide what room is the best in the house." Remember that *not enough milk* and *the best in the house* in these examples are purely arbitrary phrases with meaning only for the author, not for Inform.

To use a decision phrase, we can assign its result to a variable:

```
let sets be sets needed to win;
```

...or just use it directly:

```
say "In today's match, players must win [sets needed to win] sets."
```

It's important to understand that as soon as a decision phrase reaches a line beginning **decide** or **decide on**, it stops running and immediately returns the result to the calling phrase. Any further lines in the decision phrase will not be executed. This means that we could rewrite the above as:

```
To decide what number is sets needed to win:
    if tournament play is true, decide on 5;
    decide on 3.
```

...without changing its meaning. Although this makes your source text shorter, it does not necessarily make it clearer; my personal preference in a case like this is the more explicit style, where the block indentation helps preserve the decision's logic.

Deciding If

Phrases to decide are often used with the truth state kind of value to return either true or false. In fact, this is so useful that Inform provides two shortcuts. You may replace "To decide which truth state is" with the clearer "To **decide if**." Additionally, instead of "decide on true" and "decide on false," you can say **decide yes** and **decide no**.

Imagine we had a series of courts with varying lengths, and needed a way to check whether a particular one was regulation. Check rules would be inappropriate, since the ruling might not be directly tied to a player action. Instead we'll use a decision phrase:

```
Length of court in feet is a number variable. Width of court in feet is a
    number variable.

To decide if court is standard:
    if length of court in feet is not 78, decide no;
    if width of court in feet is not 27, decide no;
    decide yes.
```

This phrase checks each relevant attribute for an invalid value, and only if everything passes the test is the final "decide yes" reached. If later we had to amend this rule to allow for the possibility of doubles courts (36 feet wide), we could amend this definition to take that into account as it makes its decision.

We can make use of this phrase as follows, perhaps in a different named phrase or action rule:

```
if court is standard, say "All seems to be in order.";
```

Phrases with Variable Inputs

In addition to optionally providing output, phrases can also optionally take input. Deciding on the legality of a tennis court would be much more useful if the phrase could be used for multiple courts. Let's set up some infrastructure:

> A tennis court is a kind of room. Every tennis court has numbers called length and width. Court 9 is a tennis court with length 78 and width 27.

Next, we need a new phrase that lets us submit values. To do this, we leave empty spots in the name of the phrase that will be filled in by variables whenever a decision is needed. We fill in these blanks with parenthetical clauses that define a temporary variable to store those values in, and the kind of that variable. Let's look at an example:

> To decide whether a court (court length - a number) by (court width - a number) is standard:
>
> if court length is not 78, decide no;
>
> if court width is not 27, decide no;
>
> decide yes.

You could then use a phrase like the following in another rule:

> if location is a tennis court and a court length of location by width of location is standard, say "All seems to be in order.";

Here, we've named the phrase *a court ____ by ____ is standard*, and declared that both the first and second blanks should be filled by numbers. We've set up two temporary number variables, *court width* and *court length*, to hold the values passed in by the calling phrase (which is the example above might be *length of Court 9* and *width of Court 9*). Now, within our decision phrase we can make use of these temporary variables to help determine what decision to make.

Here are some other examples:

> To decide which person is the spouse of (character - a person):
> To decide which liquid level is the fullness of (item - an object) after (X - a number) swallows:
> To decide which number is the secret number of (area - a room):

Note that it's also possible for phrases that don't decide anything to take values as input. We could redefine our first "begin the match" phrase to be more flexible:

> To begin a match between (challenger - a person) and (opponent - a person) at (arena – a room):
>
> now challenger is in arena;
>
> now challenger holds tennis racquet;

> now opponent is in arena;
>
> now the audience is in arena;
>
> say "The match begins."

To summarize, then, there are four main types of named phrases, depending on whether they accept and/or produce variables as input and output:

Input	Output	Example
No	No	To begin the match:
Yes	No	To begin a match between (challenger - a person) and (opponent - a person):
No	Yes	To decide what number is sets needed to win:
Yes	Yes	To decide whether a court (width - a number) by (length - a number) is standard:

Let's create a named phrase for *Sand-dancer* to see this in action. Our phrase will select a hint for what to do next, and display it in a new report rule for smoking. The rule itself is simple, creating a temporary text variable and putting inside it the results of our new named phrase, *best course of action*. Put this in Part - Mechanics, Chapter - Smoking:

Report smoking:

let hint be best course of action;

if best course of action is not "", say "Maybe [hint]. [run paragraph on]".

Now we'll create the named phrase itself, using conditional tests to select text that best indicates what the player should try next.

To decide which text is best course of action:

if player is in truck:

decide on "you could start by getting out of this truck";

otherwise if Crumbling Concrete is unvisited:

decide on "you could start by looking around the area, seeing if maybe there's a phone or something";

otherwise if pane of cracked glass is closed:

decide on "you could break open a window to get inside that building";

otherwise if flashlight is not handled:

decide on "you could try exploring the building by feel, even though it's so dark";

otherwise if Storage Room is unvisited:

decide on "you should poke around the building more, see what else there is to find";

> otherwise if emergency lights are switched off:
>
> > decide on "you should switch on those emergency lights in the storage room so you can get a better look at things";
>
> otherwise if Open Desert is unvisited:
>
> > decide on "you should see if the open desert has anything to offer";
>
> otherwise if strength is held and emergency blanket is not handled:
>
> > decide on "you're strong enough now to bust open that mesh cage with the blanket inside";
>
> otherwise if courage is held and duct tape is not handled:
>
> > decide on "you're brave enough to reach for that duct tape in the hole in the floor now";
>
> otherwise if duct tape is not handled:
>
> > decide on "you should investigate that hole in the floor of the staging area";
>
> otherwise if luck is held and canned oranges are not handled:
>
> > decide on "you're lucky enough now to find something to eat in the Storage room";
>
> otherwise if scent is held and Control Center is unvisited:
>
> > decide on "you should try to get up that ladder above the roof";
>
> otherwise if scent is held and gas can is not handled:
>
> > decide on "you should try to sniff out that gas now";
>
> otherwise:
>
> > decide on "".

Note that since we've specified this as a phrase to decide something, we must make a decision even if we don't have anything to say. If we don't, the phrase will decide on the default value for its kind of value (here, text). You can look up that default value in the Index panel, but it's usually easier to just specify what to decide on in every possible case.

Lists

While most variables contain just a single item, Inform also allows us to store a collection. These are called **list** variables, and let authors do some powerful things. We've seen one form of list already in text substitutions: saying [the list of open windows] does just what it sounds like it should do. But you can also create your own custom lists, unlocking a more powerful set of tools for manipulating a story.

Creating List Variables

As with singleton variables, a list variable is defined as containing a specific kind of value, and every entry in the list must be of that kind.

```
let friends be a list of people;
let primes be a list of numbers;
let forgotten items be a list of things;
```

We can also define a list already containing something, by saying **the list of** followed by any description of a set of values. While *a list of* creates a blank list of the given type, *the list of* creates a potentially populated list (assuming the description following matches anything in the story world); in either case, once it's been created and assigned to a variable, both behave identically.

```
let friends be the list of visible people;
let forgotten items be the list of handled unheld things;
let territory be the list of visited rooms;
```

If you want a list to contain specific things, you can specify them one by one by surrounding your entries in curly braces:

```
let friends be {John, Ortho, LaMont};
```

Exercise 7.2

The examples above create temporary list variables; based on your knowledge of regular variables, how would you create a list variable attached to a thing? A global list variable?

Using Lists

Once you have a list, what can you do with it?

Show Contents

As we've seen, you can use a text substitution to display the contents of a list:

```
say "It's the first day at the Academy, and already you've befriended [friends].";
```

...which generates a grammatically correct description such as "John" or "John, Ortho and LaMont". You can find out whether a list has any entries by asking whether it is **empty** (zero entries) or **non-empty** (one or more entries). Since the line above wouldn't produce satisfactory results with an empty list, a more robust implementation might be:

```
say "It's the first day at the Academy, and [if friends is non-empty]already
    you've befriended [friends][otherwise]it looks like it'll be another lonely
    year[end if]."
```

Add Things

You can add entries to a list, either alone or in groups, by using an **add to** phrase:

```
add Ortho to friends;

add Ortho to friends, if absent;

add the list of visible people to friends, if absent;
```

The optional **if absent** clause prevents Ortho or anyone else from showing up in the list multiple times. Normally, it would be okay to have a list like {John, Ortho, John, Ortho, Ortho}. If the list was storing the order in which the player has recently spoken to other characters, this might be what we wanted. In the case above, though, we're treating the *friends* variable as a collection, not a log, so we add *if absent* to eliminate duplicate entries.

Adding to and Removing from Lists

- add Albert to friends
- add Albert to friends, if absent
- add Albert at entry 1 in friends{, if absent}
- remove Albert from friends
- remove Albert from friends, if present
- remove entry 1 from friends
- remove entries 1 to 3 from friends

Remove Things

You can remove entries from a list, too:

```
remove Albert from friends, if present;
remove the list of unpleasant people from friends, if present;
```

In this case, you almost always want **if present**, since without it, you might try to remove something that's not there, which Inform would complain about with a run-time error (see below). If you're absolutely sure you're removing something that's already there, you can omit the "if present."

CAUTION

Run-time problems appear not when you compile your story, like problem messages, but during play when an unexpected situation arises (like trying to remove something from a list that isn't there). Since the compiler can't know in advance what might be in the list at the time this instruction runs, there's no way it can tell in advance that the statement might pose a problem. Run-time problems are a reason that testing is a vital part of finishing your story, as we'll see in later chapters.

Find Out What's Inside

A set of conditions exist to ascertain the content of a list. You can find out whether a particular item appears in a list with an **is listed in** condition:

    if Albert is listed in friends

    if Albert is not listed in friends

You can also find out the length of a list is with **number of entries**:

    the number of entries in friends

If you want to access a particular item in a list, you can do so by specifying its position:

    let best friend be entry 1 of friends;

This would store the first item added to the list in a new single variable of the same kind the list is defined with. If instead of the first you'd like the last item added, that can be retrieved too:

    let length be the number of entries in friends;

    let new friend be entry length of friends;

Finally, you can change a particular entry with "now":

    now entry 1 of friends is Michael;

PROGRAMMER'S NOTE

Inform's lists, unlike equivalent structures in other languages, begin with entry 1, not entry 0, and entry X is the last entry if X is the length of the list. Lists are dynamically resized as they grow and shrink, although since Inform is not designed for speed, this can be a slow operation on very large lists.

More complex structures like arrays of records can be created with a different structure called a table; consult the built-in docs for more information.

Sort

Lists can be quickly sorted in alphabetical or numeric order with the **sort** command:

    sort friends;

If instead you'd like a list to be shuffled randomly, add **in random order**:

    sort friends in random order;

Also useful is **reverse**, which makes the list run backwards:

    reverse friends;

Change Size

Finally, while you normally don't have to worry about the length of a list, there are times where you'd like to explicitly set its size. You can cut off a list by using **truncate**:

    truncate friends to the first 8 entries;

    truncate friends to the last 8 entries;

...which take the first or last eight entries of the list in question, respectively. You might use this to limit a list to the top few values:

    let invitees be friends;

    sort invitees in random order;

    truncate invitees to the first 3 entries;

    say "You've decided to pick [invitees] as the other three members of
        your squad."

CAUTION Lists are a powerful tool, but they're also more dangerous, with fiddly details that are sometimes hard to get right and the capacity of breaking your story with run-time errors and unexpected results. Refer to the chapter on Lists in Inform's built-in documentation for more technical details about lists and how to use them.

Repeating Through Lists

Other than displaying and altering its contents, what can we actually do with a list? Often we create one because we'd like to effect a change in its members. To do this, we use a **repeat running through** phrase to create a **loop**. A loop is a special kind of programming structure that repeats the same instruction multiple times, usually changing the value acted on each time through.

Here's how to construct a repeat loop in Inform:

```
repeat with current window running through the list of open windows:
    now current window is closed;
```

The text between "with" and "running" becomes the name of a temporary variable, valid only within the loop—in this case, *current window*. Each entry of the list will be put into this variable, one at a time, and the interior phrase or phrases run on each one in order. Here's a repeat loop that would surround the player with his closest friends, demonstrating using a condition inside a loop:

```
repeat with character running through friends:
    if character is not in location:
        now character is in location;
        say "[The character] arrives.";
```

PROGRAMMER'S NOTE

Inform's repeat statement works on lists with "running through," but you can use it like a standard counting loop if you change this to **running from**:

```
repeat with x running from 1 to 10:
```

...is more or less equivalent to

```
for (x=1; x<=10; x++) {
```

Inform also supports while loops and has next, break, and stop commands: see the chapter on Phrases in the built-in docs for full details.

One of the surprising things about programming with Inform is how infrequently these traditional programming concepts actually need to be employed. I've found that source text heavy with loops is likely not playing to the strengths of the language; much that would be done with a loop in another programming language can be superseded here by more powerful tools, such as phrases like *if X is listed in Y* and *now every room is dark*.

Numbers and Randomness

We've mostly avoided numbers in this book so far, unusual for a program but not for a story: it's easy to write a whole novel without mentioning a single number. Inform can work with numbers when it needs to, but does it need to?

Adjectives and custom kinds of value replace some of the things we'd use numbers for in other circumstances, but numbers are still useful on occasion:

- the time of day is represented in numbers, and a common enough feature of everyday life to warrant inclusion in certain stories (although "a hazy afternoon" often does just as well as "4:52 PM")

- when numbers have a symbolic weight or dramatic significance in a story, such as a guardian who asks a certain number of questions, or a bomb with a specific number of minutes till detonation

- statistical chances, if there are certain odds that something will happen

- detailed simulation of some aspect of the physical world: perhaps weight, magic, or dramatic tension

Use numbers sparingly in your interactive stories. The legend of King Arthur does not suffer because we don't know his dexterity score or the exact date he pulled Excalibur from the stone. Before doing something with numbers, either behind the scenes or in a form visible to the player, make sure they add something of value (pun intended).

Numbers

The **number**, representing an integer, is Inform's standard numeric kind of value.

```
let age be 23;

Every train has a number called the serial number.

The degrees Fahrenheit is a number variable.
```

Inform numbers are best with small values; if you're getting up into four or five digit territory, you might need to reconsider the information you're storing, depending on which virtual machine you'll release your game to.

PROGRAMMER'S NOTE

The number is Inform's only numeric kind: there are no other formats such as float or double (although see "Kinds of Numbers" below for one way around this). If you're compiling your story to z-code, numbers are 16-bit signed integers, so they can vary from −32,768 to 32,767. Glulx uses 32-bit numbers, meaning your integers can range roughly between positive and negative two billion.

Let's add a number variable to our example game to keep track of how many cigarettes Knock has smoked, rounding out our hint system. We'll create both a global variable, to store the original number of cigarettes, and an object variable (property) to store the current number. In Part - Mechanics, Chapter - Smoking, add:

> Original cigarette count is a number variable. Original cigarette count is 6. The pack of cigarettes has a number called count. The count of pack of cigarettes is 6.

Now, we'll want a few new action rules to incorporate this number. Add:

> Check smoking when count of pack of cigarettes is 0: instead say "You're out of cigarettes."
>
> Carry out smoking: decrease count of pack of cigarettes by 1.

We should also adjust the final report rule in this section to notify the player as to how many cigarettes are left.

> Last report smoking: say "[paragraph break]And you still haven't quit smoking. [if count of pack of cigarettes is 0]That was your last cigarette, too[otherwise]You've got [count of pack of cigarettes in words] cig[s] left[end if]."

The [s] text substitution is a useful little tool which will print "s" if the last numerical text substitution is not 1, and nothing if it is, thus allowing this line to say "one cig" or "two cigs" (and so on) as appropriate.

Lastly, if Knock's trying to quit, we should move the cigarettes somewhere less accessible: maybe the glove box of his pickup. In Part - Mechanics, Chapter - Beginning the Story, change the sentence that defines the cigarettes and lighter to this:

> The player carries a lighter. A pack of cigarettes is in the glove box. The description of pack of cigarettes is "You're kind of trying to quit, but man, [if count of pack of cigarettes is at least 1]you could really go for one right now. It looks like you've only got [count of pack of cigarettes in words] left[otherwise]you're totally out[end if]."

And finally, we need to create the aforementioned glove box. In Part - Setting, Chapter - Around the Tower, Section - Middle of Nowhere, add:

> The glove box is a closed openable container. Understand "glovebox/compartment" as glove box. It is part of the pickup truck.

(The glove box isn't described to the player yet; in a later chapter we'll be reworking some descriptions so the player is able to discover the cigarettes.)

Kinds of Numbers

By itself a number doesn't say anything about a story world's reality. The number *16* has very different meanings depending on whether it's referring to a person's age, how much money he has in his wallet, or the number of light-years to his home planet. In turn, it wouldn't make sense to compare any of these 16s to each other: though all are represented with the same numeric symbol, they are fundamentally different values. 16 years is not equal to 16 feet, and it doesn't make much sense to let both sorts of values be stored in the same kind of variable.

To address this, Inform lets us create kinds of numbers called **units**. In the same way we can make *plant* a kind of thing, we can make *age* a specific kind, too:

> An age is a kind of value. 16 years old specifies an age.
>
> A dollar amount is a kind of value. $15.99 specifies a dollar amount.
>
> A distance in light-years is a kind of value. 16ly specifies a distance in
>   light-years.

The **specifies** assertion sentence tells Inform the form we want the new kind of number to appear in, both in our source text and in messages displayed to the player. As you can see, forms can include words, abbreviations, and symbols that uniquely identify a kind of number. Now we can write phrases like:

> let price be $4.50;
>
> now the age of Suzie is 12 years old;
>
> now the distance traveled is 73ly;

...and Inform will know we're referring to variables of the dollar amount, age, and distance in light-years kinds, respectively, and that other kinds of numbers are not allowed to be stored in these variables.

While the use of 16 in the specification examples above is arbitrary, the 99 for dollar amount contains useful information: it tells Inform what the maximum allowable value is for this part of the number. If we wanted to define a height, we could say:

> 5'11 specifies a height.

...and Inform would know that 5'11 plus 0'2 equals 6'1.

You can have as many unit specifications as you like, even multiple ones for an individual unit, as long as none of the formats overlap with each other. For example, we might get tired of writing "years old" and create a second specification:

> 5y specifies an age. A person has an age. The age of Suzie is 42y.

Inform will use whichever specification you define first when displaying a unit to the player, so in this case [the age of Suzie] would still display "42 years old."

Exercise 7.3

How would you define and use a kind of number representing latitude or longitude to the level of degree and minute, such as 42 16'?

Comparing Numbers

Making a condition comparing two numbers is easy. You can write the comparison out in words, or use common math symbols as shorthand instead:

Written Out	Shorthand
if answer **is less than** 42	if answer < 42
if answer **is greater than** 42	if answer > 42
if answer **is** 42	if answer = 42
if answer **is at least** 42	if answer >= 42
if answer **is at most** 42	if answer <= 42

These can then be used like any other condition within a phrase:

if answer is 42, say "We're going to get lynched, you know that?";

When doing math or comparisons with kinds of numbers, remember to use the syntax you defined when the kind was created:

if the age of Suzie is less than 42 years old

if the price is at least $2.00

One other useful thing we can do with any type of numeric value is to make definitions that compare it to others:

Every person has an age. Definition: a person is old if its age is 65 years old or more.

This not only creates an adjective called *old*, it also creates the comparison words *older* and *oldest*, which we can freely use in conditions and descriptions. We can also check whether two values are the **same**:

if Alice is older than Bob

if Alice is the same age as Bob [shorthand for "if the age of Alice is the age of Bob"]

let matriarch be the oldest visible woman;

We can even create a person with an age exactly matching the definition:

> Dorothy is an old woman.

...will make a new female person with age set to 65 years old.

Exercise 7.4

How would you create the adjectives "young," "younger," and "youngest?"

Sand-dancer's Radio

We don't have many other uses for numbers in *Sand-dancer*, but one spot they might come in handy is the emergency radio in the break room. If we only allow Knock to reach the mysterious voice after it's been set to a specific frequency, we give the player something else to do in the early part of the game.

Let's add the radio. In Chapter - Office Interior, make a new heading called Section - Radio. Add this to it:

> An emergency radio is a device in Break Room.

We need to make a new kind of value called frequency, and then give the radio some variables to keep track of what frequency it's set to, as well as the maximum and minimum allowable values.

> A frequency is a kind of value. 100.9kHz specifies a frequency. 100.9 kHz specifies a frequency. 100.9 specifies a frequency.

> The radio has a frequency called the frequency tuned to. The frequency tuned to of the radio is 77.2kHz. The radio has a frequency called the maximum frequency. The maximum frequency of the radio is 109.9kHz. The radio has a frequency called the minimum frequency. The minimum frequency of the radio is 67.0kHz.

We should describe the radio more clearly, so the player knows how to use it:

> The description of the emergency radio is "Vintage, man. A chrome switch on the side to turn it on and off, and a big fifties dial on the front. It looks like it's tuned to [the frequency tuned to of emergency radio] right now." Understand "dial/big/fifties/knob/switch" as emergency radio.

Now, we need a new action to carry out the tuning. An extremely useful aspect of kinds of value is that Inform can understand them in the player's input, too:

> Tuning is an action applying to one thing and one frequency. Understand "tune [thing] to [frequency]" as tuning.

When we understand a kind of value in this way, a new temporary variable to go along with noun and second noun is created, called *the {value} understood*; in this case, our action rules can now make use of *the frequency understood* to find out what frequency the player used in her command.

We need a few check rules to make sure a tuning command makes sense. Asking whether a thing **provides** or **does not provide** a kind of value tells us whether it's been given one by the author.

> Check tuning when the noun does not provide a frequency tuned to: instead say "You can't tune that."
>
> Check tuning when the frequency understood is less than the minimum frequency of the noun: instead say "[The noun] doesn't go any lower than [the minimum frequency of the noun]."
>
> Check tuning when the frequency understood is greater than the maximum frequency of the noun: instead say "[The noun] doesn't go any higher than [the maximum frequency of the noun]."
>
> Check tuning when the frequency understood is the frequency tuned to of the noun: instead say "[The noun] is already tuned to that frequency."
>
> Check tuning when the radio is switched off: instead say "Not much point when it's not turned on."

Finally, we carry out the action to tune the radio, and report on its results:

> Carry out tuning: now the frequency tuned to of the noun is the frequency understood.
>
> Report tuning: say "You tune [the noun] to [the frequency tuned to of the radio]."

We'll leave it to a later chapter to define what happens when the radio is properly tuned, but hopefully this gives you a taste of using numbers and comparisons in practice.

Math

Of course, the most obvious thing to do with numbers is arithmetic. Inform's language-based syntax means it's definitely not the best programming language for working with numbers, but it can do basic math just fine.

Arithmetic

You can perform basic arithmetic on numbers (and custom kinds of numbers) either written out or with the standard abbreviations:

Written Out	*Shorthand*
now age is 7 **plus** 3	now age is 7 + 3
now health is health **minus** 10	now health is health - 10
let product be 20 **multiplied by** 15	let product be 20 * 15
now answer is 100 **divided by** the divisor	now answer is 100 / the divisor

CAUTION   When using the symbols, be sure to include a space both before and after them; otherwise, Inform might think you're trying to reference a kind of value with two components.

Division rounds down to the nearest integer if necessary. If there is a remainder, you can find it with **the remainder after dividing**:

```
the remainder after dividing 100 by 7
```

Since adding and subtracting values from a variable is such a common operation, Inform offers a shorthand: **increase** and **decrease**.

```
increase age by 1; [the same as "now age is age + 1"]
decrease answer by 36;
```

Displaying Numeric Values

You can include numbers in text substitutions, and adding **in words** to the end of the substitution will spell out the number in full:

Phrase	*Output*
say "The answer is [result].";	The answer is 73.
say "The answer is [result in words].";	The answer is seventy-three.

This works with kinds of numbers, too (although since they can be complicated, Inform can't try to write these out in words).

Phrase	*Output*
say "She was [the age of Sally]."	She was 16 years old.

Rounding

We can also round numbers, either when assigning them to variables or ad hoc when displaying them in a text substitution. Just add **to the nearest** followed by the unit to round to:

```
let approximate temperature be 76 to the nearest 10;
```
```
say "The plotted route is about [distance to the nearest 5ly] long.";
```

Note that in the second case, we're not setting or changing the value of any variable; so 87ly would display as 85ly but stay set to 87ly.

Randomness

Uncertainty is a constant companion to the human experience, and though we may fear it in our own lives, we crave it in our fiction. The reason why words and phrases like "suddenly," "by surprise," and "out of nowhere" have become cliché is that unexpected encounters and unpredictable reversals are an integral part of storytelling.

Computers, though, are designed to be the opposite of all these things: certain, expected, predictable. Unlike with people, every time you ask a computer to do something you can expect it to be done in precisely the same way as last time. How, then, to inject something of the wild flavor of real experience and exciting narratives into an interactive story?

Tabletop role-playing games hit upon the solution of random number generation some forty years ago, and computer games largely followed suit (albeit with much less rolling of dice). Though not a panacea, randomness can add a bit of variety to a story, making it feel less predictable and more real.

Random Numbers

Inform offers several easy ways to use randomness. You can request a random numeric value, and either use it immediately (perhaps in a text substitution) or assign it to a number variable:

```
say "There are [a random number from 2 to 4] lights!";
```
```
let strength be a random number from 3 to 18;
```
```
let black hole disruption be a random distance in light years from 1ly to 5ly;
```

Random Chances

Using this method, we can also simulate a chance that something will happen. Say we wanted something to happen on average one out of ten times a phrase was triggered. We could write a condition like this:

```
if a random number from 1 to 10 is 1
```

However, since this is such a common request, Inform offers us a more streamlined alternative:

```
if a random chance of 1 in 10 succeeds
```

Exercise 7.5

How would you create a condition that will be true 63% of the time?

Random Things and Values

In earlier chapters, we created text substitutions that selected a random item matching a descriptive phrase. You can use this same method to assign the result to a variable:

```
let portal be a random window;
```

```
let escape destination be a random adjacent room;
```

We can choose random kinds of value, too:

```
say "Billy's milk bottle is [a random liquid level].";
```

Random Texts

In Chapter 4, we saw how to choose a random piece of text from a list:

```
say "The weather today is [one of]clear[or]partly cloudy[or]mostly cloudy[or]
    overcast[or]raining[at random]."
```

Here's a full list of all of the possible alternatives for the final condition.

Randomness Type	Effects
at random	an equal chance that any text other than the one most recently shown will be selected; this prevents the same piece of text from being shown twice in a row
then at random	like the above, but first runs through each one in order
purely at random	an equal chance that any piece of text will be selected
then purely at random	like the above, but first runs through each one in order
in random order	choose a different piece of text at random each time until all have been displayed, then shuffle into a new order and repeat
stopping	show each piece of text in order, then repeat the last one indefinitely
cycling	show each piece of text in order, then go back to the beginning and start again

Randomness Type	Effects
sticky random	the first time this is encountered, a piece of text will be selected at random; the same text will be shown every time after that
as decreasingly likely outcomes	each piece of text is slightly less likely to be selected than the one before

Randomness is a nice tool that Inform's friendly syntax makes easy to use. I like to use a lot of randomness in my descriptions to add variety and surprise to text; it's a very cheap and efficient way of making a story world feel a little bit more dynamic.

The Kinds Index and Phrasebook

I've dumped a huge amount of information on you in this chapter, so it's understandable if you're feeling a little overloaded at this point. That's all the new material for now. Before we move on, I'll introduce a few more tools in the Inform application's Index panel to help you sort through and remember all the different syntaxes and keywords available.

The Kinds Index

Click the Index panel, then the Kinds tab to open up the Kinds Index. This page gives you detailed information about all of the kinds defined in your source text, your included extensions, and the Standard Rules. Figure 7.4 shows what this looks like for *Sand-dancer*. Depending on your monitor size, you may want to click and drag the divider between the two panes to enlarge the Index panel, so you can see all the information here more easily.

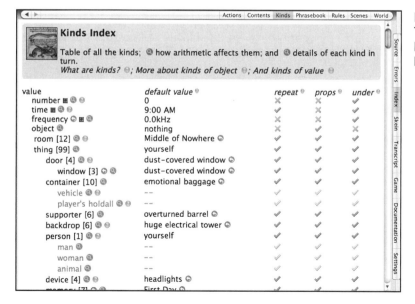

Figure 7.4
The Kinds Index of the Inform application's Index panel.

The first part of the index shows a table containing the name of each kind, links to further information, and information about what it's possible to do with that kind. The gray magnifying glass icon jumps to the details, and the blue question mark icon skips to the relevant portion of the documentation for kinds defined in the Standard Rules. For kinds you've defined yourself, an orange arrow points the way to the kind's definition in your source text.

Indented kinds are children of other kinds. The indentation levels show us that person is a kind of thing, and that woman is a kind of person. The number in brackets after the kind's name shows how many objects of that kind exist in your story world. Kinds that are defined but not actually used in your source text are grayed out.

If you create a new variable of a certain kind but do not put anything in it, Inform gives it the **default value** for that kind. The first column of the Kinds Index shows you each kind's default value.

CAUTION Generally speaking, it's best never to trust a variable to have a specific default value, but rather always give it a value explicitly before using it.

The next three columns are yes/no values that provide additional technical info for each kind. A green check in the "repeat" column means that kind can be used with a repeat loop. (Note that this is disallowed for kinds like number, where it doesn't make sense to try to go through each possible value one by one!) The "props" column shows whether a kind can have properties, and "under" shows whether you can add an understand rule to let the player refer to members of this kind in a typed command.

Below the table and its key are detailed descriptions for every kind. Reading through these is a quick introduction to some of the more advanced capabilities of Inform, some of which (like time) we'll be discussing in future chapters, and other more technical kinds we won't be making use of here.

Studying the Kinds Index is handy preparation for doing something unusual for an unfamiliar kind, to get a handle on how many objects are in your story world, and to refresh your memory on definitions.

The Phrasebook

Another tab of the Index panel, the Phrasebook, provides an index to all the phrases in your story: again, both those in the Standard Rules and the ones you've created yourself.

At the top of the Phrasebook is a list of categories, grouped first into large headings like "Control phrases," and then into more specific values like "Deciding outcomes." Click a magnifying glass to see all of the phrases related to that heading, including every alternate syntax (Figure 7.5). Click the plus icon next to a phrase to see more details of syntax and usage. Most phrases have a blue question icon that jumps you to the built-in docs for that phrase.

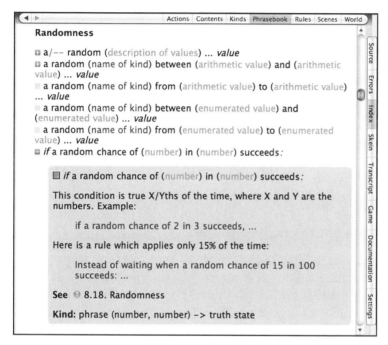

Figure 7.5
The Phrasebook of the Inform application's Index panel.

In some phrases, you'll see a slash separating two words: this indicates that either word in the list is equivalent. A slash followed by a dash means the word is optional:

Entry in Phrasebook	Examples of Usage
number of entries in/of (list of values)	number of entries in friends number of entries of friends
a/-- random (description of values)	(let portal be) a random window (let portal be) random window

Following this list of phrases is a list of words used in descriptions. This holds every adjective and kind the story understands. For instance, you can see from browsing the list that the Standard Rules define the adjectives **odd** and **even** for numbers, which lets you write a condition like "if the number of friends is even."

Next up is a list of all the relations in your story. Some of these are used internally; some, such as *holding*, whenever you write a condition like "if the player holds the piece of jade." The table also shows some details about how each relation works and what its two components ought to be.

Last is a list of verbs used in descriptions, with largely technical information you probably won't need to concern yourself with.

The phrasebook is a helpful resource if you can't remember the right way to express something. We haven't gotten to all of the concepts mentioned in here, but a quick visit through this page reveals a lot about the power and capabilities of Inform.

Expanding Sand-dancer

In the next chapter, we'll discuss time and pacing, and how to create specific scenes within your narrative. First, though, let's take some of what we learned in this chapter to create the setting for two important sequences in *Sand-dancer*: Knock's trips into the desert.

Reaching the Desert

For the purposes of our narrative, the desert is a vast blank slate, a place to be lost in. It's a boundary between the mostly realistic world of the power station environs and the mostly fantastic world of the spirit animals. This place of transition should be a little unnerving, and definitely disorienting.

We defined the Open Desert room in Chapter 5 as connected to our map in the major cardinal directions. Rather than create a series of desert rooms, we'll keep this single room and make it connected to itself on all sides. Each time the player moves, we'll vary the description, creating the illusion of a vast and trackless space. Once Knock gets to Open Desert, he shouldn't be able to backtrack: he's lost until his date with a spirit animal.

We could add the connections this way:

> The Open Desert is north of The Open Desert, northeast of The Open Desert, east of The Open Desert, southeast of The Open Desert, south of The Open Desert, southwest of The Open Desert, west of The Open Desert, and northwest of The Open Desert.

But this is fairly tiresome. Can we leverage anything we've learned in this chapter to make this more elegant?

What about using a repeat loop? Put the following in Part - Setting, Chapter - The Open Desert:

> Before going to The Open Desert when The Open Desert is unvisited:
>
> repeat with heading running through directions:
>
> change the heading exit of The Open Desert to The Open Desert.

Our repeat loop steps through every direction, placing each one in a temporary variable called *heading*, and changes the map connection accordingly. To do this, it uses the special phrase **change the {direction} exit**. Essentially, the loop runs a series of statements like the following:

> change the north exit of The Open Desert to The Open Desert;
>
> change the northeast exit of The Open Desert to The Open Desert;

...and so on.

One potential problem with this: going up or inside will also lead to the desert, which is a bit unrealistic. Let's add a definition to help distinguish between cardinal directions and special ones:

> Definition: A direction is cardinal if it is not up and it is not down and it is not outside and it is not inside.

Now, alter the "before going to the Open Desert" rule's repeat line to read as follows:

> repeat with heading running through cardinal directions:

Now, the first time the player travels to Open Desert, it will automatically be set to loop on itself in every sensible direction. This serves to illustrate that map connections are not required to line up in a grid. One way we could graphically represent this arrangement is something like Figure 7.6.

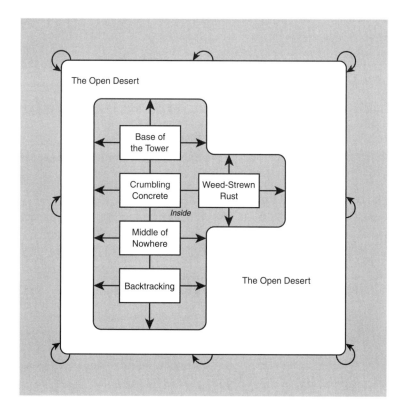

Figure 7.6
The Open Desert room surrounds the other outdoor rooms.

Remember, though, that this means Knock is stuck in Open Desert until we move him somewhere else by hand, which we won't do until the next chapter. Hope you brought some water!

We should probably add something that explains why backtracking isn't possible. Let's say that a disorienting dust storm comes up as Knock sets out.

> Report going to The Open Desert when The Open Desert is unvisited: say "You walk for a long time, thoughts turning over like the sand under your sneakers. You think about [a random thing in emotional baggage]. You think about Ocean and how pissed she's gonna be that you're not home. Like you tell her not to wait up for you but she always does anyway.
>
> Some wind kicks up and chucks sand in your face. You blink it out and kinda realize while you're doing it that you haven't really been paying attention to where you've been going. Another gust whines through the sagebrush and you realize with a kind of heavy feeling that with all the dust this wind is kicking up you can't see a damn thing. You can't see your pickup, you can't see the electrical tower. Not even your damn footprints. You're lost. Well, shit."

Describing the Desert

Now let's work on a description for the desert location. We'd like it to vary each time the player moves, to make it less obvious that we're just using a single room for this whole vast space. Let's use some inline randomness to achieve this:

> The description of Open Desert is "[one of]Clouds of dust swirl through the air[or]The dust storm rages around you[or]Your tracks are swallowed up in moments by the billowing sand[or]The desert stretches around you in all directions[in random order], and [one of]you shiver in the chill night air[or]you plod wearily through the sand[or]you wish you could see more than twenty feet in front of you[or]god damn it's dark[or]every inch of sand looks just like every other[in random order]."

This is a good start, but still gets repetitive before long, and it's lacking any specificity. Let's add a group of random scenery objects, and have one or two be around each time the player moves to a "different" Open Desert room. We'll start by creating the kind and the items.

> Desert flotsam is a kind of thing. A looming cactus is desert flotsam. A dull grey boulder is desert flotsam. A dead cow is desert flotsam. A low bluff is desert flotsam. A clutch of weeds is desert flotsam. Some dry bones are desert flotsam. Some clumps of sagebrush are desert flotsam. A dry streambed is desert flotsam. A stand of cactus is desert flotsam.

We'll give the desert flotsam kind an initial appearance that describes both itself and any other visible desert flotsam. I'll explain why this works in a minute.

> The initial appearance of desert flotsam is usually "[one of]All you can make out in the darkness [is-are a list of visible desert flotsam][or]You can sort of see [a list of visible desert flotsam][or]Nearby: [list of visible desert flotsam]. Nothing to write home about[or]Half-lost in shadows, you see [a list of visible desert flotsam] and that's about it[in random order]."

We use a couple different styles of lists to vary the feel of each descriptive line. Remember, we can use the construction *is-are* to print either "is" or "are" depending on the quantity and plurality of the contents of the list.

Writing combinatorial text like this can be tricky. For instance, you need to make sure that the static parts of your text match up with every possible substitution. What would be the problem if our description had been written like this?

> The initial appearance of desert flotsam is usually "[one of]All that's around you[or]Nearby you can see[or]Nothing much is here except[in random order] [is-are a list of visible desert flotsam]."

Close scrutiny reveals that this version could produce sentences like "Nearby you can see are a looming cactus and a clutch of weeds." Inform makes it easy to create dynamic sentences, but always keep a close eye on your construction of them to ensure they will make sense in any possible combination.

Why is only a single initial appearance sentence printed, even though each piece of desert flotsam has its own? The answer relates to Inform's complex procedures for generating room descriptions, which we'll discuss in more depth in Chapter 10. In short, Inform knows that things that are mentioned in bracketed text while printing a room description do not need to be mentioned a second time. Here, our [list of visible desert flotsam] covers everything in a single go.

Finally, we'll need a rule to move our desert flotsam around. Let's start with:

> Before going to Open Desert:
>
>> repeat with item running through visible desert flotsam:
>>
>>> now item is off-stage;
>>
>> let decorations be the list of desert flotsam;
>>
>> sort decorations in random order;
>>
>> truncate decorations to the first 2 entries;
>>
>> repeat with item running through decorations:
>>
>>> now item is in The Open Desert.

In the first two lines, we use a repeat rule to "clear the set," removing all desert flotsam from the world. Next, we create a temporary list of objects variable called *decorations* and assign to it all of the desert flotsam things we've made. Next, we put them in a random order. The next line limits the size of the list to only two entries: together, these three lines give us a list of two random desert flotsam items.

Lastly, we use a second repeat loop to cycle through our list, assigning each entry in the *decorations* list to a temporary object variable called *item* as we do, and simply move each thing in the list to the desert. Since this is a before rule, the items will appear before Inform gets around to describing the room, and it will seem as if they've always been there.

Exercise 7.6

For a less predictable experience, it might be nice for the number of desert flotsam items to vary from time to time, including a chance of having none at all. How might you simulate this with tools learned so far?

Let's compile this and take a look at how it plays out (Figure 7.7). If you want to try this yourself, you can use the ABSTRACT testing command we learned in the previous chapter to jump yourself to the desert by typing ABSTRACT ME TO OPEN DESERT. You will also need to ABSTRACT FLASHLIGHT TO ME and turn it on so you can have a look around.

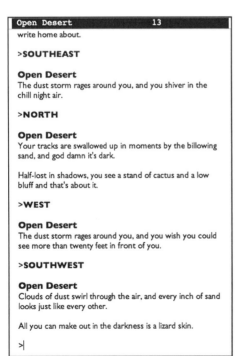

Figure 7.7
Our infinite desert in action!

Exercise 7.7

Add some more pieces of desert flotsam and some rules to defer player attempts to interact with them.

CAUTION One possible flaw with our current implementation can be seen by typing LOOK multiple times in the same desert location. Since all of the random text substitutions happen each time their text is displayed, it seems as if the description changes wildly each time, even though we haven't gone anywhere.

One solution to this is to use my extension Procedural Randomness by Aaron Reed. This lets you produce effects that are predictably random, not changing until you change the value of a seed parameter (which in this case we would do each time the player moves).

One last tweak: if the player was allowed to drop items in the desert, it would both destroy our illusion of a vast space and mean they could lose access to those objects forever, since they can't return to the desert at will. Let's forbid this:

> Instead of dropping something when location is The Open Desert: say "Sounds like a good way to lose something forever."

Though it only took a few paragraphs, this is already a passable simulation of a vast and trackless desert. Soon we'll learn how to add a dynamic sequence to this setting, which gives direction to the player's aimless wandering.

Exercise Answers

Exercise 7.1

Add descriptions referencing new door and windows. You can describe these however you like, but here's how I did it:

> The description of Crumbling Concrete is "This [building] must've been some sort of utility structure for [the huge electrical tower] to the north, now abandoned[if lit by headlights]: [a pane of cracked glass] sparkles faintly in the beam of your headlights[otherwise if lit by flashlight]: it seems dead and alone in the dusty beam of your flashlight[end if]. Tendrils of [sand] drift against [a boarded-up door] to the northeast leading inside; you could also walk around to the east or head south back to your truck."

> The description of Staging Area is "[if location is not lit by flashlight and location is not lit brightly]Faint [shafts of light] from your dimming headlights seep through the empty window frame, but you can barely make out anything of the interior[otherwise]It's obvious this place has been abandoned for years. Cold night air breathes through [holes in the roof] and everything is strewn with [sand] and [patches of mold]. [The boarded-up door] is southwest, alongside the empty window frame; other rooms lie north and east[end if]." Understand "empty/frame" as the pane of cracked glass when pane of cracked glass is open.

> The description of Base of the Tower is "Behind [the concrete building], featureless except for [a dust-covered window], [a steel girder] rises ...

> The description of Weed-strewn Rust is "Behind the rather small [building] and its [tiny frosted window] is nothing but a scraggly patch ...

> The description of Break Room is "Shadows and grime linger in dark corners of this dismal room with just one [tiny frosted window]. Some [rotting picnic tables] ...

Exercise 7.2

Create different kinds of list variables.

> The player has a list of people called friends. The friends of player are {John, Ortho, LaMont}.

> Friends is a list of people variable. Friends is {John, Ortho, LaMont}.

Exercise 7.3

Create a kind of number to represent latitude.

> A latitude is a kind of value. -42 59' specifies a latitude.

The negative sign tells Inform that it's okay for this kind of value to be negative.

Exercise 7.4

Create a set of adjectives for "young."

> Definition: a person is young if its age is 12 years old or less.

Exercise 7.5

Make a condition that is true 63% of the time.

> if a random chance of 63 in 100 succeeds

Exercise 7.6

Vary the number of desert flotsam items selected after each movement.

Replace the "truncate" line with the following two lines:

```
let density be a random number from 0 to 2;
truncate decorations to the first density entries;
```

Exercise 7.7

Extend the implementation of desert flotsam. Feel free to create whatever you like. Make sure you don't give anything a name that's a subset of an existing thing's name (like *cactus*, which conflicts with *stand of cactus*). Here's what I did:

```
A scattered patch of dying sagebrush is desert flotsam. A dead pine tree is
   desert flotsam. A weatherbeaten outcropping is desert flotsam. A lizard
   skin is desert flotsam. Instead of doing anything to desert flotsam: say
   "It's not important, man."
```

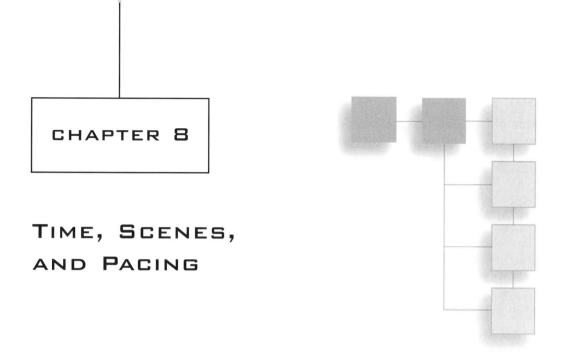

CHAPTER 8

TIME, SCENES, AND PACING

I f I handed you a random sentence from a novel and asked for your opinion, you might find it hard to answer without knowing whether it came from the beginning, middle, or end of the story. But so far in our example game, the rules and phrases we've written are timeless. They react the same way in the earliest moments of the story as they do at its conclusion.

While authors can create order and sequence through puzzles—keeping certain areas or items from the player until some task has been performed—to tell complex, interesting stories requires recognizing that not all moments are equal. To get more sophisticated with our storytelling we should learn how Inform understands time.

Inform comes with significant tools to handle chronology. It remembers whether certain things have ever been true, and how many times something has happened. It also lets us create special situations called scenes during which rules and actions behave differently from normal.

But before we learn how these tools work, let's take a step back and be sure we understand what we need them for. We'll take a whirlwind tour through traditional narrative theory, then look at how the rules of storytelling change with the complication of interactivity. As we build some of *Sand-dancer*'s dramatic scenes, we'll see how pacing, tension, and pivotal moments can contribute to an interactive fiction.

Story Structure

Most of us learned some of the basics of story structure in school. Some readers of this book may even have studied it on a more formal level. I can't begin to do justice to the topic in a few pages here, but a quick review will get the concepts fresh in our minds and help frame the techniques we'll learn in the rest of the chapter.

Structure in Traditional Narrative

People have studied stories throughout human history, and never stopped trying to categorize them, quantify them, and unlock the secrets that make them so compelling. Well over two thousand years ago, Aristotle's *Poetics* divided tragedy (the dominant storytelling form of its time) into six components: plot, characters, theme, dialogue, music, and spectacle. Shakespeare followed the Romans in breaking his plays into five-act structures, but many contemporary playwrights use three acts instead, and some screenwriters use a seven- or nine-act system to construct their scripts. Russian scholar Vladimir Propp identified thirty-one basic units of story for his 1928 book *Morphology of the Folk Tale*; in the 1940s, Joseph Campbell's *Hero with a Thousand Faces* posited a "monomyth" underlying all stories with identifiable archetypes like the wise old mentor and the princess in distress. Dramaturg Lajos Egri, in his seminal *The Art of Dramatic Writing*, maintains that every story has a premise and all the action of a story should be designed to prove that premise is true. Theorists have claimed that only a finite number of unique stories exist: forty-three, twelve, seven, five, two, or even just one (love? loss? cruelty? conflict?).

Out of all these dizzying theories of story, which are right and which are wrong? The multiplicity of analyses suggests there is no simple answer: as one of the oldest and most powerful human endeavors, storytelling is complex and not easily categorized. Even so, looking at narrative theories is a great way to get yourself thinking about what works and why in your favorite stories, and can be a useful tool to help construct the ones you want to tell.

Let's look at a few basic tropes and vocabulary common to nearly all theories of story, reviewing some useful concepts for going forward.

The Journey of the Characters

Stories are about people in motion. A character is at the heart of every story, and as the story develops, a **conflict** arises that pushes that character's life in an unexpected direction. The resulting momentum and where it leads that character form the backbone of the narrative.

A story usually has a **protagonist**, the character who undergoes the most significant change, and an **antagonist**, the character who most directly causes that change. These two roles are often taken by the hero and the villain, though not always. The protagonist of the original *Star Wars* trilogy was Luke Skywalker, while Darth Vader was the antagonist. Vader sets

Luke's journey to become a Jedi in motion by slaughtering his aunt and uncle, motivates him to train by ruthlessly pursuing the rebellion, and ultimately justifies Luke's rejection of the Dark Side by sacrificing himself to save his son's life. However, when looking at the entire six movie *Star Wars* saga, you might say that Vader is the protagonist. His character changes dramatically from pure innocence to ultimate evil to a final redemption. Vader's antagonist is the Emperor, whose actions throughout the saga cause these changes, up to and including the murderous cruelty that finally awakens the last spark of good in Anakin Skywalker.

The protagonist's journey through emotional space is usually supported by two other journeys: one through conceptual space (the plot) and another through physical space (the setting). In *The Lord of the Rings*, Frodo goes from cheerful naïveté to world-weary martyr, from inheriting a seemingly harmless magic ring to casting it into the fiery chasm from whence it came, and from Hobbiton to Mount Doom. The latter two journeys can be seen as scaffolding to support the first, and are worth discussing briefly in their own right.

The Plot

We can define the **plot** as the sequence of events the characters experience during the story: the tasks, questions, challenges, red herrings, car chases, conversations, and love scenes that make up the business of the narrative. The plot can often be surprisingly disconnected from the emotional journey of the characters: Luke's mission to save his father is not really affected by the fact that it takes place in a galaxy far, far away filled with aliens, space battles, and prissy protocol droids.

When constructing a plot, authors often work backwards from a desired moment in a character's emotional journey to set up earlier plot infrastructure that allows it to happen: this is called **plotting**. James Cameron's 1986 film *Aliens* concludes with a memorable battle between Ripley in a robotic loader and the alien Queen. To justify this scene, much earlier in the film Cameron established that the loaders are around for the colonists to do manual labor, that Ripley knows how to drive one, and that she learned because that was the only work she could get after she destroyed the Company's ship in the previous film. The sequel begins on a shot of Ripley's escape capsule drifting in deep space as a result of that destruction: we later learn that decades have past and her daughter back on Earth has grown old and died. Ripley's fight against the Queen is to protect Newt, a surrogate for her lost daughter. From the earliest frames of the film, Cameron sets up the emotional catharsis of Ripley's final battle through careful use of plotting.

A well-constructed plot takes the audience through periods of **rising action**, when the tension and stakes of a story rise and things get more exciting, and **falling action**, where the action calms down for a bit. Action rises to higher and higher peaks as the story progresses, building to a climactic encounter and the most exciting moment of the story, followed by a final period of falling action called the **denouement**.

The Setting

The plot of a story takes place in the context of its **setting**, which is one of the first things the teller must establish as the story begins. To understand the stakes of the plot, the roles and actions of the characters, and the importance of their emotional journey, the audience must know where in time, space, and genre this story is situated. Are we in the past or the future? Is the tone serious or comedic? Is this a world much like or own or wildly different, and is it one rich with detail or sparsely minimalist? What are the rewards and hazards for the characters in this setting, and what are the social structures that define or oppress their behavior?

The setting doesn't just orient the audience, it draws them in through the details that make it unique. The doomed philosophies of Rapture's failed utopia, the gritty texture of New Crobuzon's endless streets and alleyways, the strict social codes of Victorian London or Imperial China, the whimsical courses on offer at Hogwarts: all these details help pull the audience into the world of the story and make them want to spend more time there.

Show, Don't Tell

Many stories use **exposition**, a technique where the narrator or a character explains something the audience needs to know to understand details of the setting or plot. In the classic film version of *The Wizard of Oz*, Glinda appears in a iridescent soap bubble to deliver exposition about good and evil witches, the yellow brick road, and the Wizard; a more recent crowd-pleaser, *Avatar*, features an opening voice-over from its central character explaining the nature of the alien world Pandora, mankind's interest in it, and how he comes to find himself there.

Exposition can be a blunt and awkward hammer. It can insult the audience's intelligence by pointing out what they'd already understood or assumed, and often comes off as forced or trite. Often, a better solution is to remember the maxim **show, don't tell**. Rather than lecture, it's more natural to have a character, plot point, or detail of setting reveal the necessary information. In the *Lord of the Rings* movies, we don't need to be told that hobbits are a peaceful, cheerful, agrarian people: the opening shots of Gandalf arriving in Hobbiton serve nicely to convey this. In the acclaimed graphic novel *Watchmen*, newspaper headlines and television broadcasts mentioning Richard Nixon's run for a fourth term as president tell us a lot about the alternate history 1985 where the story takes place.

Structure in Interactive Stories

The desire to tell interactive stories dates back far before the computer. First performed in 1607, Francis Beaumont's *The Knight of the Burning Pestle* (Figure 8.1) opens with a heckler from the audience interrupting the Prologue to clamber up on stage and demand a story more to his liking. In the mid-twentieth century, Ayn Rand's play *Night of January 16th*, called for randomly selected audience members to fill the on-stage jury box of the story's murder trial: in the final moments, the audience jury deliberated before announcing their verdict, and the fate of the central character.

But by the late twentieth century, the desire to meaningfully participate in a story became a real possibility rather than just a dream or a stunt. With the rise of the personal computer, we now have opportunities to participate in stories every day, and construct our own interactive narratives. While participatory fiction has most of the same narrative elements as traditional fiction, the addition of audience participation adds new twists and challenges for authors.

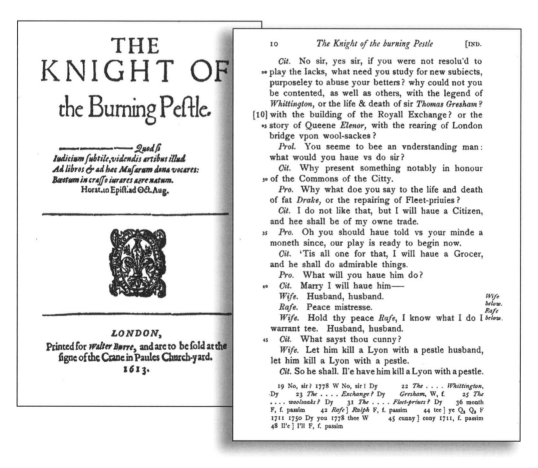

Figure 8.1 *Knight of the Burning Pestle*'s script features an early example of longing for audience interaction with story. Here, a Citizen from the audience argues with the Prologue (who traditionally summarized the upcoming story) about what the play should be about.

Since interactivity is such a recent addition to narrative, far fewer books have been written on the subject of combining them. A few recommended volumes are *Second Person*, edited by Noah Wardrip-Fruin, *Hamlet on the Holodeck* by Janet Murray, and *Cybertext* by Espen Aarseth. We mentioned this last book earlier, and borrowed from it the useful term "ergodic" (requiring non-trivial effort from the reader to continue advancing). Here are a few key points distilled from these and other volumes, serving as a brief summary of some of the chief challenges of designing ergodic narratives.

The Journey(s) of the Player

In participatory stories, the key journey is usually taken not just by the protagonist, but by the player as well. Rather than watch someone else's fall from grace or rise to glory, in a well-constructed ergodic story the players should feel these events are happening to them.

IF, with its use of the second person, present tense voice, makes the connection between player and protagonist even stronger: *you* are the one who is deciding what to do, and *you* will have to face the consequences. Making the player complicit in the emotional journey of the protagonist can be a powerful technique. In Victor Gijsbers's *Fate*, you play an expecting mother in life-threatening circumstances, and must decide for yourself how much you're willing to sacrifice your moral code to give your child a better future. Paul O'Brian's *LASH* questions the morality of the player giving commands to the player character, while my own *Whom the Telling Changed* puts the fate of the central character's people in the hands of the player's moral choices.

 Traditional narratives can use the omniscient third person voice and alternating viewpoint characters to show multiple perspectives, but interactive stories can let us become different people in the narrative, and not just see through their eyes but act through their hands. Adam Cadre's *Photopia*, one of the most acclaimed pieces of modern IF, uses this technique to great effect; *The Djinni Chronicles*, by J. D. Berry, casts the player as a series of magical servants to make a point larger than any of them about the nature of free will.

The spatial journey through the setting is also the player's in an interactive story, along with navigating the twists and turns of the plot. Riddles must actually be solved, not merely read about; enemies must be strategically defeated, not just feared. The player character's trials make the story ergodic: the player must work to navigate through them. A poor ergodic story makes this work feel unfair, meaningless, or wasted; but in a well-crafted ergodic story, it's the best part. At the end of an epic console RPG, the player feels a very real satisfaction in saving the world, having fought in the trenches through battle after battle and explored through countless dungeons and cities to attain that victory. Likewise, reaching the end of a challenging piece of interactive literature brings a sense of accomplishment more personal and deserved than merely turning to the last page a book. Like Bastian in *The Neverending Story*, we go along with our heroes in ergodic stories, sharing their pain, exalting in their joy, and finding their fates inextricably bound with our own.

While a linear story takes its hero through a predefined journey from point A to point Z, heroes of ergodic stories might take different paths. They might skip some of the points in between, arrive at them in different orders, or move through points that don't appear in other stories. They may end the story earlier or later than expected. They may spend more time and be more interested in some points at the expense of others. If each player's experience can be unique, how can an author still tell an effective story?

Back in the 1980s, working with sequences of simple black-and-white illustrations, a storyteller named Amanda Goodenough created some of the first interactive stories for young children. In the 1990 BBC documentary *Hyperland*, Goodenough justifies labeling these games as stories:

> "It's possible to combine storytelling with interactivity if you take the story apart and make sure that each thread or each branch that allows a choice is a story in itself. If you have three branches that all lead to the same ending, each one has to be an equally valid story. And that is the challenge."

Amanda grasped something the makers of many interactive stories still forget, even decades later: if the player reaches an ending of your story and feels dissatisfied, *it's your fault*. Adding agency does not remove your responsibility to tell a good story. As Amanda said, it's a challenge. But finding ways to tell interesting stories *along with* the player's choices, rather than *in spite of* or *without respecting* them, is key to writing engaging participatory fiction.

Gateways and Sandboxes

Traditional stories use rising action and falling action to control tension, but it's difficult for authors to maintain control of this pacing without removing the player's agency. An analogous structure in interactive stories is an alternation of **gateways** and **sandboxes**. A sandbox is an explorable area where the player has certain freedom in choosing what action to take next. He may explore terrain, encounter characters, solve puzzles, or fight against and enemies. Eventually, though, he'll encounter a gateway: an action or group of actions he must perform to continue. Often opening a gateway involves "using up" most of the resources in the sandbox before it: solving all the puzzles, defeating most of the enemies, exploring enough of the territory. Passing through the gateway (which might take the form of an exciting challenge) then leads to the next sandbox, and the pattern continues.

Figure 8.2 shows the rising/falling action diagram contrasted with the gateway/sandbox diagram. While similar, the two structures are not entirely analogous.

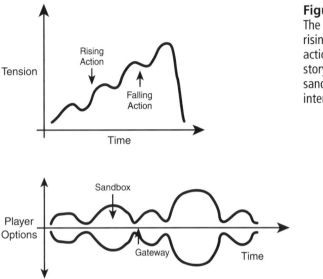

Figure 8.2
The progression of rising action/falling action in a traditional story, and gateways/sandboxes in an interactive story.

The gateway/sandbox model can stretch to accommodate a lot of different kinds of story games. Some (like *The Elder Scrolls IV: Oblivion*) are nearly all sandbox, presenting large open-ended worlds to explore with only rare moments where the player is required to do something specific to continue, while others, like (*Final Fantasy XIII*) are nearly all gateway, with many gauntlets the player must pass through in a specific order along the way. Generally, the larger your sandboxes and rarer your gateways, the more your story will be one about exploration and problem solving. Games with frequent gateways, on the other hand, are sometimes called **on rails**, meaning they're more like a theme ride at an amusement park, and they're often more about enjoying a well-crafted experience and engaging in predefined contests of skill.

Do, Don't Show

Sometimes games remove the player's agency entirely for a while, via a sequence known as a **cutscene**. Usually cutscenes are designed to advance the plot through a significant development while ensuring the player doesn't do anything to screw it up. Of course, significant moments in the plot are exactly the places a good interactive story should be letting the player participate! Video games become mere movies during cutscenes, and interactive fiction becomes, well, just fiction. Cutscenes can be the interactive story's equivalent of poor exposition: clumsy, off-putting, and not playing to the strengths of the medium.

Whereas action trumps description in traditional stories, leading to the adage "show, don't tell," letting players decide and perform a course of action themselves trumps prescribed action in interactive stories. I call this **do, don't show**. In Jeremy Freese's IF *Violet* (Figure 8.3), your failed attempts to force the protagonist to sit down and get some writing done tell you more effectively than anything else that your character is a chronic procrastinator. The portrait of the protagonist in Stephen Bond's *Rameses* emerges through his cowardly evasion or cynical shrugging off of player commands he can't imagine performing. *Photopia* features a wonderful moment where the player realizes the player character can do something unexpected; the story never tells you what it is, but when you figure it out and perform the correct action, it's a thrilling moment. Not only does "do, don't show" make for a more compelling experience, it also encourages players to think like the characters, increasing immersion in and engagement with the story.

Figure 8.3 Another piece of interactive fiction that actively engages the player in the telling of the story is Jeremy Freese's *Violet,* winner of the 2008 Interactive Fiction Competition.

Traditional stories can reveal character through careful plotting. Interactive stories can go a step further, and say things about both plot and character through mechanics. The **mechanics** of a game system are the rules the player must understand to successfully navigate it. In IF, these include the basic skills of entering commands and moving through space, but also the specific skills required by a particular story world. A powerful tool for an interactive story is to tie together the structural elements of the game mechanics with the dramatic themes of the story. In the classic Infocom title *A Mind Forever Voyaging,* you play an artificial intelligence without a physical body except in virtual reality; the limited commands available to you and the sense of being unreal and disconnected mirror the feelings of your lonely character. The controversial *1-2-3...* casts the player as a serial killer, but vastly reduces your choice of commands and ignores any attempts to run away or save your victims, forcing the player towards typing commands in the same way the character feels helpless in the face of his compulsions. In *Sand-dancer,* the player learns that by giving up memories to the spirit animals, Knock can gain the skills he needs to overcome his obstacles, representing his processing of emotional scars into the characteristics that define what sort of man he's becoming.

When playing an interactive story, the most compelling experiences are usually those you make happen yourself, not those thrust upon you unasked for. As an author, always be looking for opportunities to let your audience tell parts of the story themselves through their actions.

Structure in Inform Stories

Now that we've grounded ourselves with some basic elements of story structure, let's look at the specifics of how Inform handles beginnings, endings, and those devilish parts in between.

Interactive fiction, though a young medium, already has a certain set of established conventions for how its stories should begin and end (much as books have evolved the title page and table of contents for the early pages, and the index and snarky bio of the author for the last ones). Let's take a look at these conventions and how to make use of them in our source text.

Beginning

By convention, most IF begins with an introductory text that briefly explains the setting, introduces the player character, and establishes the player's immediate goal. Though some IF begins in situ, before the player knows what's going on, it's generally more difficult to do this effectively in IF than in traditional fiction: the player needs to know enough about the story world and the player character to feel comfortable participating.

Here are some classic IF introduction texts. The best of these immediately ground you in a story world, make clear what that world is like, and set up your place in that world and what you're supposed to be doing—or ignore this approach entirely and try to intrigue, amuse, or entice you enough to find these things out on your own.

"The picnic is going full blast, which is exactly why you've wandered away from it. It's not that you don't like your new companions; it's just that after weeks of spending each day around them, a noisy weekend cook-out isn't the way to relax. Some exploration—on your own—is an appealing thought."—*A Change in the Weather*, Andrew Plotkin

"Pig lost! Boss say that it Grunk fault. Say Grunk forget about closing gate. Maybe boss right. Grunk not remember forgetting, but maybe Grunk just forget. Boss say Grunk go find pig, bring it back. Him say, if Grunk not bring back pig, not bring back Grunk either. Grunk like working at pig farm, so now Grunk need find pig."—*Lost Pig*, Admiral Jota

"Finally, here you are. At the delcot of tondam, where doshes deave. But the doshery lutt is crenned with glauds."—*The Gostak*, Carl Muckenhoupt

"You've lived in this city all your life, but now you may be the last man left here. It's already dusk, and before the next dawn comes—well, it's not quite clear what's expected, but the whole city has fled from it. You could and should have been on that last train. You would have been on that last train but for *her*."—*Nightfall*, Eric Eve

"The sun has gone. It must be brought. You have a rock."—*For a Change*, Dan Schmidt

Inform lets us create a special rule called **when play begins** to display introductory text. This rule can also take care of any other initial setup that needs to be done before your story begins. For *Sand-dancer*, we want to jump straight into the action with the crash of Knock's pickup truck. We'll shift much of the orientation a normal introduction would provide into the room description for Middle of Nowhere, and modify it accordingly. Add this to Part - Mechanics, Chapter - Beginning the Game:

> When play begins: say "but it's too late, you're crashing, you're crashing, you crash..."

Now, adjust the description of Middle of Nowhere in Part - Setting, Chapter - Around the Tower, Section - Middle of Nowhere:

> Middle of Nowhere is a room. The description of Middle of Nowhere is "[if player is in pickup truck]You've smashed up against a [tall saguaro], which is all you can see out [the windshield] except a few feet of [desert sand], then blackness[first time]. Hell, you must have driven off the road and crashed. Ocean keeps telling you this night commute on this lonely highway's gonna kill you; maybe you should start listening[only].[otherwise]The [tire tracks] from the south stop abruptly here, but where the hell are you? [explain lighting conditions]." The windshield is part of the pickup truck.

To say explain lighting conditions: say "The [desert sand] and clumps of pale [sagebrush] are all [if lit by headlights]your dimming [headlights] pick out before barely reaching[otherwise if lit by flashlight]your flashlight picks out, other than[otherwise]you can see in the glow of[end if] [the concrete building] to the north".

 Why do we need the text substitution *explain lighting conditions*? Conditional text substitutions aren't allowed to include nested logic, which would be extremely difficult to follow without the visual cues provided by block indentation. By moving this text into its own custom text substitution, we can write a more complex phrase or set of phrases, using block indentation or other advanced tools if we wish, to precisely define our descriptive text.

As soon as *when play begins* finishes running, Inform shows the **banner**, which includes the story title, author, headline, and version. You can change the title of course, simply by adjusting the first line of source text. You can add a byline by appending it to the end of the title. Change *Sand-dancer*'s very first line to read as follows, and feel free to insert your own name if you've been customizing the story as you go along:

"Sand-dancer" by Aaron Reed and Alexei Othenin-Girard

The **headline** is a few words of text that can be used as a subtitle or indicator of the story's genre (such as "An Interactive Self-Portrait" or "A Mystery in Three Acts"). The default is "An Interactive Fiction." Let's add a touch of style to *Sand-dancer*'s, again, somewhere near the top:

The story headline is "A Desert Fable".

After showing the banner, Inform prints the name and description of the starting room exactly as if the player had typed LOOK, and then prompts the player for the first command. You can set the player's starting location by simply asserting it. Put this back in Part - Mechanics, Chapter - Beginning the Game:

The player is in the pickup truck.

Without such an assertion, the default starting location is the first room defined in the source text.

Midgame

It would seem there's not much to say about the middle of the game; or rather, that it's said by the entire rest of the book! One important tool, however, is the **every turn** rulebook, consulted after each player action. Any number of every turn rules can be created, and each will run at the end of every turn.

Every turn rules can be used to make aspects of a world seem active, and not just reactive to the player: machinery that continues to operate, weather that changes and progresses, and even characters taking their own actions from turn to turn (which we'll talk about more in the next chapter).

With every turn rules in our toolbox, we can finally finish one of the systems in *Sand-dancer* we started in Chapter 3. Recall that we created a new relation, suggestion, to link memories to specific items in the story world that trigger them. Whenever the player finds a new linked item, we want the related memory to be mentioned and then trapped in Knock's emotional baggage. Linked items might become visible as a result of any number of player actions (moving, opening a container, being given something) so no single action rulebook could do the trick. An every turn rule is ideal for this situation.

Let's first make a new definition in Part - Mechanics, Chapter - Memories:

> Definition: a thing is charged if it suggests a memory which is not in emotional baggage.

We also want to tweak our definition of the suggestion relation to make it easier to refer to things related by it. Change the definition to look like the following:

> Suggestion relates various things to one memory (called the suggested memory).

Now we can ask for *the suggested memory of* something, and Inform knows we mean the one memory it's linked to through the suggestion relation. If there isn't anything linked through that relation (such as if we asked for *the suggested memory of the player*), the answer is **nothing**, which is a special value we can use in conditions to make sure we have a legitimate result.

Now that our infrastructure is in place, we can write our every turn rule.

> Every turn when a charged thing (called the item) is visible: move the suggested memory of the item to emotional baggage; say "Something about [the item] makes you want to brood about [suggested memory of item]."

Similarly, we can make an every turn rule that points out the importance of items related to plans. We created our two plans, *staying the night* and *fixing the truck*, and the "requirement" relation to link them to the items necessary to carry them out. First, let's skip down to Chapter - Plans, and modify our relation, again to add a helpful identifier:

> Requirement relates one plan (called the objective) to various things.

Now we'll make a property that tracks whether we've noticed one of these useful items yet, and if not, hint to the player that it might be important. We'll use an every turn rule to check the noun of the player's current action, so that any attempt to interact with a key item, successful or not, triggers the hint message.

> A thing can be noted as useful. Every turn when noun is a thing and noun is required by a plan and noun is not noted as useful: note noun as useful.
>
> To note (item - a thing) as useful: now item is noted as useful; say "Hey, that [item] might be useful if you decide on [objective of item]."

We need to add *when noun is a thing* to our every turn rule so Inform doesn't try to use relations with nouns that don't support them, like compass directions.

Ending

Good stories must end. Without resolution, it's hard to judge the meaning of a character's emotional journey, or understand the author's intent in taking us on it. This partly explains why the story component of most online multiplayer games, which are usually designed to offer an infinite play experience, is often ignored by players, if it's even present at all.

The earliest adventure games tended to end in one of two ways: victory or death, with the latter much more common. Inform no longer assumes your story will end so operatically: instead, the phrase **end the story** simply prints a special message called the **obituary** (by default, the text "The End") and brings the action to a halt. You can define a different obituary by adding **saying** and some text, such as *end the story saying "So it goes."*

Obituaries should be no longer than a few words. A longer piece of text can and should be displayed before invoking a game-ending phrase, to tell the player what triggered the story's conclusion.

In fiction, death is not always permanent; and in interactive fiction, not always final. Before the obituary is displayed, one last rulebook is checked: **when play ends**. Any when play ends rules you create can decide the story isn't over after all by calling the phrase **resume the story**, perhaps only if a particular condition is true. Usefully, you can declare some endings more conclusive than others by adding the word **finally** to a story-ending phrase, as in *end the story finally* or *end the story finally saying "The nightmare is over."* This produces no effect by itself, but in a when play ends rule you might check whether *the story has ended finally* and do something differently if it has.

Sometimes you'd like to have the player give a yes or no answer in response to some question. To do so, you can use the special condition **if the player consents**, which is true if the player types Y or YES and false for N or NO. The player may not type any other commands until they answer the question.

Exercise 8.1

How might you add a feature to the end of *Sand-dancer* that asks whether the player is satisfied with the ending, and if not, restores the story to an earlier state for replaying? (Assume that moving the player to the "Roof" location is all that needs to be done to restore the story to the earlier state.)

Sand-dancer's design document calls for three endings (Figure 8.4), based on whether Knock barters with his final spirit animal for honor, spirit, or freedom. We haven't written the story's climax yet, but let's say that after Knock trades with Sand-dancer for the chosen talent, the lizard vanishes, and the game ends when the player makes his first movement back towards ground level. In all of our endings, we'll further personalize them by referencing the player's other two chosen talents.

Figure 8.4
A flow chart of *Sand-dancer*'s basic story structure.

Let's write the most disturbing ending first, where the player takes Sand-dancer's danger-ous bargain and tries to change the rules of fate. Add this to a new chapter heading in Part - Mechanics called Chapter - Ending the Story:

> Instead of going when player holds freedom: say "You go, with a strange, kinda tingly feeling in the backs of your hands and inside your eyes. You feel powerful[if player holds strength], stronger than wind now[otherwise if player holds courage], braver than the sun now[end if] and free, most of all free. You walk backwards across the sand to your truck, sucking up your footprints as you go, and slip behind the wheel. There's this crazy wrenching bang and you jerk backwards as the engine starts, uncrashing your pickup off the cactus and juddering back onto the highway, and you smile. You're going back, back to a second chance, back to make it all right.

> You speed up, drive backwards at a thousand miles an hour to work, and unclean bathrooms and repack inventory in a flash, faster and faster. The days rewind like videotape, unwork, unsleep, giving back kisses from Ocean one by one[if player holds scent], and the smell of the past unfurling is like wine and ozone[end if]. And then it's that night, the night you made the Big Mistake[if player holds luck] before your luck started turning around, yeah, cause[otherwise], but[end if] this time you make it backwards, and the moment unpasses and your future is safe and uncomplicated, no kid, no nightmares, no arguments, no lectures, and you just have to get this thing out of reverse now and do it right this time (or mebbe not at all, it's too hot anyway ya know babe?) and this time you'll make everything perfecto.

> But you don't turn around. You try, but it's kinda like trying to stop falling, and you suddenly get that you [italic type]are[roman type] falling, plummeting back faster and faster like you got pushed off the cliff of now. You're unmeeting Ocean and unditching school and unsmoking for the first time behind the dumpsters, faster and faster, stomach in your throat, memories blowing back your hair as they rocket past. You're a kid again unskateboarding and unlearning video game combos, screaming backwards faster and faster and you get it now, you get the lizard's joke. He's making you free by unmaking you, fixing the burden by erasing the guy who's bearing it, and you're unlearning to read and unlearning to walk and uncrawling and uncrying and then some brilliant moment of light and noise and chaos comes shrieking towards you hella fast, fast, faster than anything and it's too late, you're crashing, you're crashing, you crash..."; end the story.

Now, we'll make the ending where the player chooses honor, fixing Knock's truck and returning to his pregnant girlfriend with a new commitment to stick by her.

> Instead of going when player holds honor: say "You go, and when you get back outside the clouds are gone and the stars are so bright you squint. You patch the fuel line and refill the tank and she starts like a beauty, and then you're back on the highway again, headed for Ocean, [if player holds luck]and you've never felt luckier[otherwise if player holds scent]and the urge to breathe the same air as her leads you on like a bloodhound[end if].

> You shut off the headlights as you pull up to the trailer, and climb in through her window for old times sake[if player holds courage], crazy courage her sister at least appreciated if not her old man[otherwise if player holds strength] even though you think you're finally strong enough to take her old man[end if]. She's awake of course, always no matter how quiet you are, and she holds out a hand from somewhere under the blankets. And as she's doing it you're suddenly exhausted, beyond exhausted but also safe, warm even before you slip under the covers. She half turns to kiss you as you fumble with the blankets but you're so tired all you can do is push your face against her neck and slip an arm around her warm skin, and she starts to ask you something but it's too late, you're crashing, you're crashing, you crash..."; end the story.

The last ending is spirit, where Knock decides on the life of a wanderer, tied to no one.

> Instead of going when player holds spirit: say "You go, and the night collapses in on you so hard you barely remember curling up in a corner with the blanket[if player holds courage], not afraid any more[otherwise if player holds strength], strong enough now to wait out the night[end if].

> In the morning some highway patrol dude shakes you awake with a lecture and a ride back to town. Oro Oeste? he asks but you tell him no, take a left instead, and you end up on a street corner in Pobre Vista and keep going. Seven Sticks and then Gallup and then Flagstaff, hitching west. The cash in your wallet runs out but a trucker buys you a value meal and [if player holds luck]with a little more luck you keep from being hungry[otherwise if player holds scent]you seem to have a knack for sniffing out enough to stay fed[end if] and your blanket keeps you warm and you keep going.

> When you hit the Pacific you roll up your jeans and wade into the surf for the first time in your life. And it's warm on the top and cool underneath and this is all you want, this moment, this here and now. You'll find work and you'll find love but you'll never find home and that's okay. It's okay. You wade deeper and the waves lap higher and then a big one rolls in, blue and white, and you feel [if player holds strength] strong, strong[otherwise]crazy brave[end if] as it crests and smashes into you with the force of all the water in the world, and you laugh and try to stay on your feet but it's too late, you're crashing, you're crashing, you crash..."; end the story.

After the final text and the obituary, Inform politely asks whether it should start over, restore a saved position, or quit. This is the universally recognized sign that the story is well and truly over, although some authors have been known to tamper even with this (the surreal *Shrapnel* makes involuntarily restarting the story part of its reality-bending narrative).

How Inform Sees Time

Inform tracks a great deal about the history of the story world and the passage of time within it. Learning to properly access and utilize that history is a key part of creating strongly plotted stories.

Turns

As we've seen, the flow of time in IF takes the form of call and response. The computer displays some text, then waits for a command from the player. One such iteration through this pattern is called a **turn**, and the turn is thus the atomic unit of time in Inform. (We've referenced turns already in the every turn rules and the built-in *turn count* variable.)

In nearly all interactive fiction, no measureable time passes while the story waits for input from the player; the story does not know or care whether it took the player half a second or a thousand years to submit the next command. The turn is all that matters.

Inform comes with a second mechanism for tracking time, a built-in simulation of a standard twenty-four hour clock. Every move the player makes advances this clock by one minute. Perhaps surprisingly, though, it's a rare story that actually needs to make use of this precision. While the ticking bomb can be a powerful plot mechanism in a linear story, interactivity muddles the picture: what happens if the player gets delayed on the way to defuse it? Meetings with shadowy contacts at particular times of day sound intriguing, but if players get interested in something else and miss the rendezvous, what then? Are you prepared to describe your story world differently at 4:30 PM than at 11:30 PM, or 6:30 AM?

Keeping track of a clock can be useful in some sorts of stories (and is discussed at length in the Inform documentation) but also stirs up a host of problems: make sure you actually need it before you bring it in. The preternatural night of *Sand-dancer*'s desert, for instance, has no use for the measured precision of clocks.

Remembering Past Events

Most of the verbs we've used in assertion sentences and conditions have been in the present tense, like *is*. Inform also understands three forms of past tense, which let us access a story's historical record. Using these past tenses, we can write elegant phrases that often eliminate the need for our own bookkeeping to track the player's interactions.

Past tense conditions always refer to the state of the world at the very beginning of a turn, after the player has entered a command but before the story has begun to process it. This positioning is deliberate and often useful, as we'll see below.

Present Perfect

Most broadly, we can check if something **has been** or **has not been** in a given state on any turn from the beginning of the game until the present moment.

> if emergency lights have been switched on
>
> if player has been holding duct tape
>
> if Sand-dancer has not been visible

If it helps, try thinking of these phrases in slightly longer formats: "has ever been" or "has never been". The last condition above will be true as long as the player has never seen Sand-dancer, and false indefinitely ever afterwards. The middle condition tests whether the player "has ever been" holding the duct tape, even if only for a single turn.

One use of the present perfect is to make actions behave differently after the player has learned a certain piece of knowledge. For instance, if we wanted the player to catch a glimpse of Sand-dancer earlier in the game, we could write a rule like this:

> Instead of going to Open Desert when Sand-dancer has been visible: say
> "Now that you know there's some huge-ass lizard out there? No way, man."

Past Tense

The simple past tense, invoked with **was** or **was not**, is concerned with whether or not a condition was true at the start of the current turn. It doesn't have a long term memory: it just remembers the state of the world as it was moments ago when the player typed the most recent command.

This is most useful when we'd like to report on the results of an action in a way that ties into the way it's changed the world. In *Sand-dancer*, let's have the radio's report rule differ based on whether the frequency we just tuned it away from had signal or not. In Part - Setting, Chapter - Office Interior, Section - Radio, replace the current carry out and report rules for tuning with the following lines:

> The emergency frequency is a frequency variable. The emergency frequency is
> 102.3kHz.

> Carry out tuning: now the frequency tuned to of the noun is the frequency
> understood.

> Report tuning: say "You tune [the radio] to [the frequency tuned to of the
> radio][if the frequency tuned to of the radio is the emergency frequency], and
> the static resolves into a clear signal[otherwise if the frequency tuned to of
> the radio was the emergency frequency], and the voice dissolves into
> static[end if]."

The second condition in the report rule checks whether the frequency *was* the one with the voice at the beginning of the turn, before the carry out rule ran and changed it. On the next turn, though, checking this same condition would now produce a result based on the frequency at the beginning of the new most recent turn.

Past Perfect

Finally, we can use the past perfect tense to ask if a condition **had been** or **had not been** true at the start of the current turn. We can think of this as working like the present perfect "has been" but excluding the current moment from consideration, in the same way the past "was" ignores the current moment, too. The past perfect checks whether something had been true at any point from the beginning of the game until the end of the previous turn, regardless of whether it's true or not at present. (Figure 8.5 demonstrates all three forms of the past tense.)

```
if the player had been holding the wallet

if the emergency lights had not been switched on
```

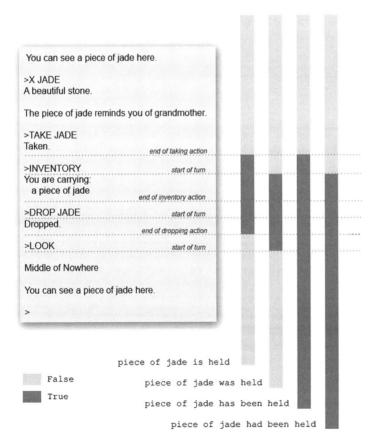

Figure 8.5
Demonstration of the time spans covered by is, was, has been, and had been.

Again, it might be helpful to think of these conditions a little more expanded out, as "had ever been, ignoring the present" and "had never been, ignoring the present." The second condition above is checking whether the emergency lights had been consistently off throughout the game, regardless of whether they were turned on during the present turn. We might use the past perfect to make something happen one time only, after some important event takes place.

> Every turn when emergency lights are switched on and emergency lights had
>   not been switched on: say "As your eyes adjust to the brightness, you notice
>   how shabby this place is."

This isn't obviously useful for *Sand-dancer* (we could just incorporate this message into the report switching on rule), but this method could be handy were there other ways the emergency lights could come on (another character activating them, or a mysterious power surge).

CAUTION Most variables may not be used with past tense conditions, since the value of the variable (and thus the history being referenced) might have changed over time. Specifically, temporary variables, and action variables like *noun* and *second noun*, are never allowed. Inform makes an exception for global variables like *the player*, in which case it tracks the history of the variable itself, separately from the different things that have been stored in it: this can lead to confusing results without careful consideration. Whenever possible, it's best to use the past tense with specific objects, not variables.

Repetition

In addition to conditional information about the history of the story world, Inform also keeps track of numerical histories: during how many consecutive turns a condition has been true. You can add the words **for X turns** to the end of a condition to check this:

> if flashlight is held for three turns

> if flashlight is held for at least three turns

In the former case, the condition will be true only on the third consecutive turn the object is held and not on the fourth; in the latter, it will be true on the third and every subsequent turn that the flashlight continues to be held.

We can track history in action rulebooks, too:

> Report going for ten turns: say "You're starting to get tired."

> Instead of waiting for at least five turns: say "You're too bored to wait
>   any longer."

Similarly, we can also keep track of how many **times** a thing has been true. A condition has been true one time after it's been true for any number of consecutive turns; for it to be true two times, it must be false for at least one turn before becoming true again.

> if the One Ring is worn for the seventh time, end the story saying "You have fallen into shadow.";

This means the player character can put on the ring, wear it as long as he likes, and take it off on a total of six occasions before this condition would be true. Again, we can add "at least" to make the condition true on the eighth and ninth times (and so on) as well. Conversely, we can have something be true only until a certain number of times with **less than**:

> Report wearing the One Ring for less than seven times: say "The burden grows heavier."

> Report wearing the One Ring for at least the fifth time: say "Soon, you will no longer be able to bear it!"

Exercise 8.2

How would you write rules to prevent Knock from smoking twice in a row, or to respond differently after smoking (or attempting to smoke) more than three times?

Remembering Past and Present Actions

Sometimes it's helpful for a rule outside of an action rulebook to know what the most recent action is. This is kept during a turn in a global variable called *the current action*.

> if the current action is switching on the flashlight

> if the current action is switching on something

> if the current action is doing something to the flashlight

As shorthand, you can instead say just **we are**:

> if we are switching on something

The current action is a held in a variable of kind **stored action**, and as with any other kind we can make new stored actions, and set, change, and retrieve their values:

> let the funniest attempt be a stored action;

> now the funniest attempt is the current action;

> now the funniest attempt is the action of chopping the mightiest tree with the herring;

We can also find out whether an action has ever successfully taken place, by asking if **we have** done it:

> if we have opened the boarded-up door

> if we have gone north

Note that while checking whether "we are" doing something will be true even on turns when the action failed, "we have" done something will not be true for unsuccessful actions, since the attempted action did not actually occur. This distinction is important since "instead" rules and other circumstances might interrupt the normal flow of an action, causing it be recorded by Inform as unsuccessful regardless of whether your rule had a positive or negative result for the player.

When we learned about action rulebooks in Chapter 5, we learned about two phrases that override the normal behavior of rulebook processing: *stop the action*, which immediately causes action processing to come to a halt, consulting no further applicable rules or rulebooks, and *continue the action*, which will continue even for a type of rule that would normally end the sequence (such as an instead rule). Two other phrases that are useful to more finely control the behavior of action rules are **rule succeeds** and **rule fails**. Both of these act like *stop the action*, except they explicitly record that action as having either succeeded or failed for the story's historical record.

These phrases are useful because sometimes the easiest way to implement a successful but unusual action is through an instead rule, which (since it defaults to failure) will not make an entry in the story's historical record that the action has succeeded. For instance, if you checked the condition *if we have thrown anything at a window* after the player had gotten inside the building, it would be false: the instead rule we wrote to handle the special case of breaking windows does not convey that the action succeeded. We could add *rule succeeds* as the last phrase of our instead throwing rule if we needed to use a condition like this elsewhere in our source text.

While you can use vague present tense action conditions like *we are opening something*, you cannot do the same with past tense action conditions like *we have opened something* or *we have done something to the door*; past tense checks on actions must involve both a specific action and a specific noun.

Future Events

In addition to Inform's wizardly ability to retrieve information about the past, it can also send information into the future, at least to a limited extent. In our source text, we can create a special kind of phrase that executes not at the time it's called, but a certain number of turns later. This is sort of like setting an oven timer: the story can go ahead and continue with its business, forgetting about the timer until it goes off and the phrase is triggered.

To achieve this effect, we need to do two things. To create the phrase that will run when the timer goes off, we begin with the words **at the time when**, followed by the name we want to give to our phrase. Then, when we want to set the timer, we invoke this phrase adding the words **in X turns from now** to the end of its name, where X is the number of turns we want to delay the execution by.

> Instead of complaining for the third time: say "The waiter apologizes profusely and promises your food will appear shortly."; the food is delivered in 35 turns from now.
>
> At the time when the food is delivered: move lobster fettuccine to table; say "Your food finally arrives!"

CAUTION Though occasionally useful, this technique can sometimes be a bit of a gamble. There's no way to cancel execution of a timer in progress, so you must be absolutely sure the delayed action will still be relevant when it finally occurs. (In the example above, what if the player got bored and left the restaurant in the meantime?) In addition, the passage of time might alter any variables in your "at the time when" phrase (especially ephemeral ones like *noun* or *location*) to be different than you expect them to be. Use this technique with care.

Scenes

While some stories are set in a single place over a continuous span of time, more often stories shift between several places and times as they progress. Especially in film, these transitions are often instantaneous: moments where the set, props, or other details abruptly change as the next part of the story begins. Inform lets us create such moments by making a new **scene**.

Scenes can also be used to create situations where the normal rules established by the story world temporarily change. In *Jurassic Park*, moments when the characters are hiding from the predatory dinosaurs have different rules than other moments: speaking, for example, would be disastrous. The students in *Harry Potter* can wander freely through Hogwarts during the day, but face consequences if they do so at night. In *Neuromancer*, what's possible while a character is jacked in to cyberspace changes drastically from what's possible in the real life of the Sprawl. This notion of chronological portions of a story that begin and end at certain moments and have different rules in between can be simulated with scenes.

Both uses of scenes—to alter the story world in particular ways when a certain triggering condition is met, or to establish an altered set of rules for a specific time—help create a stronger sense of forward momentum in a story.

Creating a Scene

Creating a scene is simpler in Inform than in real life (where it generally requires something like a stressful day and a rude waiter). Simply assert a scene and give it an optional description property, which as shorthand can be just the quoted text immediately following the scene definition. Let's add our first scene to *Sand-dancer*, the storm that happens between the visit with the first spirit animal and the second. Make a new part heading called Part - Scenes, and a new subheading within called Chapter - Rainstorm.

> Rainstorm is a scene. "Rain starts to come down, pattering on the desert sand. Soon it's gonna be a muddy deathtrap out here."

CAUTION Take care when naming scenes. The most obvious names often mention items, rooms, or characters appearing in your story, which can confuse Inform as to whether you're talking about the object *steak* in the room *Dining Room*, or the scene *Steak in the Dining Room*. I try to give scenes short, unique names that don't conflict with anything else in my source text: *Dinner Incident* or *Suppertime* might be better names for the above scene. Since players won't ever see scene names, you can make them goofy or self-referential if you want: you might call this one *Medium Rare* or *Where's the Beef*.

The scene now exists, but without further instruction, it will never actually happen. We need to give Inform a condition that, when true at the end of a turn, causes this scene to start. We do this with the special word **begins**. The rainstorm should get going as the player returns from the desert after the meeting with the rabbit.

> Rainstorm begins when Rabbit's Offer ends.

Other than displaying its description (if one is provided), by default nothing happens when a scene begins. We can change this by defining a **when X begins** rule for the scene, declaring within what should happen at the moment the scene begins. Let's make a scenery object to represent the rain and move it into place when the storm begins.

> The rain is a backdrop. "Rain batters down on the desert."

> When Rainstorm begins: now the rain is in Around the Tower.

We can also define a condition under which a scene ends, and what happens when it does. The storm should end shortly after the player has used the rabbit's talent to gain the first significant item; the rain itself should go away along with the storm. Remember, beginning and ending conditions for scenes are checked at the end of every turn, after all actions have been processed and all every turn rules have run.

> Rainstorm ends when at least one thing required by a plan has been carried and Control Center is visited and location is not Roof and a random chance of 1 in 4 succeeds.
>
> When Rainstorm ends: now the rain is off-stage; say "The rain's dying down, the sounds of the storm fading, water sinking into the thirsty sand leaving only the smell of sage behind."

We can use the keyword **during** and the name of a scene at the end of any rule to make it apply only while that scene is happening—that is, after it's begun but before it's ended. The gameplay purpose of the rainstorm is to keep Knock from returning to the desert before the Coyote is ready for him. Let's add this, as well as some other rules, to add flavor to this sequence.

> Instead of going to The Open Desert during Rainstorm: say "That's not the best idea in a storm like this."
>
> Instead of listening during Rainstorm: say "You can't hear anything at all above the pounding noise of water slapping sand."
>
> Report going from Crumbling Concrete to Staging Area during Rainstorm: say "Gratefully, you slip inside the building, out of the storm."

You can find out if a scene is underway by using the words **is happening**, which means a scene has begun but not ended:

> if Rainstorm is happening
>
> if Rainstorm is not happening

You can also find out if a scene has ever begun with **has happened**, and whether a scene has ever finished with **has ended**:

> if Rainstorm has happened
>
> if Rainstorm has not ended

Normally, a scene will only run once: after it begins, any subsequent turns when its starting condition is true produce no effect. However, we can also create **recurring** scenes, which can happen again and again whenever they're not happening and the starting condition is true. Make a new heading called Chapter - Pursuit and start out with this:

> Pursuit is a recurring scene.

We'll go back and fill out this scene in a moment. Let's also create the Rabbit's Offer scene we mentioned, so our source text will continue to compile. In a new heading called Chapter - Rabbit's Offer, add:

> Rabbit's Offer is a scene.

Variant Scene Endings

As soon as the final scene of *Hamlet* begins, anyone familiar with the story knows how it will end. In interactive stories, the outcome can be less certain. One key feature of Inform scenes is that we can define different ways they can end. We do this by adding a few words to the end of the scene's ending condition that distinguish it from other endings:

> Countdown ends with a bang when the timer of the atom bomb is o.
>
> Countdown ends victoriously when the atom bomb is switched off.

We can then later check how a scene ended:

> if Countdown ended victoriously

Scene Variables and Properties

One last note on scenes: like variables of any other kind, they can have their own variables and properties, meaning you can write rules applying to whole groups of scenes at once. For example, your game might include dramatic scenes that preclude a lot of dawdling actions like examining. Let's create this for *Sand-dancer* with the following: put this under Part - Scenes, before any of the individual chapters begin:

> A scene can be dramatic. Instead of smoking during a dramatic scene: say "This isn't really the best time for that, man."

The "Rabbit's Offer" scene we created earlier should be marked as dramatic. Now we can look through our source text for any actions that seem inappropriate during exciting events, and as long as we remember to declare all appropriate scenes as dramatic, we can keep the player from doing things at inappropriate times.

Exercise 8.3

How would you make a scene that makes Knock crave a cigarette after he's smoked more than a certain amount?

Pursuit: Tracking the Rabbit

Let's set up a more complicated scene and some associated rules, this time for luring the player to the rabbit's burrow. This sequence should begin once the player has finished the initial exploration of the area and turned on the lights. We'll create a darting shadow leading off into the open desert, and see if we can get the player to follow it. Since the player can choose not to take the bait and wander off in a different direction, we make the scene recurring, so it can start up again later on to give the player another chance. In Chapter - Pursuit, add:

> The darting shadow is a thing.

We don't include a description for the scene here: we need to do some set up when the scene begins that affects how it's described to the player, so we'll do that by hand in a moment.

First, we need to say what triggers this scene. Scenes often function as a gateway, requiring a set of earlier tasks to be complete before they begin: and this is indeed how we're using *Pursuit*. Because of this, the triggering condition can sometimes be quite complicated. Two techniques to help minimize confusion in this case are to use optional indentation, and to separate parts of the condition into their own definitions. We use both techniques here:

> Pursuit begins when
>   player holds flashlight and
>   emergency lights are switched on and
>   the shadow appears.
>
>
> To decide whether the shadow appears:
>   if location is The Open Desert for at least six turns, decide on whether or not
>   a random chance of 1 in 4 succeeds;
>   if location is Roof, decide no;
>   if location is in Around the Tower, decide on whether or not a random chance
>   of 1 in 3 succeeds;
>   decide no.

To satisfy our story conditions, we need a number of things to be true before the player is allowed to visit the rabbit. The player should have a light source, and have switched on the emergency lights (meaning the building is explored). But also, we're very particular about which rooms the player can be in when this scene begins and how likely it is to do so in various cases, so we put all the logic for this within the simple phrase deciding whether *the shadow appears*. The scene can happen in either the desert or any room in the Around the Tower region except Roof, and it's less likely once the player gets to the desert, providing an opportunity to feel lost briefly before the story continues.

When this scene begins, we want the shadow to appear and tempt the player. More specifically, we're trying to get the player to move towards the desert. From the desert itself, of course, any direction will do; when near the tower, west does the trick from any room except Weed-strewn Rust. Once we've settled on a direction, we want the shadow to remember that direction as long as the player does, which sounds like a great place to use a variable.

> Understand "movement/moving/something" as darting shadow. The darting shadow has a direction called the path.

> The initial appearance of darting shadow is "[one of]Hey, there it is again[or]Yeah, you're sure you saw it[or]It's gone now... no, wait[in random order]-- [one of]something's moving[or]movement[or]a darting shadow[in random order], to the [path of darting shadow]."

The player shouldn't be able to do anything to the shadow like taking it or even really getting a closer look at it:

> Instead of doing anything to the darting shadow, say "Hey, you're not even sure you saw it."

Now, let's define what happens when our scene begins.

> When Pursuit begins:
>
> > let desert connection be an object;
> >
> > if location is The Open Desert:
> >
> > > now desert connection is a random cardinal direction;
> >
> > otherwise if location is Weed-strewn Rust:
> >
> > > now desert connection is east;
> >
> > otherwise:
> >
> > > now desert connection is west;
> >
> > now path of darting shadow is desert connection;
> >
> > move darting shadow to location;
> >
> > if darting shadow is visible, say "[one of]Out of the corner of your eye you spot a glimpse of something moving in the darkness, off in the desert to the [path of darting shadow][or]You see that weird movement again, out in the shadows to the [path of darting shadow][stopping]."

Let's say that the player has to pursue the shadow three times before it leads him to the rabbit. We'll use another variable to keep track of how many times it's been followed.

> The darting shadow has a number called times followed. The times followed of darting shadow is 0.

Now, we'll increase this number each time the player moves in the direction we've stored in the shadow's *path* variable. If the player moves in a different direction, though, we'll reset the counter, making the trail go cold and the quarry disappear.

> Before going during Pursuit:
>
>> if noun is path of darting shadow:
>>
>>> increase the times followed of darting shadow by 1;
>>
>> otherwise:
>>
>>> now times followed of darting shadow is 0;
>>>
>>> now darting shadow is off-stage;
>>>
>>> say "You lose sight of whatever it was."

To make the pursuit seem more unpredictable, we should vary the direction the shadow is seen in after each time it's been followed, and also show some text acknowledging the player's pursuit:

> Carry out going path of darting shadow when darting shadow is visible during Pursuit:
>
>> say "[if times followed of darting shadow is 1]You head off in the direction of the movement, scanning with your flashlight over the skittering shadows.[otherwise if times followed of darting shadow is 2]You chase after the shadow, faster and faster, breath misting in the cold air.[otherwise]Some crazy thrill comes over you. You feel like a hunter. You can almost smell the thing you're chasing in the air. You [italic type]can[roman type] smell it, sweaty fur and terror. You race after it.[end if]";
>>
>> now path of darting shadow is a random cardinal direction.

Finally, if the player has successfully followed the darting shadow four times, we want to do something much different. Instead of the results of a regular going action, we move the player to a new location and explain what's happened:

> Instead of going path of darting shadow when times followed of darting shadow is at least 4 and darting shadow is visible:
>
>> say "Dodging after the fleeing, skittering shadow, you're almost caught up to it when your foot trips on a rock and you stumble to the ground. But the ground doesn't stop your fall, it collapses, and you're tumbling in a shower of dirt clods down a hole, rolling down some crazy underground tunnel clutching at mud and roots, till finally you slide into some damp, fetid place, and come up a stop against something soft, huge, warm. And furry.";
>>
>> now player is in Burrow;
>>
>> now darting shadow is off-stage.

Let's create the new location, in Chapter - Rabbit's Offer:

> Burrow is a room.

 Why didn't we make use of Inform's ability to track consecutive events here, introduced earlier in the chapter? It's because our condition is slightly more complicated than this allows for. Since the player can do something other than move and still continue the pursuit, we don't know exactly how many turns the pursuit might take; and since Pursuit is a recurring scene, we don't know how many times it might begin or end.

There's almost always more than one way to do anything in Inform; don't let the existence of certain techniques blind you to other solutions.

All good. We should end the Pursuit scene here: but also, it should end whenever the player loses the trail of the darting shadow. Since it's recurring, this gives the player the chance to find it again when the scene restarts. The latter condition covers both ways the scene can end:

> Pursuit ends when darting shadow is not visible. When Pursuit ends: now times followed of darting shadow is 0.

The following scene, The Rabbit's Offer, doesn't necessarily begin when Pursuit ends; instead, we'll tie it to the arrival at the correct location. Add this in Chapter - The Rabbit's Offer:

> The Rabbit's Offer begins when location is Burrow.

Since *Pursuit* is a recurring scene, we also want to make sure it's never triggered again after *Rabbit's Offer* has happened. Add the following condition to our *Pursuit begins when* rule, before the final line:

> The Rabbit's Offer has not happened and

Incorporating Scenes into Your Narrative

What role should scenes play in your story?

Scenes have always been present in adventure games to some extent. Even *Adventure*, the original, ends with a climactic sequence that shifts the player to a new location and changes existing rules. However, explicit support for scenes in Inform signifies a shift in modern IF towards the story side of the story/game dichotomy.

We can say a story that uses scenes frequently is **strongly plotted**, meaning it will feel closer to the experience of reading a book or watching a movie. A story without scenes will feel more open-ended and gamelike. *EVE Online* lets players explore a vast universe of star systems, pirates, and moneymaking opportunities, and has very little that we'd call a scene in

Inform's sense; a game like *Heavy Rain*, on the other hand, is basically nothing but scenes, each one linked to those before and after and pushing the story forward with a firm, relentless hand. Compelling experiences can be created using either approach, as each of these successful games demonstrates (Figure 8.6): figuring out where on the spectrum your story lies is up to you.

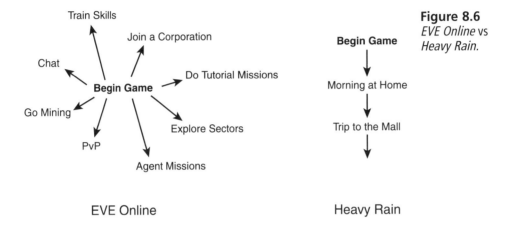

Figure 8.6
EVE Online vs *Heavy Rain*.

EVE Online

Heavy Rain

Scenes can also be used more radically. While rooms and the movement between them has traditionally been the foundation of IF narrative, we could instead create a series of linked scenes each taking place in a single location and remove movement from our command set entirely. This would make an IF that felt more like a stage play, where each scene occupies a specific point in time and space and the connections (physical and temporal) between them are skipped over as uninteresting or irrelevant.

Scenes can also be used on a smaller scale to represent sustained moments within larger plot structures. Nothing prevents multiple scenes from running at the same time, so you could perhaps measure the level of intensity with a condition like *if at least three dramatic scenes are happening*, or move the plot of a horror game forward to a climax with something like *if four scary scenes have ended*. You might even have scenes play out differently in different contexts with a rule like *When George's Visit begins during a tragic scene*.

Another use for scenes is to create flashbacks or flash-forwards. You might start with *A scene can be a flashback*, and then define a procedure to store the important things about the player's current state (position, inventory, time of day) whenever a flashback begins, and restore that situation when it ends. In between, you move the player to a new set of rooms unconnected to the main map representing some part of the player character's past, perhaps changing what he's wearing, his appearance, or even his identity. After performing in the flashback for a while, the player triggers the flashback's ending condition, and is restored to the "present," the situation he was in when the flashback began.

In the end, scenes are just another tool. It's possible to construct any sort of game without them using other techniques, but they often provide a useful shortcut and a helpful way of thinking about how the dramatic events of your game fit in to its gameplay components.

What Scenes Can't Do

An often forgotten point is that scenes cannot be stopped or started at will. Only when the condition defined in a begin rule is met will the scene take place, and it's invalid to write a phrase like *now George's Visit begins.* The good part is that it's impossible for a scene to begin except under the exact conditions you designed it for. The bad part is that it can make testing scenes problematic. One solution is to create custom commands that set up the conditions necessary to trigger each scene, and remove these before releasing your game to the public.

It's also worth noting that using scenes requires precision in both design and execution. Recurring scenes in particular are notorious for coming back when you least expect them to; and it's often frustrating when you expect a scene to trigger at a certain time and it mysteriously fails to begin. The error nearly always lies in an imprecisely defined starting condition covering more or fewer situations than you intended. Careful study of the scene definition will often reveal the culprit

Testing Scenes

Another tab of the Index panel, the Scenes Index, shows some helpful info about all the scenes in your game. When your scenes aren't working as expected, it's often because Inform has misunderstood something about your intent, and the Scenes Index is a good way to double-check this (Figure 8.7).

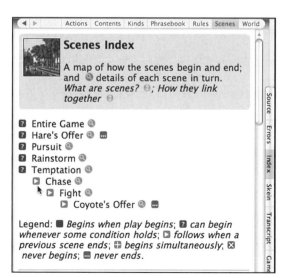

Figure 8.7
The Scenes Index.

Index: Scenes

At the top of the index you'll find every scene defined in your story. As usual, the gray magnifying glass will jump down the index page to more detailed information. A group of icons also shows at a glance some properties of your scenes, as defined by the key below: useful icons include the ellipsis, indicating a scene with no defined ending condition, and the series of orange icons that show scenes linked to one another by a rule like *George's Visit begins when Suppertime ends.*

Following the summary are details for each scene: all the rules that apply to it, including when it begins and ends, what happens at these times, and any rules that apply during. The orange arrow jumps to the definition of the relevant scene or rule.

At the bottom of the index are some general rules applying to scenes. We can see here that the *scene description text rule* is responsible for printing a scene's description when it begins; if we wanted, we could add other rules to these two rulebooks to create universal effects whenever any scene in our story began or ended, or unlist this rule to stop printing scene descriptions. Lastly is the scene-changing machinery itself, which is probably best left alone except for advanced Inform hacking.

The SCENES Testing Command

Type SCENES during an unreleased game to have Inform display a message whenever a scene begins or ends. It will also tell you how scenes with custom endings ended. SCENES OFF will turn off this info.

Temptation: Tracking the Coyote

Let's create a more elaborate sequence for the second introduction of a spirit animal, the Coyote, taking advantage of our knowledge of scenes and timing to build a dramatic sequence of events.

As with Pursuit, we need to start by luring the player into the desert. Let's start with a figure on the horizon who begs investigation. This scene should begin once the player has found the first quest item, as well as used a talent to investigate the Control Center. Put this in Part - Scenes, under a new heading Chapter - Temptation:

> Temptation is a scene.
>
> Temptation begins when
>
> > Rainstorm has ended and
> >
> > Control Center is visited and
> >
> > location is not regionally in Office Interior and
> >
> > location is not Roof and
> >
> > location is not Control Center.

> When Temptation begins: say "You stop in mid-stride as your eyes flick to the horizon. Way out in the desert, silhouetted on a rise, a [distant figure] stands. As you watch he raises a hand and waves."; move distant figure to Around the Tower.

To simplify, this time we'll make the lure a backdrop, visible from all outdoor locations, and let the scene linger as long as it takes for the player to investigate. We'll keep reminding the player about the distant figure in the meantime.

> The distant figure is a backdrop. Instead of doing anything to the distant figure, say "He's too far away. You can barely see him." Instead of waving hands during Temptation: say "The figure waves back, then seems to beckon you forward."

> Every turn during Temptation: if a random chance of 1 in 4 succeeds and location is not regionally in Office Interior, say "The [distant figure] waves again, out in the deep desert."

Our temptation scene ends as soon as the player takes the bait.

> Temptation ends when location is The Open Desert. When Temptation ends: now the distant figure is off-stage.

Once the player has entered the desert, we'll have a pack of mostly unseen coyotes stalking him. Make a new heading, Chapter - Chase:

> Chase is a dramatic scene. Chase begins when Temptation ends. Chase ends when Chase is happening for six turns.

> Carry out going during Chase: say "[one of]You move nervously forward.[or]You jog forward, eyes snapping left and right at the moving shadows around you.[or]You're running now, jumping over sagebrush and stumbling on rocks, as snarling animal forms close in around you.[or]You run.[stopping]".

> Every turn during Chase: say "[one of]Something snarls off in the distance, a warning growl.[or]A howl from behind you, and an answer from somewhere ahead. Coyotes. Hungry, sounds like.[or]Coyotes call all around you now, circling in the dark, unseen, but coming closer, closer.[or]You can smell them now, wild, feral. Shifting shadows whirl around you, panting, whining with the thrill of the chase.[or]The pack's at your heels, snapping, growling, and you've never in your life been this terrified.[or]Snarls and teeth and mangy fur on every side.[stopping]".

We should add an object and some rules to instantiate the phantom coyotes in the story world:

> The snarling shadows are an undescribed animal. When Chase begins: move snarling shadows to Open Desert. When Chase ends: now snarling shadows are off-stage. Understand "moving/shadow/animal/form/forms/snarl/growl/howl/coyote/sound/sounds/coyotes/wolf/call/feral/wild/shifting/pack/snarls/teeth/mangy/fur" as snarling shadows. Instead of doing anything to snarling shadows: say "All you can do is run."

Finally the player is surrounded by snarling coyotes. He'll have to use his talent (either strength or courage) to scare them off, at which point one figure remains... Coyote himself. Add another heading, Chapter - Fight, and then:

Fight is a dramatic scene. Fight begins when Chase ends.

When Fight begins: now circle of snarling coyotes is in location; say "It's over. They've caught you. They surround you, circling, growling, looking for weakness, moving in for the kill."

The circle of snarling coyotes is an animal. Understand "coyote " as circle of snarling coyotes. Every turn when circle of snarling coyotes is visible: say "[one of]A coyote snaps his teeth, lunging forward then fading back into the pack.[or]The circle of snarling coyotes tightens.[or]The coyotes growl, pulling closer, snapping at your heels.[in random order]".

Instead of going when circle of snarling coyotes is visible: say "You try to flee and instantly teeth and claws block your path; you pull back to the center of the circle, terrified."

Fight ends in cowardice when Fight is happening for six turns. When Fight ends in cowardice: say "It's over. The coyotes dive in for the kill, jaws snapping, and you cower in fear.

But then one of them flicks his head and bares his teeth, and the others pull back. He's not bigger or stronger or anything but there's something about him that's different. He takes the littlest step forward and the others scatter, mangy shadows slinking away into the desert and then you're left alone with the leader, the alpha coyote."

Fight ends in bravery when we are attacking. Instead of attacking during Fight: say "It's over. The coyotes dive in for the kill, jaws snapping, [if player holds strength]and without hardly realizing what you're doing you make a fist and slam it into the one that's closest.

The coyote squeals, flung sideways by the strength of your punch, blood dripping from its nose, and the rest of the pack pulls back in sudden caution. Another coyote makes to lunge and you whirl towards it in fury, pulling back for another blow, but the pack breaks in some collective decision and scatters[otherwise if player holds courage]and suddenly this bolt of courage runs through you and without even thinking about it you leap towards the biggest coyote with a terrible scream.

It flinches back, suddenly unsure, and you charge at it full speed, still screaming, arms outstretched, until it turns tail and bolts away. The other coyotes circle uncertainly, but you turn your snarling furious rage on them too and then they're all scattering[end if], mangy shadows slinking away into the desert. Except for one last coyote who stands his ground."

> Instead of throwing anything at circle of snarling coyotes during Fight: say
>   "Maybe you could just attack them directly."
> When Fight ends: now circle of snarling coyotes is off-stage.

The last coyote, of course, is the Coyote himself—who, along with the rabbit, we'll introduce in the next chapter. For now, put this in a last new heading, Chapter - Coyote's Offer.

> Coyote's Offer is a scene. "And then you blink, and realize he's not a coyote
>   after all. Just... just a guy." Coyote's Offer begins when Fight ends.

Extensions for Time and Pace Control

Different authors have different conceptions of how time and pacing should work. As usual, the extensions page offers a variety of plug-and-play solutions for extending or altering Inform's handling of time and events.

The built-in **time of day** functionality, though not technically an extension, supports precise tracking of the time of day quite comprehensively, simulating a standard twenty-four hour clock. One turn is considered equivalent to one minute, so every move the player makes advances this clock by one minute. The Standard Rules keep track of a global variable called **time of day** that holds the current time. You can manipulate this variable like with any other:

> now the time of day is 4:15 PM;
> increase the time of day by 15 minutes;

Time of day is a variable of type "time"; thus, you can create other variables to store times, create new actions that understand times in player commands, do math with times, and so on. Using times in complex ways requires more advanced techniques, so refer to the built-in documentation if you're interested in this.

If the built-in time of day functionality isn't advanced enough for your needs, Variable Time Control by Eric Eve lets you define how long specific actions should take down to the second, so that taking something and waiting around can advance the clock by different amounts.

Scheduled Activities by John Clemens lets you define a series of events that will happen at specific times, with advanced support for later cancelling them, checking whether events are scheduled for certain times, and defining with more precision the effects of overlapping or consecutive events.

<u>Weather Effects</u> by Mikael Segercrantz defines a large set of scenes tied to certain seasonal and weather-related conditions, letting you write tests like *if it is March* or *if it is snowing*.

<u>Basic Real Time</u> by Sarah Morayati lets you write games that take note of how much time has passed on the player's end, useful to create a sense of a dynamic world evolving in real time, or to create added time pressure on the player to submit commands before it's too late.

Exercise Answers

Exercise 8.1

Add a feature that lets the player try out a different ending.

```
When play ends:
    say "Are you unhappy with this ending? ";
    if the player consents:
        now player is in Roof;
        resume the story.
```

Since a powerful theme of *Sand-dancer* is commitment to choices, this option feels thematically inappropriate to me, so I'm leaving it out of the version constructed in this book. But feel free to include it in your own if you disagree.

Exercise 8.2

How would you write rules to prevent Knock from smoking twice in a row, or to respond differently after smoking (or attempting to smoke) more than three times?

```
Instead of smoking for at least two turns: say "Hey, go easy on those."
Report smoking at least three times: say "You're smoking like a chimney.
[run paragraph on]".
```

Exercise 8.3

Make Knock crave a cigarette after he's smoked more than a certain amount. We'll build a more detailed implementation of this later in the book, but for now, here's a basic solution.

```
Craving is a scene. Craving begins when the count of pack of cigarettes is
    less than 4. Every turn when a random chance of 1 in 30 succeeds during
    Craving: if a dramatic scene is not happening, say "Damn, you could
    really go for a cigarette right now.
```

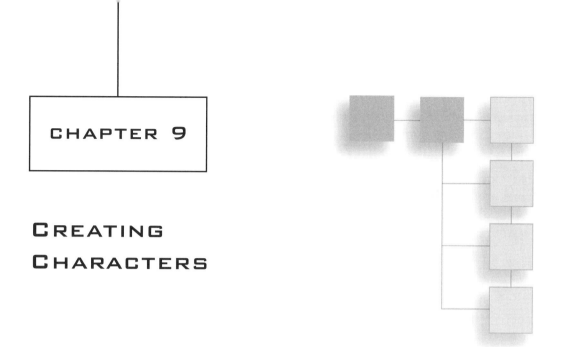

CHAPTER 9

CREATING CHARACTERS

In October 2005, film critic Roger Ebert made a casual comment in his Answer Man column for the Chicago Sun-Times: "As long as there is a great movie unseen or a great book unread, I will continue to be unable to find the time to play video games."

Ebert was responding to a reader comment on his review of *Doom*, the much-reviled game-to-film adaptation. Over the next few months, in a series of further columns, Ebert clarified his opinion: "I believe the nature of the medium [video games] prevents it from moving beyond craftsmanship to the stature of art. ...That a game can aspire to artistic importance as a visual experience, I accept. But for most gamers, video games represent a loss of those precious hours we have available to make ourselves more cultured, civilized, and empathetic."

In the years since Ebert's revelation, many gamers have tried to convince him that games can be art, often using specific examples. 2007's *BioShock* might have seemed like a prime opportunity to convince a non-believer: it garnered perfect scores and "game of the year" awards from dozens of members of the gaming press. Reviewers called it "the most creative and compelling experience of its generation" (*360 Gamer* magazine) and "one of the most playable, thought-provoking, and just downright impressive games... ever" (GamePro). No less prestigious a home of art critics than the *New York Times* named *BioShock* "among the best games ever made."

But the GamePro review admits: "The storyline is certainly thoughtful and well crafted, but make no mistake: *BioShock* is squarely a first-person shooter," a genre which, by Wikipedia's definition, "centers the gameplay around gun and projectile weapon-based combat... [and focuses] on action gameplay, with fast-paced and bloody firefights." And indeed, for all its beautiful art deco stylings and elaborately crafted backstory, the vast majority of play time in *BioShock* is spent murdering human-like characters with wrenches, guns, and genetically-enhanced superpowers gained from injecting yourself with colorful syringes. Blood smears the floor and screams constantly echo through the art-deco corridors; the player must kill hundreds of characters to finish the game.

Five years later, Ebert remains unconvinced. In early 2010, he reaffirmed his opinion that games are inherently artless, saying that the examples he's been shown "do not raise my hopes for a video game that will deserve my attention long enough to play it. They are, I regret to say, pathetic."

Figure 9.1
Ebert: "No one in or out of the field has ever been able to cite a game worthy of comparison with the great poets, filmmakers, novelists and poets." (Sketch by Amber Fitzgerald.)

I do not agree with Ebert that games cannot be art. But I also cannot blame him for getting that impression from the mainstream game industry. In his original review of *Doom* the movie, he lambasted a sequence that "abandons all attempts at character and dialogue and uncannily resembles a video game." For Ebert, character is the polar opposite of game: they are incompatible and anathema. In this chapter I'll try to prove otherwise, demonstrating how interaction with a character can be a mature, fascinating, and, yes, artistic part of an interactive story, and how games can draw from traditions more rich than the action movie.

Characters are the most important component of story, but also the most complicated. Interactive fiction has always been a vanguard for advancing the state of interactive characters, from the thief in *Zork* through *Planetfall*'s Floyd and the unforgettable title character of *Violet*. In fact, many of the most acclaimed modern interactive fictions such as

Galatea, *Varicella*, *Everybody Dies*, *Lost Pig*, and *Make It Good* are centered around fascinating characters.

In *BioShock*, the only way of interacting with a character is the decision to kill or not kill. IF allows for more subtle alternatives. We might be able to give things to other characters, engage them in conversation, flirt with or seduce them, bore them, outsmart them, or order them around. Subtleties of gesture or facial expression can reveal story details or emotional variables. The viewpoint character's descriptions of others might be colored by personal opinions, memories of past behavior, hopes, dreams, prejudices, and affectations.

The possibility space is intriguing—and for authors, perhaps a little terrifying. We'll start with a few definitions to ease us into this brave new world that has such people in it.

Defining Interactive Characters

Usually when we speak of characters in games, we're talking about **non-player characters** (NPCs), all of the people you encounter during play. But the **player character** (PC) whose actions you control is also worth talking about, not the least because this character can be surprisingly schizophrenic.

All of You

IF writers almost always use the second person voice: most of the action happens to someone called "you." But this *you* does not refer to the player, who sits in a chair tapping at a keyboard rather than exploring caves or riddling with demons. Permit me a grammatical *faux pas* in asking, then, who is you?

The Player Character

It's usually the player character, the actor in the story world whose actions are primarily driven by the player. While NPCs tend to be like characters from traditional media, with names, identities, and personalities, PCs can vary on a spectrum from fully characterized (as in *Sand-dancer*) to completely nondescript and anonymous (as in *Zork* or *Adventure*). A blank-slate character is sometimes called a puppet, and a fully-realized one a role: the terms imply how this difference in characterization affects the experience of play.

Positioning a player character somewhere on this spectrum should be a deliberate authorial choice, but any position can lead to an interesting experience. The minimalist PC-as-puppet approach can create a greater sense of immersion: the PC disappears and it becomes "you the player" exploring the story world, invoking games of make-believe. A detailed PC, on the other hand, creates something more story-like, with a protagonist who experiences emotions and undergoes changes: entering such a character's body can be a little like stepping on stage to perform a part (Figure 9.2).

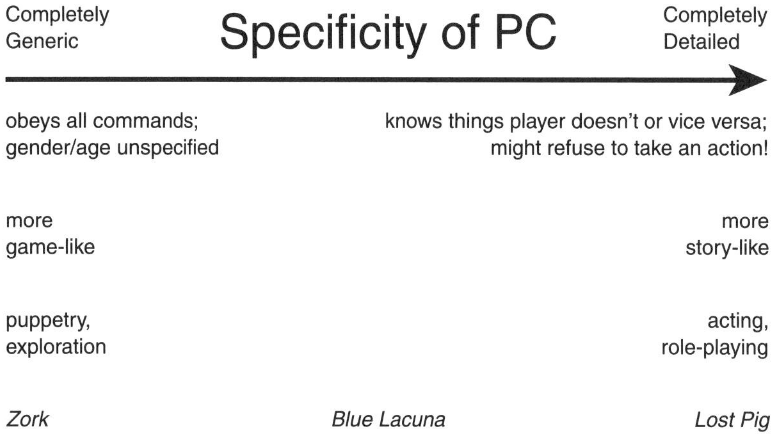

Completely Generic	Specificity of PC		Completely Detailed

Figure 9.2
Puppet PCs versus detailed PCs.

obeys all commands; gender/age unspecified		knows things player doesn't or vice versa; might refuse to take an action!
more game-like		more story-like
puppetry, exploration		acting, role-playing
Zork	*Blue Lacuna*	*Lost Pig*

The Parser/Narrator

The first time explorers of the original *Adventure* were killed, they saw this message:

```
OH DEAR, YOU SEEM TO HAVE GOTTEN YOURSELF KILLED. I MIGHT BE ABLE TO
HELP YOU OUT, BUT I'VE NEVER REALLY DONE THIS BEFORE. DO YOU WANT ME
TO TRY TO REINCARNATE YOU?
```

This might seem straightforward enough until we start to wonder who is speaking: now there's not just a *you*, but an *I*. The speaker can't be the player character (now deceased). It doesn't seem to be any NPC we know of. It's not the player, who is the one being addressed (also, hopefully, not dead). Who, then, are we speaking to this time?

It's the **parser**, who can usually be thought of as the **narrator** as well. The parser acts as a kind of go-between for the player and player character, converting the player's text commands into actions by the PC, and explaining what happens as a result. *Adventure*, again, explained the concept perhaps as succinctly as anyone could:

```
I WILL BE YOUR EYES AND HANDS. DIRECT ME WITH COMMANDS OF 1 OR 2
WORDS.
```

While we can usually trust the narrator of *Adventure* to be honest, traditional literature has often explored the notion of an unexpected, unreliable, or just plain unlikeable narrator. Some modern IF has followed suit by giving the parser a character of its own. The parser in Tommy Herbert's *Bellclap* is an obsequious angel relaying the commands of a deity (the player) to a worshipper (the player character) taking shelter in your temple during a storm. The player's commands are literally taken as such: orders given by a god to a supplicant, with the parser translating back and forth between the two. The response to the command GO OUTSIDE is "He is refusing, sir. Citing the dangers of the rain and lightning." Submitting the command a second time results in: "I shall try again…"

In another memorable example, Andrew Plotkin's *Spider and Web* casts you as a secret agent lying to an interrogator about how you infiltrated his base. Your actions are frequently interrupted by the interrogator suspiciously pointing out the holes in your story, after which you are returned to an earlier position and asked to tell the truth this time. "Don't be absurd," he says if you try to leave early on, "if you'd had enough sense to walk away from that door, you wouldn't be here. You don't and you didn't and are; we caught you. And you're going to start by telling me how you got through that door. Do you understand me?" Here, the *I* is the interrogator, judging your commands not by whether they make sense in an objective model of the story world, but whether they make sense in his subjective one.

Subtle characterization was given to the parser even from the earliest interactive fictions, often as if the parser was some winking ghost in the machine bemused by the endless series of armchair adventurers attempting to uncover its secrets. While this approach is shied away from in modern IF, it worked particularly well in games like Infocom's *Hitchhiker's Guide to the Galaxy*, which responded to attempts to interact after the PC's death with messages like "You keep out of this, you're dead and should be concentrating on developing a good firm rigor mortis."

Exceptions aside, the narrator and parser are most often invisible: we don't care or think about who is telling us this story or why. A common alternative technique that works well for stories with detailed PCs is to write the narration as if the player character is describing the events, almost like an interior monologue. In *Sand-dancer*, we've written events and descriptions from Knock's point of view, colored by his unique dialect and perspectives on the world.

The Player

Of course, the ultimate "you" is the one sitting at the keyboard, typing text: the player (also sometimes called the interactor). While the relationship between this figure and those in the story is usually uncomplicated, one interesting exception can be seen in the 2010 documentary *Get Lamp*, where blind IF fan Austin Seraphin recalls first being told he couldn't do anything because he didn't have a light source. Unlike most players, Austin's response to *You can't see any such thing* is an indifferent *So what?*

Further Permutations

Some stories try to eliminate the parser/narrator entirely by creating an experience explicitly about directing a remote character who reports back his progress. One example is Jon Ingold's *Fail-Safe*, where you receive a distress call and must assist a surviving crewmember on a crippled spaceship. "What do I do?" he asks in desperation, and takes all your commands as suggestions to act. Misunderstood commands are explained away by the signal's poor connection: "What was that..? The radio.. <crackle> ..ing up, Moon's interference, something..."

Fail-Safe illustrates another useful distinction to make when considering the IF "you": between the player character, the protagonist, and the **viewpoint character**. The viewpoint character is the one from whose point of view the story is told. While usually the same as the player character and the protagonist, these roles may also be complicated with interesting effects. Scott Starkey's *The Beetmonger's Journal* tells the story of a famous explorer from the point of view of his loyal assistant. Though the commands the player types become the explorer's actions, it's the assistant who tells us about their enaction and results.

Stories can also have multiple player characters, switching control between them at scene breaks or at will through a player command. Paul O'Brian's *Earth and Sky 3* (Figure 9.3) lets players swap off being either member of a sibling superhero team. Some stories that do this alter descriptions based on which character you're playing, making the choice of whose eyes and hands to use in a scene part of the exploration and puzzle solving experience.

Figure 9.3 Cover art for *The Beetmonger's Journal* and *Earth and Sky 3*, two stories with interesting variations on the traditional role of the PC.

Achieving these sorts of unusual effects often requires altering Inform's Standard Rules. We'll talk more in the next chapter about how to do this, but for most stories, the standard setup—with a strong link between player, player character, viewpoint character, and a mostly invisible parser/narrator—works just fine.

Revealing the PC's Character Through Game Mechanics

Let's add a minor but conceptually rich element to *Sand-dancer* that will help tell the story of our PC, Knock. We've tied his cigarettes into the basics of a hint system, and given him only a limited number to smoke. But let's also create some consequences for smoking: the more the player makes Knock smoke, the more likely it is that Knock will start smoking by himself, reducing the number of available hints.

First, let's create a scene that starts after a few cigarettes have been smoked, which creates a small chance each turn that Knock will be craving another. In Part - Mechanics, Chapter - Smoking, add:

> Jonesing is a scene. Jonesing begins when count of pack of cigarettes is original cigarette count - 2. Every turn when a dramatic scene is not happening and we are not smoking and a random chance of 1 in 30 succeeds during Jonesing: say "[one of]Hey, you really need a cigarette[or]Man, you could really go for a smoke right now[or]You're really jonesing for a smoke[or]You'd kill a hobo for a smoke right now. Well not really but you know[cycling]."

We add the condition *we are not smoking* to prevent this message from being triggered on the same turn as a smoking action, which would seem awkward.

If the player smokes even more, we can create a second scene that causes Knock to smoke by himself.

> Addicted is a scene. Addicted begins when count of pack of cigarettes is original cigarette count - 3.
>
> Every turn when a dramatic scene is not happening and we are not smoking and a random chance of 1 in 30 succeeds during Addicted:
>
> say "[one of]You can't help it. You need another cigarette[or]What the hell, another cigarette won't kill you[or]You really need another smoke[cycling].";
>
> let old count be count of pack of cigarettes;
>
> try smoking;
>
> if old count is count of pack of cigarettes [meaning smoking was unsuccessful]:
>
> say "[one of]Damn[or]Tonight sucks[cycling]."

The *try smoking* phrase will automatically run all the relevant check and before rules related to smoking (meaning if the lighter or pack isn't held, the player character will try to take them, delivering appropriate errors if these attempts fail, and so on). If the smoking action is unsuccessful (which we check by seeing if the *carry out smoking* rule's instructions to reduce the *count* variable have succeeded), we print an irritable rejection.

Note that the smoking action's report rules will also fire, meaning this will display a hint just as if the player had tried smoking. You might feel this is too annoying, since players might not want hints. You could alter the behavior here to suppress the normal report rules by adding a *last carry out* rule that prints a more generic message and then stops the action.

All of Them

Intriguing exceptions aside, the majority of characters in a story are non-player characters: villains and friends, supporting actors, and memorable guest stars. Let's look at a couple of roles NPCs can play in an interactive story.

Sources of Knowledge

Perhaps the most common use of NPCs in IF is to provide exposition, either in a static monologue or by answering questions. It's certainly easy to create this kind of NPC, who is basically just another object in your story world (staying in one place, responding predictably to a set of inputs, and so on).

Nevertheless, the static, information-dispensing NPC is a cliché, and one you should try to avoid whenever possible. It's also a weak story element, ignoring both "show, don't tell" and "do, don't show." Finding ways for your players to learn the same information through action might provide a more compelling experience.

Enemies

Despite the generally less bloody stories in the IF world, NPCs as opponents are still common in IF. This is partly because a good story always needs conflict, and partly because, like dispensing information, physical confrontation is another mode of human interaction that's easy to simulate. It's easier to calculate how many hit points a man has left than what motivated him to leave his wife.

Enemies can be simple cannon fodder to be defeated, but confrontation can take more creative forms, too. *Adventure* had dwarves throwing nasty little knives, but also featured an enemy who stole from you and could only be "defeated" by stealing back (the pirate), another whose weakness was bravado (the dragon), and a third who couldn't be attacked, only tricked through non-confrontational magic (the troll).

Outside of fantastical contexts, enemies in modern games can act like antagonists: motivating the player character through indirect action, appearing in key scenes to shake things up, and otherwise complicating things in dramatically provocative ways.

Gateways

Often, NPCs are used as gateways to prevent premature forward motion in the plot. Until the appropriate time, nothing will successfully overcome, persuade, or bypass the NPC to get to the parts of the story on the other side. An ogre guarding a door was a classic gateway NPC in the early 1980s; in a modern IF, friends who won't let you leave a party might fill this role.

As Plot Devices

NPCs can serve as important parts of your plot, even if they only make rare appearances or never appear at all. Godot in an interactive "Waiting for Godot" would require no lines of code. Similarly, the princesses in *Super Mario Brothers* and, more recently, *Braid*, only appear at each game's conclusion, and yet provide the player character's motivation for the entire story. In my IF *Blue Lacuna*, the sisters Phoebe and Lethe are on-stage only briefly in dreams or flashbacks, but their story forms a major component of the plot.

Conversational Partners

Conversing with other characters purely for the delight of conversation, not just to reveal important plot exposition, is something that IF does well, perhaps better than any other interactive storytelling medium. Emily Short's stories are among the best known and loved for this: her *Best of Three* and *Alabaster* eschew exploration and puzzle solving entirely to focus on a single, wide-ranging interactive conversation with an intriguing subject. Some IF combines puzzles with conversation, as in Chrysoula Tzavelas's *shadows on the mirror*, where you're trapped in a car with your kidnapper and have to find a way through his stoic exterior before it's too late. Conversation can even be used to paint details of setting and social milieu, as in the stark portrait of American ex-pats in Cambodia seen in Michael Whittington's *Love Is as Powerful as Death, Jealousy Is as Cruel as the Grave.*

It's relatively easy to set up NPCs in Inform to respond to simple conversation attempts, harder to produce more elaborate simulations of conversation. We'll explore doing both later in the chapter.

Extras

Sometimes, an NPC can just be an incidental character needed only for a single scene, or to add color to a background: a clerk, a passing knight, a space hobo. Creating this kind of NPC in IF is much like implementing scenery objects, with perhaps a little more attention to detail.

Major Characters

The most challenging NPCs to create are those who take an active role in the story: moving around, taking action, seeming to have goals and motivations. Major characters might be companions who follow the player character and assist; they may be rivals actively working to thwart the PC's plans; they could be love interests or children or supervisors or trench-mates. Any character the player can interact with in multiple contexts and throughout significant portions of your game can be put in this category.

When characters in an interactive story take center stage like this, creating the illusion of intelligent behavior becomes exponentially more challenging. There are a wide variety of ways players might reasonably interact with other people, and to keep track of these from moment to moment across a number of different states (conversing, traveling, waiting, exploring) can be a significant challenge. The rewards can be an incredibly compelling and memorable experience for your players, but think carefully before adding such a character to your game without good reason.

Making a Character

The job of creating life might seem daunting, but, like Victor Frankenstein, we'll take it one step at a time. The good doctor started by finding himself a body. We'll start with that, too: the brain can wait for later.

The Person

To create an entity in Inform that's assumed to have an animus of its own (be it a small child, a robot, a cat, or a shambling fiend from another dimension), we use a kind called the **person**. People differ from things in a few fundamental ways: they can't be taken, respond differently to many core commands (pushing a person produces "That would be less than courteous"), and can be acted upon with a number of targeted actions such as kissing, attacking, and asking. We can create *Sand-dancer*'s first two characters with one simple line. Create a new top-level heading called Part - Characters (which should be before Part - Scenes), and then add:

> Sand-dancer is a person. The rabbit and the Coyote are people.

Gender

People also differ from regular things by being gendered **male**, **female**, or **neuter**. The gender of a person only affects what pronoun is used to describe them (he, she, or it). We can create a person of each gender by using one of the subkinds, **man**, **woman**, or **animal**, or we could simply create a *male person*. With the latter approach, gender can be changed mid-story with a phrase like *now the Coyote is female*, which would change the default response of the giving action (for instance) to "She doesn't seem interested."

As with any kind, you can create your own subkinds of person. Let's do that for *Sand-dancer*, to easily differentiate our spirit animals from other characters. Change the line we added above:

> A spirit animal is a kind of person. The rabbit, the Coyote, and Sand-dancer are
> male spirit animals.

We're going to have non-magical versions of the animals around to make our environment seem more alive, so let's go ahead and give them a kind as well.

> A normal animal is a kind of animal. A desert hare and a brown lizard are normal
> animals.

The Player's Identity

By default, a person called *yourself* is created when play begins to represent the player character. You can create a more specific player character if you like: let's go ahead and do so. Add this to Part - Mechanics, Chapter - Beginning the Story:

> The player is a man called Knock. The description of Knock is "You don't really
> want to think about what you look like right now, especially when there's a
> totally legit likeness on the driver's license in your wallet."

As the line above implies, *the player* is just a global variable holding the person object controlled by the user. Setting the variable to a different person will make that character the one controlled by the player, and the one whose eyes the narrator sees through. We could take our story in a much different direction by adding a line like:

> Instead of sleeping: now the player is Sand-dancer.

CAUTION Though it's technically trivial to change the player to another character, in practice a lot of authorial work must take place to base a compelling narrative around this idea. Each character probably perceives the world differently, which ought to be reflected in descriptions; or they might have different limitations on actions. Be aware of the workload involved before jumping into a story based around multiple player characters.

Describing People

People, as with other things, can have an initial appearance and a description, which appear after the room description and in response to the examining action, respectively.

When describing people, it's helpful to again remember BENT. If you mention that a barista is wearing a nose ring and a black t-shirt in your descriptive text, bracket them both, which will help you remember to implement them in your world model. Let's put this into practice by writing a description for the Coyote. Back in Part - Characters, create a new heading called Chapter - The Coyote, and add this underneath:

> The description of the Coyote is "You can barely see him in the darkness, can't tell whether he's old or how old, what color his [dusty hoodie] is, and with those [sunglasses] you can't even tell whether he's smirking at you or just twitching his mouth. There's a weird smell coming off him, sweat and dirt and a little wet dog and something deeper, earth, desert, rain, all mixed with [cigarette] smoke."

Possessions

NPCs can carry and wear things just as the player can. Add this:

> The Coyote holds a thing called a cigarette. He wears some sunglasses and a dusty hoodie.

The player can try the taking inventory action to learn what's being carried or worn, but there's no default way to find out what an NPC carries. Inform assumes you'll mention any visible possessions in your description, as we did above. If Coyote's inventory was more variable, we might need to use a text substitution like [the list of things held by Coyote] in his description.

If you don't want to reveal all of the things a person is carrying, you can simply leave them unmentioned. Still, all things carried by an NPC are in scope, meaning a clever player can refer to them by figuring out what they're called. If you want NPCs to carry concealed items, one quick fix is to not actually give them to that NPC until the moment they're revealed.

A more robust solution to the problem above is to use the "deciding the concealed possessions of" activity. We'll talk more about activities in Chapter 10, but if you'd like to learn more about concealed possessions now, look up "Concealment" in the built-in documentation.

As descriptions or other text properties get more complicated, you might wish you could embed more robust logic within them. The easiest way to do this is to have the property consist only of a custom text substitution and a period. You can then create as complex a structure as you like when defining the substitution. We could do something like this:

> An inner glow is a thing. The description of the Coyote is "[Coyote's appearance]."

> To say Coyote's appearance:

> let items be the list of things held by Coyote;

> remove the secret map from items, if present;
>
> if Coyote holds a talent, add the inner glow to items;
>
> say "He's got [items]".

Omitting the period from "He's got [items]" prevents Inform's default behavior of printing a line break at the end of a phrase; the period back in "[Coyote's appearance]." then handles this as expected.

Actions Done to People

Inform has a large set of built-in actions for interacting with NPCs, though most of these actions are just **stubs**, bare-bones definitions that let you build your own rules to support them. By opening the Actions tab of the Index panel, you can see a list of these actions and find out more about them under the heading "Standard actions concerning other people." Let's do a quick run-through.

Actions Involving People as Indirect Objects

> Giving it to
>
> Showing it to
>
> Throwing it at
>
> Asking it for

These are all ways you might try to engage an NPC with an item you carry (first three cases) or she carries (last case). The Standard Rules define a few basic check rules for each one (such as preventing you from throwing something you aren't holding), but in most cases stop the action before the carry out stage with a final check rule that always matches and refuses to take the action (something like "He doesn't seem interested").

To give one of these actions your own set of carry out and report rules, you'd first need to **unlist** this final check rule, which you can do from the Actions tab of the Index panel by looking up the action in question, finding the name of the relevant rule, positioning the cursor at an appropriate spot in your source text, and clicking the "unlist" icon next to the rule's index entry. Next, you'd add your own carry out and report rules to make the action actually do something if it succeeds.

Actions Directly Involving People

Attacking

Kissing

Waking

(Pushing)

(Touching)

(Listening to)

Often attempted, rarely successful, the first three actions here are again only stubs which do nothing by default. The last three are other actions that players might try with NPCs that ought to respond appropriately in a well-implemented game.

Actions Indirectly Involving People

Waving hands

Buying

These are both exceedingly rare, and can probably be ignored or removed, but the stubs exist if you want them. The built-in Recipe Book contains examples of creating a system of money and transactions that makes use of the buying action.

Action Involving Conversation

Asking it about

Telling it about

Answering it that

Saying yes

Saying no

Saying sorry

(Going)

(Waiting)

The classical model for NPC conversation is based around commands like ASK COYOTE ABOUT THE DESERT. Inform makes it relatively easy to include basic conversation like this, which we'll discuss more later in the chapter. Less common cousins of ASK are TELL and ANSWER, and Inform also recognizes (but does not do anything interesting with) YES, NO, and SORRY.

Going and waiting are not conversational actions, but ought to be responded to if they happen in the middle of one.

Sorting Through Actions

We've just listed twenty actions a player might expect to use with an NPC, which doesn't include plenty of other things a reasonable player might expect to work (the Standard Rules have no commands for HELLO and GOODBYE, for example). *BioShock*, with a team of dozens of developers, offered only one action: attacking, and now maybe we see why. How is a designer to make sense of this overwhelming possibility space for player behavior, and create a character that could hope to respond intelligently or consistently to a player armed with all those verbs?

Keep in mind that the list of actions above is a menu, not a blueprint. For any given project, you'll only use a small subset that works for your story. Once you've found a workable set, you can block the others with instead rules or even remove them from your story entirely.

In *Sand-dancer*, for instance, the story doesn't ever require Knock to SHOW something to anyone. Let's simply redirect this action into GIVE. In Part - Mechanics, Chapter - Customizations, add:

> Before showing something (called the item) to someone (called the viewer): try
>   giving the item to the viewer instead.

Exercise 9.1

What would be an alternate way of achieving the same effect as the above, but actually remove the SHOW action from the story?

Due to their relative simplicity, animals are often easier to create than people. Let's create one of our normal animals to demonstrate how to respond to a range of possible player actions. Under Part - Characters, make another new heading called Chapter - Normal Animals, and add the following:

> The brown lizard is in Middle of Nowhere. "[if player is in pickup truck]Through
>   the windshield, you see a little lizard clinging frantically to the
>   [Saguaro][otherwise]A brown-colored lizard clings to the cactus[end if]."
>   Understand "brown-colored/colored/sand-dancer/dancer" or "sand dancer" as
>   brown lizard. The description is "[one of]He looks pretty pissed that you
>   crashed into his cactus. What did grandma used to call those little dudes?
>   You can't remember any more[or]Oh yeah, you remember, she called them
>   sand-dancers. This little sand-dancer still looks pissed[or]The little sand-
>   dancer lizard stares at you with one slitted eye[stopping]."

> Instead of giving anything to the lizard: say "You dangle [the noun] in front of it, but it just flicks its tongue in and out a little faster, staying put." Instead of attacking or taking or pushing or touching the lizard: say "You reach out to grab it, but in a flash it scurries around to the other side of the cactus and disappears."; now lizard is off-stage. Instead of kissing the lizard: say "Someone in elementary school dared you to do that once and you beat him up."

Actions Done by People

When IF characters do more than just react, they really start coming to life. Conveniently, every action in your story can be performed by any person, whether they're the PC or an NPC. Whereas the PC's actions are invoked by the player during play, NPC actions are invoked by the story's author in its source text, using a **try** phrase:

> Every turn when Emma holds the hot potato: try Emma dropping the hot potato.

Actions generated from a try phrase are processed just like player actions, with check, instead, and other action rulebooks consulted as normal. If the player can see the actor and the action succeeds, a message explaining what happened is displayed, like "Emma drops the hot potato."

If you've ever opened up the Standard Rules and looked at the action definitions, you might have noticed that most of them are written in the form "Check an actor taking" rather than just "Check taking." When action rules have the words **an actor** added to the rulebook name, they will apply to any character in the game performing that action. Otherwise, they will apply only to the player. One way to think about this is imagining that *the player* is always inserted when the person performing the action is omitted: "Check taking" is the same as "Check the player taking."

In fact, we can put any description that evaluates to a character or group of characters in this position, leading to rules like *Check a spirit animal taking* or *Instead of Emma giving* or *After a cruel person attacking*. In rules like these, it's sometimes helpful to determine who exactly is performing the action: we can use the person variable **the actor** within action rules, as with *the noun* or *the second noun*.

Letting other characters take actions is a powerful technique, but it creates significant hurdles for an author. Each rule you write, and especially those for newly created actions, must be scrutinized to see how its conditions, effects, and descriptions might need to vary based on which character is involved. For many games, this may be overkill. The characters in *Sand-dancer*, for example, never take actions in the Inform world-model sense, largely because most of what they do breaks the world model's conception of reality: appearing and disappearing, changing size, gifting talents, and so on. Since their appearances are so brief and stage-managed, we don't need to give them the ability to take action.

If we did, though, we'd need to know how to make them act at appropriate times. Let's talk a little about giving NPCs plans.

People with Plans

Triggering actions one at a time for NPCs with try phrases is one thing, but how do authors give characters the appearance of agency, working from turn to turn towards goals? There are a couple of basic methods.

Every Turn Rules

You can have an NPC seem to respond when a certain situation arises by using an every turn rule. For instance, say Emma was a vegetarian. We could define a rule like the following:

```
Every turn when eating meat and Emma is visible: say "[one of]'Oh, yuck,'
    Emma says. 'Don't you know that's made of dead animals?'[or]Emma frowns
    disapprovingly at you.[stopping]".
```

 An easy way to make NPCs seem less robotic or artificial is to prevent them from ever repeating an exact piece of text twice. Inform's text substitutions provide us an easy way to do this, either by randomly varying the components of a response, or shifting it to a non-verbal message on subsequent occasions.

At the Time When

We can also use Inform's time-keeping system to make NPCs seem motivated.

```
After saying hello to the guard: say "'You've got three minutes, buddy,' he says,
    glowering."; the guard's patience runs out in three turns from now. At the
    time when the guard's patience runs out: if the guard is visible, say "'All
    right, time's up,' the guard says."
```

Pathfinding

If you need an NPC to move through your story world seeking a certain destination, Inform offers a handy **pathfinding** tool. We simply use the phrase **the best route from** to find out how to get where we're going:

```
let course be the best route from location of Emma to location of Roger;
if course is a direction, try Emma going course;
```

The *if course is a direction* test will be false if there is no way for Emma to get to Roger's location, or if she's already nearby. If you put these two phrases within an every turn rule, Emma would always follow Roger wherever he went, catch up with him if she got separated, and wait around once she reaches him.

Exercise 9.2

Using every turn rules and pathfinding, how could you make the desert hare move around at random, but only through rooms it makes sense for it to be in, including reporting on its movement with some custom text?

Orders

Another way of dealing with characters is to allow the players to direct their actions. The traditional syntax for giving an order is by prefacing a regular command with the character's name and a comma, as if you were speaking to them:

>EMMA, TAKE THE ROSE

This is converted to the action *asking Emma to try taking the rose*. This is an action in its own right, and we can write any standard action exception rules for it that we like. We can also create less specific rules if we need to:

Instead of asking Emma to try taking the rose

Instead of asking Emma to try taking something

Instead of asking Emma to try doing something to the rose

Instead of asking Emma to try doing something

You could get rid of ordering entirely in a game with a rule like this:

Instead of asking anyone to try doing anything: say "Orders are not necessary in this story."

Unless the NPC in question is a robot, it's not very believable for orders to be blindly followed. Normally, orders to NPCs will fail with a message like "Emma has better things to do." But if you do want to let certain actions succeed, you can define a new sort of rule called a **persuasion rule**. We write a persuasion rule for a certain action (or class of action, as above) as follows:

Persuasion rule for asking Emma to try taking the rose: persuasion succeeds.

As with rules to decide things, we can put any number of phrases inside before making a final verdict: in this case, using one of the phrases **persuasion succeeds** or **persuasion fails**. If persuasion succeeds, a new action begins (in this case, it would be *taking the rose*, with *the actor* set to Emma) and processed as normal.

Extensions for People

Several extensions exist to enhance NPC behavior.

Intelligent Hinting by Aaron Reed is designed to tell the player what action to take next, but can also be used for NPCs. For instance, an author could decide that in a certain scene an NPC needs to burn a note. The extension would automatically have the NPC move to the note's location, pick it up, move to the fire's location, and throw it in.

Planner by Nate Cull approaches the same problem as the above in a different way, letting authors build libraries of plans which NPCs can deploy to solve problems.

Mood Variations by Emily Short lets you define a set of moods for a character, and then include text substitutions like [when upset] to customize text related to that character based on his or her mood.

Simple Followers by Emily Short lets characters (including the player) follow or be followed by other characters.

Conversation: Three Systems

The idea of having a conversation with a voice inside the computer is as old as computers themselves. In the late 1960s, two seminal artificial intelligences caught the imagination of computer enthusiasts: the fictional HAL, and the real-world ELIZA. While HAL could converse in natural English sentences, offer opinions about art, and even plan and execute a murder, he was only celluloid fantasy. ELIZA, meanwhile, actually existed, in a few hundred lines of data and computer code that could be interacted with. But the longer you spent with ELIZA, the more you realized she was just a simple set of instructions producing a simple set of outputs: in the end, nearly as much of an illusion as HAL.

More than forty years later, we still can't create autonomous AI like HAL, but we have gotten a lot better at faking it. Many interactive fictions have featured fascinating conversations with fictional characters. Much like a good author creates an engrossing physical space for players to explore, we can think of writing IF conversations as sculpting a particular conversation space in which exploration yields interest, surprises, and treasure.

How best to model conversation has been and remains one of the most common points of disagreement among IF authors. There are almost as many conversation systems as there are games with conversation. Is it best to use a conversation tree, as most commercial games do, or keep the conversation topics hidden? If the conversation offers no real choice points, should there just be a TALK TO command without the need for guessing what to talk about? Should characters respond differently to being asked about, told about, or shown something, and if so, how can it be made clear to the player that this is the case?

In this section, we're going to take three conversation systems, the first built-in to Inform and the latter two added through extensions, and take a close look at both interacting and authoring with them. All three systems are based around Inform's ASK and TELL verbs, which are the most common foundation for approaching character conversation in IF. Afterwards, we'll talk briefly about some alternate conversation systems. Hopefully after reading through this material, you'll have a good sense of what's possible in IF conversation and what tools you might like to use in your own stories.

 Conversation varies enough from one IF to another that it's very important to make clear to players how to converse with your characters. A tutorial message the first time a conversation begins (perhaps with a rule like *Before asking for the first time*) is one way to do this.

ASK/TELL

The baseline for IF conversation is what's known as the classic ASK/TELL model. Let's start by looking at an excerpt of this system in action, from Steve Meretzky's Infocom sci-fi dystopia, *A Mind Forever Voyaging*. In this story, you play an artificial intelligence that's been prematurely awakened from your simulated life to help with a project vitally important to the beleaguered United States of North America.

>ASK PERELMAN ABOUT SENATOR RYDER

"Ryder's a Senator from... I'm not sure. Oklahoma? Alabama? Anyway, he's one of the big driving forces behind the Plan. Gives speeches about it all the time. He introduced the bill to Congress. He's really photogenic, very popular. I've got sort of mixed feelings about him."

>ASK HIM ABOUT THE PLAN

"The Plan. It's full name is the Plan for Renewed National Purpose, a typical bit of linguistic obfuscation. A group of politicians and businessmen are trying to take advantage of the clamor for change, any kind of change."

>ASK HIM ABOUT CONGRESS

[I don't know the word "congress".]

>TELL HIM ABOUT MYSELF

It doesn't look as though Dr. Perelman is interested.

>ASK HIM ABOUT THE PLAN

"The Plan. It's full name is the Plan for Renewed National Purpose, a typical bit of linguistic obfuscation. A group of politicians and businessmen are trying to take advantage of the clamor for change,
any kind of change."

The transcript reveals both the strengths and weaknesses of ASK/TELL. On the plus side, it's simple to understand, and makes it easy to review information later since the response to a single topic stays the same no matter how many times it's been asked about. For authors, ASK/TELL conversations are simple to create and test, since they're typically **stateless**, meaning that any given turn during a conversation is no different from any other.

While this means it's hard to create a broken conversation, it's also one of the principal weaknesses of this sort of system: it can feel extremely artificial for a character to simply repeat the same words on request, over and over. Another more serious difficulty: since the available topics of conversation are hidden from the player, it's easy to get frustrated when topics aren't understood—any given character might be reasonably expected to know about hundreds of things even in a small story, and most authors don't have time to write responses for all of them. This makes it hard also to know when a conversation is over: in the excerpt above, is there nothing else to talk about, or have we just not thought of the right topic to try next? It's also obnoxious to have to type ASK PERELMAN ABOUT over and over again to converse.

Let's look at the source text that would be required to produce a transcript like the following in Inform 7, abbreviating some of the text strings to save space.

Instead of asking Perelman about "plan/renewed/national/purpose": say
    "'The Plan. It's full name is the Plan for Renewed National Purpose...'".

Instead of asking Perelman about "Senator/Richard/Ryder": say "'Ryder's
    a Senator from... I'm not sure. Oklahoma? Alabama? Anyway...'".

Instead of telling Perelman about something: say "It doesn't look as though
    Dr. Perelman is interested."

ASK/TELL has the advantage of being built in to Inform, so no new actions, rulebooks, or extensions are required to make it work. As seen above, all that's needed is an instead rule for asking about or telling about a string of quoted text (with multiple matched words separated by slashes). We could also put a bracketed object name in the quoted topic string, to match any word in that object name.

Since Inform interprets standard double quotes as marking the beginning and end of a string, you can't use them within a string to show quoted dialogue. Instead, use single quotes, which will be displayed as double quotes to the player. Inform normally is smart enough to preserve the single quote in a contraction like *don't*, but if it ever guesses wrong, we can use the text substitution ['] to force a single quote and [quotation mark] to force a double quote.

To a certain extent, we can make ASK/TELL more powerful by adding some of the time-tracking capabilities we learned in the last chapter. We could, for instance, add something like this:

> Instead of asking Perelman about "plan" for at least the second time: say
>   "'There's not much more to say, PRISM, unless you want to access GovNet
>   and read all four thousand pages of the bill yourself,' Perelman says wryly."

> Before telling Perelman about something for the third turn: say "'Whoah, slow
>   down!' he says, grinning. 'I can't answer everything at once!'".

For the most part, though, if you feel the need to start enhancing ASK/TELL at all, you're probably better off setting up a more advanced conversation framework. ASK/TELL is a basic tool that works in stories where conversation is rare or incidental, but you'll probably want something more elaborate to tell a story with real conversations.

One useful feature of ASK/TELL, though: another built-in verb, CONSULT, works on exactly the same mechanism, except it's designed to be used on things that aren't people. For instance:

> An issue of Dakota Online is a thing. Instead of consulting Dakota
>   Online about "Senator/Ryder": say "The article on Senator Ryder
>   contains a brief history of his rise to fame, starting as a young Free
>   Party activist and concluding with his triumphant 2030 reelection."

This model of interaction actually makes a lot more sense for inanimate objects than for real people.

Exercise 9.3

Allow the guidebook in Weed-strewn Rust to be consulted about the various animals the player might encounter.

Conversation Framework by Eric Eve

One of the major competing IF languages, TADS, has long been based around a more complex conversation model than Inform's ASK/TELL. Conversation Framework by Eric Eve, and a series of optional plug-in companion extensions, add similar functionality to Inform.

Let's see what Conversation Framework looks like in action, when partnered with a companion extension, Conversation Suggestions. The excerpt below is from Eric Eve's *All Hope Abandon*, which is not an Inform game, but includes a conversation system much like the one Eric's extensions emulate. In this excerpt, after unexpectedly dying at a conference on religious scholarship, the player character finds himself outside the gates of hell, framed by an inscription reading, unexpectedly, ABANDON HOPE ALL YE THAT ENTER HER.

A workdemon is standing on top of the ladder, chiselling away at the lettering above the gate, but seemingly making very slow progress in removing it. So far as you can see he's still chipping away at the final E that's no longer there.

>SAY HELLO

"Hello there!" you call up at the demon. The demon looks down from the ladder and gives you a cheery wave, "Why, hello mate!" he replies, "I don't see many folk round here these days!"

(You could ask him about God, hell, heaven, the gate, Satan, death, life, the notice, himself, or work.)

>ASK HIM ABOUT THE GATE

"This gate appears to be closed," you remark. "That's right, mate," the demon agrees, "firmly and finally closed."

>A HELL

"What's happened to hell?" you ask, nodding towards the sign on the gate. "Closed for good, mate." he informs you sadly, "So if it's eternal torment you're after, you're out of luck, I'm afraid. Apparently it's no longer Theologically Correct."

>A SATAN

"Is Satan around anywhere?" you ask. "Don't ask," he replies, "you don't want to meet him."

>ASK ABOUT THE RIVER STYX

"I was hoping you could tell me something about..." you say. "Hoping?" the demon echoes, "Look mate, I may be removing this here inscription, but hope's totally out of place here, believe me!

>TOPICS

You could ask him about demythologization, hell, heaven, the gate, Satan, death, life, the notice, himself, or work.

Figure 9.4
Detail from Rodin's
"Gates of Hell."

While using the same verbs as ASK/TELL, we can see already that this system has a number of advantages:

- It adds the notion of conversations beginning and ending, with actions for HELLO and GOODBYE.

- It offers the convenient abbreviation "A" for ASK {SOMEONE} ABOUT.

- It reveals the available conversation topics to the player both when the conversation begins and on request afterwards via a TOPICS command.

- It allows the author more control over the flow of a conversation, such as introducing new topics only after others have been mentioned, or removing topics once they've been adequately discussed.

- It lets us ask about both abstract concepts as well as specific objects in the story world, which gives us the advantage of automatically understanding something like ASK HIM ABOUT HIMSELF.

Though not obvious from this transcript, another advantage of the Conversation Framework system is that it is **state-based**; a memory is retained about which topics have been discussed, allowing for more complex and dynamic conversations.

Conversation Framework requires a little more setting up and management than plain ASK/TELL. Let's take a look at how the code for this sequence might have appeared were it written in Inform 7 using Eric's extensions, abbreviating again some of the strings.

> The ask-suggestions of the demon are {God, hell, heaven, the huge gate, Satan, death, life, the notice, the demon, demon's work}.

> After saying hello to demon: say "'Hello there!' you call up at the demon. The demon looks down from the ladder and gives you a cheery wave...".

> The huge gate is a closed locked door north of Hell's Gate. After quizzing demon about huge gate: say "'This gate appears to be closed,' you remark. 'That's right, mate,' the demon agrees...".

> hell is a familiar thing. After quizzing demon about hell: say "[add demythologization ask suggestion]'What's happened to hell?' you ask, nodding towards the sign on the gate. 'Closed for good, mate.' he informs you sadly... ".

> After quizzing demon: say "'I was hoping you could tell me something about...' you say. 'Hoping?' the demon echoes, 'Look mate, I may be removing this here inscription, but hope's totally out of place here, believe me!'".

From this code, we can observe a number of things about how the extensions function. The new actions *saying hello* and *saying goodbye* have been added, and you can create rules for them as usual. Here, we create a specific response for greeting the demon: since we use an after rule, it will only be seen if the saying hello action succeeds (the rule would fail if we've already greeted the demon, for instance). Saying hello will automatically take place even if the player just walks up and starts asking questions.

Quizzing is the action the extension creates for asking about things; we can also use *informing* for telling. In the code above, we wrote rules for quizzing about a specific object in the story world (the huge gate) as well as an abstract concept (hell) which we created as a thing that's not located anywhere in the game world. To make hell available in conversation, we gave it the adjective *familiar*, a feature of a prerequisite extension for using this conversation package, Epistemology by Eric Eve.

 Epistemology adds the concept of familiar and unfamiliar things to Inform. Anything the player has ever seen is familiar. Conversation Framework uses this to only allow conversation about things the player has encountered already: we predefine hell as familiar here, since we assume the player has heard of it.

Conversation Framework also contains the idea that certain characters should only be able to talk about certain concepts. Each person in the game is given three lists of object variables (*ask-suggestions*, *tell-suggestions*, and *other-suggestions*) which define what subjects that character can be asked, told, or bothered about. (*Other-suggestions* can add suggestions for non-conversation actions to the topics list, like attacking, waiting, or giving something.) In the source text above, we make a new conversation topic available by using a text substitution defined by the extension, which adds it to the ask-suggestions list of the workdemon.

Conversation Framework is part of a robust set of extensions by the author that can be mixed and matched in several ways. Another member of the family, Conversation Nodes, is designed for conversations that move forward through a series of significant points, useful for conversations with a more directed or tighter pace. Explore the components of the system on the Inform 7 extension page by looking for extensions by Eric Eve beginning with the word "Conversation."

Threaded Conversation by Emily Short

Threaded Conversation by Emily Short is the product of several years of testing and refinement by one of IF's most acclaimed conversation-based storytellers. This robust extension allows for richly detailed and highly stateful conversations with other characters. While not yet publicly released at the time this book went to press, the plans are for Threaded Conversation to become one of the default extensions bundled with Inform.

Let's take a look at Threaded Conversation in action. In this excerpt from *Alabaster*, you play the hunter asked by your queen to take Snow White into the woods and bring back her heart. As you converse with the seemingly helpless girl, though, the motives of all parties involved become suspect, and surprising truths rise to the surface.

"What are you?" you demand. "No ordinary girl would have lasted a night march into the dark woods."

"Oh, I dare say she would, if she were tied up and taken along by force! It is not as though you stopped to ask how I was feeling."

You might ask if she is a witch, ask whether she will keep the pact, or ask why she drinks red wine.

> ASK IF SHE IS A WITCH

"Are you a witch?" you ask, "Is that what you don't want the Queen to know?"

She ponders your question for a moment, then replies, "'Witch' is not a good description of what I am; but then, so few people understand witches."

You can ask why so few people understand witches.

> A WHY

"Why don't they understand them?"

"There's so much superstition and fancy going around. People are so taken by it. More so," she adds, "than by real witches."

You could ask whether the Queen herself made the magic mirror or ask if the Queen is a witch.

>A IF THE QUEEN MADE

"Did the Queen make the magic mirror herself? Or did it come to her from elsewhere?"

"Yes, and yes." She shivers. "It came to her as an empty vessel; she filled it. It is she who chose a suitable voice and soul for the mirror, and made the sacrifice of their living donor."

You could ask whose voice the mirror has, ask where the Queen got the mirror, ask whether the Queen killed someone for the mirror, or ask what powers the Queen dabbles with.

Threaded Conversation clearly represents the most sophisticated conversation system we've seen yet. The available topics change each turn in response to the direction of discussion, and a complex system of interrelatable subjects lets the extension automatically suggest related topics, keep track of mood and changes of subject, and do much more to make conversing with an IF character seem more realistic and narratively coherent.

Let's take a look at some of the source text behind this extract. Here, the strings are more complicated, so we'll reprint them in full.

```
what she seems is a questioning quip.

The printed name is "what she is". The true-name is "what she seems".

Understand "is" as what she seems.

It mentions Snow White.

The comment is "'What are you?' you demand. '[if scariness is greater than o]No
    ordinary girl[otherwise]No other girl your age[end if] would have lasted a
    night march into the dark woods.'".

The response is "'Oh, I dare say she would, if she were tied up and taken
    along by force! It is not as though you stopped to ask how I was
    feeling[pathetic].' ".

It quip-supplies Snow White.

It is negated by magic-revealed, vampirism-revealed, snow-white-possessed.


if she seems a witch is a questioning quip.

The printed name is "if she is a witch". The true-name is "if she seems a witch".
```

Understand "is" or "whether" as if she seems a witch.

It mentions Snow White, witchcraft.

The comment is "'Are you a witch?' you ask, 'Is that what you don't want the Queen to know?'".

The response is "She ponders your question for a moment, then replies, '[']Witch['] is not a good description of what I am; [scary]but then, so few people understand witches.'".

It quip-supplies Snow White.

It is negated by vampirism-revealed, snow-white-possessed.

It is listed.

why so few people understand witches is a weak questioning quip.

It mentions witchcraft.

The comment is "Why don't they understand them?'".

The response is "'There's so much superstition and fancy going around. People are so taken by it. More so,' she adds, 'than by real witches.'".

It quip-supplies Snow White.

It directly-follows if she seems a witch.

It is negated by snow-white-possessed.

It is listed.

whether the Queen herself made the magic mirror is a questioning quip.

Understand "if" or "who" as whether the Queen herself made the magic mirror. The comment is "'Did the Queen make the magic mirror herself? Or did it come to her from elsewhere?'".

It mentions witchcraft, magic mirror, queen.

The response is "'Yes, and yes.' She shivers. 'It came to her as an empty vessel; she filled it. [scary][Queen-made-mirror]It is she who chose a suitable voice and soul for the mirror, and made the sacrifice of their living donor.'".

It quip-supplies Snow White.

It is listed.

Conversation topics are called "quips" in Threaded Conversation. Quips can be associated via themes; the suggestion message before each prompt can automatically mention thematically related quips, as well as those the author has manually decided should come next. Threaded Conversation also allows for the player and other characters to learn nuggets of information called "facts," and only make certain quips available when the related facts are known. Let's see how the source text above achieves all this.

A quip *quip-supplies* a character if it can only be said by that character. Here we can specify that a certain topic is "owned by" a specific character. (Compare this with Conversation Framework's ask-suggestions list.)

We see that the player character's *comment* is separated from the NPC's *response*. This allows the possibility of creating interesting effects, like having the NPC decide not to answer, or even interrupt the player in mid-sentence!

Threaded Conversation defines a relation called *mentioning* that links quips to things in the game world representing general subjects of inquiry. In addition to providing a mechanism that thematically links individual quips, it will also redirect attempts to converse directly about that subject (like *the Queen*) to a disambiguation question asking which of the available quips about the Queen you want to discuss.

A quip can *directly-follow* another quip, meaning it's only available immediately after the first quip is discussed; this is useful for fleeting conversation opportunities that wouldn't make sense to be invoked after a move or two have passed.

You might notice the unusual text substitution [Queen-made-mirror]. This is a *fact* that's been defined by the author; invoking it in this fashion doesn't display anything to the player, but notes internally that all characters present now know about this fact, which can unlock new quips, as seen in the final topics line of the transcript.

 Alabaster keeps track of two number variables that represents Snow White's affect: scariness and anger. The text substitution [scary] increases the scariness number, which can then be used to alter the text shown to the player (as we see in the first quip above, where any earlier unsettling behavior from the girl causes the hunter's question to have a more suspicious edge). This functionality is not a core part of Threaded Conversation, but is a good example of how text substitutions can easily add more complexity and flavor to a conversation, whatever system you're using.

Threaded Conversation comes with a companion extension designed for use only by authors, not players, called <u>Conversation Builder by Emily Short</u>. With this extension, authors testing a conversation can iteratively add new topics from within the game itself, simply by typing a command referring to an unrecognized topic like ASK HER ABOUT REAL WITCHES. The extension then asks the author a series of questions to define the new quip, and type in the comment and response. Upon request, the generated Inform 7 source is displayed, which can then be copied and pasted back into the game's code. This clever approach lets you effectively modify conversations while still inside them.

It's clear that Threaded Conversation is the most advanced of the three systems we've looked at. It allows for NPCs who are much more dynamic and proactive, able to respond to changes of topic, change the subject themselves, respond if the player stops speaking, and exhibit other lifelike behavior. It gives extreme flexibility to the author to control the flow and pacing of a conversation, and even offers an iterative design tool. However, not all games will need this level of complexity, and depending on the focus of your story, you might find that the advanced tools hinder rather than help to tell it. For games with strong conversation, though, Conversation Builder is one of the best options available.

Other Conversation Systems

Some conversation systems eschew the asking and telling actions for their own unique paradigms. Here are a few counterexamples that can also be used to create talkative NPCs.

Some of my own recent stories have displayed conversation topics in colored text and then let the player type that word directly to talk about that subject, without using a verb like ASK (Figure 9.5). My extension Keyword Interface by Aaron Reed provides the basis for the highlighting, but doesn't have an integrated conversation system; Keywords for Conversation by Matt Wigdahl is one solution, merging Keyword Interface with Conversation Framework.

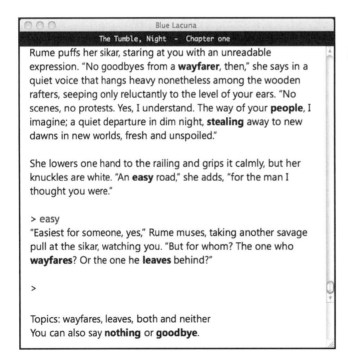

Figure 9.5
Blue Lacuna using Keyword Interface.

An approach common to some early adventure games, and still thriving in places like PC RPGs, is the **conversation menu**. Under this model, the player sees a list of possible things to say next, usually full lines of dialogue. While this method solves a number of interface and characterization problems, many in the IF community have shied away from it for two major reasons: it offers an abrupt break from the control scheme used by all other input in an interactive fiction (imperative commands), and also removes any element of surprise or intuition from participating in a conversation. Conversation menus can also result in the **lawnmower effect**, where players feel obligated to exhaust every possible conversation option so as not to miss any important plot points, an exercise which can feel as repetitive and tiring as yard work. Despite these caveats, many successful interactive fictions have used conversation menus: if you'd like to try them yourself, Quip-Based Conversation by Michael Martin and Simple Chat by Mark Tilford are two extensions that add menu-based conversation interfaces to a story.

Other interactive stories outside the IF world have used a wider variety of conversation tools. *Heavy Rain* and *Mass Effect* use two variants on the conversation menu, letting the player choose from brief snippets that signify the desired direction the conversation should move in, like *angry* or *persuade*. Some ambitious stories like *Façade* attempt a natural language interface where the player can type plain English; complex AI attempts to then convert the player's input into a form the story world can understand. Though at publication time there are fewer Inform 7 extensions supporting these more experimental methods of conversation, as time goes on I hope that new systems and ideas continue to proliferate.

Sand-dancer's Characters

Reviewing our concept document, we see that *Sand-dancer* involves as many as five conversations, perhaps overly ambitious for an example game. Let's break down each one to see what function each fulfils in the narrative.

1. Radio voice (First contact). Establishes the stakes: Knock must either fix his truck or stay for the night. A storm is coming in.
2. Radio voice (Later). Reveal that all is not as it seems; the voice as the fearful parts of Knock's subconscious.
3. The rabbit. Let Knock bargain for strength or courage; make explicit that strength is the path of staying the night and abandoning Ocean, and courage is the path of fixing the truck and going home to her.
4. The Coyote. Lets Knock bargain for luck or scent.
5. Sand-dancer. Makes Knock confirm his decision; tempts him with Freedom; resolves the plot.

The last three all seem vital to the plot, and the first conversation with the radio is useful to set the stakes. The second radio conversation seems less important, however. Let's keep this story beat, but present it as a series of non-interactive transmissions interrupted by the static of the storm. This will save a lot of authoring time without losing too much plot. We'll tackle the conversations with the first two spirit animals in the remainder of this chapter.

The next step is to determine what sort of conversation system would be best for our story. The meaningful moment of interaction in each of the spirit animal conversations is the player's choice of a talent. But we'd like to build up to that moment in a short but directed conversation beforehand. ASK/TELL is definitely too simple for this, but since each conversation is very short, Threaded Conversation might be overkill. We'll take the middle road and go with an approach centered around Conversation Framework.

Setup

It's very rare that something as complex as conversation will work exactly how you want out of the box, and *Sand-dancer* isn't an exception. You'll usually need to fiddle around to get things to work the way you envision them for your game.

In order to save space in the book, and to prevent future updates to the relevant extensions from causing confusion, I've created a single stable extension that takes Eric Eve's extensions and combines them with a number of unique customizations for *Sand-dancer*. Go ahead and download <u>Conversation Framework for Sand-dancer by Aaron Reed</u> from the Inform extensions page and install it, then add this line to the top of your source text:

    Include Conversation Framework for Sand-dancer by Aaron Reed.

While this conversation system works almost identically to the one we profiled in the second example above, there are a few changes. I've extended the vocabulary for conversing, made an easier way to move topics into and out of scope, and made certain actions disallowed during conversation (to prevent, for example, the player from walking away in the middle of an important scene). As with *Alabaster*'s system, we also show the list of available topics after every move during a conversation.

There's nothing wrong with spinning some of the source text of your game out into its own extension, even if you don't plan on using it in another project. The act of isolating the code for a particular system is often useful for ensuring it's complete and clean, and has the advantage of making it easy for you to test it in a simpler context through a new project. If you do decide what you've created is useful on its own, consider submitting it to the Inform 7 extension page so others can benefit from your work.

CAUTION The rest of this chapter contains a lot of source text for two of Sand-dancer's conversations. Remember, code for each chapter is available on the book's website (www.courseptr.com/downloads); rather than typing all this in, you might want to copy and paste from there. Alternatively, you could try writing your own versions of these conversations, putting a personal spin on the characters or direction of discussion.

Before we start in on the conversation proper, let's create the trading mechanic that allows Knock to gain talents.

Trading

Each of the three conversations with a spirit animal rely on choosing certain memories of Knock's to exchange for a chosen talent. To instantiate this, we'll need to create a new action, trading, and its associated rules.

First, we set up how many memories each animal demands for a talent. Under Part - Characters, create a new heading called Chapter - Trading with the Spirit Animals, and add this:

> A spirit animal has a number called price. The price of the rabbit is 1. The price of the Coyote is 2. The price of Sand-dancer is 3.

Now let's make the action.

> Trading is an action applying to two things. Understand "trade [something preferably held] for [something]" as trading.

[something preferably held] simply means that the parser is more likely to match an object in the player's inventory than something else. (The dropping action is defined with a syntax like this, to help avoid embarrassing disambiguation questions like "Which do you want to drop, the model of the Eiffel Tower or the Eiffel Tower?")

While the trading action only has two components (the memory to trade and the talent traded for), there's an implied third element not mentioned: the person we're trading with. Since in our story only one spirit animal will ever be present at a time, it's safe to leave this out. But it might be nice, for the benefit of our action rules, to know who's being traded with on a particular action. We can create an **action variable** to keep track of this. Action variables are set up when the action begins and last only as long as it takes for all of its associated rulebooks to run. Let's add one to *Sand-dancer* to illustrate:

> The trading action has a person called the trader. Rule for setting action variables for trading: now the trader is a random visible spirit animal.

Now we have a variable called *the trader* that we can use in any action rulebook related to trading. You can make action variables for any action, new or built-in.

 Why do we have to ask for a random spirit animal, when we know there will only ever be a single spirit animal present? Here's the catch: we know that, but Inform has no way of knowing it's not possible for multiple spirit animals to appear in the same location at once. We can say "a random" in a case like this and be sure of getting the right result, in the same way we could ask for "a random number from 1 to 1" and be sure of getting the entirely non-random result of 1.

Let's add check rules for trading, to ensure it only can happen in an appropriate context.

> Check trading when the trader is not a spirit animal: instead say "There's no one here to trade with."
>
> Check trading when the noun is not a memory: instead say "'I'm only interested in trading memories,' [the trader] says."
>
> Check trading when the second noun is not a talent: instead say "'I only have talents to offer you,' says [the trader], '[list of visible not held talents].'"
>
> Check trading when the second noun is held: instead say "You've already got the talent of [second noun]."
>
> Check trading when the noun is not in emotional baggage: instead say "You've already traded away that memory."
>
> Check trading when trader needs more memories: move the noun to the trader; instead say "[The trader] touches your fingertips and pulls [the noun] through your nerve endings. 'Good,' he says, 'I'll take that, although it's not enough to complete the trade.'[paragraph break]Somewhere inside you, things are shifting, moving, growing."

In the last check rule, we reference a truth state, *{someone} needs more memories*. Since our check rule is happening before the item transfer, we need to make sure that the amounts will be correct if the action happens. Let's add the rule.

> To decide whether (trader - a person) needs more memories:
>
> > let the projected total be the number of memories held by trader + 1;
> >
> > if the projected total is less than the price of trader, decide yes;
> >
> > decide no.

The way we've structured these check rules means we can easily override them with a more specific rule for a particular character if we wish.

Now, carry out the trade.

> Carry out trading:
>
> > move the second noun to the player;
> >
> > repeat with item running through visible not held talents:
> >
> > > now item is off-stage.

And at last, a report rule, to explain what happened.

> Report trading: say "[The trader] nods. 'Yes,' he says, 'a fair trade.' And
> something happens inside you as he says it. [The noun] shifts and wriggles
> and fades away and it's still there, but now it's shifted, become something
> else. And yeah, it kinda does feel like you could call it [the second noun].
> Cool."

Again, we can write character-specific messages by adding more targeted report rules.

Finally, let's add a few action exception rules for existing actions, to help direct players into using our new trading action instead.

> Instead of taking a not held talent when a spirit animal (called the potential
> trader) is visible: say "'You can't just have it,' [the potential trader] says.
> 'That's not how it works. You have to TRADE something for it.'".
>
> Instead of giving something to a spirit animal (called the potential trader): say
> "'No, not like that,' [the potential trader] says. 'You have to TRADE it for
> something.'".

We also ought to restrict using any actions other than asking about or trading on a talent.

> Instead of doing anything other than quizzing, implicit-quizzing or trading to a
> not held talent: say "It's just potential, or something."

...which reminds us, we ought to modify the earlier rule like this we created for memories. In Part - Mechanics, Chapter - Memories, Section - Brooding, change the instead rule to:

> Instead of doing anything other than brooding or trading to a memory, say "As
> if. All you can really do is BROOD ABOUT it."

Now that our conversation system and our trading mechanics are in place, we're ready to write our first conversation.

The Rabbit

The first spirit animal is the rabbit, encountered by the player after chasing the mysterious shadow into the desert. We previously created a scene for this conversation called the Rabbit's Offer, and defined it as beginning when the player arrives in the Burrow. Let's say that it ends when the player leaves this room: add the next line to Part - Scenes, Chapter - The Rabbit's Offer:

> Rabbit's Offer ends when location is not Burrow.

We'd like to give the player one turn to take in their sudden change of surrounding before beginning conversation. Let's schedule an event for one turn in the future (a trick we learned in the last chapter) to do this.

> When Rabbit's Offer begins: Rabbit's conversation starts in 1 turn from now.

For the conversation itself, let's put it along with the other code related to our character. Add this to Part - Characters, under a new heading called Chapter - The Rabbit:

> At the time when Rabbit's conversation starts: try quizzing the rabbit about
>   introduction; try listing suggested topics.

Let's sketch in the details of his appearance and surroundings.

> The description of Burrow is "Roots push through the earthen roof, casting
>   weird shadows in the beam of your flashlight. It's round and small and
>   underground in here and filled with hot sweat and animal stench. But mostly
>   filled with something big and alive." Some roots are scenery in Burrow.

> The rabbit is in Burrow. The initial appearance of the rabbit is "[one of]It's huge,
>   covered in sweaty fur stained with mud, and a huge eye stares out you above
>   long black whiskers. You can feel its breath on your face and its heartbeat
>   thudding through the floor and you cringe back in terror against the wall.
>   It's... well.[paragraph break]It's a rabbit.[or]The rabbit stares at you, whispers
>   twitching, and it's freaking you out.[stopping]". The description of the rabbit
>   is "The closer you look the weirder it gets, like it doesn't start or end in any
>   one place or something all new-agey like that."

And now for the actual conversation. Let's begin.

> introduction is a familiar thing. After quizzing the rabbit about introduction: say
>   "The rabbit breathes and stares. You wonder if it's going to start talking like
>   in some crap disney movie and then jesus christ it does...[paragraph break]'So
>   what'd you expect from an animal guardian?' it says, but like not with its lips,
>   somewhere in your head instead. 'Were you thinking big, nasty, sharp, pointy
>   teeth? Waistcoat and pocket watch? Nah. Tricks are for kids. What's up,
>   Knock?' Its whiskers twitch.[add rabbit ask suggestion][add go insane other
>   suggestion]".

For abstract concepts that aren't represented by preexisting objects in the game world, we need to create them: here, we instantiate "introduction" as something existing in the story world that our conversation verbs can act upon. We make it *familiar* so it's available to be discussed.

The two text substitutions at the end of the quoted text use Conversation Suggestion's framework to add two possible responses to the list of available topics. These topics should only be available during this conversation: the player should certainly never get a response from Coyote when talking to the rabbit, for instance. Normally we'd have to manage this by hand, but one tweak we've added in our custom version of the extension is to automatically make available any topic held by an NPC at the start of a conversation. So as we define our further topics, we need to remember that they should be held by our NPC.

Remember, as per Conversation Framework we use "quizzing" for topics the player asks about, and "informing" for topics the player tells about. Other suggestions (which we define as misc-suggestion objects) are for things the player might type that don't begin with ASK or TELL.

> go insane is a misc-suggestion. It is held by the rabbit. The printed name is "just, you know, go insane". Understand "go insane" as a mistake ("I know, right? Looks like it's too late though.") when location is Burrow.

This conversation sadly doesn't have a lot of real choice (partially to keep it manageable enough to fit in this book!) but a few moments such as the above that allow for a bit of characterization are worth including.

> After quizzing the rabbit about the rabbit: say "[remove go insane other suggestion]'Oh come on, pal, you know me,' he says with this kind of stupid cheerful tone, and suddenly he looks more like Buster from Arthur, scrawny and poorly animated. 'I've been keeping an eye on you from the TV all these years. Your grandma asked me to, remember?' He grins, buck teeth protruding.[add grandma ask suggestion][add how he's not real tell suggestion]".

Our modified extension automatically removes topics from the relevant suggestion lists as we discuss them, but we still need to do some hand tweaking. In this case, the "go insane" option really only makes sense at the very beginning of the conversation, so we remove it from the topic list if the player chooses the other option.

> grandma is held by the rabbit. After quizzing the rabbit about grandma: say "'She was wrong about lots of stuff,' Buster says, scratching himself with a hind paw thoughtfully, 'but right about lots too. Oh, lots.'"; try quizzing the rabbit about rabbit's judgment.

> how he's not real is held by the rabbit. After informing the rabbit about how he's not real: say "'Oh, don't say that!' the rabbit says, animated eyes going round like saucers. 'Then it'd be just you here all alone, and wouldn't that be boring. It's much more interesting if I'm really around.'"; try quizzing the rabbit about rabbit's judgment.

To hurry the conversation along, and make it seem as if the rabbit is a more active conversational partner, we only allow the player to talk about one of the two topics here, before speeding things along to the next major point.

In this next topic, we'll show one of three different segments based on how the player has played the game so far: whether they've smoked a lot, broken more windows than they needed to, or done neither. This ties into our theme of choices with consequences: while it won't affect the plot of the game, Knock's actions are referenced here to make them become part of his personal story of growth and change.

> rabbit's judgment is held by rabbit. After quizzing the rabbit about rabbit's judgment: clear all topics; say "[one of][if count of pack of cigarettes is less than original cigarette count - 1]'Yo, you started smokin['] again?' Buster asks, sniffing disdainfully, except he's not Buster any more, more like Eminem. 'I thought you quit that shit, dawg. It's cool, I won't tell your grandma, but it makes Thumper cry a little, you know what I'm sayin[']?' [otherwise if at least 2 windows are open]'Yo, nice work breakin['] all those windows,' Buster says, except he's not Buster any more, more like Eminem. 'Way to stick it to the man. You hella bad, dawg. Maybe you can tag some shit when you get back to town too.' [otherwise]'Hey yo, you been hella good about keepin['] off those cancer sticks,' Buster says, except he's not Buster any more, more like Eminem. 'Don't think I ain't watchin['] ya.' [end if](Oh hey, Rabbit Smith, you get it.)[or]The rabbit just scratches his ear with a hind paw, smirking.[stopping][add how he knows so much about everything ask suggestion]".

> how he knows so much about everything is held by the rabbit. After quizzing the rabbit about how he knows so much about everything: say "'Hey, back off, man,' he says, 'it's my ****in['] job.' And there's actually like a bleep, too, and now that you think of it you only ever saw 8 Mile on TV."; try quizzing rabbit about down to business.

Again, we hurry the conversation on to the next major mode, where we ask what Knock feels about Ocean. From a game perspective, this tells the player that the choice of talents is connected to his choice of paths, which in turn determines the destiny of his relationships.

> down to business is held by the rabbit. After quizzing the rabbit about down to business: clear all topics; say "'Anyway, look, man, we both know you're in trouble. I just gotta ask you one question.' And he changes again into like a giant silhouette, and it's the Playboy Bunny, ears and bow tie and all. 'Do you love her?'[add yes-no-suggestion other suggestion][add don't know if I love her other suggestion]"; move the bunny's bow tie to location.

The yes-no-suggestion is one of the shortcuts offered by Conversation Suggestions, that adds both saying yes and saying no as options to the topics list; we can also invoke them individually with yes-suggestion and no-suggestion.

We'll use this opportunity to throw in another memory, a fairly ambivalent one that adds to our portrait of Ocean. To make this choice have weight, staying with Ocean shouldn't be the "obvious" thing to do; if they're not in love, is a life together really the best thing? Put this up in Part - Mechanics, Chapter - Memories, Section - Memory Collection:

> The bunny's bow tie suggests a memory called her graduation night. Understand "Ocean's/Oceans" as her graduation night. Instead of doing anything to the bunny's bow tie: say "It's just a few lines on a silhouette." The description of her graduation night is "She grinned when you picked her up, and you drove on in to Mike's and the lot was filled with trucks and Mike's was filled with Indian guys and Indian girls and she was still the most beautiful, and you danced a lot and drank some and left early to go lie down under the stars and count the shooting ones.
>
> And that was maybe you think the first time she said she loved you, and you said it back cause it felt all right and shit, but you didn't really know if you meant it, or if she did, or what it even really means. I mean you like Ocean a lot, really a lot, but then you also aren't really sure you even know her, anything about her that's important or real or meaningful. She could be anyone, really, on the inside. So could you."

And now, back in Part - Scenes, Chapter - Rabbit's Offer, the three answers to the love question. At the end of each, we'll call a new named phrase, *introduce rabbit's choices*, that will move the plot forward.

> Instead of saying yes when yes-no-suggestion is familiar and location is The Burrow: say "'Then you should probably get home and tell her,' the bunny says. 'Patch up that truck and fly down that highway before she gets away.' It winks."; introduce rabbit's choices.
>
> Instead of saying no when yes-no-suggestion is familiar and location is The Burrow: say "'Then what are you still doing with her?' the bunny says. 'Get out while the getting's good. You think either of you will be happier if you put that off? There's fish in other oceans kid. You've got your whole life ahead to swim.' It winks."; introduce rabbit's choices.
>
> don't know if I love her is a misc-suggestion. It is held by the rabbit. The printed name is "tell him that you don't know". Understand "that/you" as don't know if I love her. After informing the rabbit about don't know if I love her: say "'Yeah,' the bunny says, 'well this is the night to figure it out. Whether you decide to go home to her tonight or take care of yourself tonight might have consequences on a night with a storm like the one that's coming. Just sayin['].' It winks."; introduce rabbit's choices.

Now, the real choice in the conversation: the setup of the talents.

> To introduce rabbit's choices:
>
> > clear all topics;
> >
> > now bow tie is off-stage;
> >
> > move strength to location;
> >
> > now strength is familiar;
> >
> > move courage to location;
> >
> > now courage is familiar;
> >
> > move easter basket to location;
> >
> > say "[line break]'Look,' he says, and now he's big and fluffy and smells like springtime and peeps. 'I can help you make your decisions. I'll trade you for one of these talents.' He holds out an [easter basket filled with plastic green easter grass]; in it are two glowing orbs.[paragraph break]'Strength,' he says, pointing to the first one, 'and courage. Pick whichever one you think will be most useful, but you have to give me something back. Something real, something I can work with.'[add more about trading ask suggestion][add strength ask suggestion][add courage ask suggestion][add trade-for-strength other suggestion][add trade-for-courage other suggestion][add take-inventory other suggestion][add don't want to trade other suggestion]".

> There is a thing called an easter basket filled with plastic green easter grass. Instead of doing anything to easter basket: say "You aren't sure you believe in it enough for that.".
>
> After quizzing the rabbit about strength: say "'Might be useful for surviving through the night,' he says, 'if that's what you're planning.'".
>
> After quizzing the rabbit about courage: say "'You're going to need it to get home to Ocean,' he says, 'if that's what you want.'".
>
> more about trading is a familiar thing held by the rabbit. After quizzing the rabbit about more about trading: say "'You won't lose what you trade entirely,' he says, twitching his whiskers, 'but it will change, transverse, be resurrected as something else. Reborn.'".
>
> trade-for-strength is a misc-suggestion. It is held by the rabbit. The printed name is "trade something for strength". trade-for-courage is a misc-suggestion. It is held by the rabbit. The printed name is "trade something for courage".
>
> you don't want to trade is a misc-suggestion. It is held by the rabbit. The printed name is "tell him you don't want to trade". Understand "i" as you don't want to trade. [This is so we can also recognize "i don't want to trade".]

> After informing the rabbit about you don't want to trade: say "[remove you don't want to trade other suggestion]'I came all this way to help you,' the rabbit says, 'I'm even missing the big parade,' and it wiggles its tail with a smell of sugar and frosting. 'I think we'd better make a trade.'"
>
> take-inventory is a misc-suggestion. It is held by the rabbit. The printed name is "take inventory of what you've got".

That last one is just to remind the player that the inventory command will show what Knock's holding, including the memories in his emotional baggage.

Let's customize rabbit's responses a little.

> Check trading when the noun is not a memory and the trader is the rabbit: instead say "'No, no, I don't want that,' says the rabbit, twitching its nose indignantly. 'For a talent like this, you ought to put up something real. Something you care about.'[line break]".

Finally, the conclusion.

> Report trading when Rabbit is visible: clear all topics; now more coming is familiar; try quizzing the rabbit about more coming; stop the action.
>
> more coming is a thing. After quizzing the rabbit about more coming: say "'The others are coming,' he says, 'they'll be here soon,' and now he looks like Frank from Donnie Darko and his face is behind that freaky metal mask and his voice is distorted and makes your skin crawl.[paragraph break]'Watch out for them,' he says. 'We all want to help, but... the others are wilier than me. Look up.'[paragraph break]'Look up, Naki,' he says again."; now lookup-suggestion is familiar; reset the interlocutor. lookup-suggestion is an unfamiliar misc-suggestion with printed name "look up".

Reset the interlocutor is a named phrase from our conversation extension that lets us immediately end a conversation without saying goodbye. We abruptly stop the conversation here to make the transition from Frank's suggestion to the player typing LOOK UP as abrupt as possible. The sudden disappearance of the conversation suggestion line should strengthen the tension at this moment.

> Instead of examining up when lookup-suggestion is familiar: say "Stupidly, you tilt your head back and stare up at the dirt ceiling, and all you can see is blackness.[paragraph break]No wait... there's patterns, slowly shifting, barely visible in the darkness, and miles away. Like clouds. And then a drop of water falls on your face, and then another, and you realize suddenly you're outside, and it's starting to rain..."; move player to Backtracking; now lookup-suggestion is unfamiliar.

It was a lot of words for a pretty short scene, but we now have an interactive conversation that lets the player steer the plot, with some great character moments for both Knock and his spirit guardian.

When working on a complex scene like this in the middle of your game, testing it can be a challenge. In Chapter 11 we'll talk about some useful tools for this, but one quick solution is to add a When play begins rule at the bottom of your story file (so it happens after any others) that sets things up for testing. To test the rabbit conversation, we might make one like this:

> When play begins: move flashlight to player; now flashlight is switched on; move player to Burrow.

The Coyote

Coyote presents himself to the player as a man, one of the coyotes who smuggle people across the border from Mexico to the United States. Always a trickster, Knock's second spirit animal takes this form to suggest our protagonist's own transitions, from child to man, city to desert, real to unreal.

When defining our lead-in scenes in the last chapter, we created the Coyote's Offer scene and its starting condition. Let's define how it ends, and begin the conversation: add this in Part - Scenes, Chapter - Coyote's Offer.

> Coyote's Offer ends when location is not Open Desert.
>
> When Coyote's Offer begins: move the Coyote to Open Desert; Coyote's conversation starts in 1 turn from now.

Now, in Part - Characters, Chapter - The Coyote, the result:

> At the time when Coyote's conversation starts: try quizzing the Coyote about introduction; now Coyote holds down to business; try listing suggested topics.

This scene takes place in our previously created Open Desert location, so we don't need a new room. We set up a description for Coyote earlier; let's give him an initial appearance now.

> The initial appearance of Coyote is "The Coyote watches you intently." Understand "guy/man" as the Coyote.

Now, on to the conversation.

> After quizzing Coyote about introduction: say "He wears a couple days of stubble, a [dusty hoodie], and, ridiculously in the darkness, a pair of cheap [sunglasses]. He lights a [cigarette], then holds up a hand in annoyance to block your flashlight beam. 'Turn that thing off,' he says, and either you do it or it goes off by itself, because the next thing you know it's darker and he's closer and the only light comes from the red glow of the cigarette.[paragraph break]'That's better,' he says. He takes a drag on the cigarette, then pulls another from behind his ear and offers it to you. 'Smoke?'[add yes-no-suggestion other suggestion]".

Let's keep our world model consistent with the text we used in the introduction:

> When Coyote's Offer begins: now flashlight is switched off; now Coyote is lit. Instead of switching on flashlight during Coyote's Offer: say "You think you'd rather keep him on your side."

Somewhat sneakily, we give Coyote himself the *lit* property, so that we can still interact with him and the other objects like talents even though the objective light source is gone.

Now, let's deal with the repercussions of the Coyote's offer.

> Instead of taking cigarette: move cigarette to player; try saying yes. Instead of dropping cigarette: now cigarette is off-stage; say "You drop it to the ground and stub it out with your foot." Instead of smoking when player holds cigarette during Coyote's Offer: say "You take a drag, thoughts and adrenaline whirring through your head." Instead of smoking during Coyote's Offer: try saying yes.

> Instead of saying yes when yes-no-suggestion is familiar and Coyote is visible: say "You pull out your pack and [if count of pack of cigarettes is 0]see that it's empty, but Coyote grins and hands you his last one[otherwise]he grins, like he knew you'd say yes[end if], and leans forward for you to light up off him. His sunglasses reflect back nothing but your own face weirdly lit by the glow from the cig, and for a moment it's like the blackness behind them is deep, deeper than the sky, deeper than the universe..."; if count of pack of cigarettes > 0, decrease count of pack of cigarettes by 1; Coyote-talks.

> Instead of saying no when yes-no-suggestion is familiar and Coyote is visible: say "He shrugs, takes a puff on his, and exhales the smoke into the desert night. Wind whips it away and he stares towards the horizon, forehead wrinkling in something (annoyance, maybe contemplation) you can't read through the sunglasses."; Coyote-talks.

> To Coyote-talks: clear all topics; say "[line break]'Gotta keep an eye on the horizon,' he says in a scratchy, slow voice[if we are saying yes] as you step back, inhaling the dry smoke[end if]. 'Always someone hunting. Border Patrol, National Guard, INS, Minutemen. You want to help people get where they're going out here, you need more than [if player holds strength]strength[otherwise]courage[end if]. You need to learn how to hide.'[paragraph break]'I'm the Coyote,' he says. 'And we've been hiding from each other for a long time.'[make rabbit known][add rabbit ask suggestion][add Coyote ask suggestion][add advice ask suggestion][add down to business ask suggestion]".

Since the topics in this conversation can occur in a slightly more flexible order, let's add a say suggestion that lets us insert a bit of **business** into the dialogue. Business is a theater term for an unimportant but character-building action taken by an actor, often in the background. We'll use it here to remind the player of details of the setting and Coyote's physicality.

To say Coyote-business: say "[one of]smoke gusting from his lungs in clouds[or]scratching his stubble with the hand that holds the cigarette[or]itching underneath his jacket, slowly[or]the red tip of the cigarette glowing as he takes another drag[cycling]".

advice is held by the Coyote. After quizzing the Coyote about advice: say "He laughs, [Coyote-business]. 'Kid,' he says, 'you don't want my advice. I could tell you some stories and you'll smile and be sure they'll never happen to you. I could tell you some stories and you'll yawn and think you know them already. I could tell you some stories and you'll think they're wise and not realize you don't understand them until you make the same mistakes yourself and try to turn your failure into advice and fail at that, too. I could tell you some stories.' He looks off towards the horizon, [Coyote-business]. 'But it's not my stories that will help you.'".

After quizzing Coyote about Coyote: say "'You know who I am,' he says, [Coyote-business]. 'I'm the one who runs on both sides of the fence. I'm the one who scouts ahead. I'm the one with songs in my blood and dirt under my nails and people owe me money in every trailer park town from here to Yuma, or maybe I owe them money but anyway they don't want to see me. You know who I am, Knock.'".

After quizzing Coyote about the rabbit: say "He grins, not unkindly but not exactly kindly either. 'That cute little jackalope?' he says, [Coyote-business]. 'He's got his upsides, I guess. [if player holds strength]Strength[otherwise]Bravery[end if] has its place. But if you're always in the spotlight, you'll never learn how to live in the shadows. And most of us spend a lot of time in the shadows.'".

Once the player has asked all they want of Coyote, we get on to the trading.

After quizzing Coyote about down to business: clear all topics; move luck to location; now luck is familiar; move scent to location; now scent is familiar; say "He presses his hands together, still clutching the cigarette with thumb and index finger, and smoke rises past his hidden eyes as he slowly rubs his palms together. He mutters something rhythmic to himself and you realize it's a song, and you can't quite make out the lyrics but the melody is simple and makes you think of Johnny Cash and the end of the world. And then he stops, and pulls his hands apart, and in each he holds a talent.[paragraph break]'Here we have luck,' he says, bobbing the left, 'and scent. And look, I'll be straight with you. These are precious things and I can't afford whatever blue light special deal the bunny gave you. I need double his price. I need two memories to part with one of these. Oh, they're worth it, believe me. Both have saved my ass more times than you'd believe. Both could save yours. But it's up to you. Which'll it be?'[add luck ask suggestion][add scent ask suggestion][add trade-for-luck other suggestion][add trade-for-scent other suggestion][add take-inventory other suggestion]".

After quizzing Coyote about luck: say "[if player holds strength]'Looks like you're already pretty tough,' he says appraisingly, looking you over. 'With a little luck, you ought to make it through the night and get on with the rest of your life.'[otherwise]'You found some cojones, kid,' he says, looking you over appraisingly, 'which'll be good for fixing your truck and getting back to your girl. I don't know if luck'll help you out much there, though.'".

After quizzing Coyote about scent: say "[if player holds courage]'You found some cojones, kid,' he says, 'If you can just sniff out the right finds, you can probably get back to that little lady you're so fond of, if that's what you want.'[otherwise]'You're pretty tough,' he says, 'but I don't know that a good nose is going to help you make it through the night and get on with the rest of your life, if that's what you're trying to do.'".

trade-for-luck is a misc-suggestion. It is held by Coyote. The printed name is "trade something for luck".

trade-for-scent is a misc-suggestion. It is held by Coyote. The printed name is "trade something for scent".

Report trading when Coyote is visible: clear all topics; now more coming is familiar; try quizzing Coyote about more coming; stop the action.

After quizzing Coyote about more coming: say "He tucks the other talent back in his pocket, and without its faint glow it seems darker than ever, the pulsing red tip of his cigarette all you can see.[paragraph break]'The last of us is coming,' Coyote's voice says out of the black, 'last and most powerful, and most dangerous, and most afraid. Sand-dancer. Be careful of him, Knock. [if player holds strength]Stay strong[otherwise]Stay brave[end if]. [if player holds luck]Stay lucky[otherwise]Keep your nose to the wind[end if]. Remember the shadows.'[paragraph break]And it seems like he's growing, larger and larger, the red tip of his cigarette pulsing and glowing now high up in the sky, and you stumble back, shivering, and suddenly remember your flashlight in your hand and switch it on..."; reset the interlocutor; now flashlight is switched on; move player to Base of the Tower.

The player character has once again returned to relative normalcy, this time armed with two talents to help him.

With the knowledge of how to build characters and conversations under our belts, we've mastered the last major skill area lacking in our Inform 7 knowledge. We could take what we've learned already and tell interactive stories on the same level as the adventure games from the '80s, which included some amazingly sophisticated stories like *A Mind Forever Voyaging* and one of my favorite interactive fictions ever, *Trinity*. In the next few chapters of the book, we'll learn how to challenge some of Inform's assumptions about how a story world should work, talk in depth about techniques for testing, debugging, and polishing a story, and get a roadmap for where to turn after the book has ended to keep learning more.

Exercise Answers

Exercise 9.1

How would you remove the showing action from a story entirely and redirect it to giving?

> Understand the command "show" as something new. Understand "show [something] to [someone]" as giving it to.

Exercise 9.2

Make the hare animal into an active character.

> The desert hare is in Base of the Tower.
>
> Every turn when a random chance of 1 in 4 succeeds:
>> let starting point be the location of the desert hare;
>> let destination be a random room which is adjacent to starting point;
>> let heading be the best route from starting point to destination;
>> if heading is a direction and destination is regionally in Around the Tower, try the desert hare going heading.
>
> After the hare going a direction (called way): if the hare is visible or the hare was visible, say "The hare hops [way]wards."

Exercise 9.3

Let players look up things in the guidebook.

> Instead of consulting the guidebook about "sand-dancer/sand/dancer/lizard/lizards/brown": say "You look up the brown-colored lizard in the guidebook and quickly identify it: those eyes are a dead giveaway. The entry says it's a 'rare subspecies of the common desert lizard found only in the deep desert near Oro Oeste, and known to native peoples as a [italic type]sand-dancer[roman type]. In legends, the sand-dancer was a clever trickster and twister of words, who created night by tricking the sun into spending half the day underground.' Huh."

You could then add as many other entries to the guidebook as you wished.

CHAPTER 10

CHALLENGING ASSUMPTIONS

While we've learned a lot about how Inform works, we haven't questioned its underlying assumptions very much. Both on large and small scales, from describing a room to choosing a pronoun, we've basically just accepted the way the Standard Rules say things should work.

But as you get more experienced, and your projects get more challenging, you'll inevitably want to change these defaults—not all of them, but in any given project at least one. From a certain perspective, nearly *all* IF programming is setting up exceptions to default behavior: every instead rule effectively says "Well, normally nothing would happen here, but in this case..."

Since many of these default behaviors are hidden in the Standard Rules, overriding them can be confusing. In this chapter we'll go through many of the most common ways you might want to alter the core functionality of an Inform story. In the process we'll learn some of the nuts and bolts of the underlying machinery that make these stories work.

Basic Changes

A lot of the standard behavior of an IF story, both in terms of appearance and functionality, can be easily customized. Let's go over some of the most common things you might want to change.

The Command Prompt

Normally, the IF prompt is a simple greater than sign, a tradition dating back to *Zork* and the command-line interface of the operating systems that first ran it. For the computer-savvy, the prompt is an indication that a program is awaiting input from the user to continue. However, you might want it to look like something else for various reasons, one of which might be helping new players understand what to do when it appears. It's simple enough to change the prompt's appearance by altering the global text variable *the command prompt* within a phrase or rule:

```
now the command prompt is "Knock should ";
```

Any text, including text substitutions, can be given here: if you wanted each command numbered, you might set it to "[turn count]>". The command prompt can be changed at will, but a good place to change it for the duration is in a when play begins rule.

Status Line

The status line at the top of the screen normally shows the current room (on the left side) and the number of moves made (and score, if any) on the right. We can change this by changing the text variables *the left hand status line* and *the right hand status line* within a rule or phrase.

```
now the left hand status line is "Talents: [the list of held talents]";
now the right hand status line is "Cigs: [count of pack of cigarettes]";
```

Keep in mind that people read IF on screen sizes ranging from giant monitors to cell phones, so the space available in the status line may be much larger or smaller than it appears on your screen. It's recommended to keep both sides to just a few words in length.

Extensions allow for fancier tricks with status lines. Basic Screen Effects by Emily Short lets you center things in your status line, or give it more than one row.

Directions

Inform comes with built-in directions for connecting rooms: the eight cardinal points, plus in, out, up, and down. However, you can freely extend this set by creating your own directions. You must always assert new directions in simple sentences and along with an opposite that defines its reverse (like east and west):

```
The starboard is a direction. The opposite of starboard is port. The port is
    a direction. The opposite of port is starboard.
```

Once created, new directions can be used exactly as any built-in direction can.

> The galley is starboard of the kitchen.
>
> Understand "p" as port.
>
> Check going starboard: ...

Exercise 10.1

If you write *Understand "s" as starboard*, the letter s will now refer to two different directions (starboard and south), producing a disambiguation message. Can you think of a tool you've learned for reducing disambiguation messages that could be used to avoid this whenever possible?

Plural Things

Inform's concept of a thing normally assumes that it represents one singular object. You can create something that acts plural by defining it with the pronoun *some* (as in *some marbles*). But what if you actually want duplicate objects (*six marbles*), or more complex use of pronouns (*a bunch of marbles*)? Inform offers a number of flavors of plurality for the adventurous to dig into.

Plural-Named Things

For things representing a collection of objects that always act as one unit, we use the pronoun *some* in our assertion sentence.

> Some cobwebs are a thing in the hole in the floor.

Creating an object this way actually does two things: it sets the **indefinite article** text property of the thing to "some," and also makes it **plural-named** (the default for a thing is **singular-named**). While this is almost always what we want, we can set these two values by hand if we need to.

We ought to fix one case of a mismatched plural in *Sand-dancer*. The emergency lights should use the singular definite article (the) since we're mostly referring to them as a collective noun, but they should be plural for the purpose of writing a message like "They're hardly portable." Amend the declaration of the lights in Part - Setting, Chapter - Office Interior, Section - Storage Room to read as follows:

> The emergency lights are a plural-named fixed in place device in Storage Room.

CAUTION

Players often try to refer to plural objects in a singular form, but unless we explicitly define these variations, Inform won't be able to parse them. You can use understand rules to catch both singular and plural versions.

> Some delicious sandwiches are a thing. Understand "sandwich" as
> sandwiches.

Mass Nouns

Some nouns in English refer to aggregates that do not contain easily divisible items: these are called mass nouns, and examples include water, sand, and bread. While "some" is indeed the correct article for these, they do not use plural verb forms: it would seem unnatural to read "The water are already here." We can create mass nouns by asserting them with a singular article, to set plurality, but a hand-set indefinite article:

> The water is here. The indefinite article is "some".

Now the above message would correctly describe "some water" in room descriptions, but refer to it in error messages like "The water is already here."

Multiple Distinguishable Objects

Sometimes you might want two or more objects in the same room that are similar, but not identical: a series of doors, a stack of books, three marble statues. Since each object must have a unique name, it's important to find some easy way to distinguish between them: a *screen door* and a *heavy oak door*, or maybe the *painting by the window* and the *painting above the door.*

Sometimes, though, lists of such objects in room descriptions can be awkward: we might have something like: "You can also see a statue of David, a statue of Medusa, and a statue of Cheech Marin here." One trick for resolving this is to make the statues scenery, and refer to them in your room description with a phrase like "three statues." You can add an understand rule to make "statues" match each object (or the statue kind, if you've created it). Now the response to a command like EXAMINE STATUES is "Which do you mean, the statue of David, the statue of Medusa, or the statue of Cheech Marin?" This unclutters our main description until such time as the player actually needs to distinguish between the similar objects.

Indistinguishable Objects (Duplicates)

Sometimes, you really do want to create a group of identical objects—ten wooden blocks, thirty silver pieces, eight packages of Ramen—and allow the player to treat them as distinct objects that can each be picked up and moved around at will. This introduces a great deal of complexity, but to get started, all you need to do is define a kind, and then assert that some number of that kind exists:

> A wooden block is a kind of thing. Ten wooden blocks are in the Playroom.

CAUTION

Be forewarned: while Inform makes duplicates technically possible, creating them invites a host of headache-inducing problems. If you've created ten wooden blocks, how should they be described if the player has taken some but not all of them? All of them but one? What if some of them are on a supporter in a room and the others are on the ground? Should they appear as ten separate items in the player's inventory or be grouped together?

Think carefully before you introduce this level of complexity into your story: often, you can get away with a simpler implementation. However, if you want to dive in, check the official documentation's chapter on Activities, in particular "printing the plural name of something," "printing a number of something," and "grouping together something."

Exercise 10.2

Knock's cigarettes are currently implemented with a number variable *count* attached to the *pack of cigarettes* thing. How would you instead create each cigarette as a specific object in the story world? What would be some of the advantages and disadvantages of doing so?

Games in Different Languages

Though Inform's syntax would seem to couple it closely to the English language, there have long been substantial IF communities working in many other languages, and Inform's various versions have supported these efforts. The Inform site hosts a number of extensions (under the category Translations) for modifying the language of play, which define the basic fundamentals of grammar (how to count, say words like *he* and *she*, conjugate fundamental verbs like *to be*, and so on). Many of these extensions also fully translate the library messages produced by the Standard Rules—such as "You can't see any such thing," which is rendered in <u>Italian by Massimo Stella</u> as *Non si vede niente del genere*.

What's left, of course, is all the text of the story itself, which it's up to the author to write. One potential snag is that many non-English languages use unusual characters, from accented letters to punctuation marks not appearing on English keyboards, to complex symbols not appearing on any keyboard.

Inform understands most kinds of accented letters common to Romance languages natively, and these can be used anywhere regular letters can, such as in story titles or object names. The Inform parser can also distinguish between, for instance, an e and an é.

PROGRAMMER'S NOTE

The exact set of characters Inform understands natively is an old IF standard called ZSCII, based on 8-bit ASCII but modified to squeeze in characters likely to be useful to Western authors. ZSCII is fully documented on the official site for Inform 6, linked to from the main Inform site.

Any other character you can get your computer to type can be used within quoted text. Characters that can't be typed can be used if you find their Unicode ID number, using a text substitution like [unicode 716]. Two built-in extensions, <u>Include Unicode Character Names by Graham Nelson</u> and <u>Include Unicode Full Character Names by Graham Nelson</u>, allow for use of the official names for the first 2,900 and 12,997 Unicode characters, respectively, letting you write things like [Unicode Hebrew letter alef].

CAUTION Authors must consider that many players may not have access to a font that can display unusual characters, a concern of increasing urgency the more obscure a character you try to use.

Use Options

Use options, introduced in Chapter 5, are assertions that set some basic either/or rules about how your story should operate. They're mostly used to address conflicting schools of thought on the best default behavior. Here are the most important use options you'll run into.

The Use Option	*Notes*
Use American dialect	Uses American spellings in the Standard Rules messages, as well as American methods of writing numbers. The British versions are used by default.
Use the serial comma	By default, a list of three objects will read "apple, orange and pear"; adding this option will include an extra comma after the penultimate item (producing "apple, orange, and pear"). The serial comma is more commonly used in American English, although it mostly boils down to a matter of grammatical preference.

The Use Option	*Notes*
Use no scoring	We've already enabled this for *Sand-dancer*: it disables Inform's built-in system for keeping and displaying a score.
Use memory economy	If you're trying to fit a game into the smaller z-machine format, this line will buy you a little extra room, at the expense of losing the ability to effectively use testing commands while debugging.
Use authorial modesty	Prevents an extension (or any extensions by the project author, if used directly) from appearing in the credits generated by the VERSION command. Created not for bashful extension authors, but to prevent extensions designed for your internal use only from showing up in this list.
Use fast/slow route-finding	Changes the algorithm used for pathfinding; most authors won't need to worry about this, but see "Adjacent rooms and routes through the map" in the built-in docs for the nitty-gritty.
Use undo prevention	Disables use of the UNDO command.
Use no deprecated features	Disallows the use of any phrases that may be removed from future versions of the language.

If necessary, you can create a condition to test whether any use option is set by using syntax like *if the undo prevention option is active*.

CAUTION

Particularly in light of *Sand-dancer*'s themes of committing to decisions, and the impossibility of going back to change the past, should we disable UNDO?

This presents an interesting dilemma about the balance between gameplay and story. Story-wise, it is absolutely right to disable undo: if the player can see all the endings to the story in quick succession by just undoing and trading for different talents from Sand-dancer, much of the permanence of our final words is lost. However, from a gameplay perspective, disabling undo is problematic at best and infuriating to your players at worst: it's a commonly accepted part of a player's toolkit, and forbidding access to it can feel like having a limb amputated. Then again, the use of UNDO destroys our "smoking as hint system" mechanic as well: the player can get free hints whenever, then just UNDO with no consequence to Knock.

I'll leave this thorny decision up to you. If you decide to get rid of undo, add "Use undo prevention." to the top of your story file. For more complex handling of undo, check out the extensions <u>Conditional Undo by Jesse McGrew</u> or <u>Undo Output Control by Erik Temple</u>.

Not listed here is a group of technical use options that extend the allowable numbers of certain constructs in a story. To better manage errors in the Inform compiler, some of these limits are set relatively low, and in medium to large stories you may on occasion see an alarming-looking error (Figure 10.1).

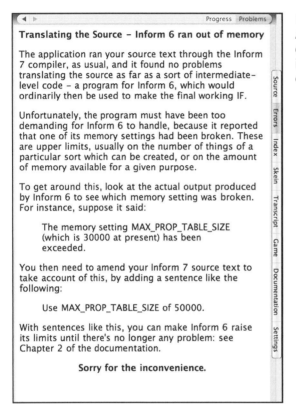

Figure 10.1
An error message produced upon exceeding one of the built-in constants.

The instructions in this message are fairly reassuring and complete: select the Progress tab of the Errors panel and look for the "fatal error." This will give you a variable name all in capital letters and its current numeric size—something like "The memory setting MAX_OBJECTS (which is 512 at present) has been exceeded." All that's needed is a use option setting this to a larger number—doubling is usually a safe bet. In this case, you'd write:

Use MAX_OBJECTS of 1000.

Recompile and you're off and running again.

Activities

We've seen how to change lots of surface components of a story world's presentation. But how do we get in and change the inner workings of the Standard Rules, Inform's primary engine? To do so, we'll need to introduce a new concept.

We've spent a lot of time talking about actions (performed by characters in your story), and their associated default and exception rulebooks (check, instead, carry out, and so on). However, much of the Standard Rules' behavior is not directly related to actions. Printing a list of things, deciding whether there's enough light to see, displaying an error after an invalid command: these all happen while simulating the model world, regardless of a character's actions. These jobs are performed by **activities**.

To better explain the difference between actions and activities, imagine you're driving your car. You might take actions like *depressing the accelerator, tuning the radio, turning on the wipers,* or *opening the glovebox.* These **actions** all have effects on the car's behavior. However, the computers and devices in the car are doing their own things, not all of which are related to the driver's input: things like *charging the battery, shifting into third gear* (in an automatic), *lighting the seat belt sign,* or *deploying the air bag.* These **activities** are also vitally important to the car's operation, but usually not anything the driver needs to worry about... unless they aren't behaving the way you want them to.

One of the basic activities in the Standard Rules is *printing the name of something,* which simply displays the printed name of an item whenever it needs to be identified. While this wouldn't seem to be a particularly interesting or noteworthy activity, we'll shortly see how tweaking even basic behaviors can produce interesting results.

Activity Rulebooks

Like actions, activities have a set of rulebooks associated with them. Any rules in an activity's **before** rulebook run immediately before the activity begins. An activity's single **for** rule defines what that activity does. Finally, all of an activity's **after** rules run immediately after the for rule finishes. Adding or replacing these rules gives authors tremendous flexibility to adjust Inform's default behavior.

For instance, try temporarily adding the following line to *Sand-dancer*:

```
Before printing the name of something: say "stupid ". [Note space at end]
```

Now we get text like "In the stupid pickup truck you can see a stupid piece of jade." While perhaps not the most sophisticated example, it's clear how just a single change to an activity's behavior can produce wide-reaching changes across an entire story.

More usefully, we might check which items we've forgotten to get BENT with by adding a rule like this:

> For printing the name of something: say "XXX".

This lets us see at a glance which items we forgot to bracket in our room description text, possibly meaning we forgot to create an object representing that text in the story world, too (Figure 10.2). Note that while any number of *before* rules can run, only one *for* rule is allowed. Our rule here overrides the *for printing the name of something* defined in the Standard Rules, since it appears later in the source text.

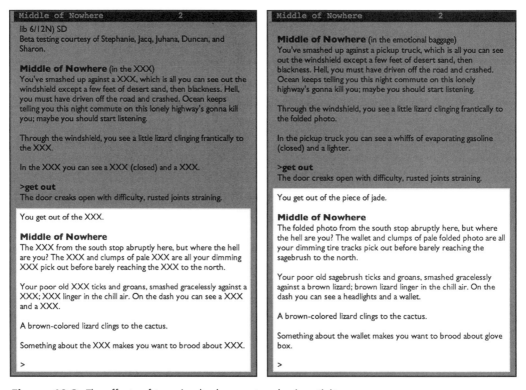

Figure 10.2 The effects of two simple changes to a basic activity.

Less usefully (at least for this story) we could introduce utter chaos with something like:

> For printing the name of something: say the printed name of a random visible thing.

Another example of an interesting usage can be seen in my previously mentioned extension <u>Emphasized Keywords by Aaron Reed</u>, which uses the before and after rules of printing the name of something to change the color of the text, thus making all notable things visually distinctive.

As with action rules, we can also make an activity rule more specific by applying it only to a certain thing or category of things:

> Before printing the name of a memory: say "the memory of ".
> After printing the name of the rabbit: say ", or whatever it is".

You can make activity rules apply only in specific circumstances by adding the word **while** at the end of their definition, followed by a condition. In Part - Mechanics, Chapter - Smoking, add:

> After printing the name of the pack of cigarettes while taking inventory:
>   say " you should have given up months ago".

 Before and after activity rulebooks will run in the order they are defined in your source text. Only the first defined "for" rulebook at a given level of specificity will run (meaning a *for printing the name of the pickup* rule and a *for printing the name of a container* rule can both coexist, in the same way action rules are ordered).

Exercise 10.3

How would you write an activity rule that would visually flag the objects you haven't written a description for? Or visually mark anything portable, to be sure you don't have scenery items the player could walk off with? Can you use the latter trick to find something in the building that's portable but shouldn't be?

Exercise 10.4

How would you describe objects in a subtly different fashion after Knock has acquired a talent that might alter his perception of them?

Some Useful Activities

Let's take a look at some other activities frequently used by Inform. A full list of Inform's activities can be found in the "Activities" chapter of the built-in docs, along with more details about each one. These are just some of the highlights, to give you a sense of what kinds of things activities are used for.

Printing Room Description Details of Something

Not as sweeping as it sounds, this activity is responsible only for showing the parenthetical clauses that sometimes appear after an item mentioned in a room description: things like (closed) for containers or (providing light) for lit objects. We might decide these are mere distractions, and abolish this activity:

> Rule for printing room description details: do nothing.

Alternatively, we might decide we could usefully display some additional details here:

> Rule for printing room description details of something required by a plan: say " (hey, looks useful)".

Supplying a Missing Noun

If you define a noun-less understand rule for an action that normally requires a noun, you can get the parser to assume the most likely object by creating a *for* rule for the *supplying a missing noun* activity. For instance, one useful trick might be to get the command SMOKE to work the same as SMOKE CIGARETTES. Let's add the following to Part - Mechanics, Chapter - Smoking:

> Understand "smoke" as smoking. Rule for supplying a missing noun while smoking: now the noun is the pack of cigarettes.

Now the parser will assume the noun "pack of cigarettes" when the player doesn't provide one for smoking. One catch: since the cigarettes might not actually be visible, we should account for this and give a different message. Adjust the rule above to read as follows:

> Rule for supplying a missing noun while smoking: if pack of cigarettes is visible, now the noun is the pack of cigarettes; otherwise say "You slip your hand into your pocket and remember you don't have your smokes on you."

Printing the Banner Text

The banner is normally displayed after any *when play begins* rules and before the description of the first room, displaying the title, author, and version information somewhat akin to the title card of a movie This is something of a convention, but if we wanted, we could create a simpler introduction for *Sand-dancer* (in Chapter - Beginning the Story):

> Rule for printing the banner text while turn count is 1: say "[paragraph break]   S A N D - D A N C E R[paragraph break][paragraph break]".

Note that we specify this should only happen during the first turn. The banner text is also displayed in response to the VERSION command, which displays information about the story format and other bibliographic details it would be considered bad form to completely omit.

Room Descriptions

Among the most complex set of Inform's activities are those dealing with describing a room and its contents. While the process may seem simple at first, there are a surprisingly large number of situations this code must consider: what order should objects be described in? How should things be described if the player is inside an enterable transparent box? Or a closed opaque one? What should be visible if the player brings a flashlight into the box?

Then, too, are the stylistic choices enshrined into the Standard Rules. What if we'd prefer a different style of listing miscellaneous objects than the straightforward one generated for us? If we want a single paragraph for all the objects with initial appearances? If we don't want to list the contents of an open container in the room description?

The Standard Rules break down every step of describing a location into a series of activities, from the overall *printing the locale description of something* to our humble friend *printing the name of something*. Ten different activities can potentially get involved in the process. Let's do a brief overview of the most important.

Activity	*Description*
printing the locale description of something	runs for every "locale" the player is in: usually just the room, but might also include, say, Knock's pickup truck if you were inside it
choosing notable locale objects for something	builds and prioritizes the list of what objects in a locale need to be described. Rules can set the *locale priority* of items to a number lower than 5 (which will make them appear earlier in the room description) or greater than 5 (to appear later)
printing a locale paragraph about something	decides whether to print anything for each item on the prioritized list
writing a paragraph about	prints an initial appearance or similar text, if any
listing non-descript items of something	considers the list of miscellaneous items (anything on the prioritized list that has not yet been mentioned)
listing contents of something	prepares and prints the list
grouping together something	for each object in the list, decides whether it can be grouped with any other objects
printing room description details of something	displays parenthetical details like "(closed)" or "(providing light)" for objects in the miscellany list

We don't have the space to discuss each of these in depth (again, the built-in documentation is your friend), but we'll talk about some useful examples.

Creating More Natural Prose with Writing a Paragraph About

One useful activity is *writing a paragraph about*, which gets triggered for every visible object in a room. Normally, this only does something for objects with an initial appearance, not only displaying the given text but marking that item **mentioned**. Every visible item starts the room description process set to **unmentioned**, and as each is described, it's changed to mentioned. If an object doesn't have an initial appearance, *writing a paragraph about* ordinarily does nothing, leaving it to later activities to describe anything left unmentioned at the end.

One neat trick is to create a *for writing a paragraph about* rule that describes several objects at once. We can do this by bracketing their names in the text, or manually setting them to mentioned afterwards; in either case, Inform understands that the item does not have to be described again later, potentially leading to more elegant prose.

For instance, we could declutter the description of the Storage Room by merging the text describing the emergency lights and the crumbling shelving. If you like, replace the initial appearance text for the emergency lights and the crumbling shelving with the following, in Part - Setting, Chapter - Office Interior, Section - Storage Room:

> For writing a paragraph about the emergency lights: say "Near some [rows of crumbling shelving] supporting hundreds of dusty [cans of food] [if emergency lights are switched off]you spot a dark[otherwise]is the[end if] control panel for the building's emergency lights."; now cans of food are mentioned.

Exercise 10.5

Create a writing a paragraph about rule for the Roof location that describes in a single paragraph the barrel and the rungs to the Control Center, varying the text appropriately based on the barrel's position and the player's talents.

Grouping Together

One way to make a list of things sound more natural is to group together similar entries. The *grouping together* activity can allow for this, and it's most useful within a before rule for another activity, *listing contents*. You can invoke the former activity within the latter by simply requesting that objects matching a description be grouped together. In Part - Mechanics, Chapter - Customizations, add:

> Before listing contents while taking inventory: group talents together.

This would make *Sand-dancer*'s inventory listings a little more succinct. We could write another line like the following:

> Before listing contents while taking inventory: group things required by a plan together. Before grouping together things required by a plan: say "useful stuff: ".

In tandem, all three activity rules would produce an inventory listing like this:

> You are carrying:
>
>   a denim jacket (being worn)
>
>   useful stuff: canned oranges and emergency blanket
>
>   luck and strength

Extensions for Describing Rooms

IF author Emily Short has written a number of extensions that make the process of adjusting how room descriptions work a little easier.

Room Description Control by Emily Short provides a framework for substituting different styles of room description. For instance, when combined with Tailored Room Descriptions by Emily Short, it describes objects in rooms without the parenthetical asides like "(closed)" or "(providing light)" the Standard Rules normally generate; instead, this information is integrated more naturally into the text.

Complex Listing by Emily Short lets you define your own ways of listing items, producing lists perhaps like "an apple; an orange; a pear."

Assorted Text Generation by Emily Short gives authors more tools to use in describing groups of similar objects, allowing for the automatic production of sentences like "There are three doors here. None of them are open."

Introductions by Emily Short creates an easy way to describe things differently the first time they're encountered than on subsequent occasions.

Changing Library Messages

Sometimes you don't want to change Inform's built-in behaviors, just its built-in responses. Several hundred pieces of text are part of the Standard Rules and appear in response to unsuccessful player commands:

> You aren't holding that!
>
> Are you sure you want to restart?
>
> That's fixed in place.
>
> You can't put something on top of itself.

...and sometimes successful ones:

> Taken.
>
> You are carrying:
>
> You switch the flashlight on.

Sometimes we'd like to give these responses more character, or remove what character they do contain (such as the vaguely prissy tone the standard error messages sometimes exude).

While a built-in solution for customizing library messages is in the works for a future version of Inform, for now the best solution is to use the extension <u>Default Messages by David Fisher</u>. Including this lets you change most library messages with a single phrase. For instance, the stock response to typing in dirty words is "Real adventurers do not use such language." This isn't appropriate to *Sand-dancer* for several reasons. With Default Messages installed, we can change it by adding a phrase like this to a *when play begins* rule:

```
set LibMsg <block swearing obscenely> to "Mos def, bro.[/n]";
```

(Most library messages ending with a period need a line break; the extension doesn't add this by default since not all library messages have one. Default Messages defines the [\n] text substitution as a handy shorthand for [line break].)

While the full list of library messages is immense, and includes many messages that occur only infrequently or require more than a single line to effectively replace, below is a subset containing some of the most common messages you might encounter and want to change. The list here is sorted alphabetically by message; simply match the message text in the left column to the library message name on the right. The documentation for <u>Default Messages</u> contains a list sorted by category, as well as the more obscure messages omitted here, such as those related to reporting an NPC's actions or features of Inform not covered in this book.

Many library messages need to respond slightly differently based on the plurality, gender, or name of the object being acted on. To modify these, you'll need <u>Plurality by Emily Short</u>, which we discussed previously. One trick not already introduced: if a Plurality text substitution like [is-are] needs to appear as the first word of a sentence, you can simply capitalize its first letter, as in [Is-are]. The messages in the table below all use Plurality's formatting to make it easy to see how to construct a proper replacement.

Library Messages

Text of Message	LibMsg Name
Are you sure you want to quit?	<confirm Quit>
Are you sure you want to restart?	<confirm Restart>
But it's dark.	<look under while dark>
But it's dark.	<search while dark>
But you aren't holding [that-those of main object].	<cannot wave something not held>
Cutting [that-those of main object] up would achieve little.	<block cutting>
Darkness	<dark room name>
Darkness, noun. An absence of light to see by.	<examine while dark>
Dropped.	<report player dropping>
Failed.	<Restart failed>
Futile.	<throw at inanimate object>
I beg your pardon?	<empty line>
I didn't understand that sentence.	<command not understood>
I didn't understand the way that finished.	<command badly ended>
I don't suppose [the main object] would care for that.	<cannot take other people>
I don't think much is to be achieved by that.	<block climbing>
I only understood you as far as wanting to	<command partly understood>
If you think that'll help.	<report player touching self>
[It-they of main object] [is-are] fixed in place.	<cannot pull something fixed in place>
[It-they of main object] [is-are] fixed in place.	<cannot push something fixed in place>
[It-they of main object] [is-are] fixed in place.	<cannot turn something fixed in place>
It is now pitch dark in here!	<entering darkness>
It is pitch dark, and you can't see a thing.	<dark description>
Keep your hands to yourself!	<report player touching other people>
Keep your hands to yourself.	<squeezing people>
Keep your mind on the game.	<block kissing>
No, you can't set [that-those of main object] to anything.	<block setting to>
Not that way you can't.	<pushed in illegal direction>
Nothing is on sale.	<block buying>
Nothing obvious happens.	<report player pulling>
Nothing obvious happens.	<report player pushing>
Nothing obvious happens.	<report player turning>
Oh, don't apologize.	<block saying sorry>
Ok.	<Restore succeeded>
Ok.	<Save succeeded>
[']Oops['] can only correct a single word.	<oops too many arguments>
Please answer yes or no.	<yes or no prompt>

Library Messages (continued)

Text of Message	LibMsg Name
Please give one of the answers above.	<restrict answer>
[bracket]Please press SPACE.[close bracket]	<page prompt>
Putting things on [the main object] would achieve nothing.	<cannot put onto something not a supporter>
Quite.	<block swearing mildly>
Real adventurers do not use such language.	<block swearing obscenely>
Restore failed.	<Restore failed>
Save failed.	<Save failed>
Sorry, that can't be corrected.	<oops failed>
Sorry, you can only have one item here. Which exactly?	<single object disambiguation>
Taken.	<report player taking>
That seems unnecessary.	<block waking other>
That was a rhetorical question.	<block saying no>
That was a rhetorical question.	<block saying yes>
That would be less than courteous.	<cannot pull people>
That would be less than courteous.	<cannot push people>
That would be less than courteous.	<cannot turn people>
That's not a direction.	<not pushed in a direction>
That's not a verb I recognize.	<unknown verb>
[That-they of main object]['s-'re] plainly inedible.	<cannot eat unless edible>
[That-they of main object]['s-'re] fixed in place.	<cannot take something fixed>
[That-they of main object]['s-'re] hardly portable.	<cannot take scenery>
[That-those of main object] seem[s] to be a part of [the main object].	<cannot take component parts>
[That-those of main object] seem[s] to belong to [the main object].	<cannot take possessions of others>
The dreadful truth is, this is not a dream.	<block waking up>
There are none at all available!	<no objects available>
There is no reply.	<block answering>
There is no reply.	<block asking>
There is nothing on [the main object].	<nothing found on top of>
There's not enough water to swim in.	<block swimming>
There's nothing sensible to swing here.	<block swinging>
There's nothing suitable to drink here.	<block drinking>
Think nothing of it.	<oops no arguments>
This dangerous act would achieve little.	<block burning>
This provokes no reaction.	<block telling>
Time passes.	<report player waiting>
Violence isn't the answer to this one.	<block attacking>

Text of Message	LibMsg Name
What a good idea.	\<block thinking>
Which do you mean,	\<which disambiguation>
Who do you mean,	\<who disambiguation>
You achieve nothing by this.	\<block rubbing>
You already have [that-those of main object].	\<cannot take something already taken>
You are always self-possessed.	\<cannot take yourself>
You are carrying	\<Inventory initial text>
You are carrying nothing.	\<Inventory no possessions>
You are unable to climb [the main object].	\<cannot go up through closed doors>
You are unable to descend by [the main object].	\<cannot go down through closed doors>
You are unable to.	\<cannot pull scenery>
You are unable to.	\<cannot push scenery>
You are unable to.	\<cannot turn scenery>
You aren't feeling especially drowsy.	\<block sleeping>
You aren't holding [that-those of main object]!	\<object not held>
You aren't holding [the main object].	\<cannot give what you have not got>
You aren't holding [the main object].	\<cannot show what you have not got>
You can hardly repeat that.	\<cannot do again>
You can only do that to something animate.	\<verb cannot have inanimate object>
You can't go that way.	\<cannot go that way>
You can't see any such thing.	\<unknown object>
You can't see inside, since [the main object] [is-are] closed.	\<cannot search closed opaque containers>
You can't talk to [the main object].	\<cannot talk to inanimate object>
You can't use multiple objects with that verb.	\<verb cannot have multiple objects>
You can't wear [that-those of main object]!	\<cannot wear something not clothing>
You can't, since [the main object] leads nowhere.	\<nothing through door>
You can't, since [the main object] [is-are] in the way.	\<cannot go through closed doors>
You close [the main object].	\<report player closing>
You discover nothing of interest in [the main object].	\<block player consulting>
You eat [the main object]. Not bad.	\<report player eating>
You feel nothing unexpected.	\<report player touching things>
You find nothing of interest.	\<cannot search unless container or supporter>
You find nothing of interest.	\<look under>
You give [the main object] to [the second noun].	\<report player giving>
You have died.	\<you have died>
You have won.	\<you have won>
You haven't got [that-those of main object].	\<cannot drop not holding>

Library Messages (continued)

Text of Message	LibMsg Name
You hear nothing unexpected.	<block listening>
You juggle [the main object] for a while, but don't achieve much.	<cannot give to yourself>
You jump on the spot, fruitlessly.	<block jumping>
You lack the dexterity.	<cannot put onto something being carried>
You lack the nerve when it comes to the crucial moment.	<block throwing at>
You look ridiculous waving [the main object].	<report player waving things>
You must name something more substantial.	<something more substantial needed>
You must supply a noun.	<noun needed>
You must supply a second noun.	<second noun needed>
You open [the main object].	<report player opening>
You put on [the main object].	<report player wearing>
You see nothing special about [the main object].	<examine undescribed things>
You see nothing unexpected in that direction.	<examine direction>
You seem to have said too little!	<command incomplete>
You seem to want to talk to someone, but I can't see whom.	<cannot talk to absent person>
You smell nothing unexpected.	<block smelling>
You switch [the main object] off.	<report player switching off>
You switch [the main object] on.	<report player switching on>
You take off [the main object].	<report player taking off>
You talk to yourself a while.	<telling yourself>
You taste nothing unexpected.	<block tasting>
You wave, feeling foolish.	<block waving hands>
You would achieve nothing by this.	<block jumping over>
You would achieve nothing by this.	<block tying>
You'll have to say which compass direction to go in.	<block vaguely going>
You're already wearing [that-those of main object]!	<cannot wear something already worn>
You're not holding [that-those of main object]!	<cannot wear not holding>
You're not wearing [that-those of main object].	<cannot take off something not worn>
Your singing is abominable.	<block singing>
[The main object] cannot be pushed from place to place.	<block pushing in directions>
[The main object] do[es]n't seem interested.	<block giving>
[The main object] has better things to do.	<person ignores command>
[The main object] [is-are] currently switched [if main object is switched on]on[otherwise]off[end if].	<examine devices>
[The main object] [is-are] empty.	<nothing found within container>
[The main object] [is-are] unimpressed.	<block showing>

If you come across a library message not listed here that you'd like to change, one way to find its name is to temporarily add a phrase to your story that will display the identification for any library message:

> When play begins: change library message debug to dbg_on.

Now you'll see messages like this as you test:

>DROP BALL

{LibMsg <cannot drop something already dropped>}

The ball is already here.

Exercise 10.6

Library messages related directly to actions are usually triggered by action default rules. What would be a different way to replace the message above that wouldn't require the Default Messages extension?

A larger extension, <u>Custom Library Messages by David Fisher</u>, allows for more complex manipulation of library messages. Specifically, it enables authors to switch the tense, inflection, and person of library messages at will, so "You can't see any such thing" could become "Knock couldn't see any such thing."

Writing good replacement library messages is trickier than it might first appear. Many of the messages that seem to have awkward phrasing are written that way in order to cover a range of circumstances that might not be immediately apparent. For instance, the old standard "You can't seen any such thing" is carefully constructed to not imply anything about the plurality or gender of the unrecognized word: something like "That's not here" would sound weird in response to a command like TALK TO GEORGE or GET MARBLES. This message also has to work equally well for things the player has seen before that are no longer in scope, and things that don't exist in the story world.

A few other examples: "You hear nothing unexpected" covers a wider gamut than something like "You don't hear anything," which could seem rather out of place in the midst of a jet engine takeoff or wild party. "I don't think much is to be achieved by that," the standard response to climbing, carefully avoids mentioning whether the item in question could potentially be climbed on (like a boulder) or couldn't (like a smell of rose petals) since the parser by default has no idea. However, the standard response to eating, "That's plainly inedible," could stand a change: it assumes it's the player, rather than the author, who has made a mistake. Much more likely is that the player has tried to eat something perfectly edible which was not marked as so by the author. A more neutral message might be something like "That's not something you can eat in this story."

Other tips for writing good library messages: remember that each of these messages is in effect a sort of magic trick, attempting to respond sensibly to something the parser couldn't understand. The shorter your message, the less likely you are to put your foot in your mouth and say something weird and incongruous. Try to never remove any useful information from a message, since the point is to indicate to the player what's gone wrong; likewise, be wary of adding information that may not hold true for all the instances the message might appear for. Jokes about the parser's inability to understand get old fast. Most of all, never assume a message is the result of the player doing something stupid or wrong: it's almost always the reverse, and any messages that are smug or chiding will be infuriating.

Exercise 10.7

Write some new library messages for our story that feel more appropriate to its tone, keeping in mind that things are mostly narrated from Knock's point of view.

Rules and Rulebooks

Activities are the machines that drive a story, but rules are the individual gears. Meddling with rules is one of the most direct and powerful ways to influence your story's behavior, and can be highly confusing if you don't know what you're doing. Let's refresh our memory of how to interact with rules, and then learn about some built-in ways to keep tabs on them.

A Review of Rules

We defined rules and rulebooks back in Chapter 5, but it's worth revisiting the definition now that we've seen all the things you can do with them. A rulebook is a collection of rules to be consulted under particular circumstances, usually to decide whether something succeeds or fails, but sometimes merely to make preparations for something else to happen. Each rule within a rulebook runs in sequence, and has the opportunity to affect the rulebook's decision or behavior. So the *check taking* rulebook runs when the player tries a taking action, and individual rules like the *can't take scenery rule* help decide whether the rulebook returns success (so the action happens) or failure (so it does not).

You can unlist rules from particular rulebooks or any rulebooks in which they might appear:

> The can't take scenery rule is not listed in the check taking rulebook.

> The can't take scenery rule is not listed in any rulebook.

You can also suggest rules be listed first or last, or before or after another rule in a particular rulebook.

> The can't take scenery rule is listed first in the check taking rulebook.

> The can't take scenery rule is listed before the can't take other people rule in the check taking rulebook.

...although note that you can't guarantee placement since another assertion could request a different rule be put in the same position, bumping the previous champion down a slot. For the most part, you don't need to worry about the precise positioning of rules in rulebooks: or if you do, you can use the simplest method of positioning, the order they appear in your source text.

A final trick is to request that a particular rule be listed instead of another rule:

> The customized can't take scenery rule is listed instead of the can't take scenery rule in the check taking rulebook.

An assertion like this implies the need for another syntax: how do we create a standalone rule that isn't attached to any existing rulebook? We simply assert its existence:

> This is the customized can't take scenery rule: say "You can't take scenery... yet."

Rules can invoke other rules with phrases requesting to **consider** or **abide by** them; the difference is that in the former case, we'll ignore the results of any decision the rule makes and continue as normal, and in the latter, we'll make the requested rule's decision our decision too.

> This is the customized can't take scenery rule: if size of player is gigantic, continue the action; otherwise abide by the can't take scenery rule.

The Rules Index

The last tab of the Index panel to be introduced is the Rules panel, also called the Rules Index, which offers a great way to get an overview of all the rules currently defined in your story, which rulebooks and activities they're associated with, and what order they're listed in.

When you open the Rules Index, you'll see a list of rule categories and a brief description. Most of these categories concern fundamental aspects of the simulation of a story world, and don't need to be worried about; but try opening some of these categories to get a look at the ugly details beneath an Inform story (no offense, *enable Glulx acceleration rule*). From any category, you can click "Back to full view" at the top of the tab to return to the main page.

Some categories do contain information you may want to consult often. "Rules added to the sequence of play" shows all of the when play begins, every turn, and when play ends rules in your story. Since these are most likely declared in lots of different places throughout your source text, it's often very handy to see them all in one location.

"How commands are understood" shows all the rules related to parsing the player's input, such as any *does the player mean* rules for disambiguation, and rules for the various activities related to parsing such as *deciding the scope*.

"How actions are processed" does not contain information on the action rulebooks: remember, all of this info is important enough to merit its own tab, "Actions." The actual rules listed in here are foundational and usually don't need to be meddled with.

At the bottom of the list of categories, you'll find separate sections for any extensions you've included that define their own rulebooks or activities. <u>Conversation Framework for Sanddancer</u> uses a rulebook to build the list of suggested conversation topics, so it shows up here.

On all the category pages of the Rules Index, each rulebook or activity receives its own shaded box with the name of the rulebook/activity in bold, a question mark icon that takes you to the documentation for it (if it's from the Standard Rules), and a set of code icons labeled either *name* (for activities) or *b*, *f*, and *a* (for before, for, and after): clicking this code icon will paste in the name of the relevant rulebook at the cursor position in your source text.

Below, you'll find each associated rule in that rulebook, with either its given name (if it was asserted with one) or the first phrase within it. Most rules have *name* code icons and also *unlist* code icons, which will paste the name of and code for getting rid of that rule, respectively, into your source text (Figure 10.3). Rules defined in extensions will show an orange *e* icon, and those defined in your source show with an orange arrow icon, which you can use to skip to the rule's assertion sentence in the appropriate document.

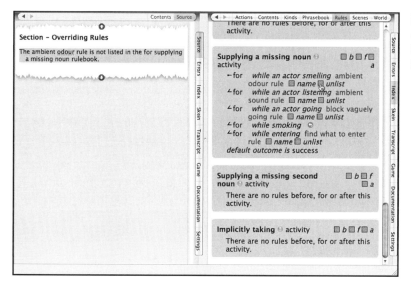

Figure 10.3
An example of using the Rules Index icons to unlist a rule.

Now is also a good time to remind you of the RULES testing command: typing it in an unreleased game will show a list of each rule that's consulted as you play through your story, which can be immensely useful for tracking down errors.

The Rules Index rounds out a great set of fantastic alternate views for the information in your source text and the Standard Rules. Flip through these tabs often to keep a handle on your story.

Scope and Reachability

When the Standard Rules decide what the player can see or touch, they use activities and action default rules to know that, for instance, something inside a closed transparent container is visible (if there's a light source present) but not touchable. But what if these assumptions are wrong?

We can leverage our new knowledge of activities and rules to override the built-in assumptions about visibility and reachability if we need to. The *deciding the scope of something* activity can contain after rules with the phrase **place {something} in scope** to make the item mentioned (and its contents, if an open container or a room) able to be referred to on the current turn by the player in commands. We use this when we want the player to be able to interact with something that couldn't ordinarily be seen.

Imagine, for example, we decide it's too cutesy to have the player actually carrying around the emotional baggage as a visible container. We could keep it as a storage place for discovered memories, but keep it out of play so the player doesn't know it exists. Normally, the player wouldn't be able to refer to its contents, since they wouldn't be in scope. We could change this with a rule:

> After deciding the scope of the player while brooding or trading: place the emotional baggage in scope.

Notice that we only adjust the scope when the two actions related to memories are attempted. It's as if the story world only knows the memories exist when the player is brooding about or trading them, which is perhaps more accurate.

If you try this out, though, you'll see that it doesn't work, producing instead the enigmatic message "That isn't available." This is the Standard Rules trying to cough politely and indicate that we've tried to act on something that's in scope with an action that requires the noun to be touchable. Really? Is that how we defined brooding? Let's take a look back at our definition:

> Brooding is an action applying to one thing.

Though we didn't explicitly state it, Inform assumes we meant "one *touchable* thing," since this makes sense for almost all actions. If we want to define an action as requiring only visibility, not touchability, we need to explicitly state this:

> Brooding is an action applying to one visible thing.

Perhaps counter-intuitively, *visible* here means "visible but not necessarily touchable"; the parser won't care whether the item is touchable or not, just whether it's visible. Making this change would allow us to successfully brood about what's in our emotional baggage, even though it's nowhere to be seen in our story world. (Of course, this method has disadvantages: the most major of which is it gives the player no way to review what memories they've found, which will be vital for trading.)

What if we want to be able to touch something we ordinarily couldn't? For instance, imagine our emergency blanket inside the wire mesh cage. Shouldn't the player be able to touch it, even if can't yet be taken?

Let's first add the following rule, in Part - Setting, Chapter - Office Interior, Section - Break Room:

> Instead of touching blanket when blanket is in cage: say "You can touch the warm wool through the mesh, but you can't get it out."

If we try this, though, we see that our rule never runs: instead, trying to touch the blanket produces a flat refusal, "The wire mesh cage isn't open." Before our instead rule runs, the Standard Rules are saying this action isn't even possible, because the blanket is inside a closed container.

To override this assumption, we need to add a rule to a built-in rulebook called *reaching inside something*. The Standard Rules populate this rulebook with a single rule something like this:

> Rule for reaching inside a closed container: deny access.

If we create a more specific rule that returns the result **allow access** instead of **deny access**, any action checking whether this item is touchable will decide it is. If we restrict this to a specific action or set of actions, we can produce the result we're looking for. Add this:

> Rule for reaching inside the wire mesh cage when we are touching: allow access.

Now, as desired, we can touch the blanket but still not take it.

Exercise 10.8

Add a small object inside the cage that can be taken even when the cage is closed.

A complementary rule is *reaching outside*, which we might use if we wanted to let the player touch something outside the pickup truck while still inside it.

As another example, let's create the folded photo Knock carries that we've alluded to in previous text. When opened, it finally reveals the nature of the problem he's put off thinking about: the baby. This revelation can come only after Knock's done enough brooding, probably not until he's returned from his conversation with the rabbit. Create a new section in Part - Mechanics called Chapter - The Photo, and add the following:

> The player holds a photo. Understand "photograph/pic/picture/folded/unfolded" as photo.

To use the advantage of our existing system that suggests memories, we can put the contents of the photo "inside" it, so they're only revealed (and the memory suggested) after it's opened.

> The photo can be open. The photo can be openable. The photo is closed and openable. The printed name of photo is "[if closed]folded [end if]photo". The description is "[if closed]You just can't deal with that right now. Maybe after you've spent more time brooding.[otherwise]It's [an ultrasound of Ocean's baby]. Your baby too." Inside the photo is an ultrasound of Ocean's baby.

> Instead of opening photo when the number of retrieved memories is less than 4: try examining photo. Understand the command "unfold" as "open".
> Understand the command "fold" as "close".

But since the photo otherwise doesn't act like the sorts of containers that Inform is used to, we can use the reaching inside rule to keep the player from, say, removing the ultrasound from the photo.

> Rule for reaching inside photo: say "Just a photo."; rule fails. Instead of inserting anything into photo: say "Just a photo."

Let's go ahead and write the memory, while we're at it. Put this up in Chapter - Memories, Section - Memory Collection.

> The ultrasound suggests a memory called when you heard the news. Understand "i/baby/ocean's" as when you heard the news. The description of when you heard the news is "Four weeks ago now, a little colder and a little darker. On a night just like this one except you didn't drive off the road and crash into a cactus, you got off work and drove the state highway in the dark and crossed over the edge of the res to Ocean's dad's trailer, and she told you that night while you were dead exhausted, Knock, I'm pregnant.
>
> And all you could think was how totally not real it seemed, after an hour of blackness and Arizona night streaming by, bugs exploding in tiny tragedies on your windshield, you just felt like driving on, like this thing was some podunk town you could breeze by, no services, ranch exit only. And you thought of every movie they ever made you watch in school and every lecture and every living example, the drunken uncles and snaggle-toothed coworkers who knocked up their high school sweethearts and started families on minimum wage and no prospects and never went anywhere and never did anything and what did you do? How could this happen? Why were you both so stupid?
>
> Ocean's aunt is paying for the baby but it's been made clear the money stops when the baby's born. Ocean wants to keep it, she's always wanted to be a mommy. But you never thought you'd be a daddy. And when she pushed this into your hand last night she told you, Knock, it's time to decide. If you aren't with me on this, if you don't want this as much as I do, then this can't go on anymore and you should go. Fly. Head west. Visit Nakaibito. She smiled just a little and traced your ear.
>
> But decide soon, Knock. Decide soon."

The built-in documentation covers scope and reachability in greater detail, including rules for changing the default behavior in darkness, in the chapters on Advanced Actions and Activities.

Changing the Style of Play

Of course, the most drastic change one can make is to do away with the Standard Rules altogether and make something that parses input totally differently. Keep in mind that such major surgery may mean Inform is no longer the best tool for the job: it's designed to tell stories with the parser and Standard Rules, and bypassing them is really working against that design. But if you want to experiment, here are some extensions that implement alternate formats of storytelling.

A simpler model of interactive storytelling is the **choice-based narrative**, perhaps most familiar in popular culture as the "Choose Your Own Adventure" series of books. Two extensions, <u>Simple CYOA by Mark Tilford</u> and <u>Adventure Book by Edward Griffiths</u>, both offer ways to recreate this experience within Inform. Rather than typing commands, players choose from a list of options presented to them. Tilford's extension offers a basic implementation of this concept to create stories much like those you'd see in a printed gamebook, while Griffiths' allows for more complex effects such as inventory and variables.

<u>Interactive Poetry by Michael Bacon</u> eschews the standard parser and world model in favor of a dynamic text that the player can alter by typing specific keywords. Each author-defined keyword changes some of the poem's text in a predefined way. <u>Interactive Poetic Interludes by Kazuki Mishima</u> lets you drop a similar sequence into the middle of an otherwise normal Inform story.

<u>Questions by Michael Callaghan</u> lets the player respond directly to questions asked; though designed for implementation into an existing game, it could be used to create an entirely question-and-answer based story.

Filling in the Corners of *Sand-dancer*

We're nearly complete with our implementation of *Sand-dancer*; just a few major setpieces remain to be created. Let's close out the chapter by creating two of these: the conversation with the voice on the radio, and the dramatic arrival of Sand-dancer himself.

The Voice on the Radio

The radio, sitting tantalizingly in the darkened break room when Knock first encounters it, can be activated once the emergency power is switched on. We previously created the radio and a way to tune it to a custom kind of value called a frequency, and defined an emergency frequency variable. Let's give the player a way to discover this frequency. In Part - Setting, Chapter - Office Interior, Section - Foreman's Office, add this:

> A faded safety poster is in Foreman's Office. "Tacked to the wall is a peeling safety poster, text almost faded away except for a section mentioning an emergency radio frequency." Understand "peeling/text/section/emergency/radio/frequency" as faded safety poster. The description is "According to the poster, the emergency radio frequency is [the emergency frequency]." Instead of taking poster: say "It would disintegrate if you tried to remove it from the wall."

Let's make a better response for turning on the radio, back in Section - Radio.

> After switching on radio: say "You flip a bulky switch on the radio's side. A hiss
> of static pours from the speakers[one of], like tons of sand sliding over
> metal[or][stopping][if frequency tuned to of radio is emergency frequency],
> then quickly resolves into nothing more than a quiet hum[end if]."

Also, we should prevent the player from operating the radio until the emergency power is activated.

> Check switching on radio when emergency lights are switched off: instead say
> "You flip the switch back and forth, but there doesn't seem to be any power.
> Damn."

Now for the conversation itself. Since making the radio itself a conversant might be awkward, let's make a character called *the voice* to fill this role. We could write a rule to place the voice in scope when the radio is switched on, but this might produce difficulties with our conversation system. In this case, a simple parlor trick is all that's needed; we'll just move the voice into the location when the radio is switched on and tuned correctly, and remove the voice after the conversation ends.

Let's put the rest of this conversation in Part - Characters, under a new heading called Chapter - The Radio Voice.

> The voice is an undescribed man.

> Every turn when radio is switched on and frequency tuned to of radio is
> emergency frequency and voice has not been visible:
>
> move voice to location;
>
> try quizzing voice about introduction;
>
> try listing suggested topics;
>
> set pronouns from voice.

The final stipulation in the every turn rule (*voice has not been visible*) makes sure this scene will only happen once. But what's that last phrase in the rule doing? The Inform parser recognizes pronouns like he, she, and it automatically, but normally the referents are set in response to player commands. Since here the player hasn't typed a command where the voice is the direct or indirect object, the parser won't know who is meant if the player tries to ASK HIM something. You can **set pronouns from** a thing to update the relevant pronouns.

For our first topic, we'll re-use the introduction object we previously created for the conversations with the rabbit and the Coyote.

> After quizzing voice about introduction: say "Not like you think anything's going to happen, but what the hell. You grab the dusty old mike, press the call button, and ask is there anybody[paragraph break]'...out there?' the speaker blurts and holy crap, someone's responding, and they say 'Roger roger, tower station nineteen, read you now loud and clear, what's your forty?' and the voice is staticky and whirled through with weird rhythmic distortions but you can hear it just fine and now what?[add what that means ask suggestion][add being lost tell suggestion][add never mind tell suggestion]".

This conversation serves a very important gameplay mechanic of introducing the stakes to the player: setting up that Knock must make one of two choices. To that end, we'll make it fairly short and to the point. Feel free to extend the dialogue here if you like.

> never mind is held by voice. After informing voice about never mind: say "[remove what that means ask suggestion]You mutter something about how you think you've made a mistake and you have to go but the voice interrupts. 'Hang on, hang on, son, there shouldn't be anybody out there. Not at all, especially not this late. Why don't you tell me what's going on?'".

> what that means is held by voice. After quizzing voice about what that means: say "You try to make some joke about not having forty of anything, but the voice cuts you off. 'Ten forty means situation report, son. Obviously you're not on duty. Ain't nobody on duty out there anymore, specially not this time of night. What's going on?'".

> being lost is held by voice. Understand "Im/I'm" or "I am" as being lost. After informing voice about being lost: say "[remove what that means ask suggestion][remove never mind tell suggestion]Feeling a little stupid, you come clean and tell the voice that you drove off the road and aren't sure really exactly where you are.[paragraph break]'Copy that,' the voice says briskly after a moment. 'You're at tower station nineteen, son, about thirty-two miles southwest of Oro Oeste, fifteen miles or so from the state highway.' And if the mike wasn't attached to the radio you'd drop it on the floor. Fifteen miles? How in the [italic type]hell[roman type] could you have driven fifteen miles off the road and not remember? How is that even possible?[paragraph break]'Hello?' the radio says. 'Hello, son, do you copy?'[add yes-suggestion other suggestion][add switch-off-radio other suggestion]".

Again, remember that our modified conversation extension automatically removes topics we discuss from the list of available ones, but we still need to do some hand tweaking. The response to "What's your 40?" only makes sense right after the radio voice says it; likewise, telling the radio about being lost means the other introductory topics aren't relevant any more and should disappear from the list.

> After informing voice about yes-suggestion: say "You jabber something positive and sit back, still shaken.[paragraph break][voice explains choices]?".
>
> switch-off-radio is a misc-suggestion held by voice with printed name "switch off the radio". Instead of switching off radio when current interlocutor is voice: say "You reach for the switch, but hesitate, hand hovering above it as the static whirls and roars.[paragraph break][voice explains choices]?".
>
> To say voice explains choices: say "'Look, son,' the voice says, 'I don't know how you got out there but that's not important right now. Weather report's coming in and there's a cold front the size of Texas coming your way. I don't want to scare you but if you don't find a way home, or figure out some food and shelter for the night, you could freeze to death. You hear me? Now on account of the cutbacks I don't have anyone to send out there until morning. But there may be parts around that old tower you can use to patch up your truck and make it back to the highway. Or, there may be emergency supplies that would get you through the night. This storm's gonna blow out all our communication, so you're gonna be on your own. It's up to you. Over and out.'[paragraph break]You rub your face tiredly. Ocean was expecting you tonight after your shift, like usual. If you don't make it she'll be worried sick. Then on the other hand maybe you should worry about yourself first for a change. You feel like you need a cigarette and then you remember you quit. Hell, can't anything be easy"; reset the interlocutor; now voice is off-stage.

The choice we give the player here is actually a false choice: other than a different introduction, both options produce mostly the same response. It's okay to do this on occasion, but be mindful of why you're sacrificing the player's agency. Here, we're doing so because it's critical to set up the reason for the player's game choice, regardless of how the player navigates the conversation.

The last two phrases end the conversation immediately (so we don't get an erroneous topics line this turn) and move the voice character back off-stage. One last piece of business: now that this conversation is in place, we want to keep the player from visiting the open desert (and discovering the rabbit) until afterwards. In Part - Scenes, Chapter - Pursuit, change the starting conditions to add the bolded line below:

> Pursuit begins when
>
> > player holds flashlight and
> >
> > emergency lights are switched on and
> >
> > The Rabbit's Offer has not happened and
> >
> > **voice has been visible and**
> >
> > the shadow appears.

More Radio Conversations

In our concept document, we described the radio as one of the key signs that Knock's reality is getting fuzzy. After the conversation with the rabbit, we want the voice to return but more sinister, mocking the player character and questioning his choices.

Let's say the radio is in this period from the end of the player's meeting with rabbit until the beginning of Sand-dancer's arrival. Our design suggests using a scene to create this condition. In Part - Scenes, make a new heading called Chapter - Sinister Voices, and add:

> Sinister Voices is a scene. Sinister Voices begins when Rabbit's Offer ends.

Now, let's have the radio spring to life at random when the player passes near it while this scene is underway.

> Every turn when going and location is Break Room during Sinister Voices: now radio is switched on; now frequency tuned to of radio is emergency frequency; say "[one of][sinister-radio-1][or][sinister-radio-2][or][sinister-radio-3][stopping]."

Since there are quite a lot of different things the voice can say, we split them out into three text substitutions.

> To say sinister-radio-1: say "With a sudden growl of static the radio springs to life and it freaks the hell out of you. The voice weaves in and out of crazy whirling distortion and shifting blasts of static. 'Hey... receiving? ...never told... you'll never, never--' A wail like an 8-bit banshee screams through the signal. '...waste of time... who do you think?...' Static, static. 'Very soon now, Nak... akaibito... very...'[paragraph break]Uh. You're pretty sure you never told that dude your name. Maybe you're just hearing things[if radio was switched off]?[paragraph break]Come to think of it, you're [italic type]damn[roman type] sure you left that radio off, too[end if]".

> To say sinister-radio-2: say "The radio growls to life again, the voice distorted now under a constant barrage of electronic rain. 'Where do you think you're going?' it says. 'What are you trying to do? You can't...' A snap, some syncopated crackles. '...can see you, Na... know where... never going to work. Never g--' And the voice cuts off, replaced by a low, tooth-rattling hum.[paragraph break]The voice sounds different than before. I mean it still kind of sounds like the first guy you talked to but it sounds like someone else now too, someone you know, you've known for a long time. Someone you're afraid of".

After these two preliminary interruptions, we'll have the remainder of the radio tirades be tied to various conditions the story might be in. We only want each of these to appear a single time, so we'll create a series of truth state variables to ensure this.

> plan-threatened, memory-threatened, talent-threatened, and final-threatened are truth state variables.

> To say sinister-radio-3:
>> if plan-threatened is false and the player holds something required by a plan (called the item):
>>> now plan-threatened is true;
>>> say "Static squeals from the radio. 'Hey,' the speaker shouts, 'hey, do you really think that [item]'s going to help you with anything? You can't even--' and static reclaims it again";
>> otherwise if memory-threatened is false and emotional baggage contains a memory (called the selected memory):
>>> now memory-threatened is true;
>>> say "The static on the radio resolves into overlapping whispers. 'It makes for a nice story,' the whispers say, 'but you're remembering [the selected memory] all wrong. That's not really how it happened, was it? Was it, Knock? Was--' and they repeat and overlap and echo and fade back into the mutters of the static";
>> otherwise if talent-threatened is false and the player holds a talent:
>>> now talent-threatened is true;
>>> say "'You think just because you've got [a random talent held by player] now you're going to be anything other than a pathetic failure?' the radio squawks angrily, before dissolving into harsh buzzing distortions";
>> otherwise if final-threatened is false and the player holds a talent:
>>> now final-threatened is true;
>>> say "'You're nothing,' it spews, 'your [list of talents held by player] [is-are] worthless. You'll never amount to anything, and neither will your kid, just another half-breed loser destined to die in poverty and live in debt, isn't that right, Knock?' and with a sudden shock you realize why the voice sounds so familiar. It's your voice. It's your own god-damned voice";
>> otherwise:
>>> say "[one of]The radio fizzles and growls through weird twists of distortion[or]Angry distortion bubbles and pops from the radio speaker, twisting in weird rhythmic patterns[stopping]".

All this provocation will doubtless make the player stop and try to mess with the radio, so we want to have a wide range of responses.

> Understand "unplug [radio]" as a mistake ("[one of]You rip the cord out of the wall[if radio is switched on], but the speaker keeps buzzing and the lighted dial keeps flickering[end if].[or]Damnit, you already did![stopping]").

> Instead of attacking radio: say "[one of]You slam a fist into the top of the radio, but it just keeps hissing with static.[or]You kick the radio off the table and it clatters to the ground, but still keeps laughing with hisses and whines.[or]You smash the radio over and over again, until it lies in pieces on the ground, but the static still continues, and more and more it sounds like sand.[or]The radio is destroyed, but the sound still plays, echoing and reverberating through the room.[stopping]".

Finally, the player might try to talk back:

> Before saying hello to the emergency radio: if emergency radio is switched off, try switching on emergency radio instead; otherwise say "You try to raise someone, but there's no response[if frequency tuned to of radio is not the emergency frequency], at least on this frequency[end if]." instead.

Sand-dancer's Arrival

Now, let's create maybe the most exciting scene of all: Sand-dancer's dramatic entrance.

This scene is triggered when the player has collected at least two items required for a plan, although we want to wait until the player is positioned correctly. Since we know Knock has to be inside the building to receive the second required item, we'll wait until the next time he tries to leave. We'll force him to run to the roof with rising sand chasing him the whole way.

In Part - Scenes, create a new heading called Chapter - Sand-dancer's Arrival, and add this:

> Sand-dancer's Arrival is a dramatic scene. "There's like this faint tickle through the soles of your feet, some vibration, almost like whispers in the sand. You want to bend down, put your ear to the ground, listen forever.[paragraph break]And then the ground drops out from under you, heaves, and drops again. Struts groan and boards snap and then with a whooshing bang sand starts pouring in through the window and every crack, jets of sand, and already it's shin-deep and holy christ you've got to get out of here."

One potential snag in our plan: since a scene's starting conditions are not checked until the end of a turn, after the player's command has been processed, the player will actually end up outside (as a result of the going action) before the scene begins. This isn't what we want, since for our dramatic escape to work the player must be trapped. So we want to prevent leaving on the turn that will trigger our scene. This means we need to check its starting conditions in at least two places, so we should put them into a definition.

> To decide whether time for arrival: if the number of complete plans is 1 or the number of in progress plans is 2, decide yes.

Since there are also a couple of commands that might result in the player leaving the building, we'll create a kind of action, too.

> Going outside is leaving the building. Going southwest is leaving the building. Entering a window is leaving the building.

Now we can set up the initial denial and then the scene-triggering payoff.

> tried to leave is a truth state variable. Instead of leaving the building when time for arrival: say "[one of]You start to go out, but then you stop. Something's not right. Something's... weird.[or]The building's sinking into the sand! You've got to get out some other way![stopping]"; now tried to leave is true.
>
> Sand-dancer's Arrival begins when time for arrival and tried to leave is true.

We should say when this scene ends, too: we want the player to flee through the building towards the Roof.

> Sand-dancer's Arrival ends when location is Roof.

And while we're at it, we no longer want the ominous radio voices to be triggered once this sequence has begun. Back in Chapter - Sinister Voices, add:

> Sinister Voices ends when Sand-dancer's Arrival begins.

We want to create some dramatic tension during this sequence, so let's continuously remind the player of the danger Knock's in. Return to Chapter - Sand-dancer's Arrival, and add:

> Every turn during Sand-dancer's Arrival: say "The building shakes and groans as sand continues to pour in, rising higher and higher."

We can also describe movement to reinforce the danger:

> Report going during Sand-dancer's Arrival: say "You wade through the sand, which is rising all the time."

This is a good start. But playing through this sequence now (Figure 10.4) reveals a major problem: rooms are still described normally, in detail that seems inappropriate considering the singular focus of Knock's attention, and including descriptions of items that ought to be getting covered by sand. How can we make this more realistic?

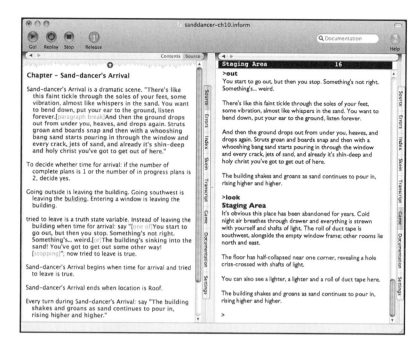

Figure 10.4
The beginning of the
Sand-dancer's Arrival
scene, so far.

Let's create a custom rule for describing a room, which will behave differently if this scene is underway. First, let's find out what rule is responsible for printing a room's description. Consulting the Actions Index in the Index panel, we click on "looking" and see that it's the *room description body text* rule, part of the *carry out looking* rulebook. We can use the trick we learned earlier in the chapter for replacing rules to swap this out for our own rule:

> The Sand-dancer room description body text rule is listed instead of the room
>   description body text rule in the carry out looking rules.

Now we'll write this rule, which should behave exactly like its counterpart except in this special circumstance.

> This is the Sand-dancer room description body text rule: if Sand-dancer's Arrival
>   is happening and location is in Office Interior, describe sand-filled room;
>   otherwise abide by the room description body text rule.

Let's make the referenced phrase show a more appropriate description.

> To describe sand-filled room: say "[one of]Waves of sand flow like water through
>   the room, filling it higher and higher[or]Knee-deep sand fills the room, rising
>   at a terrifying rate[or]The deluge of sand thunders in from every side, filling
>   the room[at random]."

The one piece of information from the room description we ought to preserve, however, is the exits. We can create another rule to list these:

> The Sand-dancer emergency exit rule is listed after the Sand-dancer room description body text rule in the carry out looking rules. This is the Sand-dancer emergency exit rule: if Sand-dancer's arrival is happening and location is in Office Interior, say "You glance wildly at the exits [list of viable directions]."

"Viable" is an adjective defined in the <u>Small Kindnesses by Aaron Reed</u> extension; if you aren't using it, the definition line is as follows:

> Definition: a direction is viable if the room it from the location is a room.

Exercise 10.9

How might you spice up the room descriptions during this scene by describing some random item present in the room being buried under the sand?

If the player makes other attempts to escape, we should redirect him to our intended destination: the Roof.

> Instead of throwing something at a window during Sand-dancer's Arrival: say "It's no good; the window shatters and sand rushes in through it."; now noun is off-stage.

And we ought to prevent any inappropriately mundane behavior, too:

> Doing something to the radio is wasting time. Doing something to cans of food is wasting time. Examining something is wasting time. Before wasting time during Sand-dancer's Arrival: say "There's no time, man! The room's filling with sand!" instead.

As the player arrives at the Roof, we should show a special description:

> After going up during Sand-dancer's Arrival: say "Barely able to reach the ladder through sand up to your waist, you haul yourself up the rungs and pull free just in time."; try looking.

And since the building has now sunken nearly completely into the sand, we need to do some re-landscaping.

> Before going up during Sand-dancer's Arrival:
>
>> now description of Roof is "Except it's more like a foundation now, the building's sunken almost entirely into the sand.";

> now metal rungs are off-stage;
>
> now huge metal barrel is off-stage;
>
> change the up exit of Roof to nothing.

Our final scene, Sand-dancer's Offer, will be cued to begin as this scene ends. We'll save it for the next chapter, which will focus on finishing up a project and getting it released.

Exercise Answers

Exercise 10.1

Disambiguate between two directions with the same abbreviation. We can create a *does the player mean* rule to instruct the parser that the player is very unlikely to mean a direction that does not connect to any room:

> Does the player mean going starboard when the room starboard from
>   location is not a room: it is very unlikely. Does the player mean going
>   south when the room south from location is not a room: it is unlikely.

We make south "unlikely" rather than "very unlikely" to prevent both directions from being equally unlikely to be matched (thus resulting again in unwanted disambiguation).

Another approach from an example in the built-in docs is to define a class of rooms where nautical directions are expected. We might start with these two assertions:

> A room can be nautical or earthbound. Before going starboard in an
>   earthbound room: say "Nautical directions can only be used on board
>   ship."

Exercise 10.2

How would you create individual cigarette objects?

> The pack of cigarettes is an openable container. A cigarette is a kind of
>   thing. In the pack of cigarettes are five cigarettes.

We'd want to modify the smoking verb to use cigarettes, not the pack itself, as well as the description of the pack to describe its contents directly rather than via the count variable. Then, we'd want to remove each cigarette from play once smoked:

> Carry out smoking: now the noun is off-stage.

It's hard to see what we'd gain from this implementation, though, other than a mountain of extra code to write: initial appearances for an individual cigarette left in a room, instead rules to prevent plausible actions such as dropping them in the desert to mark the way. Unless there's some pressing need for the accuracy—and it doesn't seems as if there is in *Sand-dancer*—you're often better just sticking with the simplest implementation that allows you to tell your story.

Exercise 10.3

Write activity rules to flag objects without descriptions and portable objects.

> After printing the name of something (called item) while the description of item is "": say "*". Before printing the name of something (called item) while item is portable and item is not part of something: say "__".

By walking around inside the building, we can use the second rule to discover that the radio in the Break Room should be fixed in place. Feel free to fix this now.

Exercise 10.4

Describe objects differently after Knock has acquired certain talents. A basic start to this might be something like the following, in Part - Mechanics, Chapter - Talents:

> Before printing the name of cobwebs when player holds courage: say "hardly noticeable ". Before printing the name of cage when player holds strength: say "flimsy-looking ". Before printing the name of piece of jade when player holds luck: say "lucky ". After printing the name of pickup when player holds scent: say ", still smelling liked spilled gas".

Exercise 10.5

Describe the barrel and rungs on the Roof in a single paragraph. Replace the initial appearance of the metal rungs with the following:

> For writing a paragraph about huge metal barrel: say "[The rungs] once led to a control booth higher up the tower, but the lower handholds have rotted away and collapsed. [if huge metal barrel is placed correctly]You should be able to clamber up onto the [huge metal barrel] underneath, though[otherwise if player holds courage]You're pretty sure you could make the leap, though[otherwise if player holds strength]You could probably push that [huge metal barrel] over underneath, though[otherwise]A [huge metal barrel] rusts quietly some distance away[end if]."

Exercise 10.6

Replace the message for dropping an unheld thing without using the Default Messages extension.

> Instead of dropping something not held: say "You don't have [that-those of noun], man."

Exercise 10.7

Feel free to create any messages you want, but here's one example of a good start (in Part - Mechanics, Chapter - Customizations):

> Include Default Messages by David Fisher.

> To say bro: say "[one of]bro[or]man[or]dude[or]holmes[or]amigo[or]brohim[or]dawg[or] gangsta[as decreasingly likely outcomes]".

> When play begins:

>> set LibMsg <block swearing obscenely> to "Mos def, [bro].[/n]";

>> set LibMsg <empty line> to "Say what?[/n]";

>> set LibMsg <unknown object> to "Uh, not sure about the noun there, [bro].[/n]";

>> set LibMsg <Inventory initial text> to "You've got";

>> set LibMsg <cannot take yourself> to "Yeah, you do need to get a hold of yourself.[/n]";

>> set LibMsg <cannot take other people> to "What is this, [bro], weight training?[/n]";

>> set LibMsg <cannot take something already taken> to "You already got that shit, [bro].[/n]";

>> set LibMsg <report player taking> to "[one of]Snagged[or]Got [if noun acts plural][']em[otherwise]it[end if][or]Sure thing, [bro][at random].[/n]";

>> set LibMsg <examine undescribed things> to "About what you'd expect.[/n]";

>> set LibMsg <look under> to "[one of]Nada[or]El zilcho[or]Nothin[at random].[/n]";

>> set LibMsg <cannot eat unless edible> to "You ain't that hungry, [bro].[/n]";

```
set LibMsg <report player touching things> to "No surprises.[/n]";

set LibMsg <report player touching other people> to "He's real.[/n]";

set LibMsg <block climbing> to "Uh, [bro], probably not a good plan.[/n]";

set LibMsg <block attacking> to "Come on [bro], they already think you
    have anger management issues.[/n]";

set LibMsg <block burning> to "Heh heh... fire... fire.[/n]";

set LibMsg <block throwing at> to "Hey, let's not just piss people off for
    no reason.[/n]";

set LibMsg <block sleeping> to "For whatever reason you've never felt
    more awake.[/n]";

set LibMsg <block waking up> to "Good call, [bro], but you can't seem to
    snap yourself out of whatever this is. Doesn't feel like a dream,
    anyway.[/n]"
```

Be careful not to overreach. Look for opportunities to include messages that can be taken more than one way: "You ain't that hungry" could be a joke, for something obviously inedible, or a simple statement of fact.

Exercise 10.8

Add a small item in the cage that can be taken even while the cage is closed.

```
A scrap of paper is in wire mesh cage. Rule for reaching inside cage when
    we are touching: allow access. Rule for reaching inside cage when we are
    taking: if noun is scrap of paper, allow access. After taking scrap when
    scrap was inside cage: say "Reaching carefully through the mesh, you
    snag an end of the scrap and pull it out."
```

Exercise 10.9

Enhance room descriptions during Sand-dancer's Arrival to mention an appropriate piece of detritus swirling in the sand. We'd first need to create a definition that would prevent items from appearing that wouldn't make sense in this context:

```
Definition: a thing is detrital: if it is the player, no; if it is a window, no; if it
    is a door, no; if it is scenery, no; if it is enclosed by player, no; yes.
```

Then, we could amend the *describe sand-filled room* phrase to add the following to its conclusion:

```
"; [the random visible detrital thing] [one of]surfaces for a moment then
    gets buried[or]tumbles in the flow[or]vanishes under the sand[at
    random]."
```

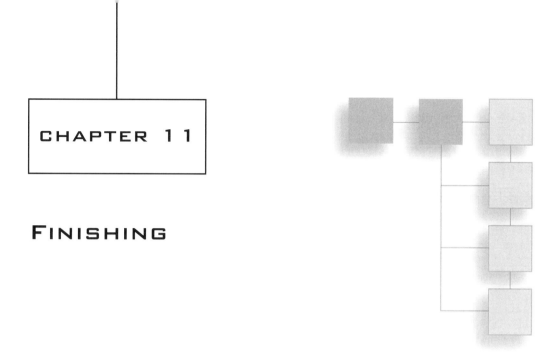

CHAPTER 11

FINISHING

A few weeks before a play opens, the actors are still running through scenes or acts in isolation and out of order. The lighting designer is still playing around with cues and hanging lamps in hard-to-reach places. The set builders are hauling lumber and wielding drills, the costumers are sewing, the musicians, if any, are starting to learn their parts. But the week before opening brings a time of reckoning known as tech week (or, less charitably, hell week) where everything comes together for the first time: the actors perform the whole play in costume, on sets, under lights, with music, and the director discovers at last how well the whole thing fits together.

Usually the seams are rough at first. Maybe the actors can't possibly perform the fight scene in their elaborate costumes, or there's no way the floor crew can change the scenery during the composer's brief interlude. Solutions must be devised: simplify the fight or the costumes, write longer music for the set change, or hire more crew. In addition to these major changes, any number of minor tweaks are made: moving an actor's mark a foot or two sideways to better catch the light; speeding up the pace here and slowing it down there; playing one line for laughs that just wasn't working as a dramatic moment.

An IF author goes through a similar process as a project nears completion, although usually playing all the above roles at once. Once each element is finished—each character, location, prop, and scene—the next step is to find out if they all work together to tell the story the author set out to tell. Both minor tweaks and a few redesigns are usually required before a project is ready to be released.

This chapter discusses the three major stages required to carry your project through the finish line. **Polishing** involves filling in all the missing corners, making sure you've implemented everything from your original concept document, and adding the finishing touches that make a story shine. In **testing**, you'll play through looking for both game failures and story failures, first on your own, then with the help of others. Finally, **releasing** a game prepares it to be discovered, played, and enjoyed by its audience, so all your hard work doesn't go to waste.

Adding the Polish

As you turn to the final stages of your project, you need to make sure you've built everything needed, but also look for opportunities to add some flavor. To begin the process, though, you'll need to look backwards.

Review the Concept Document

Reading your original design near the end of a project can be a surprising experience. While it's natural for a story to evolve as you construct it, it's also very easy to get lost in the details and forget some of the big picture. You may discover you've left out some major part of your original vision, and have to decide whether to go back and add that component, or whether you no longer need it.

I put the concept document for *Sand-dancer* at the end of Chapter 1. Reviewing it now, our design seems to capture most of what we set out to do. (We'll create the final conversation with Sand-dancer himself, the only major scene not yet written, later in this chapter.) One component we seem to have left out is much of the early motivation for Knock's activity: we haven't much described the frigid night air that compels him to seek shelter or the problem with his pickup truck in the early parts of the story.

One simple way to make the coldness more present is to remind the player about it at intervals. We don't want to overdo it, but we could add this to Part - Mechanics, Chapter - Customizations:

> Every turn when a dramatic scene is not happening and a random chance of 1 in
>   40 succeeds: say "[one of]You shiver in the cold air[or]The cold night air
>   swirls around you, and you pull your jacket closer[or]The air is frigid, and
>   turns your breath into clouds[at random]."

To tell the player the problem with the truck more explicitly, we can give it a description, and some responses to likely interactions. Put this in Part - Setting, Chapter - Around the Tower, Section - Middle of Nowhere:

> The description of the pickup truck is "[if player is in truck]You can't tell what
>   the damage is from in here[otherwise][first time]Getting down on your knees
>   in the cold sand, you look underneath. Sure enough; you ripped up the fuel
>   line and all your gas has drained away, sucked dry by the thirsty desert sand.
>   [only]You'll need to find some way to patch up the line, plus some fuel, to
>   have any hope of fixing her[end if]."

> Understand "fix [pickup]" or "repair [pickup]" or "use [duct tape]" or "tape [pickup]" or "fill [pickup]" or "put [gas can] in [pickup]" or "use [gas can]" as a mistake ("You should wait until you've got everything you need before you start making repairs.").
>
> Instead of switching on or switching off pickup truck: say "The engine just turns over. It won't start."

Finally, while we establish much of Knock's back story with the memories, his wallet contains a driver's license that ought to provide a description. Let's add that, too: a good spot might be in Part – Mechanics, Chapter – Memories, Section – Memory Collection where the license is defined.

> The description of driver's license is "When the highway patrol pulls you over they see your kind of crazy uncombed hair (morning), your brown name (Nakaibito Morales) and brown skin (actually more kinda tan), your D.O.B. (eighteen years ago just barely) and tribal affiliation card (expired) and assume you're either some kind of native eco-terrorist, illegal drug-running border jumper, or delinquent high school dropout (all lies except for kinda maybe the last one a little). Unless it's Jimmy Kay who pulled you over since he usually just wants to buy you a beer and talk about your dad, which is weird but better than getting a ticket."

Sand-dancer Himself

The other major component to add is the conversation with Sand-dancer himself, the climactic scene of our story. We've previously written his dramatic arrival, as well as the final denouement sequences, but not the conversation in between.

We left Knock standing on the roof of the now-sunken building. First, create a new heading within Part - Scenes called Chapter - Sand-dancer's Offer. Let's create a scene for this sequence and set the stage.

> Sand-dancer's Offer is a scene. "The sand swirls and churns like something liquid or alive around you, and then you look and see it is alive, thousands and [thousands of lizards], little sand-dancers, are burrowing up from somewhere underground, scattering and writhing in some complex pattern in a huge circle all around you.[paragraph break]Then, suddenly, everything stops.[paragraph break]And with a mighty heave, a huge lizard crests through the sand right in front of you."
>
> Sand-dancer's Offer begins when Sand-dancer's Arrival ends.
>
> When Sand-dancer's Offer begins: now Sand-dancer is in location; now thousands of lizards are in location; now Sand-dancer holds advice; Sand-dancer's conversation starts in 1 turn from now.

We should give descriptions to the lizard and his supplicants. Since the final spirit animal's name is a bit of a revelation, we'll create a variable to track whether the player has learned it or not:

> Sand-dancer can be named. The initial appearance of Sand-dancer is "[if Sand-dancer is named]Sand-dancer[otherwise]The huge lizard[end if] sits before you, breathing, watching." Understand "lizard/huge/sand/dancer" as Sand-dancer.
>
> The description of Sand-dancer is "His scales are thick, sand still spilling off them in rivulets and trickles, and they recede and collide in fractal complexities that make you dizzy. He rumbles somewhere inside him, and the sand jitters at his feet."
>
> The thousands of lizards are an animal. "Thousands of lizards writhe in the desert around you." The description is "They crawl over and under and around each other, restless, always moving."

As we did with the Coyote, we'll create a text substitution for this character that will let us add some asides to his dialogue text:

> To say SD-business: say "[one of]and his voice shakes the earth and creaks the rusty joints of the tower[or]flicking his tongue in and out, slowly[or]his great slitted eye blinking slowly[or]sighing as the lizards in the desert writhe and twitch[cycling]".

Now, the conversation itself. For the conversations with the first two spirit animals, we created a dummy object called "introduction," which we can reuse again here.

> At the time when Sand-dancer's conversation starts: try quizzing Sand-dancer about introduction; try listing suggested topics.
>
> After quizzing Sand-dancer about introduction: say "The lizard's tongue snakes through the air, tasting it, tasting you. One slitted eye studies you intently. It pauses, as if waiting for you to say something.[add hello other suggestion][add Sand-dancer ask suggestion][add thousands of lizards ask suggestion]".
>
> hello is held by Sand-dancer. The printed name is "say hello". Instead of hailing when Sand-dancer is visible: say "[remove hello other suggestion]The ground rumbles as the lizards shift. 'Hello,' he says, [SD-business]. 'Yes, hello, little one. Strange thing to say when I've always been with you, watching, waiting. But hello, hello at last, Nakaibito.'".
>
> Sand-dancer is familiar. After quizzing Sand-dancer about Sand-dancer: say "[remove hello other suggestion]'I am Sand-dancer,' he breathes, [SD-business]. 'I am the desert and the dust and the rain and the wind. I was there the first time you went hungry and the first time you made love and the last time you asked for help, but I could not help you then. But tonight, Nakaibito, tonight I can.'"; try quizzing Sand-dancer about final choice; now Sand-dancer is named.

> After quizzing Sand-dancer about thousands of lizards: say "[remove hello other suggestion]The lizards hiss and writhe as you ask, almost as if they are laughing. 'Little sand-dancers,' he says, [SD-business], 'they come with me wherever I go. They will not bother you.'".

We want Sand-dancer in this scene to offer the player a choice between confirming the path he's been following, or taking the easy way out by choosing freedom. But if the player has chosen two non-complementary talents, and thus acquired items from two different plans (such as the duct tape and the canned oranges) we don't know which plan the player wants to try. Let's write a conditional sequence to make sure the player has committed to one choice or the other. Remember that we've previously defined the adjectives *in progress* and *complete* for plans, so we can leverage that definition here:

> Instead of quizzing Sand-dancer about final choice when the number of complete plans is 0: try quizzing Sand-dancer about path selection.

> path selection is held by Sand-dancer.

> After quizzing Sand-dancer about path selection:
>> clear all topics;
>> say "'Much has happened tonight. You've made bargains and plans. [Sand-dancer talent summary]But these things together do not help you. No, you still haven't decided.' The lizard stares at you with one eye, [SD-business]. 'But now is the time.'[paragraph break]";
>> let unclaimed things be the list of things required by a plan;
>> remove the list of held things from unclaimed things;
>> repeat with item running through unclaimed things:
>>> now item is in location;
>> say "The ground shudders and shifts beneath you, and out of the sand rise [unclaimed things with indefinite articles].[paragraph break]'The tape and the gas can will return you to her. The blanket and the can of food will look out for you. Take one.'[add grab something other suggestion]".

> grab something is held by Sand-dancer. The printed name is "take [the list of visible not held things required by a plan]".

> To say Sand-dancer talent summary:
>> if player holds strength, say "You carry strength that ripped warmth from walls. ";

if player holds courage, say "You hold courage that earned you a tool for mending. ";

if player holds luck, say "You wear luck that filled your belly. ";

if player holds scent, say "You have scent that brought you liquid motion. ".

After taking something required by a plan during Sand-dancer's Offer:

now noun is handled;

let unclaimed things be the list of things required by a plan;

remove the list of held things from unclaimed things;

repeat with item running through unclaimed things:

now item is off-stage;

say "As you take it, [unclaimed things with definite articles] sinks into the sand.[remove grab something other suggestion]";

try quizzing Sand-dancer about final choice.

Now Knock's definitely committed to one plan or the other: staying with Ocean or leaving her. Sand-dancer teases Knock by asking him whether he's happy with this choice. Note the use of the text substitution [a random complete plan] below: though *we* know there will logically be only one complete plan at this point, the Inform compiler has no way of knowing this.

The final choice is a familiar thing held by Sand-dancer.

After quizzing Sand-dancer about final choice: clear all topics; say "'By your actions and through your talents, you have chosen [a random complete plan],' he says, [SD-business]. 'You have looked into yourself and found your story, the path you will walk tomorrow.'[paragraph break]He breathes. 'And are you happy with your story?' he asks, and there's some dangerous undertone to the question and you don't know why. The lizards tense, quivering, twisting their little heads back and forth as they await your answer.[add yes-no-suggestion other suggestion][add not sure if I'm happy other suggestion]".

Instead of saying yes when yes-no-suggestion is familiar and Sand-dancer is visible: say "'Yes?' Sand-dancer says, and the lizards quiver anxiously. 'You're happy with the path you've chosen? [SD-tease].'"; try quizzing Sand-dancer about doing the trade.

Instead of saying no when yes-no-suggestion is familiar and Sand-dancer is visible: say "'No?' Sand-dancer says, and the lizards quiver anxiously. 'You're not happy with the path you've chosen? [SD-tease].'"; try quizzing Sand-dancer about doing the trade.

To say SD-tease: say "[if a random complete plan is staying the night]A life on the run, alone, work time in one town, jail time in another, no job, no skills, no family?' [otherwise]Trying to build a family out of nothing, spin futures from government handouts and dusty trailer parks, raising another generation of hopeless dropouts and messed-up losers?' [end if]The lizards scurry angrily, snapping and clawing at each other, with a sound like static and sand.[paragraph break]'It doesn't matter,' he says more calmly, as the lizards subside, 'since you have already made your choice. You cannot take back your actions. You cannot unmake the past.' The lizards around him tilt their head, edge forward cautiously, and he seems to grin. 'But I can".

not sure if I'm happy is a misc-suggestion. It is held by Sand-dancer. The printed name is "tell him you're not sure if you're happy". Understand "you/you're/I/I'm" as not sure if I'm happy. After informing Sand-dancer about not sure if I'm happy: say "The lizard turns his head sharply, and all the lizards in the desert around writhe angrily, clawing and biting at each other in agitation. 'And when will you know, Knock?' the lizard asks. 'When will you own your life? When will you become a man? Tonight. It must be tonight.'"; try quizzing Sand-dancer about doing the trade.

Though it's too late to back down on the choice, Sand-dancer tempts Knock with an alternative: freedom.

spirit, honor and freedom are familiar.

There is a thing called doing the trade. It is held by Sand-dancer. The printed name is "ask him about getting on with the trading". Understand "getting/on/with/trading" as doing the trade.

After quizzing Sand-dancer about doing the trade:

clear all topics;

if staying the night is complete, now spirit is in location;

otherwise now honor is in location;

now freedom is in location;

now spirit is familiar;

now honor is familiar;

now freedom is familiar;

> say "A glistening egg rises from the sand, glowing with neon potential, and the lizard glances down at it almost dismissively. 'This is [if staying the night is complete]spirit[otherwise]honor[end if],' he says, 'the last talent you need to achieve your goal, and you can have it for three memories. But perhaps I have something else to trade.'[paragraph break]The lizards whisper in anticipation as a second egg rises. This one's bigger, and almost blinding with its intensity, and the lizards draw back, chittering in awe and amazement. 'This,' Sand-dancer says, 'is freedom. Pure, undiluted, and absolute. Many crave it and few get a chance to take it. I offer it to you, Nakaibito, but it does not come cheaply.' He grins. 'For freedom, you must give up everything. You must give me all your memories.'[paragraph break]The lizards begin to circle restlessly as they wait for you to choose. Sand-dancer merely watches, and waits.[if spirit is visible][add spirit ask suggestion][add trade-for-spirit other suggestion][otherwise][add honor ask suggestion][add trade-for-honor other suggestion][end if][add freedom ask suggestion][add trade-for-freedom other suggestion]".

> After quizzing Sand-dancer about spirit: say "'You have the warmth and energy you need to stay through the night,' he says, 'but to continue looking out for yourself, you will need spirit.'".

> After quizzing Sand-dancer about honor: say "'You have the tools to fix your truck,' he says, 'but to return to Ocean and stand by her side you will need honor.'".

> After quizzing Sand-dancer about freedom: say "'With freedom, Nakaibito, you can make your troubles vanish. True freedom is the power of unmaking the past, of undoing what's done and regretted. This power is great and terrible, but I promise you.' He flicks his tongue. 'It will set you free.'".

> trade-for-honor is a misc-suggestion. It is held by Sand-dancer. The printed name is "trade something for honor". trade-for-spirit is a misc-suggestion. It is held by Sand-dancer. The printed name is "trade something for spirit". trade-for-freedom is a misc-suggestion. It is held by Sand-dancer. The printed name is "trade something for freedom".

We've already set up a named phrase to determine whether a spirit animal has received enough memories (based on the *price* number variable each one has). Sand-dancer's price is more complicated, though, since the player might be buying one of three talents, the last with a different metric to determine its price. The phrase below illustrates how we can override one phrase to decide something with a more specific version. In the general rule, we decide whether *trader - a person* needs more memories. Here, we narrow the criterion: the rule below will match only when we're trading with Sand-dancer, and the more generic rule otherwise.

To decide whether (trader - Sand-dancer) needs more memories:

> if the number of memories in emotional baggage is at least 2 and the second noun is freedom, decide yes;

> let the projected total be the number of memories held by trader + 1;

> if the projected total is less than the price of trader, decide yes;

> decide no.

Now, we'll write a more specific rule to make the act of trading with the lizard more dramatic:

> Check trading when the trader needs more memories during Sand-dancer's offer: move the noun to the trader; say "He flicks out his tongue and pulls [the noun] from [one of]your head[or]your heart[or]your gut[or]your palm[or]your core[or]your soul[in random order], swallowing it whole. '[one of]A good start,' he says, 'but you must trade more'[or]Yes,' he says, 'but more'[or]More,' he says[or]Still more,' he says[or]I must have more,' he says[or]Give me more,' he says[stopping]." instead.

Finally, we'll report the results of the trade.

> Report trading when Sand-dancer is visible: clear all topics; say "'The choice is made,' he rumbles, 'your path is set. Goodbye, Nakaibito.' And he turns and dives into the sand. The lizards twist and writhe and follow him.[paragraph break]And then, just as quiet settles, another huge rumble shakes the ground, and, almost like an afterthought, the building breaches the sand and rises to the surface."; now Sand-dancer is off-stage; now thousands of lizards are off-stage; reset the interlocutor; move player to Crumbling Concrete; stop the action.

We've previously defined the story-ending messages as being triggered when the player moves after holding one of the final talents, so we shouldn't need to do anything else to guide the player to one of the story's conclusions.

Verify Your Story Is Completable

Once everything's been created, the next step is to see if you can play your story from beginning to end. While you can iteratively test parts of your story as each one is designed and coded, you usually can't effectively play through the entire game until most of it has been written. Doing so inevitably reveals messy seams. In *Sand-dancer*, we often wrote the ending conditions for one scene well before we started work on the follow-up scene, so we'll want to check and make sure these transitions work the way we planned them to: we can use the Scenes Index in the Index panel to check this.

Exercise 11.1

Try playing through your local version of *Sand-dancer* (or download the "Chapter 10" version from the book's website) and see if you're able to traverse the story from beginning to one ending. Note any problems you discover along the way.

One rough seam in *Sand-dancer* is the series of rules controlling when the player can visit the Open Desert. The complexity of this decision (with multiple reasons to both allow and disallow the movement) means that it's hard to tell if it works the way it should. Getting this right is crucial: since there's no way for the player to escape the Open Desert other than successfully concluding a scene, getting there at the wrong time could strand him indefinitely, which isn't a very fair or interesting conclusion to the story. Also, the repetition of conditions in these rules (such as checking whether the flashlight is held and turned on) isn't very efficient design.

Let's re-do this all as a single rule, bringing the logic together. In Part - Setting, Chapter - The Open Desert, replace the three instead rules related to going to the desert with this single before rule:

> Before going from Around the Tower to Open Desert:
>
> > if flashlight is not held, instead say "[if headlights are switched on]Outside the wavering glow of your headlights, i[otherwise]I[end if]t's black. Pitch. Storm must have rolled in; there's no stars above, no anything but blackness around. Only the smell of the desert tells you it's still out there.";
> >
> > if flashlight is not switched on, try switching on the flashlight;
> >
> > if emergency lights are switched off or voice has not been visible, instead say "You heft your flashlight nervously, licking your lips, but decide not to head out into the desert just yet. There might be more around here you should investigate before taking such a drastic step.";
> >
> > if Rainstorm is happening, instead say "In a storm like this? No way.";
> >
> > if Coyote's Offer has ended, instead say "You have some feeling that when the last spirit animal decides to make an appearance, it will find you.";
> >
> > if Pursuit is not happening and Temptation is not happening, instead say "On a night as freakishly dark as this, that's insane."

Now, we can easily see at a glance that our logic is sound. The most pressing denials (such as not holding a flashlight) will override the more specific ones that come later. In our final line, we explicitly prohibit travel to the desert unless it's during our two lure scenes, meaning we can feel much more reassured that the player won't end up there at an inappropriate time.

Adding Candy

Much of the joy of a good IF comes from all the pieces that aren't vital to the story, but provide for a rich, compelling experience regardless. One of the best places to insert these tidbits is in interesting responses to unexpected commands. A pair of extensions can help track down the best spots for these.

<u>Property Checking by Emily Short</u>, when included with a project, will generate a list of all the things and rooms in your story world without a description property. While this often can produce false positives (such as our conversation topics in *Sand-dancer*, which don't need descriptions) scanning the list is still a great way to catch opportunities for description you might have overlooked.

For instance, the piece of jade in Knock's pickup truck ought to be described, since it's presumably important to our central character (not to mention being one of the first objects encountered, and thus part of a player's first impressions of the story). Add this to Part - Mechanics, Chapter - Memories, Section - Memory Collection:

> The description of the jade is "Grandma said it will bring you luck, which hasn't really been working out. You can't remember now how it ended up in your pickup truck. Maybe someday you'll see someone lucky and you can throw it at him."

We also ought to give the cactus, which so violently begins our story, a description of its own, in Part - Setting, Chapter - Around the Tower, Section - Middle of Nowhere.

> The description of the tall Saguaro is "The cactus seems totally undamaged. Go figure."

<u>Object Response Tests by Juhana Leinonen</u> adds a testing command that will try every available command on a particular object. It's easy to forget all of the built-in actions, and this often reveals great spots where customization can improve your story. It's also great for catching places where the library messages don't make sense.

For instance, this extension reveals that we haven't written a response for attacking the pickup truck, something a frustrated player might try to do. Add this in the same section:

> Instead of attacking pickup truck: say "You smack [if player is in truck]the wheel[otherwise]the hood[end if] in exasperation. How did you get into this mess?"

The default response to taking the sand, "That's hardly portable," is also not particularly interesting. Let's create something better:

> Instead of taking the desert sand: say "[if Rainstorm is happening]More like mud right now.[otherwise]You kneel down and let some run through your fingers, vague memories of better times slipping through your fingers. But the ground is freezing and you get back to your feet."

> **Exercise 11.2**
>
> Use these two extensions to look for other descriptions and action responses you feel *Sand-dancer* ought to have. Don't just write these blindly: look for places where a response will help entertain your players, set the scene, hint at what to do next, or reveal more about the characters.

Rewriting

Don't neglect your story's prose when looking for things to improve. Often, your descriptions and responses are written while your mind is still worrying about the technical details of coding or designing a scene. Giving the text another pass while focused more on the writing will dramatically improve its quality.

Of course, the code itself also benefits from a second pass. On revisiting a rule, you might notice some obvious flaw you overlooked when first designing it. In the light of later changes, older source text may no longer be up-to-date. Taking the time to reread, revise, and rewrite earlier material is always time well spent.

Testing and Debugging

The word "bug" has always had ugly definitions. Before it meant creepy crawly insects, it suggested scary things that roam in the night (this sense survives in the words *bugbear* and *bogy*). We tell people who are bugging us to bug off, we worry about bugs on our phone lines, and our eyes bug out when we see something unpleasant. Engineers have long referred to problems in mechanical systems as bugs: Thomas Edison wrote to a friend that, after the initial burst of intuition accompanying any new invention, "'Bugs'—as such little faults and difficulties are called—show themselves and months of anxious watching, study, and labor are requisite..." Today, programmers still use this term to refer to all the annoying problems, ranging from minor niggles to fatal crashes, that make certain programs just seem totally buggered.

As Edison knew, with any new invention the exciting phases of design and construction must inevitably end, and the business of getting the thing ready to be used must begin. While debugging is often considered the least fun part of a project, it's also among the most essential, separating enjoyable, worthwhile, and memorable stories from the frustrating and forgettable ones.

Bugs can completely derail a story, rendering it unfinishable; more commonly, they prevent the correct response to commands, producing output that's incoherent or just wrong. Each response like this takes players out of the story world: if they get jerked back to reality enough, they may decide to stay there.

Some bugs are caused by bad code, but they might also arise from bad design or bad prose. We'll talk in this section about how to find bugs, identify their cause, and squash them.

Playing Like a Tester

The first stage of testing is to run through your story wearing one of two hats: either earnest user or devious troublemaker. Both approaches will ferret out their own types of bugs.

Playing as earnest user means trying, as much as possible, to play the story exactly like you imagine its audience will. Pretend you don't know how to solve the puzzles, what the story's about, or even what verbs or nouns are implemented, and start typing commands. You'll immediately notice interactions you've overlooked, descriptions that omit important details, and sequences that need more context for the player to make sense of.

Playing as devious troublemaker, on the other hand, means specifically looking for weak points in the game: trying to break it, ignoring the story in favor of getting the program into unexpected situations, and discovering places where the rules break down. What happens if we run away instead of talking to a character? Try to pick up unexpected items? Perform actions in unusual orders? Do things repeatedly or not at all? Playing this way often reveals broken **edge cases** (conditions on the boundary of what is allowed by the rules) and mistaken assumptions about how players will interact or what it's possible to do within the story world.

As you find bugs, you can fix them as you go, or compile a list and fix a swarm of them at once. I'll discuss fixing bugs more in a bit, but first let's learn some tools for finding and diagnosing them.

Review of Testing Commands

I've introduced a series of testing commands across the book, but let's recap them all to get them fresh in our memory.

ACTIONS

The ACTIONS testing command will display every action attempted by the player or any other game character, as well as the results of that action (success or failure), interleaved with the normal text of the story and marked with square brackets. This is useful to find out which action results from a particular verb. If your story features rules that redirect one action to another (like *Instead of listening: try waiting*) the ACTIONS output makes these redirections immediately apparent.

Type ACTIONS to turn this mode on, and ACTIONS OFF to disable it again.

RULES

The RULES testing command identifies every rule consulted in the course of a turn, using either its given name or its header (the part describing the name of the rulebook and conditions under which this rule applies). This can be used to determine which rule results in a particular text appearing. For instance, *looking* while in Middle of Nowhere with rules testing enabled tells us which rule is responsible for describing the pickup truck's contents:

> [Rule "describe what's on scenery supporters in room descriptions rule" applies.]
>
> In your pickup truck you can see a piece of jade.

Type RULES to activate this mode, and RULES OFF to turn it off. RULES ALL will display a list of *every* rule in your story each turn, including those that don't apply in the current situation: this list will be extremely long but is sometimes useful.

SCENES

The SCENES command turns on notification of the moments that scenes begin and end. If a scene isn't behaving quite the way you expect, this command, particularly in conjunction with the ones above, can reveal whether it's starting or ending at an unexpected moment in the turn sequence.

Type SCENES to enable this mode, and SCENES OFF to disable it.

RELATIONS

The RELATIONS testing command shows a complete list of all the custom relations in your story, sorted by type. The style of the connecting arrow indicates the type of the relation (one to one, one to various, and so on). This command, for instance, reveals the connections between plans and objects in *Sand-dancer*:

> Requirement relates one plan (called the objective) to various things:
>
>   spending the night here >=> the canned oranges
>
>   spending the night here >=> the emergency blanket
>
>   fixing your truck and getting out of here >=> the gas can
>
>   fixing your truck and getting out of here >=> the roll of duct tape

Simply type RELATIONS to display the information.

TREE

The TREE command will show the object tree for the whole story world or a given subset, with indentation for things enclosed by other things. This is a good way to verify that Inform's conception of where something is matches your own.

Type TREE alone to show your whole story world, or TREE {something} to show that thing and all it encloses.

SHOWME

The SHOWME testing command reveals detailed information about a certain object in the story world, including the status of all its properties, its location, anything it encloses, and anything it relates to.

Type SHOWME alone for information on the current location, or SHOWME {something} for information on that item.

ABSTRACT

The ABSTRACT testing command can move any object in the story world to another spot on the object tree. For instance, ABSTRACT DUCT TAPE TO ME instantly gives the player the duct tape. This is great for quickly testing interactions with items, or bypassing puzzle gateways, but be careful that doing so doesn't break any logic of your game that expects objects to be acquired in a particular way or rooms to be entered in a certain order.

SCOPE

We'll round out the set with one new testing command, SCOPE, which will show a list of everything that's currently in scope (able to be interacted with by the player). This can be useful if you're facing problems with disambiguation, or adjusting the default scope (as we learned how to do in the previous chapter) and trying to make sure things are working as you expect.

Creating Test Scripts

During testing, you'll often need to quickly input a series of commands to get to the spot in the game you want to test. One quick way to do this is to create a **test script**. These can be created in your source text by defining a one-word name and a sequence of commands separated by slashes. For instance, we could add this to our source text:

```
Test interior with "get out / north / throw lighter at window / in".
```

Now, within the story, we could type TEST INTERIOR as the first move to have these four commands quickly input, bringing us to the Staging Area location. Note that this would only make sense when this command was issued as the first move of the game. A more general way to write a test script is to stipulate that it must take place *in* a certain location or *holding* a certain item; the item or player will be moved accordingly before the script begins. We could write a script like this:

> Test guidebook with "turn on flashlight / get guidebook / read it / consult guidebook about sand-dancer" in Weed-strewn Rust holding the flashlight.

A few other useful tidbits about test scripts: one script can invoke another by including a TEST command as one of its commands. You can type just TEST at a prompt to see a list of all the test scripts you've defined. Finally, test scripts are not included in a released game, so you don't have to worry about your players accidentally stumbling across them.

Debugging with showme

Very often while playing through a bugged sequence trying to work out exactly what's wrong, you'd like more information than is normally displayed. You can use a phrase called **showme** in your source text to display information about a variable, property, or descriptive clause. At the time that phrase is encountered (and only in unreleased versions of your story) the kind and current value of that variable will be displayed.

For example, say we were having difficulties with trading memories for talents. We could add the following line to our source text:

> Before trading: showme the trader; showme the price of the trader; showme the number of memories held by the trader.

This might produce output like the following:

```
>TRADE STORIES FOR STRENGTH

trader = person: rabbit

price of the trader = number: 1

number of memories held by the trader = number: 0
```

If one of these values wasn't what was expected, we'd have a good clue about the source of our bug.

Exercise 11.3

How could you use the showme phrase to notify the user on any turn when an item without a description is visible, excluding scenery?

Note that the showme phrase (which authors can write into source text) is different than the SHOWME testing command (which would be typed as a command while the game is running); the latter provides more information, including the values of all of a thing's properties, but can only be used on a specific item, not a variable, list, or description of a group of items.

Sections Not for Release

While showme phrases and test scripts will be automatically excluded from a released version of your story, sometimes you'd like to make your own testing tools and be sure they won't accidentally survive into a final release. Inform allows you to include the words **not for release** as part of any heading, indicating that everything under that heading (and any subheadings) should not be included in a released story. We could add the following custom testing command:

```
Section - Progress (not for release)

Understand "progress" as requesting progress. Requesting progress is an
    action out of world applying to nothing. Carry out requesting progress: say
    "Handled items required by a plan: [the list of handled things which are
    required by a plan]." After printing the name of a thing (called item) which
    is not a plan while requesting progress: say " ([a random plan which requires
    item])".
```

Useful Debugging Extensions

Here are a few more helpful extensions for use during testing.

Simple Debugger by Michael Hilborn adds a phrase similar to showme, but with the added benefit that each phrase can be attached to a particular item, and debugging output for each item can be turned on and off individually. You might set up a series of phrases to show diagnostic information about a conversation, for example, and not have to worry about them unless you type DEBUG COYOTE.

Flexible Windows by Jon Ingold (only available when compiling to Glulx) lets you create multiple output windows in the interpreter. While not primarily written as a testing tool, for debugging something complicated it's often nice to open a secondary window just to display all your debugging information, so the main story window doesn't get cluttered and unreadable.

Debugging Strategy

Fixing a bug is a bit like playing detective: you need to ascertain means, motive, and opportunity, and once you've eliminated the impossible, whatever remains, however unlikely, must be the truth.

It's helpful to start by breaking down the kinds of bugs you can expect to find. Here's a quick overview:

Common Effects of Bugs

Observed Effect	Description
Prose problem	Misplaced commas, misspelled words, extra/missing line breaks or spaces. On a larger scale, poor writing, missing information, or bad combinations of substitution-heavy text.
Implementation problem	No response or incorrect response to a command that should have one.
Logic failure	Something you thought should be allowed is not allowed; something you thought should be forbidden works.
Problem message	Invalid source text that prevents your story from compiling.
Run-time problem	Unexpected situation produces an error message during play.
Parsing problem	Problems with disambiguation, understanding actions, or commands being misinterpreted.
Game-breaker	A bug, usually a malformed rule, that puts your game in a state from which it's impossible to finish the story.
Game-crasher	A bug that actually causes the story file to stop executing, lock up, or crash the interpreter.

The first step in fixing a bug is working out exactly what's causing it. Usually, there's an obvious first place to look, but sometimes bugs lurk in less obvious corners: Inform source text is highly interrelated, with rules and objects affecting each other across your own source text, the Standard Rules, and any included extensions. If you're having trouble working out the origin of a bug, try using the ACTIONS and RULES commands to see if you can spot exactly where in the turn sequence it appears. From there, you can add a series of showme phrases to the relevant rules to get more information.

One nice trick is to have showme display text in addition to values. You might alter a rule to look like this:

```
Before going to Open Desert:
    showme "Beginning before going to Open Desert rule. Removing items:";
    repeat with item running through visible desert flotsam:
        showme item;
        now item is off-stage;
    showme "Finished removing items.";
    ...
```

Code like this should let you work out the exact phrase within a rule that's causing the problem.

From there, it's a matter of working out what that phrase is doing wrong. While the list above represents the different effects of the bugs you'll encounter, it might also be useful to break down their most common causes. Here are likely culprits for Inform bugs.

Common Causes of Bugs

Cause	Description
Conflict with Standard Rules or an extension	You misinterpreted or overlooked some aspect of existing code, leading to incorrect behavior (perhaps you tried to create an action that already exists, or used a global variable name claimed by an extension).
Misunderstandings	Inform understood part of your source text as meaning something other than your intent. Perhaps you referenced an object vaguely and Inform guessed incorrectly, or you indented a conditional phrase improperly, distorting your logic.
Numerical mistake	A part of your code dealing with numbers is doing the arithmetic incorrectly, possibly producing results off by 1 (such as saying *greater than* instead of *at least*).
Missing code	You simply forgot to write source text to deal with a particular situation.
Logical flaws	The structure of your source text doesn't cover all the possible states the story can be in, or handles some incorrectly.
Infinite loops	Almost all bugs that cause the game to lock up and not respond after a command are the result of source text that refers to itself (such as writing a rule for printing the name of something that shows the printed name of that thing, which calls the rule for printing the name of something...)
Bug in Inform	Rarely, you might find a bug caused by a problem in Inform itself rather than your own source text. This is especially likely to be the case if you can isolate the bug in a new, stripped-down story and the behavior is clearly contrary to that laid out in the built-in documentation. Visit inform7.com for information on reporting bugs.

One tip for thorny bugs is to try simplifying the problem. Try to recreate the situation in as basic a form as possible in a new, temporary story file. Can you get the bug to recur? If so, keep removing places for the problem to hide by further simplifying your test code, phrase by phrase, until the bug goes away: the last phrase removed is likely your culprit. You can then devise a solution in this test-tube environment before applying the fix to your main source text.

If you can't get the bug to happen in isolation, either it's not in the part of your source text you think it is, or it's a result of an unexpected interaction between multiple systems. Try disabling extensions one at a time, or commenting out parts of your code, until you find a pattern that points to the bug. If you can't, you haven't tracked down the phrase that's causing problems yet: keep simplifying until you do.

Once you find the bug, you may discover that it reveals a flaw in your underlying design that requires more extensive changes. Many bugs can be patched with the addition of a phrase to circumvent the problem, but often a better solution is redesigning the broken component.

Imagine we'd written one piece of the code for the windows like this:

> A tiny frosted window is a window. It is outside of Break Room and inside from Weed-strewn Rust.
>
> Instead of entering tiny frosted window: say "It's too small for you to wriggle through."

This looks fine, but there's a bug here: if the player types GO OUTSIDE or GO INSIDE, the going action is used, not the entering action. Our instead rule never runs, and the player can travel through this window and bypass the introductory scene in Staging Area. Which of the following solutions to the bug is better?

Instead of going through tiny frosted window: say "It's too small for you to wriggle through."	Instead of entering tiny frosted window: say "It's too small for you to wriggle through." Instead of going inside when location is Weed-strewn Rust: say "It's too small for you to wriggle through."

The solution on the left is clearly better: it repairs the problem ("going through" catches any attempt to move via a window, regardless of the action), rather than simply patching it by adding another rule.

Fixing a bug is sometimes as simple as adding a tab stop or tweaking a rule, but in more complicated cases, the solution may require more serious changes to your source text. Sometimes bugs can reveal an underlying problem with a part of your story that needs redesigning. Take the time to think through whether something should be patched or rebuilt from scratch.

As you continue iterating your story, you'll want to start making use of a more powerful testing tool to help ensure your fixes aren't breaking other parts of your code. We'll turn to this major feature of the Inform application next.

Using the Skein and Transcript

Two panels of the Inform interface we haven't looked at yet are the Skein and Transcript. These two tools work together to form an extremely powerful device for testing your game. Let's get familiar with them and see how they work.

 If you haven't been using the Skein, it's probably a good idea to trim it before you start playing with it in the rest of this chapter. While the Skein panel is open, click the Trim button along the top. (Macs only: Move the slider all the way to the right towards "Trim a lot," then click "Trim the skein".) This will start you with a fresh and unknotted skein.

The Skein

The word "skein" means a length of thread, coiled or knotted together. In Shakespeare the word appears twice, both times in the midst of vicious diatribes of insults, so it's perhaps appropriate that it's been repurposed to name a debugging tool. Before you curse someone for an indistinguishable cur of monstrous arrogance, try taking a look at what Inform's Skein can do to reduce your stress.

The Skein panel shows a series of knotted threads representing all the recent traversals of your work in progress. Each knot is a single command, and each thread below that knot leads to all the different commands recently entered next (Figure 11.1). The Skein updates automatically in real time as you play in the Game panel.

Around this framework hangs a number of tools to make testing a complex story easier. The most basic mode of interaction with the Skein is to double-click any knot. The story will restart and play through to that moment, issuing every command in the selected branch. This works similarly to the Replay button, except you can access several past traversals, not just the most recent, and stop at an earlier place than you did previously.

Hovering your mouse over any knot reveals a series of icons that offer more advanced functionality (Figure 11.2). (On Windows, right-click a knot for a menu with the same controls.) In the center is a lock: clicking this will lock that branch, meaning it will be preserved indefinitely. (Normally, old branches are pruned automatically as the Skein gets too full, or when you use the Trim button.) A locked branch will be shown with a solid line, while unlocked branches have a dotted one. The branch representing the game currently or most recently in progress is shown with a thick dotted line, and yellow knots instead of green ones.

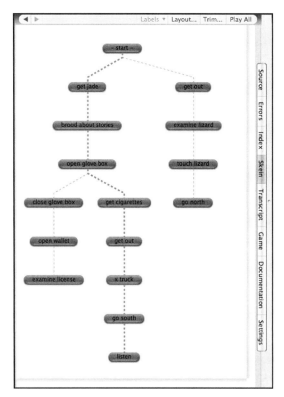

Figure 11.1
The Skein, showing several recent traversals through *Sanddancer*.

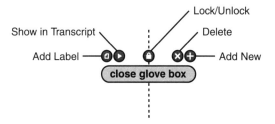

Figure 11.2
The options available when hovering over a knot in the Skein (Mac only; on Windows, these options are available by right-clicking on the knot.)

With what we've learned so far, we could define a couple of pathways through a story, locking each one as we finish, and from then on easily jump to any moment in the chosen versions of the story to test from that point. This is already useful, but some of the other buttons that appear when hovering over a knot add more functionality.

We can get rid of a knot and anything beneath it by clicking the X button. Add a new branch below a knot by clicking the + button, or insert a knot between two knots in an existing thread by right-clicking (Command-clicking on Macs) and choosing Insert Knot. If you want to change the command issued by a certain knot, click once on it then type in the new command (on Windows, right-click and choose Edit Knot).

In larger projects, it may be useful to label your knots. The blank page button can do this: the label will appear in a bubble over the knot. You can then use the Labels drop-down along the top of the Skein panel to quickly jump to any knot with a label, letting you efficiently navigate large or complex skeins.

The other buttons along the top of the panel are also useful: Layout lets you adjust the spacing between knots to a comfortable level (Mac only); Trim, as we've seen, prunes old and unlocked threads; and Play All will run through every blessed transcript. We'll discuss what a blessed transcript is in a moment, as we turn our attention to the Transcript panel.

The Transcript

Much like the Skein, the Transcript panel shows you another record of recent traversals of your story, this time preserving not only the commands submitted but also the text returned. You can easily switch between the same point in either panel: from the Skein, right-click on a knot and choose Show in Transcript; from the Transcript, click the Show Knot button. The Play to Here button in the Transcript works much like double-clicking a knot: the story will restart, if necessary, and play through to that moment.

The Transcript is divided into two halves (Figure 11.3). The left side shows what's happened on the most recent (or in-progress) traversal. The right side shows the **blessed** version of that move in the transcript. A move that's been blessed is one that you've decided is the correct version of that move: the output to the command is exactly how you'd like it to appear in the final game. You can easily bless an entire transcript by using the Bless All button along the top of the panel, or bless individual moves by clicking the button between the left and right halves of the Transcript.

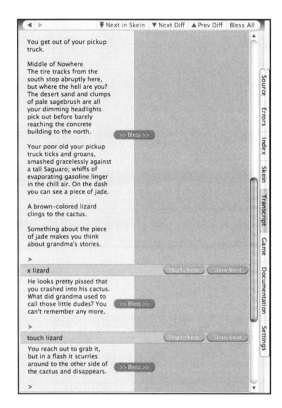

Figure 11.3
Inform's Transcript panel.

Once a transcript has been blessed, things get a little more interesting. When you navigate a blessed thread, any output that looks different from the blessed version will show up in red in the Transcript's left panel, and be given a red badge in the Skein. On Macs, you can use the Next Diff and Prev Diff buttons in the Transcript panel to jump up and down through these differences.

Effectively, this lets you see at a glance when new or revised source text causes unexpected disruptions elsewhere in your story. Once you've blessed a transcript containing a complete traversal from the beginning to an ending, you can continue making changes to your source text, and at any time double-click your blessed thread's final knot to have Inform quickly run through the entire story looking for changed text. If a change you made to one part of the story caused an unanticipated change somewhere else, you can immediately see the difference, and decide either to accept it (by blessing the red knot) or revise your source text to restore the blessed behavior (Figure 11.4).

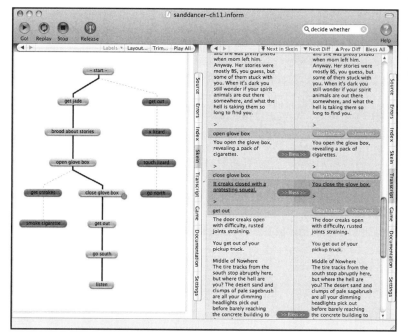

Figure 11.4
The Transcript panel showing game output text, which differed from the blessed (expected) output.

CAUTION   If your story includes randomly generated elements, it can be difficult to effectively use the Skein and the Transcript. Random directions or randomly timed events might mean the precise list of commands required to traverse your story changes on each playthrough. Random variations in descriptive detail mean many trivial differences in prose would clutter up the significant changes in blessed transcripts. Fortunately, Inform offers a solution: in the Settings panel, click the box labeled "Make random outcomes predictable while testing." This will ensure that the same sequence of random events will happen each time you test your story.

Maintaining a blessed transcript takes time, but it makes the Skein and Transcript instrumental tools in debugging your story. In a few moments you can verify that your story is still completable, or jump to any portion of it for detailed testing. It helps catch surprise bugs that often creep into complicated stories. You can also output information from the Skein into a text file for testers or users; we'll see how in the section called "Releasing." The multilinear nature of the Skein embraces the multiple pathways you might build through your story, letting you debug and maintain each of these alternatives with ease. While the Skein may seem like an unfamiliar concept at first, learning to use it pays extraordinary dividends.

Outside Testing

Everybody thinks differently. The moment someone other than the author gets their hands on an interactive fiction, a whole new slew of bugs inevitably arise. What's obvious to you may not be at all obvious to your players, and certainly what's obvious to them will be surprising to you: things so simple you can't believe you missed them, or so baffling you can't imagine why anyone would try to do such a thing (until the next player does it too). For these reasons and many others, getting second opinions is a vital step before your IF project is ready to be released.

While it sounds discouraging, outside testing can actually be one of the most fun parts of the process. Since testers expect a work in progress, you don't have to cringe as dramatically when they uncover errors. Testers will come up with great ideas for commands you should implement, alternate solutions for puzzles you should consider, and give you invaluable insight into how your story comes across to someone not intimately familiar with it. Besides, it's incredibly rewarding to finally watch someone play with the story you designed and built, even if everything isn't yet working quite the way you'd like it to.

Finding Testers

The community resources discussed in Chapter 1 are a great place to look for experienced testers. A good start is a post politely requesting volunteers for a test run, along with a brief description of your story to generate interest. Friends and family can often be recruited to test as well: feedback from people unfamiliar with interactive fiction is vital to making sure your story isn't just written for the initiated.

Wherever you find your testers, make sure to thank them profusely for their generous offer to help, both one-on-one and in the credits of your game. If they're fellow authors, offering to test their next work in progress is a friendly gesture. In fact, let's take this opportunity to thank *Sand-dancer*'s testers. Place this somewhere near the top of the story file near the inclusions:

> After printing the banner text: say "Beta testing courtesy of Duncan Bowsman, Jacqueline A. Lott, Juhana Leinonen, Sharon R., and Stephanie Camus."

Working with Testers

If some of your testers have never played IF before, you'll want to help them find an interpreter and get it installed. (Testing with a web-based or other nonstandard interpreter can make it difficult to collect the feedback you need.) For everybody, you'll want to provide a copy of your story file and instructions on what sort of testing you're looking for (earnest user? devious troublemaker?) and what feedback you expect, when you expect it by, as well as anything unusual about your story they ought to know in advance

We'll talk about releasing in greater detail later in the chapter, but for now, all you have to do is click the Release button in the Inform interface to export your story into a playable format.

 If you want to keep all of the testing commands and other material intact (which can be help-ful for experienced testers), choose the "Release for testing" option from the Release menu to export a version identical to the one in the Game panel of the application.

You can get feedback from your testers in a couple of ways. You might tell them to take notes on any problems they find and report back to you afterwards. If your testers are local, you might watch them play and take notes. The best solution I've found is to have testers save a transcript of their play sessions and send it to me afterwards along with any additional comments. This lets me see, move by move, exactly how they played and what happened, and also lets me catch all kinds of more subtle bugs the testers themselves might not even notice.

You can collect transcripts a couple of different ways. Many interpreters support using the command SCRIPT to begin saving the output to an external file; SCRIPT OFF will stop this logging. The testers can then email you the resulting file. Another method is to ask your testers to simply copy and paste the contents of their story window into a text file or message. This works as long as the interpreter doesn't crash or have a limited scrollback, and your game doesn't clear the screen or use other nontraditional effects. Both methods rely on your testers remembering to make use of them, so be sure to remind them about transcript procedure when you send out the story file for testing.

But then again, maybe we're going about this all wrong.

While testers are great at fixing the bugs in your game, there's a pretty sharp limit on the extent of the changes you'll be able to make in the final stages of your project. If your testers have problems with the overall structure, the characters, the style, the conversation system, the pacing, or the mechanics—you know, the actual game itself—the best you can hope to do is slap some patches on the underlying problems (which are likely to introduce new bugs and be less-than-ideal solutions anyway).

Professional computer games these days are play-tested for years before they're released. As soon as there's something that compiles, no matter how rickety, unfinished, disconnected, or unrefined, testers start playing it and making observations. This ferrets out problems with the basic mechanics of the game: this isn't fun, that takes too long, these things will suck no matter how slick the final presentation.

Obviously the average IF author doesn't have the resources of a major game studio, but that doesn't mean this model is useless for us. A better approach to IF testing might be to assemble a core group of testers not when you're finished, but before you've even begun, who will be with you through the whole process of creating the story. As you code new puzzles or systems, you can have your testers fiddle with them and give feedback; when the game starts coming together, you can have them test it for flow, pacing, and logical problems even before you've implemented all the scenery and invested yourself in the specifics. If the end result is interactive, the process of creation ought to be too.

Of course, the trick is finding such a group. One great strategy would be to partner up with a group of other IF writers online or in person to create a team of perpetual beta buddies who are all willing to help iterate each other's projects. Several IF writers groups like this are springing up around the country. Everyone's projects benefit from both the iteration and the discussions that will inevitably ensue over what works and what doesn't.

Signposting

While testers are great for finding bugs (and find them they will!) what they're really useful for is working out conceptual problems with a story. Looking at a tester transcript, it's immediately obvious what's clear and what isn't in your descriptions, where people need a nudge forward, which parts of your story are moving too quickly or slowly. Quite often advancing through an IF narrative requires learning a series of facts that ultimately combine to indicate the next sequence of actions, and it can be very difficult for designers to unlearn those facts well enough to adequately explain them to the player.

This explanation is called **signposting**, and it's crucial to do. For instance, the mention of the building to the north in the room description for Middle of Nowhere is a signpost, indicating that going north might be a useful action to perform for a player just getting out of the pickup truck for the first time. We use a more subtle signpost when the player tries to enter the building's door: "You slam your hands against the boards in frustration, causing a nearby window to quiver in the reflected light." Here, we draw attention to the window, hopefully sparking a realization that it might be another way to gain access to the interior.

Exercise 11.4

One spot in *Sand-dancer* that we haven't signposted very well is the guidebook. Since the consulting action is rare, you might want to indicate more strongly how it can be effectively used, and understand a broader range of commands referring to it than normal.

Debugging Sand-dancer

In the rest of this section, we'll talk about some real bugs, large and small, discovered during *Sand-dancer*'s external testing. You may have noticed some of these yourself if you've been following along. For each one, we'll talk about how the bug was tracked down as well as the strategy used to fix it.

The Lighter

Several testers attempted to use Knock's lighter as a light source in dark places. Here's a great example of an obvious solution to a problem that I simply overlooked in my design. What we have here isn't so much a bug as a failure to implement.

The most common command tried was LIGHT LIGHTER. The Standard Rules contain an action, burning, which results from several verbs, including LIGHT. The default response to burning something is "This dangerous action would achieve little." Even if we override this with a more Knock-appropriate version, a default message isn't going to be a helpful or appropriate response.

Could we let the lighter be a light source? Worth considering, but it further complicates the story's model of different levels of illumination. We'd have to write even more variable text substitutions to take lighter-lit rooms into account. This also would bypass our puzzle with finding the flashlight in the darkened Staging Area. This isn't itself a problem—players are supposed to be finding ways to bypass puzzles, right?—but because we've designed this sequence so carefully, we'd have to start again from scratch to allow this additional complexity. In addition, using the lighter as a long-term light source creates realism problems: shouldn't Knock's thumb start to burn if the lighter is lit for too long? Will the lighter run out of lighter fluid? Your mileage may vary, but for my money, letting the lighter be a light source creates more problems than it solves.

Can we get rid of it? Not really—it ties into the cigarettes and our whole smoking mechanic, which is part of both gameplay (hints) and story (Knock's efforts to quit). We don't want to lose these systems over this problem.

What we're left with seems like a weak alternative at first: writing a rule explaining why what the player is trying doesn't work. We can make this a stronger solution by giving the player something in exchange for the idea: rather than just an excuse, we'll hint towards something more useful to try. Failing that, we'll at least use this as an opportunity to reinforce the idea of the supernaturally oppressive darkness so integral to our story.

In Part - Mechanics, Chapter - Lights, add a new heading called Section - Lighter:

> Instead of burning the lighter:
>
>> if it's effectively dark, say "You flick the lighter, but the light seems grey and tiny in the face of the dark. All you can really see is[if location is Staging Area] [a desk] by your feet, and[end if][if there is at least one brighter direction] a slightly brighter place to [the list of brighter directions][otherwise] your shivering hand[end if]. As your thumb starts to burn you let the puny light go out.";
>>
>> otherwise say "You flick it open and shut a few times, an old habit."

> To decide whether it's effectively dark: if location is Staging Area and Staging Area is dim, decide yes; if in darkness, decide yes; decide no.
>
> Definition: a direction (called thataway) is brighter if it is viable and the room thataway from the location is lighted.
>
> Instead of switching on or switching off lighter: try burning lighter.

While we're at it, we should redirect another likely command, LIGHT CIGARETTE, to the appropriate action (in Chapter - Smoking):

> Instead of burning the pack of cigarettes: try smoking the pack of cigarettes.

Extended Hints

While we're here in Chapter - Smoking, we can add a few more hints to our "decide which text is the best course of action" rule, leveraging some of the skills we've gained since we created it. Just before the "otherwise if strength is held" clause, add:

> otherwise if Burrow is unvisited:
>
>> say "you should try to catch up with that weird shadow";

Before "otherwise if Open Desert is unvisited," add:

> otherwise if voice has not been visible:
>
>> say "you maybe should see if you can call for help with that emergency radio in the break room";

Finally, before "otherwise if luck is held..." add:

> otherwise if there is an in progress plan and Temptation has not happened:
>
>> say "you ought to head back to the desert and see if you can find that rabbit dude again";

Make sure to keep your indentation correct.

Notification Failure

The four story items required by plans are each supposed to trigger a message the first time they're interacted with, indicating that they're important: "Hey, that emergency blanket might be useful if you decide on spending the night here." However, one tester noticed that you don't get these messages for the gas can or the canned oranges. Investigating, we discover it's because neither of those objects are actually visible until after the player claims them: the gas can is represented only by a smell, while the oranges don't appear until Knock is lucky enough to find them.

To fix this, we can invoke the phrase we created to display the message by hand, whenever these proxy objects are first manipulated. In Chapter - Plans, add:

> Every turn when doing something to smell of gasoline and gas can is not noted
>   as useful: note gas can as useful. Every turn when doing something to cans of
>   food and canned oranges are not noted as useful: note canned oranges as
>   useful.

We also should describe these items more generally before the player has discovered that they exist:

> For printing the name of canned oranges while canned oranges are off-stage:
>   say "food". For printing the name of gas can while gas can is off-stage: say
>   "gas".

Radio Troubles

One tester tried the command SET RADIO TO 107.3, and received the response "No, you can't set that to anything." We didn't define SET as a synonym for our tuning action, so what's going on?

By using the ACTIONS testing command, we see that SET becomes the action *setting it to*. Looking this up in the Actions Index, we discover it's defined by the Standard Rules; but rather than using our custom *frequency* kind, it uses a text value instead, rendering it incompatible with our tuning action.

Since nothing else in our game needs to be set to anything, the simplest solution is simply removing the *setting it to* action, and redirecting SET to tuning. We can do this easily enough. In Part - Setting, Chapter - Office Interior, Section - Radio, after the tuning action has been defined, add:

> Understand the command "set" as something new. Understand the command
>   "set" as "tune".

The same tester also noticed that you can pick up the radio and walk off with it. You might have found this too, if you used a trick in a previous chapter to look for mistakenly portable items. If you haven't fixed this already, go ahead and do so now:

> The radio is fixed in place.

Warm Blanket

A simple oversight: several testers tried to wear the warm-looking blanket after they acquired it. This certainly makes sense and doesn't seem to harm anything, so let's make it work. In Section - Break Room, add:

> The blanket is wearable. After wearing blanket: say "You wrap it around your shoulders, and soon your shivering stops."

CAUTION   Even innocuous changes like the above can be a source of problems. If we had defined any rules as contingent on the player *carrying* the blanket, these would fail if the player was *wearing* the blanket instead. (The solution would be to use the broader condition *holding*, which applies to things either worn or carried.) Also, we might want to revisit any text mentioning the cold to see if it should differ when the blanket is being worn.

Entering the Building

One tester tried the command ENTER BUILDING from Crumbling Concrete; since we defined the building as a scenery object, this doesn't work. In Chapter - Around the Tower, Section - Crumbling Concrete, add this:

> Instead of entering concrete building when location is Backtracking or location is Middle of Nowhere: say "You aren't close enough to the building." Instead of entering concrete building: try going inside.

However, recompiling and testing this again reveals a new problem: now, ENTER BUILD-ING tries to go in through the window. This is because of the door we created northeast of Crumbling Concrete that can't be opened; instead, we expect the player to use the window (mapped inside from the same location). Unfortunately, most players would expect their character to try the door before the window, and this spoils the surprise of figuring out the window is a way to get in. Let's add a rule to fix this:

> Instead of going inside from Crumbling Concrete when pane of cracked glass is closed: try going northeast.

Too Much Distance and Other Signposting Problems

Several testers responded to the hint about breaking the windows ("Nice thought, but the last thing you need is a sliced open hand. Maybe if you could get a little distance.") by attempting to move to a different location, indicating that we signposted this puzzle incorrectly: our text is being taken too literally. Let's modify it, in Section - Windows:

> Instead of attacking a window: say "Nice thought, but the last thing you need is a sliced open hand. Maybe you could use something less likely to bleed."

This wording might imply a command like BREAK WINDOW WITH JADE. We can understand this as another form of throwing it at, but notice that the nouns are in the wrong order than the throwing action expects (throwing the jade at the window). You can add the parenthetical phrase **with nouns reversed** to the end of an understand line to account for this:

> Understand "break [something] with [something preferably held]" as throwing it at (with nouns reversed).

Similarly, our text for trying to move into the desert without a light ("It's black. Pitch. Storm must have rolled in; there are no stars above, no anything but blackness around. Only the smell of the desert tells you it's still out there.") caused testers to next move in the opposite direction, indicating that they thought they had actually moved into a dark area. We can clarify this with a more explicit statement rejecting the movement, maybe by just adding the sentence "Better not." at the beginning of the text.

Two Birds

While we're on the subject of throwing things, one tester pointed out that it seems awkward that almost anything can break a window, including the receipt from Knock's wallet. While this isn't a major problem (since most players wouldn't think to try throwing something unusual anyway), it makes our story seem more mechanical if discovered, and it's easy to fix. Back in Section - Windows, add the following, before any other *instead of throwing* rules:

> A thing can be hefty. A thing is usually hefty. The driver's license, receipt, pack of cigarettes, and photo are not hefty. Instead of throwing something not hefty at a closed window: say "Like that's going to break anything."

Now that we've created this definition, we might as well use it to fix another infelicity:

> Instead of inserting something hefty into the wallet: say "Not gonna fit."

Figure 11.5 Debugging can be depressing. I thought this motivational image might cheer you up. You're almost finished! Photo by H. Kopp-Delaney.

Brooding about the Wrong Thing

Several testers tried a command sequence like the following:

> Something about the piece of jade makes you want to brood about grandma's stories.
>
> >BROOD ABOUT JADE
>
> Eh. You couldn't really get into a good brood about that when it's this damn cold.

Arguably, our text doesn't suggest strongly enough that the item to be investigated is the stories, not the jade—perhaps because concepts and memories are only rarely implemented in interactive fiction. Instead of rewriting our message, we can make a new rule that explains more clearly what should be done. In Part - Mechanics, Chapter - Memories, Section - Brooding, add:

> Instead of brooding when noun suggests a memory: say "It's not [the noun] you want to brood about, it's [a random memory suggested by the noun]."

Better Cobwebs

The cobwebs in the Staging Area's hole were a frequent source of frustration, largely due to the poor implementation: they don't respond to any command other than take. Let's amend this, in Part - Setting, Chapter - Office Interior, Section - Staging Area:

> Instead of touching or rubbing or attacking or pulling the cobwebs when player holds courage: try taking cobwebs. Instead of touching or rubbing or attacking or pulling the cobwebs: try taking the duct tape. [Since we already have a nice response for the duct tape about being too afraid to reach in the hole.]

Inappropriate Discussions

One thing lacking from our conversation system is a way of defining which "people" in a story can be conversed with and which can't. Our story contains several characters (such as the normal animals seen around the tower, or, in fact, Knock himself) who we should-n't be able to start a conversation with. In Chapter - Customizations, add the following:

> Before saying hello to when noun is not a spirit animal and noun is not voice: instead say "You can't really get into a good conversation right now."

Not Enough Memory

One wily tester discovered that it was possible (if difficult) to reach Coyote's Offer with only one discovered memory, making it impossible to trade with him and end the scene. Our first reaction might be to dismiss this scenario as unlikely, but it's always a bad idea to assume how your story will be navigated. An order or state that seems unlikely to you may seem perfectly natural to somebody else. A player might be uninquisitive, or might be replaying and deliberately skipping past introductory material he's already seen. Regardless, it should never be possible to get stuck without enough memories to trade.

One solution is simply to add more memories, but this just makes the problem less likely, not impossible. The best solution is to prevent access to each spirit animal sequence until the minimum number of memories is held. Let's create a new phrase to decide this. Put this in Part - Mechanics, Chapter - Memories:

> To decide whether insufficient memories found:
>
>> if Pursuit is happening and the number of memories in emotional baggage is less than the price of Hare, decide yes;
>>
>> if Temptation is happening and the number of memories in emotional baggage is less than the price of Coyote, decide yes;
>>
>> if time for arrival and the number of memories in emotional baggage is less than the price of Sand-dancer, decide yes;
>
> decide no.

Since we've already compiled all the conditions for visiting the Open Desert in one rule, we can just add a new condition to it. Back in Part - Setting, Chapter - The Open Desert, change the third condition in the "Before going from Around the Tower to Open Desert" rule to add the bolded text:

> if emergency lights are switched off or voice has not been visible **or insufficient memories found**,

We also need to change the starting conditions for Sand-dancer's Arrival, in Part - Scenes, Chapter - Sand-dancer's Arrival:

> Sand-dancer's Arrival begins when time for arrival and tried to leave is true **and not insufficient memories found**.

This shows a handy, if awkward, way to reverse the sense of any decision: simply add **not** before it. (The reason for the difference here is that in the first case we're restricting behavior, and in the second we're defining a triggering condition.)

Dropping the Flashlight

Another case of unlikely player behavior is dropping the flashlight at various inconvenient times. A player who does this in hare's burrow, for instance, loses the light for good once the scene ends, and is unable for lack of a light source to get back to the desert for the scene with Coyote. We pretty much want Knock to always have the flashlight with him once found, and enforcing this does not seem to reduce the player's freedom in a meaningful way. Add this to Part - Mechanics, Chapter - Lights:

> Instead of dropping flashlight: say "Better keep it with you. It's hella dark out."

Talent Issues

Here's an odd one: a tester noticed that you can trade the same memory with a spirit animal multiple times, even after you're no longer holding it. Referring to our definition of the trading action, we see that it ought to be applied only to things held by the player. What's going on?

Further investigation revealed the traded memory was returning to the player's inventory immediately after being traded away. Use of the RULES testing command narrowed this down to a rule identified as "Every turn when a charged thing (called the item) is visible". Searching for this rule, we see that it's the one that captures and notifies about discovered memories.

And when we look at the definition of *charged*, we see the problem: "a thing is charged if it suggests a memory which is not in emotional baggage." Trading moves the memory from the emotional baggage to the trader: but because it remains visible, it becomes a charged visible memory again, triggering the every turn rule that "discovers" it and moves it back to the emotional baggage.

There are a couple of ways we could fix this, but the clearest is to make our definition apply only to memories that have never been claimed. Rather than creating a new property to track this, we might make our own tongue-in-cheek solution (in Part - Mechanics, Chapter - Memories):

> The subconscious is a container. When play begins: now every memory is in the subconscious.

Now alter the definition as follows:

> Definition: a thing is charged if it suggests a memory which is in the subconscious.

While we're fiddling, we might notice that our report trading rule for talents isn't firing. Why not? Again using RULES, we can see that the rules we've created for each spirit animal to finish up the conversation match first, leaving the generic report rule out in the cold.

We could write our own text for each spirit animal in their existing report rules to describe the results of the trade. Another solution would be to make sure the generic report rule comes first, then continues on to allow the others to fire. If we change "Report trading" to "First report trading," this is what will happen.

Finally: another little oopsie with potentially serious consequences. Add this to Chapter - Talents:

> Instead of dropping a talent: say "You can't imagine being without it, now."
>   Instead of inserting a talent into something: try dropping noun.

And they probably ought to have a description, too:

> The description of a talent is usually "[if held]It's just kind of part of you now.[otherwise]It glimmers and sparkles."

Releasing

"Good films are never released, only abandoned," goes the saying among filmmakers, not all of whom are aware that nearly every artistic medium has a similar expression. IF is no different: while it sometimes feels like you could keep testing, debugging, and fiddling forever, at some point you have to release your story into the world. Here's how to take the final steps.

Format

Inform can release stories in two major formats: z-code or Glulx. We discussed the difference between these two formats briefly back in Chapter 1, but to quickly re-iterate: z-code is an older and smaller format, while Glulx is newer and has a larger capacity. While z-code is supported on a wider range of devices (including obscure ones like calculators), Glulx is rapidly catching up and is the format of the future. Games produced with Inform 7 use data structures that tend to fill up the limited space available in z-code files rapidly, so I recommend using Glulx for most new IF projects these days.

Format	Extension	Maximum File Size	Best Feature
z-code	.z5, .z8, .zlb, .zblorb	256KB (v5), 512KB (v8)	Playable almost anywhere
Glulx	.ulx, .glb, .gblorb	4GB	Multimedia support, virtually no size restrictions

To select which format your story is released to, open the Settings panel and choose a format from the list. The checkbox "Bind up into a Blorb file on release" will produce stories in the newer .zblorb or .gblorb formats, which automatically include bibliographic data and cover art, and is recommended for all new stories.

Bibliographic Info

Several thousand interactive fictions have been released in the past twenty years, and the problem of archiving and indexing all these stories led in 2005 to the creation of a cross-language standard for IF bibliographic data called the Treaty of Babel. By asserting a value for a series of built-in global variables, you can make this data accessible to interpreters and websites that know how to extract it from your story file.

Variable Name	Variable Type	Description
story title	text	Normally set by the quoted text that begins a source text
story author	text	Normally set by adding a byline to the above
story headline	text	The subtitle that appears after the title in the banner text
story genre	text	Recommended to be one of Comedy, Erotica, Fairy Tale, Fantasy, Fiction, Historical, Horror, Mystery, Non-Fiction, Other, Romance, Science Fiction, or Surreal
release number	number	An integer representing the version of this release of the story

Variable Name	Variable Type	Description
story description	text	The equivalent of a book's back cover: a paragraph or two enticing potential readers
story creation year	number	The four-digit year of the story's first release

Let's add the uncreated values here to *Sand-dancer*, up near the top of the source text:

The story description is "It figures that your pickup would die on a night like
this and leave you stranded in the dark New Mexico desert. But nothing else
figures about this night, man. Nothing at all."

The story genre is "Fiction".

The story creation year is 2010.

Releasing With

Inform comes pre-packaged with a bunch of great options that let you more easily promote your story to players. You invoke each of these by simply adding an assertion sentence to your source text like *Release along with a website*. More details on each of these in the built-in docs, but here are some of the neat things you can do, at a glance.

Cover Art

If you add the following line to your source text:

Release along with cover art.

...Inform can package up an image you've prepared into your story file in a format that most interpreters can read and display when play begins. This image will accompany your story and might become its icon in Windows or its Quick Look preview on Macs. The cover art should contain an intriguing image, the title of your story, and (optionally) the author's name.

For the command to work, you need to prepare a large and small version of your image, conforming to the specifications below:

Image Version	Dimensions	Format	Filename
Large	960x960 pixels (recommended)	JPG or PNG	Cover.[jpg/png]
Small	120x120 pixels (exactly)	JPG or PNG	Small Cover.[jpg/png]

These two image files should then be placed in the Materials folder for your project. This is a folder that will appear in the same directory as your project the first time you compile it. You can jump to this folder by choosing Release > Open Materials Folder from the menu bar.

Much as it does with books, IF cover art helps sell the story at a glance to a potential reader. If you're not an artist, you can often find people willing to do cover art for new projects by asking nicely in the community forums, or looking for images released under the Creative Commons license on a photo-sharing site like Flickr.

An Introductory Booklet

If you *Release along with an introductory booklet*, Inform will place an eight-page PDF file in the Release folder with your story. This is an elegantly-designed primer on how to play and enjoy IF, and can be freely copied and distributed. It's a great way to ensure your game comes with some basic instructions for people new to the medium.

A Website

If you *Release along with a website*, Inform will create a functional website for your project, with links to download the story file, as well as any other items you've released along with it (such as the introductory booklet). Your bibliographic data and cover art will appear on the home page (index.html), along with a link to the story file and instructions for how to play. Now, you can simply upload the contents of the Release folder to an empty folder on your website to create a web presence for your story.

The built-in docs have information about more advanced features related to releasing with a website, such as the use of different templates.

An Interpreter

Adding the *Release along with an interpreter* option creates another link on your released website that lets people play your story file online from within their web browsers via JavaScript. This makes for a wonderful way to release your story in a format where people can start interacting effortlessly, without having to download a separate interpreter program and your story file. Playing IF within a web browser is slower than playing offline, and some features will be missing. However, it's a great option to encourage the casual play of your stories.

At publication time, this feature was officially restricted only to stories compiled in the smaller z-machine format. However, support for Glulx stories via an interpreter called Quixe was moments away from realization. Search for "Quixe" online for the latest on releasing web versions of Glulx stories.

The Source Text

Release along with the source text generates an elegant series of web pages that showcase the complete source text for your story in a nicely styled fashion, broken into individual pages for each heading. This will automatically be linked to the main page if you're releasing along with a website.

Releasing along with source text is a great way to let other authors take advantage of your skills and see how something was done.

A Solution

Release along with a solution will let you automatically turn a line of your Skein into a text file containing a walkthrough of your game. While less elegant than hints, a walkthrough has often been a required component for submissions to IF contests, so judges can verify that the game can be completed, and is useful for players as a last resort in case they absolutely can't figure out what to type next.

To mark a branch of your Skein as one that should be used for your walkthrough, simply give the final move a label beginning with "***". (Any other labels will appear in the walkthrough as annotations.) If you include multiple variations, all versions marked with three asterisks will be organized in the walkthrough as multiple variations on the sequence of play.

Custom Files

You can include any bonus files you want within the Materials folder for a project, and specify that they should be released along with your project; these will be copied to the Release folder and linked to from the website, if you're releasing with that option.

> Release along with a file of "Desert Survival Handbook" called "handbook.pdf".

Extra bonus features like this are called "feelies" by the IF community, and are a tradition dating back to the exciting packaging that Infocom used to sell their games, which often included all manner of goodies (such as a glow-in-the-dark magic stone with *Wishbringer*). Maps, mood-setting audio files, illustrations, hints, and any other materials can make good feelies. Just make sure you don't include any materials you don't own the copyright for, which could complicate the ability to share and archive your story.

Interpreters

A multitude of IF "terps" (interpreter programs) exist for a multitude of computing environments, with popular opinion about which are best or fastest changing from year to year. Increasingly, the rise of browser-based terps coded in languages like Flash, Java, and

JavaScript means many players don't have to worry about terps at all. However, for both authors and the discerning fan of the medium, finding a favorite interpreter and customizing it to your preferences is essential.

Owning multiple terps is useful for authors to ensure that a new story plays correctly on each of them. Much as web designers should test their pages in multiple browsers, a good IF author should ensure that a new game works across the major terps before releasing it (although IF formats are fortunately more stable than web standards).

If your story includes multimedia, unusual text styles or characters, extensions that make use of Glulx windows or timing effects, or other variations from the norm, cross-interpreter testing is important. Although if you work in Windows you may not have access to a Mac for testing (and vice versa), looking for at least one external tester on the other platform is always a good idea.

Where to Find an Audience

The saddest thing you can do upon finishing your project is to just put it up on your website and forget about it. You went to a lot of work to create your story! It deserves an audience.

The built-in docs have an excellent chapter called "Publishing" that's all about places you can promote your IF project and find a readership. Rather than reiterating all of the information there, I'll just say that the audience for IF today is broader than it's been at any time since the 1980s. A resurgence of interest on several fronts—the indie game scene, the electronic literature community, classrooms at all age levels—means there are more and more people interested in playing good stories. A parallel rise in handheld devices that can run IF means these people have an easy way to find and play your games.

An audience is out there. The final stage of finishing your story is getting it into their hands, so they can begin the adventure you set out to take them on.

Exercise Answers

Exercise 11.1

Try playing through your local version of *Sand-dancer*, or download the "Chapter 10" version from the book's website.

Exercise 11.2

Use the two extensions to find more places to insert color. Here's one more example:

> The description of huge electrical tower is "You can barely see it in the gloom but it's huge, like a metal spider web weaving into space. Way above, a red light blinks on, off, on, off."

Exercise 11.3

Use showme to notify about undescribed items.

> Definition: something is boring if its description is empty and it is not scenery. Every turn when the number of visible boring things is at least 1: showme the list of visible boring things.

The adjective *empty* is predefined as meaning a string with no characters inside; the opposite is *non-empty*.

Exercise 11.4

Signpost the guidebook more clearly. One approach:

> The description of the guidebook is "Most of the pages are faded or worn away, but flipping through, it looks like a guide to local animal life. You could try to LOOK UP an animal IN THE BOOK." Understand "guide/book/page/pages" as the guidebook. Understand the command "read about" as "consult".

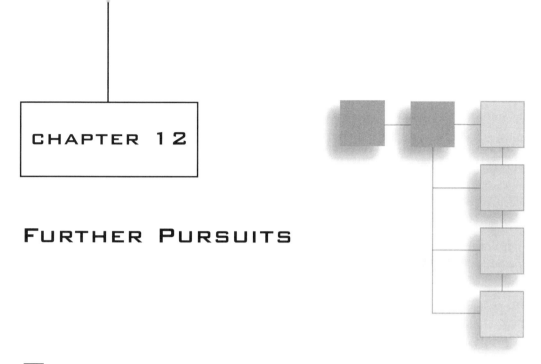

CHAPTER 12

FURTHER PURSUITS

I've taken you through the process of creating a whole project from first room through fixing bugs, and hopefully you've learned how to tell stories in Inform 7 along the way. While we haven't had space to cover everything there is to know about the language, you've gained the basic vocabulary and the tools you need to find out more.

After Release: What Next?

Once your story is being played and enjoyed, what then? Much like the many chapters Tolkien wrote after that pesky ring got thrown into the fire, there is often a lot of business left to wrap up after the end of your journey.

Fixing Bugs

What, again?

The regrettable truth is that the bug reports won't stop coming in just because your inter-actors are players rather than testers. No matter how much testing you do, the pool of play-ers will inevitably expose your story to a much broader range of commands and story states than it's seen to date, and there will almost assuredly be some bugs left to be worked out. Please see Figure 11.5 again if necessary.

The good news is that fixing bugs post-release is a lot easier with a work of interactive fic-tion than it is for a book. (The good news for *you*, I mean.) You can just correct the nec-essary issues, click the Release button again, and upload the amended file to its home on the web. Whenever you do this, though, it's a good idea to use the built-in system for tracking multiple releases by a adding a line to your source text like:

> The release number is 2.

This will help reduce confusion both for other players and yourself about which version of a story is which, since the release number is prominently displayed in the banner text when a story begins.

Some authors prefer to fix bugs and immediately post new versions, while others like to wait until a significant number of bugs have been fixed before posting an update. Either method is fine.

Adding Features

There's no rule saying you can't keep improving your story in more significant ways after you've released it, too. Often, the feedback from reviews and play will suggest new features that might improve the user experience, or new aspects of the story that could be explored. Most common is adding more implementation: descriptions and responses to commands that you didn't get to in your first release. Some stories have been known to change drastically from their first release to final version, as authors continued iterating and improving them based on feedback.

One difficulty with adding new features is that you risk adding new bugs into the mix. Be careful and thoroughly consider the ramifications of your additions across your whole story world, and for major upgrades consider running a tester or two through the new versions again before posting them. The Skein and a blessed transcript are great tools for helping catch newly introduced bugs, too.

Archiving Your Project

As time goes on and computers get replaced or upgraded, the issue of archiving your project will become important. If you lose the source text to a project, you'll no longer be able to make any changes to it, fix newly discovered bugs, or port it to a new system five or ten years down the road. It may be hard to worry much about this when you're still celebrating getting the thing out the door, but keeping a few things in mind from the beginning may prove useful.

You'll want to hold on to your Inform project file, of course, but you should also keep a copy of all the extensions you used. Extensions are frequently upgraded in ways that break stories written with their older versions, so keeping a local copy of the specific version at the time you finished your project can be crucial to getting it to compile again a year or two later. Extensions are stored on Macs in the folder Library/Inform/Extensions under your home folder, and on Windows in your Documents folder under Inform\Extensions.

It's also not a bad idea to keep a copy of the version of the Inform application you used to compile your story. Like most actively developed languages, Inform continues to be upgraded and improved, and while its authors take great pains to keep things backwards compatible, it may be easier to stick with the version of the language that was around when you wrote and released your story. For long term archival of projects, it's a good idea to create a .zip file with both the current Extensions folder and Inform application, and keep this alongside your archive of the source text itself.

Advanced Inform 7: A Brief Overview

Many of Inform's most advanced features have not been touched on in this book. Here's a quick introduction to some of the rest of what the language offers, and pointers to where you can learn more.

Indexed Text

We've worked a lot with text, obviously, but all the text we've seen has been immutable: though a text variable may be updated to hold different text, or contain text substitutions, the contents of a string never normally change in the course of an Inform game. This may seem odd for a language devoted exclusively to text. But most of the time, the hope is that authors will be able to tell stories on a larger level than worrying about individual letters and words.

But sometimes you do need to get down to this level of detail. To do so, Inform offers another, more advanced kind to hold mutable text values , called **indexed text**. Imagine we had a string variable, *invocation*, holding the text "but it's too late, you're crashing, you're crashing, you crash..." We can use a number of phrases on indexed text (or even regular text, which is automatically converted) to extract pieces and information:

Phrase	*Result*
number of characters in invocation	65
character number 1 in invocation	b
number of words in invocation	10
word number 5 in invocation	you're
number of punctuated words in invocation	14
punctuated word number 5 in invocation	,
punctuated word number 14 in invocation	...
line number 1 in invocation	but it's too late, you're crashing, you're crashing, you crash...

Phrase	*Result*
paragraph number 1 in invocation	but it's too late, you're crashing, you're crashing, you crash...
invocation in uppercase	BUT IT'S TOO LATE, YOU'RE CRASHING, YOU'RE CRASHING, YOU CRASH...
invocation in lowercase	but it's too late, you're crashing, you're crashing, you crash...
invocation in sentence case	But it's too late, you're crashing, you're crashing, you crash...
invocation in title case	But It's Too Late, You're Crashing, You're Crashing, You Crash...

A few clarifications: punctuated words counts punctuation marks (or runs of punctuation marks, like "...") as words, while asking for just words alone (or unpunctuated words) ignores punctuation. Line and paragraph counts are based on the use of [line break] and [paragraph break] text substitutions.

You can also search for text that matches various patterns:

Condition	*Result*
invocation matches the text "crash"	true
invocation matches the text "CRASH"	false
invocation matches the text "CRASH", case insensitively	true
number of times invocation matches the text "crash"	3
invocation exactly matches the text "crash"	false
word number 10 in invocation exactly matches the text "crash"	true

Variables specifically created as indexed text can also be manipulated:

Phrase	*Contents of Invocation*
let invocation be an indexed text;	{empty}
now invocation is "you're crashing";	you're crashing
replace character number 1 in invocation with "x";	xou're crashing
replace word number 1 in invocation with "he's";	he's crashing
replace the text "crash" in invocation with "fall";	he's falling

Inform's indexed text supports regular expression matching, which allows for more sophisticated matching and replacement of text. See the chapter "Advanced Text" in the built-in docs for more information on regular expressions and indexed text in general.

Advanced Inform 7: A Brief Overview   395

Tables

We've made some use of lists, which let us hold a collection of values. We can even create lists that hold a collection of other lists. But a very common way of storing data in books is to print it in a table. Because of this, Inform also lets us create **tables** that look very much like their counterparts in the print world.

The original *Adventure* ranked players at the end of a game based on their score. Were this system to be implemented in Inform 7, a table could be created that looked like this:

Table of Rankings

Min Points	Rank
35	"Rank Amateur"
100	"Novice Class Adventurer"
130	"Experienced Adventurer"
200	"Seasoned Adventurer"
250	"Junior Master"
300	"Master Adventurer Class C"
330	"Master Adventurer Class B"
349	"Master Adventurer Class A"
350	"Adventurer Grandmaster"

(The "last lousy point" separating masters from grandmasters became almost legendary, and could in fact only be gained by never saving the game.)

A table must be given a title on its own line, which begins with the word "Table." The next line must name all of the table's columns, and each line after that contains one row of information. Table columns each must be separated with one or more tab stops. The Inform application on Macs can dynamically resize columns to keep your table looking pretty.

Once you have tabular data, you can access it in a variety of ways.

Description	Result
rank in row 2 of Table of Rankings	"Novice Class Adventurer"
the number of rows in Table of Rankings	9
rank corresponding to a min points of 250 in Table of Rankings	"Junior Master"
there is a rank of "Exalted One" in Table of Rankings	false

You can also update table data: here are some simple ways.

> *Phrase*
>
> now the rank in row 1 of Table of Rankings is "Greenhorn";
>
> now the rank corresponding to a min points of 300 in Table of Rankings is "Senior Master";
>
> choose row with a min points of 300 in Table of Rankings; now rank entry is "Senior Master";
>
> choose a random row in Table of Rankings;

You can do much more with tables than is touched upon here, including sorting them, running through them one row at a time, and using them to define groups of similar items. See the chapter on Tables in the built-in docs for more information.

Styled Text

While basic standards have emerged on computing platforms for storing and displaying text itself—even in wide varieties, such as the tens of thousands of characters defined by the Unicode standard—there is still little consensus on how best to indicate style information such as bolded, italicized, or underlined text. The fact that a word is italicized in a website, a Word document, and a PDF file is stored in different ways in each of those places. Part of the problem is defining its limits. Should colored text be considered a basic style? What about size? Font? There are also matters of interpretation: to emphasize text, is it better to bold it or italicize it?

As a result, styling text in IF is more difficult than might be assumed. Inform provides base-level support for three kinds of style:

Text Substitution to Invoke	*Effect*	*Text Substitution to Disable*
[bold type]	**bold type**	[roman type]
[italic type]	*italic type*	[roman type]
[fixed letter spacing]	`fixed letter spacing`	[variable letter spacing]

More advanced styles are possible, although the situation is complicated because each of the two virtual machines, z-code and Glulx, have completely different standards for how to display advanced styles. (The situation is further complicated by the fact that Glulx's standards are currently in the process of being rewritten.)

Z-Code

Due to its venerable pedigree, the z-code styles for text seem incredibly basic: they were designed in an era when computers that could display sixteen different colors were still a novelty. The extension <u>Basic Screen Effects by Emily Short</u> provides access to z-code text effects. Either the background or foreground color can be set to white, black, or possibly garish shades of red, green, yellow, blue, magenta, or cyan, by using a phrase like *turn the background black* or a text substitution like [red letters]. The substitution [default letters] will restore the text color to its original shade.

Glulx

Glulx is a newer format for interactive stories, and one of its goals was to separate the presentation layer into its own component (much like how web designers have moved to separate content from presentation by splitting them into HTML and CSS). This unfortunately means that Glulx by itself supports very little in the way of practical styling. While there are third-party style layers (see the section on FyreVM later in this chapter) and the default layer, Glk, is in the process of being redesigned, at present it's difficult to work with styled text effectively in Glulx.

The extension Glulx Text Effects by Emily Short explains how to work with Glulx text styles, if you'd like to try anyway.

Beyond Text

Glulx games can include multiple windows, sounds, and graphics. Inform provides basic support for the latter two features natively, and the extension Flexible Windows by Jon Ingold is a good introduction to the former.

CAUTION   Before you move beyond text, think hard about whether your additions are really beneficial. If a major publisher were to release a book that came with sound effects, it would probably be seen as a gimmick, and it's hard to imagine how they would add anything to the experience of reading. On the other hand, static illustrations have had a long tradition, though they have been used much less frequency in interactive media. I'm not trying to discourage the use of multimedia here, but do think through your decision to include it.

Figures

Glulx story files can display images, which Inform calls **figures**, inline with the text. To set this up, you must first place the images you'd like to include within the Materials folder for a project, in a subfolder titled Figures. (A project's Materials folder is created the first time the project is compiled, in the same folder that the project is saved in.) The files should be saved in either the JPG or PNG formats, and keep in mind that most interpreters will not automatically resize them, which may limit your multimedia to a specific screen size or platform.

You then must create an assertion sentence that gives each image an internal name within your Inform source text. This name must begin with the word Figure, but can otherwise be anything you like:

> Figure of Wiring Diagram is the file "diagram.png".

We can then display this figure anytime we like with the phrase:

> display the Figure of Wiring Diagram;

Figures are of a kind called **figure name**, so you can create a variable to store a figure.

Sounds

Sounds in Inform work similarly to figures, and are called, well, **sounds**. The file format must be AIFF or Ogg Vorbis, and files must be placed in a folder called Sounds inside your project's Materials folder. Each sound must be asserted in your source text and given a name beginning with the word Sound:

> Sound of the desert wind is the file "desert-wind.ogg".

...and can then be played by invoking the phrase:

> play the sound of the desert wind;

Sounds are of a kind called **sound name**, so you could make a variable to hold sounds.

At present, fewer Glulx interpreters support sounds than figures. When using any sort of multimedia, it's very important to test your story with interpreters on multiple platforms to see whether the presentation is what you expect.

External Files

Usually, Inform stories exist in their own little boxes; an interpreter looks inside the box and lets you play in the world, but there's no way for the contents of the story to communicate with the outside world or vice versa. Glulx stories offer the ability to read and write files, opening up intriguing possibilities for exchanging information between stories, pulling information in from the web or other sources, and so on.

Files must be declared just as figures and sounds are, although we omit the extension (interpreters will use a platform-dependent filename), and are given names beginning with the word File; files are of a kind called **external file**. We can read and write either binary, text, or tabular data to files we create ourselves. The extension Recorded Endings by Emily Short tracks how many different endings of a story have been seen in a table called the Table of Possible Endings. It then stores this data each time the story ends:

> The File of Conclusions is called "conclusions". Before printing the player's obituary: write File of Conclusions from the Table of Possible Endings.

Then, the next time the story is started, it can reload this file to see which endings have already been reached, with the phrase:

```
read File of Conclusions into the Table of Possible Endings;
```

Other files are read-only, or read-write if we can specify the exact IFID of the story that generated that file.

For much more on working with multimedia and external files, see the chapter "Figures, Sounds and Files" in the built-in docs.

Creating Adventure Game Tropes

Inform descends in a very direct line from *Zork* and the earliest adventure games. Partly because of this, it contains a lot of features designed to emulate tropes of these early games. Many of these ideas have fallen out of fashion in the IF world, and they specifically weren't covered in detail in the book to emphasize the less-game-more-story sorts of interactive fiction prevalent today. Here's a quick overview of some of this functionality.

Score

We disabled the score in *Sand-dancer* with a use option, but by default an Inform game can keep track of points with a global number variable called *score*, which can be increased or decreased. When this happens, the player is normally notified of the score change. The score is displayed in the status line, and mentioned when the story ends (along with a rank à la *Adventure*, if we've defined a table called "Rankings").

You can find more about scoring in the section "Awarding points" in the docs.

Locks and Keys

As we saw in our example game, Inform can simulate doors representing barriers to movement between locations. One of the traditional adventure game tropes was the locked door with a key that must be found. This has since become a fairly tired cliché, but Inform will let you recreate this if you like.

A door or openable container can have the property **lockable**, and can then be set to either **locked** or **unlocked**. You can declare that something is a key by asserting that it **unlocks** something lockable. Recent games compiled with Inform will automatically open unlocked doors the player tries to go through; the extension <u>Locksmith by Emily Short</u> will also automatically unlock any locked doors if the player holds the key.

For more on doors and locks, see the sections "Doors" and "Locks and keys" in the chapter on "Things."

Carrying Capacity and Holdalls

Since the finding and managing of items is so easy to simulate, adventure game characters often accumulate large quantities of stuff. The absurdity of these large inventories often gets poked fun at (as in the *Monkey Island* fan group on Facebook, "Guybrush Threepwood Has the Most Amazing Pants in the World") since it seems ridiculous for one person to be able to carry around so many things. Early adventure games tried putting limits on the number of things that could be carried at any one time, but the result is that players end up spending a lot of frustrating time trying to remember where they left things, trekking through the world dropping off or picking up their junk, and otherwise disengaging with the story.

A compromise that many IF adventure games settled on was to introduce an item that counted towards the limit of held things, but could contain any number of additional items, like a backpack or rucksack. Inform lets us simulate this with a kind called **player's holdall**. Any item or person can be given a number variable called **carrying capacity** representing the maximum number of things it can enclose. Attempting to take something that would exceed the player's carrying capacity will automatically put something into a held player's holdall.

Most modern IF simply ignores the problem entirely, either by accepting large inventories as an accepted trope much like cardinal directions for navigation, or by creating stories that aren't so centered on the finding and managing of items.

Unusual Map Connections

It's generally assumed that if you can go north from one room, you can go south to return to where you came from, and Inform by default shares this assumption by automatically creating reciprocal directions. Early adventure games would often subvert this expectation to suggest maze-like passages or routes that curved. While they make for more interesting maps, non-reciprocal directions also make for a much more frustrating navigation experience for players, and are mostly avoided in modern IF.

However, if you do want to create them, it's simply a matter of overriding Inform's assumption of reciprocity with a contrary assertion. While:

> Meadow is east of Trail Junction.

...assumes:

> [Trail Junction is west of Meadow.]

...you can override this assumption by asserting something different.

> West of Meadow is nowhere. Trail Junction is north of Meadow. South of Trail Junction is nowhere.

Boxed Quotations

In some of the more literary Infocom games, a boxed quotation would occasionally be displayed on top of the game text. While this adds a touch of class to a game, it's become something of an overused device and much less common in the past few years. If you'd like to try it, in z-code games only, you can use the **display the boxed quotation** phrase followed by a string. Unlike regular strings, you'll have to add line breaks yourself: quotations traditionally occupied about half the total width of the screen.

Third-Party Tools

Inform 7 is still a new language, but several intriguing tools have been created to extend its functionality into different realms. Here are brief overviews of a couple.

FyreVM

In 2009, a new company called TextFyre, Inc. released its first game, *Jack Toresal and the Secret Letter* by David Cornelson and Michael Gentry. With an eye to attracting larger audiences by making a more stylish interpreter, TextFyre designed a replacement for the Glk output layer provided by Glulx stories that could create a much more flexible and graphically sophisticated interface for playing IF. That layer is called FyreVM, and in 2010 it was made an Open Source project, making it freely available for use by anyone developing interactive stories.

FyreVM works under the assumption that rather than all the output produced by your story going to the same place, information can instead be routed to a specific "channel." So rather than the score being printed in the status line, you could instead send this information to a score channel, which might then be displayed by the user interface however it likes (updating a graphical meter, playing a victory sound, and so on). A series of extensions help you set up and use the channel output scheme for your story.

The catch is that using FyreVM means you'll need to code your own interpreter in a language like C#, which is a much more daunting proposition than writing a story, or find someone else who's written a FyreVM interpreter and is willing to share. While FyreVM is not yet widely adopted among IF authors, it offers an intriguing pathway to a more visually impressive model for playing interactive stories, and will hopefully be further improved as time goes on.

Search for FyreVM online to find the latest information about the platform.

Guncho

Multi-player interactive fiction is nothing new: it's been around nearly as long as traditional IF in the form of MUDs (multi-user dungeons) and their many descendants. Even though MUDs are also text-based and share many of the same underlying world model assumptions (space is divided into rooms; people can carry around objects), the MUD community and the IF community have had surprisingly little overlap over the years. Part of the reason may be that MUDs predictably became spaces more for socialization than storytelling. (Even ifMUD, populated by many acclaimed interactive fiction authors, is hardly ever used for telling stories.) MUD systems also have traditionally featured much less sophisticated tools for world-building than their IF cousins.

Partially to address this, in 2008 Jesse McGrew created Guncho, a way to turn any Inform story into a multiplayer experience. By leveraging Inform's robust pre-existing ability for multiple characters in the world to perform actions, Guncho lets multiple players connect to the same IF world and explore it together. Of course, this implies a whole different style of design for interactive stories, since most IF is based on the assumption of only a single player!

Guncho worlds are called "realms," and can be created by uploading Inform source text via a special web-based tool to the Guncho sever. The tool can process a number of additional phrases that help stories work in a multiplayer context (such as adding the chatting action for player communication). If the realm is set to be publically available, anyone with a standard MUD client can connect and begin playing.

Persistent worlds and multiplayer puzzles open up whole new challenges for designers. While multiplayer *games* are commonplace today, true multiplayer *stories* have only rarely been told. Guncho may be the beginning of a rich new age of experimentation. Find out more at guncho.com.

Inform 6

While it may seem odd to end this forward-looking section with a look back, we'd be remiss not to mention Inform 7's predecessor, a powerful IF language of its own with a history of active usage ranging across some fifteen years. Inform 6 can do everything Inform 7 can do. In fact, it may surprise you to learn that your source text is actually converted to Inform 6 code before being compiled into a story file!

Why wouldn't we just work directly in Inform 6, then? Some people prefer to: the language is still in use. But for most of us, it's for the same reason we prefer to use a word processor over a typewriter, scissors, and glue: the elegant functionality lets us focus more on the content, not its assembly. Inform's natural language syntax lets us construct powerful programming constructs like relations, lists, and properties in an intuitive and easy-to-comprehend mode.

For dealing with certain low-level operations, though, it's sometimes necessary or convenient to use Inform 6 instead of Inform 7. You can easily include extracts of I6 code within your I7 project, making it easy to mix and match between the two. Many extensions offering advanced functionality are written in I6 with a translation layer of I7 phrases built on top.

For more about Inform 6, you can visit its website at inform-fiction.org/inform6.html. To learn the language, the best source by far is the *Inform Designer's Manual, 4th edition* by Graham Nelson, which remains one of the most erudite and entertaining software manuals ever written on any language. The DM4 is available for free online.

Some More Useful Extensions

I'd like to round out the chapter by shining the spotlight on a few more extensions that offer useful or interesting functionality to an Inform project.

Approaches by Emily Short lets players type GO TO a location to travel there, passing through intervening rooms along the way. It provides robust control over which rooms are allowed to be traveled through and how the trip should be described. This offers a great convenience for players, who after their initial exploration can ignore the compass directions entirely if they like, and simply move directly to places at will (although a disadvantage is they may be less likely to build a coherent picture of the environment, or uncover more details in seemingly uninteresting rooms frequently bypassed).

Permission to Visit by Ron Newcomb creates another intriguing alternative to compass directions by creating a series of locations that can be freely moved between, as long as the player has the correct permission. NPCs can permit or forbid access to locations, temporarily or permanently, or access can be denied until a certain item is held. This creates an entirely different model for space and time in IF, bypassing uninteresting journeys between places in favor of focusing on individual scenes where interesting things happen.

Senses by ShadowChaser adds full support for all five senses to an Inform game. You can easily define a text string representing the sound, flavor, odor, or feeling of something, or define objects as particularly noisy or pungent, which will point them out as such in a room description.

Transit System by Emily Short, Modern Conveniences by Emily Short, Computers by Emily Short, and Telephones by George Tryfonas all create kinds that let you create fully implemented rooms or things commonly encountered in modern life. Conveniences lets you create rooms for bathrooms or kitchens that come stocked with appropriate furnishings and sensible responses to using them; Transit System lets you create a vehicle that travels a fixed route through the map, stopping to let passengers on or off at assigned points.

Liquid Handling by Al Golden lets you easily simulate liquids or powders that can be mixed, divided between different containers, or consumed. It comes with properties to simulate things being absorbent, leaky, or likely to float, and for defining the effects of various combinations of substances. Another similar extension is Measured Liquid by Emily Short.

Fixed Point Maths by Michael Callaghan and Metric Units by Graham Nelson, both for Glulx only, add more ways to use numeric values to your story. The former lets you perform limited floating point operations (numbers with decimal points) while the latter encodes knowledge of the metric system into Inform, allowing you to easily add properties making use of it:

> Every thing has a mass. The mass of the anvil is 123.7 kilograms.

Basic Help Menu by Emily Short and the already mentioned Tutorial Mode by Emily Short add tools that help players new to IF learn how to successfully navigate a story. Adaptive Hints by Eric Eve or Advanced Help Menu by John W. Kennedy allow for hints to be included within the story with multiple clues that can be revealed one at a time to players feeling stuck.

More Resources

There are a couple of other useful resources for you to consider as you continue your journey through learning Inform.

Stories with Source Text

A number of authors have released the source text to their complete stories. Reading the source text to a real project, especially one you've played through to completion yourself, is an excellent way to learn more about the language. Different authors approach problems in different ways, and you'll inevitably see new techniques, styles, and ideas in someone else's code.

The IFDB (ifdb.tads.org) has a searchable tag, "I7 source available," that helps you easily find games with released source text. You can also check out the Learn > Complete Examples section of the Inform 7 site (inform7.com) for some of the early example games released along with the debut of the language.

Finally, don't forget Inform's own built-in Recipe Book in the Documentation panel. While these aren't complete games, they showcase hundreds of short examples of working source text to achieve particular goals, and make for highly informative browsing.

Our Website

This book has a companion website at courseptr.com/downloads. On the site you can find updates and errata, snapshots of *Sand-dancer* for each chapter as well as the finished and downloadable story file, and up-to-date links to other useful resources across the web.

Other Books

The Learn > Learn Inform section of the official Inform site maintains a list of other books and tutorials that have been written to help people learn Inform. Getting multiple perspectives on how to work with a language is often a useful way to gain a robust, comprehensive understanding of it. One tutorial written in an almost entirely different style than this one is Ron Newcomb's "Inform 7 for Programmers," which discusses how the language works in language familiar to experienced coders, focusing on how Inform is similar to and different from other established languages.

This portion of the site also includes links to other helpful reference materials, including a visual flowchart of the most useful parts of the Standard Rules demonstrating what happens during the turn sequence.

Is *Sand-dancer* Done?

We've built an entire playable story from the ground up as we've worked through this book. It's playable from the beginning to three different endings. But is it finished?

The answer is up to you. Are you satisfied with Knock's story? Does the telling of it provide an interesting space for readers to explore what it means to be in his shoes? If not, what might better provide that space? *Sand-dancer* is released with a Creative Commons license, so you're free to modify it and release your own version if you see fit.

Right now, memories provide story, but are interchangeable from a gameplay perspective. What if we changed this to make the choice of which memories to trade away significant, so the loss of the day you met Ocean would hurt your gameplay options, not just your soul?

Maybe our linear plot seems too constrained to you. We could modify the story world to make the Open Desert an explorable place, with each of the three spirit animals available whenever the player discovers them. We might keep track of what order they're visited and create a more flexible way to track dramatic tension, allowing for the Coyote to be the climax of the story, not Sand-dancer. Or maybe the spirit animals could become dynamic NPCs, moving around the map with their own goals, interacting with Knock more directly as he tried to solve his problems.

The possibilities are endless.

YOU ARE STANDING AT THE END OF A ROAD BEFORE A SMALL BRICK BUILDING.

-- *Adventure*, Will Crowther, 1976

The version of *Adventure* that became a classic and started a medium was not the original. Will Crowther's version created the cave system and much of the fundamentals of the experience, but it wasn't until Don Woods tinkered with, embellished, and expanded it that it took off and found an audience. That audience began with Crowther's words above, but likely ended with text written by Woods.

People continued expanding *Adventure* over the years, adding their own areas, creating new treasures, complicating or simplifying the puzzles, making it their own. One site tracks over thirty-five different major versions of the game.

Perhaps, as with so many other components of *Adventure*, this fluidity of authorship and form is a defining, differentiating feature of interactive fiction. Books and films must be published, locked into a single and immutable version preserved in paper or celluloid. But interactive stories demand interaction, not just in their enaction but perhaps also in their creation. Maybe the free exchange of source and imagination can introduce us to a new, collaborative form of storytelling for our new century.

Maybe you are standing not at the end of a road, but at the beginning.

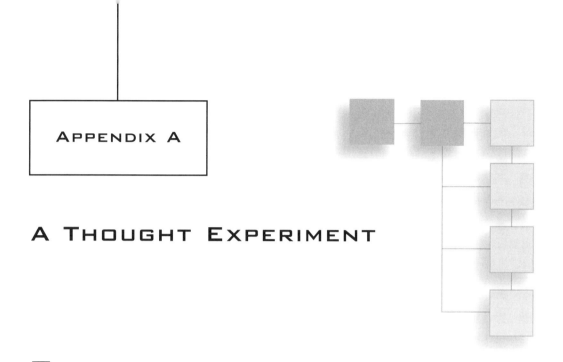

Appendix A

A Thought Experiment

Let's have a little thought experiment, here.

You're playing in a virtual world. It's got these pictures, and they're looking pretty good. And you think, "Oh, that's pretty good. I like these pictures, that's pretty good."

And it's a 3D world, but I'm only seeing it in 2D on the screen, so maybe if I got a little headset on and put it on—ah, now I can see it in 3D. But if I move my head a bit too much, ah, well—maybe if we put little sensors on so if I can move my head. Ah, yeah, now I can see it properly, ah, yes.

It's all here.

But I'm still only seeing things. Maybe I can have maybe some feeling as well. So I put a little data glove on. "Oh, this feels warm, oh, that's good."

But still, I'm not hearing things. I'm not sensing being in a place. And maybe I want to be able to move. So I say, "Well, let's get these big coffin things and fill them full of these gels." And I'll take off all my clothes and put on all these different devices, and I'll lie down and put all these electric currents through and make it feel hard or soft so it gives me an impression that I'm actually walking through grass that it's generating.

And now I begin to really feel like I'm really in one of these places.

But of course, really all that's happening here is that my senses are being fooled into this. What would happen if I were to cut out the whole business with the fingers and stick a jack in the back of your head and it goes right into the spinal cord and you're talking straight to the brain there.

All the senses that go into your brain, they're are all filtered and they're used to create a world model inside your head and imagination. If you could talk straight to that imagination and cut out all the senses, then it would be impossible to ignore it. You couldn't say, "That's just an image of a dragon." That would *be* a dragon.

And if there were some kind of technology which could enable you to talk straight to the imagination...

Well, there is. It was invented in Mesopotamia some five thousand years ago, and it's called "text."

—Richard Bartle, creator of the original MUD (Multi-User Dungeon)

As told in *Get Lamp*, a documentary about adventures in text (getlamp.com).

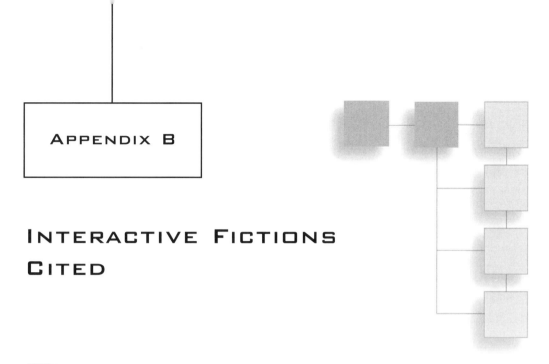

INTERACTIVE FICTIONS CITED

Below is a list of all the works of interactive fiction mentioned in this volume. Unless a publisher is listed, each work is freely available online from the IF Archive or a site like the IFDB (http://ifdb.tads.org/).

1-2-3.... 2000. Chris Mudd. Z/Inform 6.

1893: A World's Fair Mystery. 2002. Peter Nepstad; Illuminated Lantern Publishing. TADS 2.

A Change in the Weather. 1995. Andrew Plotkin. Z/Inform 6.

A Mind Forever Voyaging. 1985. Steve Meretzky; Infocom. Z/ZIL.

Ad Verbum. 2000. Nick Montfort. Z/Inform 6.

Adventure. 1976. Will Crowther and Don Woods. FORTRAN. **Source available**.

Alabaster. 2009. John Cater, Rob Dubbin, Eric Eve, Elizabeth Heller, Jayzee, Kazuki Mishima, Sarah Morayati, Mark Musante, Emily Short, Adam Thornton, and Ziv Wities. Glulx/Inform 7. **Source available**.

All Hope Abandon. 2005. Eric Eve. TADS 3. **Source available**.

Babel. 1997. Ian Finley. TADS 2.

Bad Machine. 1998. Dan Shiovitz. TADS 2.

Beetmonger's Journal, The. 2001. Scott Starkey. TADS 2.

Bellclap. 2004. Tommy Herbert. Z/Inform 6.

Best of Three. 2001. Emily Short. Glulx/Inform 6.

Blue Chairs. 2004. Chris Klimas. Z/Inform 6.

Blue Lacuna. 2009. Aaron Reed. Glulx/Inform 7. **Source available**.

Book and Volume. 2005. Nick Montfort. Z/Inform 6.

Bronze. 2006. Emily Short. Z/Inform 7. **Source available**.

Buried in Shoes. 2008. Kazuki Mishima. Z/Inform 6. **Source available**.

Child's Play. 2006. Stephen Granade. Z/Inform 7. **Source available**.

Damnatio Memoriae. 2006. Emily Short. Z/Inform 7. **Source available**.

Djinni Chronicles, The. 2000. J. D. Berry. Z/Inform 6.

Duel That Spanned the Ages, The. 2009. Oliver Ullmann. Glulx/Inform 7.

Earl Grey. 2009. Rob Dubbin and Adam Parrish. Glulx/Inform 6.

Earth and Sky 3: Luminous Horizon. 2004. Paul O'Brian. Glulx/Inform 6.

Everybody Dies. 2008. Jim Munroe. Glulx/Inform 7.

Fail-Safe. 2000. Jon Ingold. Z/Inform 6.

Fate. 2007. Victor Gijsbers. Z/Inform 7. **Source available**.

Floatpoint. 2006. Emily Short. Z/Inform 7.

For a Change. 1999. Dan Schmidt. Z/Inform 6.

Galatea. 2000. Emily Short. Z/Inform 6.

Gostak, The. 2001. Carl Muckenhoupt. Z/Inform 6.

Gourmet. 2003. Aaron A. Reed and Chad Barb. Z/Inform 6.

Gun Mute. 2008. C. E. J. Pacian. TADS 3.

Hitchhiker's Guide to the Galaxy, The. 1984. Douglas Adams and Steve Meretzky; Infocom. Z/ZIL.

Hunter, in Darkness. 1999. Andrew Plotkin. Z/Inform 6.

Jack Toresal and the Secret Letter. 2009. Mike Gentry and David Cornelson; TextFyre. Glulx/Inform 7.

Journey: The Quest Begins. 1989. Marc Blank; Infocom. Z/ZIL.

Kaged. 2000. Ian Finley. TADS 2.

King of Shreds and Patches, The. 2009. Jimmy Maher. Glulx/Inform 7.

LASH -- Local Asynchronous Satellite Hookup. 2000. Paul O'Brian. Z/Inform 6.

Lost Pig. 2007. Admiral Jota. Z/Inform 6.

Love Is as Powerful as Death, Jealousy Is as Cruel as the Grave. 2009. Michael Whittington. TADS 3.

Lydia's Heart. 2007. Jim Aikin. TADS 3.

Make it Good. 2009. Jon Ingold. Z/Inform 6.

Moonlit Tower, The. 2002. Yoon Ha Lee. Z/Inform 6.

Nightfall. 2008. Eric Eve. Glulx/Inform 7.

Photopia. 1998. Adam Cadre. Z/Inform 6.

Planetfall. 1983. Steve Meretzky; Infocom. Z/ZIL.

Primrose Path, The. 2006. Nolan Bonvouloir. Z/Inform 6.

Rameses. 2000. Stephen Bond. Z/Inform 6.

Rover's Day Out. 2009. Jack Welch and Ben Collins-Sussman. Glulx/Inform 7. **Source available**.

Sand-dancer. 2010. Aaron A. Reed. Glulx/Inform 7. **Source available**.

Shade. 2000. Andrew Plotkin. Z/Inform 6.

Shadow in the Cathedral, The. 2009. Ian Finley and Jon Ingold; TextFyre. Glulx/Inform 7.

shadows on the mirror. 2003. Chrysoula Tzavelas. TADS 3.

Shrapnel. 2000. Adam Cadre. Z/Inform 6.

Slouching Towards Bedlam. 2003. Daniel Ravipinto and Star Foster. Z/Inform 6.

Snowquest. 2009. Eric Eve. Z/Inform 7.

Spider and Web. 1998. Andrew Plotkin. Z/Inform 6.

To Hell in a Hamper. 2003. J. J. Guest. Adrift/TADS 2.

Trinity. 1986. Brian Moriarty; Infocom. Z/ZIL.

Varicella. 1999. Adam Cadre. Z/Inform 6.

Violet. 2008. Jeremy Freese. Z/Inform 7.

Whom the Telling Changed. 2005. Aaron A. Reed. Z/Inform 6.

Winchester's Nightmare. 1999. Nick Montfort. Z/Inform 6.

Zork. 1980. Marc Blank and Dave Lebling; Infocom. Z/ZIL.

Glossary

a. Indefinite article that can be optionally used or not used in source text and player commands. Within text substitutions, it will result in the thing that follows being described with its indefinite article.

abide by. A phrase that invokes a specific rule and decides on the value it returns.

absent, see if absent.

action. An event in the story world caused by a character, such as examining, taking, or waiting.

action default rulebooks. A set of three rulebooks (check, carry out, and report) defined for every action and specifying its default behavior.

action exception rulebooks. A set of three rulebooks (before, instead, and after) empty by default, which can specify exceptional behavior for an action or group of actions.

action variable. A variable that exists only while a certain action's rulebooks are being consulted.

activity. A sequence of operations performed by a story internally, not necessarily as a response to a player command. Each activity has three rulebooks (before, for, and after).

actor. A being that can take action in the story world. When "an actor" is added in the definition of an action rule, this means the rule will be checked for all characters attempting the action, not just the player. "The actor" is an action variable set to the character performing an action.

add to. A phrase that adds a new item to a list.

adjacent. An adjective indicating whether a room is exactly one map connection away from the room currently enclosing the player.

adjective. A condition, set up via a definition, that evaluates to either true or false at the specific moment of play it is tested. See also definition, either/or property.

after rulebook. An action exception rulebook for rules that changes how the result of a successful action is described. A matching rule stops the action.

always. A modifier used in assertions to indicate the required state of a property, as in "A window is always fixed in place." See also usually, never, seldom.

and. Links two conditions together, indicating that both must be true for the condition overall to be true.

animal. A kind of person not given a gender.

antagonist. Narrative term for the character in a story that causes the protagonist to change, sometimes the villain.

as decreasingly likely outcomes, see one of.

assertion. A sentence of source text that defines the existence or state of something in the story world at the start of play, like "The player wears a denim jacket."

at least, see is at least.

at most, see is at most.

at random, see one of.

at the time when. Rule which specifies what happens when a timer created by an "in X turns from now" phrase is triggered.

backdrop. A kind of thing used to represent objects that cannot be taken, are not mentioned in a room description, and can exist in multiple rooms; see also scenery.

banner. A block of information including the story's title, author, release date, and other bibliographic data, usually shown before the first turn begins.

before rulebook. An action exception rulebook for rules that makes adjustments to the story world before an action is attempted. Action processing continues after a matched rule.

begin, see block indentation.

BENT. Bracket Every Notable Thing, a design practice for writing descriptive text in Inform.

best route from. Decides on the first direction in the best path from one location to another.

bless. Mark a portion of the story transcript in the Transcript panel as the "correct" version; text that differs from the blessed version in subsequent playthroughs will be flagged in red.

block indentation. A style of source text for conditional phrases that uses tab stops to indicate nested levels of logic. Can be avoided by using begin and end phrases instead.

Book. The second-level heading in Inform source text. Books can be subheadings of Volumes, and can be further subdivided into Parts, Chapters, and Sections.

boxed quotation. A quote that can appear overlaying your main story text in z-code stories, using the phrase "display the boxed quotation."

bug. An error in source text that causes either a problem message or an unwanted result during play.

business. Theatre term for an unimportant but character-driven action taken by an actor, often in the background.

called. An optional clarifying word in assertion sentences that indicates all following text is part of the object's name, even if it contains normally meaningful words such as "and." Within rule or phrase definitions, "called" can be used to quickly instantiate local variables based on the values being passed into the rule or phrase.

calling phrase. In the context of a named phrase, the rule or phrase that invoked the current phrase and which will be returned to after it finishes.

can be. A phrase used within an assertion to indicate that a kind or object has a certain property, as in "A window can be open."

cardinal directions. The eight compass points (north, northeast, east, southeast, south, southwest, west, northwest) that define the possible directions of movement in most IF, along with four others (up, down, in, and out).

carried. An adjective indicating whether a thing is carried (but not worn) by a character; see also held.

carry out rulebook. An action default rulebook for rules that enacts the changes in the story world resulting from an action. Continue processing the action afterwards.

carrying capacity. A number variable for an object representing the maximum number of things it can enclose.

change the {direction} exit. Special phrase to change a map connection during play, as in "change the east exit of Backtracking to The Open Desert."

Chapter. The fourth-level heading in Inform source text. Chapters can be subheadings of Volumes, Books, or Parts, and can be further subdivided into Sections.

check rulebook. An action default rulebook for rules that decides whether an action is possible in the present circumstances. Continue processing the action afterwards unless the rule begins or ends with the word "instead."

choice-based narrative. A different category of text-based interactive stories based on giving the player a set list of options to perform each turn, rather than a parser and world model. The *Choose Your Own Adventure* books are the most well-known example.

closed. A property of certain kinds of things (such as doors and containers) indicating that there is a barrier to entry or access. Opposite of open.

command. A string of text input by the player at the prompt; the parser translates the player's command into an action, or rejects it.

comment. A portion of a source text surrounded by square brackets indicating that this text is meant for human readers and will be ignored by the compiler.

compass, see cardinal directions.

compiling. The process of converting your source text into a playable story, which occurs when clicking the Go! button in the Inform application.

condition. A phrase that is either true or false at any given moment, such as "the pane of cracked glass is open."

conditional test. A phrase beginning with the word "if" and followed by a condition: the following phrase or phrases will only execute if the condition is true.

conflict. Narrative term describing an event that pushes the protagonist's life in an unexpected direction. Nearly every story has conflict.

consider. A phrase that invokes a specific rule.

container. A kind of thing that can enclose other things and be either open or closed.

continue the action. Can be added to an action rule that would normally cause the action to come to a halt (such as an instead rule) to cause further applicable rules and rulebooks, if any, to be consulted. See also stop the action.

conversation menu. A style of NPC interaction in which all available conversation options are displayed in a list to the player, who selects one to continue. See also lawnmower effect.

current action. A global variable holding the action that the player attempted in their most recent command; see also noun, second noun.

cutscene. A sequence in an interactive story where the player cannot influence events, only passively observe what's happening. See also on rails.

cycling, see one of.

dark. A property of rooms which indicates that a lit object must be present to see in them; opposite of lighted. See also lit and unlit.

debugging. The act of fixing all the problems with your source text one by one until your story compiles and behaves the way you intend it to.

decide if. A decision phrase that returns either yes or no.

decide on. A phrase that returns the given value from a decision phrase to the calling phrase.

decide what. A type of phrase that returns a specific kind.

decide whether, see decide if.

decide which, see decide what.

decision phrase, see to decide.

decrease. Subtract a numeric value from a numeric variable; see also increase.

default value. The contents of a newly created variable of a specific kind, if no specific value is given.

definite article. Text property of an object indicating which definite article should be used when printing its name (usually "the"). See also indefinite article.

definition. A special type of assertion sentence that creates a new adjective.

denouement. Narrative term for the portion of a story that falls after its climax.

described. A property of things that indicates that they are automatically mentioned in room descriptions; opposite of undescribed.

description. A property of rooms and things that contains the text shown when that room is visited or that thing is examined.

device. A kind of thing that is either switched on or switched off.

disambiguation question. A question asked by the parser to clarify an ambiguous player command.

Documentation Panel. The panel within the Inform application that displays the complete built-in reference manuals, *Writing With Inform* and *The Inform Recipe Book*.

does the player mean. A type of rule that authors can use to reduce the parser's need to ask disambiguation questions.

doing anything (or doing something). Can be used in place of a specific action within an action exception rulebook to make this rule apply to all actions. Exceptions can be specified by adding an "other than" clause to the end of the rule definition.

door. A kind of thing representing a passage between two rooms. Doors can be open or closed, and locked or unlocked.

during. Causes a rule to apply only when the given scene is happening.

edge case. An unusual situation on the edge of possibility within a story world. Bugs often hide in edge cases.

edible. A property of things indicating that characters can eat them, which will remove them from the story world.

either/or property. A property with exactly two states, with a word that identifies it in the true state (such as open) and optionally a second word identifying the false state (such as closed); if a false version is not defined, the default is "not {true state}". See also adjective, definition.

else, see otherwise.

empty. An adjective for lists that indicates that the list has no entries, or for text that indicates a zero-length string (and also defined for several other kinds). Opposite of non-empty.

enclosure. A relation indicating position in the object tree: one thing encloses another if it is higher in the tree, such as a room enclosing a character who encloses an item.

end the story. A phrase that causes the story to come to an end, displaying the given text to the player. See also resume the story, finally.

end, see block indentation.

enterable. A property of containers and supporters indicating that they can enclose a character. Opposite of not enterable.

Errors Panel. The panel within the Inform application showing errors in your source text that were found the last time you compiled. Any errors shown in this panel must be addressed before your source text can become a playable story.

even. Adjective for numbers; see also odd.

every turn. A rulebook that contains rules that will be triggered on every turn of play.

exposition. Narrative term for the revelation of important plot information.

extension. A packaged-up bit of source text that allows you to easily add a piece of functionality to a project. Extensions are freely available on the Inform website. Once installed, instructions for using them can be seen in the Documentation panel.

external file. A kind representing an external data file to be read or written to at some point during play.

falling action. Narrative term for periods in a story when tension eases and pace slows down.

false. One of the two possible values of a truth state variable, along with true.

female. A property indicating the pronoun "she" should be used when describing this character.

figure. A kind representing an illustration or picture to be displayed at some point during play.

figure name. A variable holding a figure.

file name. A variable holding an external file.

finally. When added to an "end the story" phrase, causes the condition "the story has ended finally" to be true.

first. When added to the beginning of a rule definition, causes this rule to be listed first in its rulebook. If multiple "first" rules are encountered, each will claim the first spot, bumping those appearing earlier down to second, third, and so on. See also last.

first time only. A set of text substitutions, [first time][only], which will display the text in between only the first time this string is encountered.

fixed in place. A property of things that indicates that they cannot be picked up by characters in the story world; opposite of portable.

for the Nth time. When added to the end of a condition, makes that condition only apply when it has been true and then false again the given number of times.

for N turns. When added to the end of a condition, makes that condition only apply when it has been consecutively true for the given number of turns.

game. A play activity structured by a set of rules that participants agree to abide by while participating. Games present challenges that must be overcome using the rules of the game: the challenge should be difficult but possible to achieve for at least one player. The challenge often represents some real-world difficulty, providing a way for players to rehearse the act of problem solving in a safe and consequence-free environment.

Game Panel. The panel within the Inform application that lets you play your story after clicking the Go! button.

gateway. A situation in an interactive story that constrains forward motion in the plot until a number of prerequisites have been met. Puzzles are often used as gateways.

global variable. A variable that stands alone in source text and exists throughout the duration of play.

Glulx. A 32-bit standard for story files originated in 1999. Glulx is similar to z-code, but with a greatly expanded maximum file size and multimedia capabilities.

greater than, see is greater than.

had been. Uses the past perfect to check if a condition had been true at the start of the current turn, regardless of whether it is any more.

handled. An adjective for things that indicates whether the player has ever held the thing in question. Opposite of not handled.

happening. An adjective for scenes that indicates this scene has begun and not ended.

has. Used in an assertion to create an object variable, as in "The pack of cigarettes has a number called the remaining cigs."

has been. Uses the present perfect tense to check if something has been in a given state at any point from the beginning of the story until the present moment.

has ended. An adjective for scenes that indicates whether this scene has ever ended.

has happened. An adjective for scenes that indicates whether this scene has ever begun.

heading. A structural divider in Inform source text useful for telling the application and compiler where the important divisions fall, like Section - Break Room. The five levels of heading are Volume, Book, Part, Chapter, and Section.

headline. A few words of text that serve as a subtitle or indicator of an IF story's genre, such as "An Interactive Self-Portrait."

held. An adjective indicating that a thing is either carried or worn by a character.

if absent. When adding entries to a list, specifies that the item should only be added if it does not already occur in the list.

if present. When removing entries from a list, specifies that the item should only be removed if it can be verified that it currently is a member of the list.

if the player consents. A conditional test that will ask the player a yes or no question, and be true if the player types some form of yes.

IF, see interactive fiction.

implement. To create something in the story world in enough detail that it responds believably to likely player actions. Something that does not respond appropriately to sensible commands is said to be unimplemented.

improper-named, see proper-named.

in. A word used in assertion sentences, most commonly to indicate enclosure, as in "A spoon is in the Kitchen."

in random order. When used while sorting a list, repositions the order of its contents at random.

in random order (text substitution), see one of.

in words. When used in conjunction with any request to print a number, will spell that number out in words: "fourteen" instead of "14".

in N turns from now. Can specify that an "At the time when" phrase should run the given number of turns in the future.

increase. Add a numeric value to a numeric variable; see also decrease.

indefinite article. Text property of an object indicating which indefinite article should be used when printing its name (usually "a" or "an"). See also definite article.

Index Panel. The panel within the Inform application that displays a variety of indexes to the contents of your story and the Standard Rules.

indexed text. A kind of text that can be manipulated after its creation.

Inform 6. A more traditional programming language for IF, in popular usage between the mid 1990s and late 2000s.

Inform 7. A natural language approach to authoring interactive fictions by Graham Nelson, first released in 2006. Also simply *Inform*.

Inform project, see project.

Inform Recipe Book. Companion to *Writing with Inform*, a built-in compilation of all of its exercises organized by topic. Accessible through the Documentation panel.

initial appearance. A string property of a thing, to be displayed in its own paragraph when the thing is in a room being described and has never been moved.

instead. A word added to a phrase within an action rulebook to complete the action immediately, rather than consulting any more rules or rulebooks.

instead rulebook. An action exception rulebook for rules that overrides the normal behavior for an action to do something different. A matching rule stops the action.

interactive fiction. A computer-based form of interactive storytelling that uses text to describe a story world, which a player explores by entering imperative commands.

interpreter. A program for a specific computing platform that can open and run one or more kinds of story files.

is at least. Used to compare numbers; can be replaced with the >= symbol.

is at most. Used to compare numbers; can be replaced with the <= symbol.

is greater than. Used to compare numbers; can be replaced with the > symbol.

is less than. Used to compare numbers; can be replaced with the < symbol.

is listed in. A phrase that indicates whether an item appears in a list; to check the opposite, use is not listed in.

it. Pronoun that can be used in some source text phrases to refer to the last thing mentioned. Also understood in player commands to refer to the most recently mentioned singular noun. (He, she, and them are also supported.) When used within a definition, "it" refers to the thing under consideration.

kind. A subcategory or class of something, defining a more specific subset, such as "A plant is a kind of thing."

kind of value. A named parameter that can be set to one of a number of predefined types.

Kinds Index. A tab of the Index Panel that displays comprehensive information on all the kinds of value in the Standard Rules and your project.

last. When added to the beginning of a rule definition, causes this rule to be listed last in its rulebook. If multiple "last" rules are encountered, each will claim the last spot, bumping those appearing earlier down to second to last, third to last, and so on. See also first.

lawnmower effect. Criticism of conversation systems where all options are visible, noting the tendency of players to simply methodically select every available option until all are exhausted. See also conversation menu.

less than, see is less than.

let. Begins a phrase to create a temporary variable, as in "let counter be a number."

library message. A standard response to an action, specified in the Standard Rules.

lighted. A property of rooms that indicates that no light source is needed to see in them; opposite of dark. See also lit and unlit.

line break. Text substitution to add a line break to the text output. See also paragraph break.

list. A collection of objects in the story world, all of which must be of the same kind.

list of. A text substitution that can display an ad-hoc list based on a description, as in [list of visible windows]. Can also be used to populate a list variable.

lit. A property of things that indicates that they emit light; opposite of unlit. See also dark and lighted.

little. See passages.

location. A global variable holding the room that currently encloses the player; or "location of Alice" for the room currently enclosing Alice.

lockable. A property indicating whether something can be locked or unlocked by characters in the story world.

locked. A property of certain kinds of things (such as doors and containers) indicating that they cannot currently be opened. Opposite of unlocked.

loop. A phrase which instructs Inform to run another phrase or series of phrases multiple times, iterating over a group of values. See also repeat running through and while.

male. A property indicating the pronoun "he" should be used when describing this character.

man. A kind of person with the "male" property.

mapped, see change the {direction} exit.

maze. See little.

mechanics. The rules and logic of a story world, as opposed to the narrative.

mentioned. A property used by Inform's activities for describing a room, which indicates that an object has already been described. Opposite of unmentioned.

named phrase. A collection of phrases prefaced with "To" and a descriptive name.

narrator. The entity who is telling the story, usually invisible but sometimes a distinct character.

neuter. A property indicating the pronoun "it" should be used when describing this person.

never. A rare adjective used in an assertion to indicate a forbidden state of a property, as in "A window is never portable." See also usually, always, seldom.

non-empty. An adjective for lists that indicates that the list has at least one entry. Opposite of empty.

non-player character (NPC). A character in a story world who is not controlled by a player.

not for release. Specifies that the contents of a heading should not be included when compiling the story for release.

nothing. A special value that represents a null value.

noun. A global variable holding the direct object, if any, that the player used in their most recent command; see also second noun, current action.

now. A word that begins a phrase to make a condition true, as in "now the tiny frosted window is open."

NPC, see non-player character.

number. A top-level kind representing a single integer, such as 14.

number of. A text substitution that can display a numerical count matching a description, as in [number of closed windows]. See also in words.

number of entries. A phrase that returns the number of items in the given list.

object. A top-level kind which most items and concepts in a story world are part of, including things, rooms, and directions.

object tree. Inform's internal map of which objects in the story world enclose which other objects.

object variable. A variable associated with a specific object, also called a property.

odd. Adjective for numbers; see also even.

of. Used to reference an object variable, as in "battery life of the flashlight."

off-stage. An adjective indicating that an object is currently not in the object tree and cannot be found anywhere in the story world. Opposite of on-stage.

on rails. A term for a sequence or entire game where the player can interact but not significantly change the direction the story is moving. See also cutscene.

on-stage. An adjective indicating that an object is currently in the object tree and exists somewhere in the story world. Opposite of off-stage.

one of. A text substitution which begins a group of phrases, separated by [or], and ending with a substitution indicating what criteria to use in selecting a text to display. Ending substitutions include [at random], [purely at random], [in random order], [stopping], [cycling], [sticky random], and [as decreasingly likely outcomes].

opaque. A property of containers indicating that their contents cannot be seen when closed. Opposite of transparent.

open. A property of certain kinds of things (such as doors and containers) indicating that there is no impedance to entry or access. Opposite of closed.

openable. A property of certain kinds of things (such as doors and containers) indicating that story characters including the player can make them open or closed. Opposite of unopenable.

or. Links two conditions together, indicating that either condition can be true to make the condition as a whole true. When used within a text substitution, separates possible phrases that might be displayed (see one of).

order. A player command in the form "CHARACTER, ACTION" indicating that the player is asking another character in the story world to take that action. See also persuasion rule.

other side of. The room a door connects to, with respect to the player's current location.

other than, see doing anything.

otherwise. Used to indicate a phrase or phrases that will run if the preceding conditional test is false.

otherwise if. Used to indicate a phrase or phrases that will run if the preceding condition test is false and the condition test following this statement is true.

out of world action. An event that occurs outside the reality of the story world, referring instead to the player's interface with it, such as UNDO, RESTORE, or QUIT.

panel. A type of window within the Inform application that can be displayed in either of its two panes. The panels are Source, Errors, Index, Skein, Transcript, Game, Documentation, Settings

paragraph break. Text substitution that will add two line breaks (creating an entirely empty line) to the text output. See also line break.

parser. The low-level code that translates player commands into story actions. The parser can reject commands that are not understood and ask disambiguation questions to clarify unclear commands, and also handles actions out of world such as SAVE and UNDO.

Part. The third-level heading in Inform source text. Parts can be subheadings of Volumes or Books, and can be further subdivided into Chapters and Sections.

passages. See twisty.

pathfinding. Calculating the best route through a series of map connections or other relations. See also best route from.

PC, see player character.

person. A kind that represents intelligent entities in an Inform story world: predefined kinds of person are man, woman, and animal.

persuasion rule. A rule defining whether an NPC will obey a player order by deciding either "persuasion succeeds" or "persuasion fails."

phrase. A single instruction to Inform encountered during execution. Multiple phrases can be joined by ending each with a semicolon. See also named phrase.

phrases to decide, see to decide.

player (or reader). The person interacting with an IF story.

player character. The character in the story world controlled by the player, usually but not always also the protagonist and viewpoint character.

player's holdall. A kind of container with an unlimited carrying capacity.

plot. Narrative term for the sequence of events the characters experience during a story.

plotting. Narrative term for the act of arranging plot elements to culminate in an appropriate climax for a character's emotional journey.

plural-named. Property indicating that a thing represents a plural object, and should have the indefinite article "some." Opposite of singular-named.

polishing. The phase of a project where you fill in missing corners, make sure everything is implemented, and add the finishing touches.

portable. A property of things, which indicates that they can be picked up by characters in the story world; opposite of fixed in place.

present, see if present.

printed name. A text property of objects that indicate the text that should be used in place of the object's name in the source text when mentioning the object in text shown to the player.

privately-named. A property of objects indicating that the parser will not recognize words used in source text to create the object. Opposite of publically-named.

problem message. A diagnostic message shown in the Errors panel when Inform does not understand part of your source text. Most problem messages include helpful information on fixing the problem.

project. A file containing all the source text and associated files that define an Inform project.

prompt. A visual indicator, usually the symbol >, that indicates to the reader that the story is awaiting a new command

proper-named. A property of objects that indicates that no article should be used when describing this object. Opposite of improper-named.

property. A predefined variable for certain kinds of objects that can be in one of several states, such as open or closed for containers.

protagonist. Narrative term for the character in a story who undergoes the most change, usually the hero or central character.

provides. A condition testing whether an object has a certain property. Opposite of does not provide.

publically-named, see privately-named.

purely at random, see one of.

puzzle. An obstacle that prevents forward progress in the narrative, usually requiring close observation or mental effort to solve.

rails, see on rails.

random. A text substitution that can display a random selection from a description, as in [a random visible person]. Random can be used in many other contexts to select random values.

recompiling, see compiling.

recurring scenes. Scenes that are allowed to begin more than once.

region. A group of rooms, usually contiguous.

relation. An abstract connection between objects in your story world, such as the containment relation, which represents that some objects, can be inside other objects.

RELATIONS. A testing command that displays every custom relation between objects in your story world.

releasing. The phase of a project where the story is prepared for and distributed to readers.

remainder after dividing. Gets the remainder from a division operation, known as "modulo" in other programming languages.

repeat running from. A type of loop that can iterate through a group of values in order.

repeat running through. A type of loop that can iterate through items appearing in a list or description.

report rulebook. An action default rulebook for rules that tell the player the results of a successful action. Continue processing action rulebooks afterwards.

resume the story. If called during a when play ends rule, causes the story to continue as if the prior end the story phrase had not been encountered.

reverse. When used while sorting a list, reverses its current order.

rising action. Narrative term for periods in a story when the tension and stakes become higher.

room. A discrete area of space in an interactive fiction. Every item in the story world, including the player character, can be in only a single room at a time (with the exception of backdrops). Usually the player can only see and interact with other items in the same room.

rule. A collection of phrases that will be executed when this rule is triggered by another phrase, action, or event.

rulebook. A collection of rules that will be consulted one by one when the rulebook is triggered by another phrase.

Rules Index. A tab of the Index panel displaying information on all the rules defined in the Standard Rules and the project's source text.

run paragraph on. Text substitution which will indicate that Inform will not print a line break even if it normally would because of a period or other display rule.

run-time problem. A program error that cannot be detected by the compiler because it involves values of a variable that aren't known in advance.

sandbox. A situation in an interactive story where the player can freely explore and is not constrained to a particular activity.

say. A phrase that displays the following string or text substitution to the player.

scene. A kind representing a span of time in a story when some rules work differently.

scenery. A kind of thing that can usually not be taken by the player and is not automatically mentioned in a room description; see also backdrop.

second noun. A global variable holding the indirect object, if any, that the player used in their most recent command; see also noun, current action.

Section. The fifth and lowest level heading in Inform source text. Sections can be subheadings of Volumes, Books, Parts, or Chapters.

seldom. An rare adjective used in an assertion to indicate the opposite of a property's default state, as in "A door is seldom closed." See also usually, always, never.

set pronouns from. A phrase that sets the value of pronouns useable by the player like "it" to the given object.

setting. Narrative term for the story world surrounding the characters and in which the events of the plot take place.

Settings Panel. The panel within the Inform application that lets you affect basic settings about how your stories are compiled and released.

SHOWME. A testing command that displays detailed information about the current state of an object in the story world.

showme. Phrase that can be added to display diagnostic information during testing; does not output anything in a released story.

signposting. Clearly indicating to a player an implemented action or sequence of actions you'd like them to take.

singular-named. Property indicating that a thing represents a singular object, and should have the indefinite article "a." Opposite of plural-named.

Skein Panel. The panel within the Inform application that displays all the recent traversals of your story in a clickable map; you can use this panel to create sequences of commands to test your story or generate transcripts to output.

something new. Can be used in an understand rule to remove an association between a verb word and an action.

sort. A phrase to rearrange a list in alphabetic or numeric order. See also in random order and reverse.

sound. A kind representing an audio file to be played at some point during the story.

sound name. A variable holding a sound.

Source Panel. The panel within the Inform application that displays your story's source text. The Contents tab can show a summary of all your project's headers.

source text. The words that make up the definition for an Inform 7 story, more traditionally called source code.

specifies. Used in an assertion sentence to create a unit.

Standard Rules. An extension automatically included with every Inform 7 project that defines all of the standard actions, relations, and rules which set up a basic story world.

state-based. A programming term indicating that information is preserved from one cycle to the next about the prior states the system has been in. Opposite of stateless.

stateless. A programming term indicating that no information is preserved from one cycle to the next about the prior states the system has been in. Opposite of state-based.

status line. A bar displayed at the top of the screen by an IF interpreter that traditionally displays the current location, turn count and score of the story in progress.

sticky random, see one of.

stopping, see one of.

stop the action. A phrase that can be added to an action rule that would normally continue (such as before) to cause the action processing to immediately halt: no further applicable rules or rulebooks will be consulted. See also continue the action.

stored action. A kind that can hold a complete action, including the actor, action, noun, and second noun.

story. A sequence of events relating the journey of a protagonist who must fight against an opposed force in order to achieve a desired goal. A storyteller determines the arc of the protagonist's journey, adding details to keep the audience's interest, and ensuring that suspense is maintained until the protagonist is able to achieve victory, despite seemingly insurmountable odds. Stories transmit cultural information and give societies common touchstones and points of reference.

story file. A platform independent file containing all the text and logic necessary to tell a particular story. There are several major kinds of IF story files depending on which language was used to write the story and which standard it's been compiled to. An appropriate interpreter program is necessary to open a story file.

story world. The simulated world created by an interactive fiction in which the plot unfolds: the player's commands control a character in this world.

string. A piece of source text wrapped in quotation marks that may be shown to the reader at some point during play. Can contain text substitutions.

strongly plotted. A narrative term for an interactive story with an aggressive plot, which might move forward with or without player action.

stubs. An action defined in only a perfunctory way, not actually doing anything interesting. Many less commonly used actions, such as singing, are defined in the Standard Rules only as stubs.

supporter. A kind of thing that can enclose other things but never hides its contents, like a dinner plate or mantelpiece. See also container.

supporting. A relation indicating the connection between a supporter and the things it supports.

switched off. A property of devices indicating that the device is not active; opposite of switched on.

switched on. A property of devices indicating that the device is active; opposite of switched off.

table. A way of representing two-dimensional data in Inform.

temporary variable. A variable created within a phrase that only lasts while that phrase is being executed, also known as a local variable.

testing. The phase of a project where the game is played through looking for bugs and failures.

text substitution. A piece of text within a string wrapped in square brackets which can contain special commands to Inform to display customized text.

text. A kind representing a non-mutable string. See also indexed text.

the. Definite article that can be optionally used or not used in source text and player commands. Within text substitutions it will result in the thing that follows being described with its definite article.

the command. Words added to an understand rule to create verb synonyms.

thing. A basic kind which most items in a story world are part of. A thing is a kind of object.

time of day. A global variable that keeps track of time on a 24-hour clock.

To. Word that begins the definition of a named phrase.

to decide. A phrase that can return a value based on interior logic and (optionally) other values given to it.

to the nearest. Used to round a numeric value to a given amount of accuracy.

touchable. An adjective indicating whether an object can be touched by the player at the present moment. Opposite of not touchable. See also visible.

Transcript Panel. The panel within the Inform application that shows the transcript of your most recent playthrough. By using the Bless buttons in the transcript in association with the Skein, you can easily determine if any of the text output in a traversal of your story has changed since last blessed.

transparent. A property of containers indicating that their contents can be seen even when closed. Opposite of opaque.

TREE. A testing command that displays the current object tree for the entire story world or a specific object.

true. One of the two possible values of a truth state variable, along with false.

truncate. A phrase that can reduce the number of entries in a list to the given amount.

truth state. A kind of value that can be either true or false.

try. A phrase that causes a character in the story world to attempt an action.

turn. A single command from the player and response from the story, the atomic unit of time in IF.

twisty. See maze.

understand rule. A sentence in a source text that specifies how a pattern of input in player commands should be recognized by the parser.

understand as a mistake. An understand rule to respond to a non-standard player command with a message.

undescribed. A property of things which indicates that they are not automatically mentioned in room descriptions; opposite of described.

unimplemented, see implement.

unit. A custom kind of number.

unlist. Remove a rule from a rulebook, by using the "not listed in" phrase.

unlit. A property of things which indicates that they do not emit light; opposite of lit. See also dark and lighted.

unlocked. A property of certain kinds of things (such as doors and containers) indicating that there is no impediment to their being opened. Opposite of locked.

unmentioned, see mentioned.

unopenable. A property of certain kinds of things (such as doors and containers) indicating that story characters including the player cannot change their state between open or closed. Opposite of openable.

use option. An assertion that defines several basic assumptions about how your IF should operate, such as "Use no scoring."

usually. An adjective used in assertions to indicate the default state of a property, as in "A window is usually closed." See also always, never, seldom.

variable. A named container holding a value. See also temporary variable, object variable, global variable.

verb. A single word representing one way a player can give a command to create a certain action. For instance, the taking action can be invoked by the verbs GET or TAKE.

viewpoint character. The character from whose point of view the story is being experienced, usually the same as the player character.

visible. An adjective indicating whether an object can be seen by the player at the present moment. Opposite of not visible. See also touchable.

visited. An adjective indicating whether a room has ever enclosed the player. Opposite of not visited.

Volume. The top-level heading in Inform source text. Volumes can be subdivided into Books, Parts, Chapters, and Sections.

was. Uses the past tense to check whether or not a condition was true at the start of the current turn.

we are. Tests whether "the current action is" the given action.

we have. Used to create a condition that's true if the given action has ever successfully happened.

wearable. A property of things indicating that a character can wear them.

when. Used in a rule definition followed by a condition to specify that the rule only applies when the condition holds true.

when play begins. Defines a rule that will execute when the story begins.

when play ends. Defines a rule that will execute when the story ends. See also resume the story.

when {a scene} begins. A rule specifying what should happen when the given scene begins.

when {a scene} ends. A rule specifying what should happen when the given scene ends.

whether or not. Used to turn a condition into a truth state, as in "whether or not the wire mesh cage is open."

which is. Used in a phrase to include an adjective after the noun, allowing for a more specific definition to be specified.

with nouns reversed. Useful in an understand rule to denote that the order two nouns are used in a command is the reverse of the order they are defined in the action, such as the command ATTACK WINDOW WITH CAN for the action *throwing the can at the window*.

woman. A kind of person with the "female" property.

worn. An adjective indicating whether a thing is worn (not simply carried) by a character; see also held.

Writing with Inform. The main Inform manual and reference guide, built-in to the Inform application and viewable in the Documentation panel.

z-code. A 16-bit standard for story files originated in 1980 by Infocom, and later reverse engineered to create the original Inform. z-code files often have the .z5, .z8, or .zblorb extensions, and are limited to a maximum file size of 512K. z-code interpreters are available for dozens of computing platforms ranging from desktops to cell phones.

Z-Machine. The virtual machine format compiled to by z-code games.

INDEX

Note: Underlined entries denote descriptions of extensions.

Number

1893: A World's Fair Mystery, 8, 16

Symbols

*** label, using with skein, 387

: (colon), using with check rule, 108

, (comma), using, 310

< (command prompt), changing appearance of, 306

! (exclamation point), placement with quotation marks, 81

. (period), placement with quotation marks, 81

? (question mark), placement with quotation marks, 81

" (quotation marks)
  placement of punctuation with, 81
  use of, 75

; (semicolon), using with rules, 116

' (single quote), using in ASK/TELL model, 280

/ (slash) in Phrasebook, meaning of, 211

/-- (slash and dashes) in Phrasebook, meaning of, 211

[] (square brackets), using with objects, 78–79

O

P

YOUR ULTIMATE RESOURCE

Course Technology PTR is your ultimate game development resource. Our books provide comprehensive coverage of everything from programming, story development, character design, special effects creation, and more, for everyone from beginners to professionals. Written by industry professionals, with the techniques, tips, and tricks you need to take your games from concept to completion.

Introduction to Game AI
1-59863-998-6 • $39.99

**iPhone 3D Game Programming
All in One**
1-4354-5478-2 • $39.99

**C# Game Programming:
For Serious Game Creation**
1-4354-5556-8 • $49.99

**Beginning Game Programming
Third Edition**
1-4354-5427-8 • $34.99

Game Programming Gems 8
1-58450-702-0 • $69.99

Video Game Optimization
1-59863-435-6 • $39.99

**Torque for Teens,
Second Edition**
1-4354-5642-4 • $34.99

**Advanced 3D Game
Programming All in One,
Second Edition**
1-59863-575-1 • $59.99

**Multi-Threaded
Game Engine Design**
1-4354-5417-0 • $59.99

**Mastering Blender
Game Engine**
1-4354-5662-9 • $44.99